Events, Society and Sustainability

The growth of the events industry brings with it concerns of sustainable manage-ment, the sharing of available resources, and ensuring that people and places are not over-exploited. While the environmental and economic dimensions of sustainability have attracted a reasonable attention in the study of events, the social and cultural aspects of sustainability have been largely neglected. This book brings together emerging critical perspectives, innovative conceptual frameworks, and contemporary case studies. Events cannot be isolated from the actions of humans, which is reflected in the emphasis on people and society throughout. The next wave of sustainable discourse requires a critical synthesis of information and this book is the first to address the need for more critical approaches and a broader way of thinking about events and sustainability.

Divided into five thematic parts, the contributions delve into understanding the mainstream stances towards sustainability, the role events play in Indigenous cultures and in diasporic communities, and the extent to which events influence the public discourse and civic identity. Sustainability is also examined from a strategic perspective in the events sector, and consideration is given to issues such as corporate social responsibility, greenwashing, and the power of multi-stakeholder alliances in promoting sustainability goals.

Written by leading academics, this timely and important volume will be valu-able reading for all students, researchers, and academics interested in Events and the global issue of Sustainability.

Tomas Pernecky is a senior lecturer at the School of Hospitality and Tourism at the Auckland University of Technology, New Zealand.

Michael Lück is Associate Professor and Head of the Department of Tourism and Events, and Associate Director for the coastal and marine tourism research programme area at the New Zealand Tourism Research Institute, both at the Auckland University of Technology, New Zealand.

Routledge advances in event research series
Edited by Warwick Frost
School of Management, La Trobe University, Australia
and
Jennifer Laing
Monash University, Australia

Events, Society and Sustainability
Critical and contemporary approaches
Edited by Tomas Pernecky and Michael Lück

Forthcoming:

Exploring the Social impacts of Events
Edited by Greg Richards, Maria DeBito and Linda Wilks

Commemorative Events
Warwick Frost and Jennifer Laing

Power, Politics and International Events
Udo Merkel

Event Audiences and Expectations
Jo McKellar

Event Portfolio Planning and Management
A holistic approach
Vassilios Ziakas

Fashion, Design and Events
Kim Williams, Warwick Frost and Jennifer Laing

Conferences and Conventions
A research perspective
Judith Mair

Events, Society and Sustainability

Critical and contemporary approaches

Edited by Tomas Pernecky and Michael Lück

Routledge
Taylor & Francis Group

LONDON AND NEW YORK

First published 2013
by Routledge
2 Park Square, Milton Park, Abingdon, Oxon OX14 4RN

Simultaneously published in the USA and Canada
by Routledge
711 Third Avenue, New York, NY 10017

Routledge is an imprint of the Taylor & Francis Group, an informa business

British Library Cataloguing in Publication Data
A catalogue record for this book is available from the British Library

Library of Congress Cataloging in Publication Data
Pernecky, Tomas.
Events, society and sustainability : critical and contemporary approaches /
Tomas Pernecky and Michael Lück.
   p. cm.
   Includes bibliographical references and index.
   1. Special events industry. 2. Sustainability. I. Lück, Michael, 1966–
   II.Title.
   GT3405.P463 2012
   394.2068–dc23   2012027246

ISBN: 978-0-415-80993-1 (hbk)
ISBN: 978-0-203-13453-5 (ebk)

Typeset in Times New Roman
by Wearset Ltd, Boldon, Tyne and Wear

Contents

Figures

Tables

Contributors

Alison Booth's research focuses on the event production and the way in which live cultural performance events are positioned in the wider social, cultural, political, and economic contexts through stakeholder relationships and alliances. The role that popular as well as classical music productions play in profiling cultural identity, diasporic networks, and cultural representation are particular research interests. Current research focuses on the processes and relationships that support the production of cultural events, with specific reference to events that are of interest to and/or produced by New Zealand's Indian communities. Alison specialises in world music events and presents her research at international conferences and in publications. Alison's teaching speciality is in events management including coordinating courses in Event Production and Contemporary Issues in Event Management.

Adriana Budeanu is an assistant professor at Copenhagen Business School doing research in the area of sustainable tourism and international business, sustainable consumption and lifestyles, corporate social responsibility in supply chains, service innovation, and event management.

Jenny Cave is Senior Lecturer in Tourism and Hospitality Management at the University of Waikato in Hamilton, New Zealand. Her background is in anthropology, museology, and senior management of cultural attractions in Canada and New Zealand. She has been a board member of the New Zealand National Fieldays Society, which runs the largest agricultural event in the southern hemisphere, since 2004. Her research agenda addresses sustainable event management, cultural/heritage entrepreneurship, rural tourism, collaborative methodologies, and diasporan social worlds. She has published in journals and research volumes on these topics, as well as backpacker tourism and corporate macro-performance. She has guest edited three volumes on island tourism (marketing heritage, destinations, and crisis response) and is a member of the Editorial Review Board of the *International Journal of Event and Festival Management*.

Xin Chen is a research fellow at the New Zealand Asia Institute of the University of Auckland. She has been working at the Institute since 1997. Before that she was with the East–West Center in Honolulu for 11 years first as a degree fellow, then a research assistant, and finally a research fellow. During that time she also received her PhD in Political Science from the University of Hawai'i. Her research at the New Zealand Asia Institute focuses on Chinese politics, East Asian International Relations, and regional integration.

Don Clifton's commercial background is in the financial services sector having spent over 30 years in that industry. During that time he held a number of senior positions with firms involved in investment funds management and financial planning. In 2005, and following the sale of the firm for which he was CEO, Don returned to university to complete a second Master's degree in business and a PhD. He now holds an academic position at the University of South Australia's International Graduate School of Business, lecturing and researching in areas of sustainability and sustainable business.

Billy Collins is a lecturer at Thompson Rivers University in Kamloops, British Columbia, Canada in the Faculty of Adventure, Culinary Arts, and Tourism. Having had a previous career in the Canadian music industry as a manager, promoter, agent, and talent buyer, he is greatly interested in the theory that seeks to explain the global phenomenon of festivals and events, and the role they serve in creating better places to live, work, and play. His research agenda also includes sustainable transportation and tourism in mountain environments, and the heritage of National Parks as the foundation of the western North American tourism model. When not in the classroom, he can usually be found trying to entertain, or being entertained by, his dog Chester.

Deborah Edwards is a senior research fellow in Urban Tourism in the Business School, University of Technology, Sydney (UTS). Her interests are in sustainable tourism management, tourists' spatial behaviour, urban precincts, tourism planning, tourism sustainability, and festival and event impacts. Deborah has been the principal investigator on a number of projects that focus on the tourist experience of urban destinations. She has examined the spatial movements of tourists in urban destinations. Her work in this area has been conducted in Sydney, Canberra, Melbourne, and London and was the first of its kind in Australia. Deborah has published extensively in the areas of sustainable tourism and events and destination management. Strong industry collaboration underpins her approach to applied research and her links with industry ensure her research has impact.

George G. Fenich is a professor in the Department of Hospitality Management at East Carolina University. He was a practitioner in the hospitality industry for 15 years before joining academe in 1985. His PhD is in tourism planning and policy development from Rutgers University where his dissertation was entitled 'The dollars and sense of convention centers'. He has published over 40 research articles, done over 75 seminars and presentations to both academe and industry, and sits on the editorial board of six academic journals. He is the associate editor of the *Journal of Convention and Event Tourism*. His book *Meetings, Exhibitions, Events and Conventions: An Introduction to the Industry* (Prentice Hall, 2004) is one of the most widely adopted across college and universities. He has served in leadership roles for MPI, PCMA, DMAI, and ICHRIE. He continues to be actively engaged in the development and dissemination of the Meetings and Business Events Competency Standards (MBECS) and related curricular development. He has engaged in consultancy for over 40 Convention and Visitors Bureaus (DMOs) in the USA. His research and teaching interests are focused on the meetings and events industry (MICE).

Niki Harré is an associate professor at the University of Auckland where she has taught social and community psychology for 13 years. Her recent research projects have focused on sustainable communities, positive youth development, and political activism. She has worked with local councils and schools on several initiatives, including the design of injury prevention programmes and a waste minimisation project. In 2007 Niki edited, with Quentin Atkinson, the book *Carbon Neutral by 2020: How New Zealanders Can Tackle Climate Change* (Craig Potton, 2007). Niki is an active member of the Pt Chevalier Transition Town, a grass-roots group aimed at creating a sustainable community. In 2011 Niki released a book called *Psychology for a Better World: Strategies to Inspire Sustainability* (free to download).

Debra Hiom is a senior project manager at R&D/ILRT at the University of Bristol, responsible for managing the Greening Events I and II projects. Debra has been involved in internet research since 1992 with special interests in resource discovery and communication technologies. She is currently studying for a postgraduate certificate in Systems Thinking for Sustainability with the Schumacher Institute.

John S. Hull, in addition to being an associate professor in the Tourism Management Programme at Thompson Rivers University in Kamloops, British Columbia, Canada, is also CEO of John S. Hull Associates, Inc. which he founded in 2008. His present research addresses many aspects of sustainable tourism in peripheral regions with a specific focus on strategic planning and management as well as community-based tourism development. John has worked on tourism projects in North America, Europe, the Middle East, South America, Africa, and Asia. Past clients include the UNWTO, UNCBD, UNEP, UNESCO, World Bank, Nordic Council, European Tourism Research Institute, Commission on Environmental Cooperation, Canadian Tourism Commission, Tourism Atlantic, and Parks Canada. John is also a visiting professor at the University of Trento, Italy, the University of Applied Sciences, Wernigerode, Germany, and at the Icelandic Tourism Research Centre, Akureyri, Iceland. He is also a member of the New Zealand Tourism Research Institute (NZTRI).

Charles S. Johnston received his PhD in Geography from the University of Hawai'i then moved to New Zealand to work on a project related to Maori tourism. He has been a senior lecturer at the Auckland University of Technology since the final years of the twentieth century. In recent years his research interests have shifted to Asian and urban tourism, and tourist behaviour. Current projects focus on tourism's role in forging a consolidated regional identity in the Greater Mekong Subregion and whether East Asian pop culture tourism can construct a broader Asian identity.

Merrill Kaufman currently holds the position of Education Manager for the Pacific Whale Foundation in Maui, Hawaii. Her work focuses on interpretive training programmes for marine guides, as well as marine-science education programmes and outdoor learning experiences for children. Merrill is also interested in ecotourism, marine conservation, sustainable tourism, and early-childhood education.

Ian Kelly is a former geographer who switched to tourism education and directed courses at Monash and Swinburne Universities in Australia before retiring in 2000. He maintained involvement in teaching and research in an adjunct capacity at the University of South Australia and edited the annual *Australian Regional Tourism Handbook* until 2009. Research and writings on peace through tourism date from 1998. He is currently a senior consultant with the International Centre for Peace through Tourism Research and associate editor of the *Journal of Tourism and Peace Research.*

Mirrin Locke has recently completed her doctoral studies at the University of Waikato, in Hamilton, New Zealand. Her thesis is entitled 'Strategic Planning and Management for the Meetings, Incentives, Conventions and Exhibitions (MICE) Sector: A Case Study of the Auckland Region'. She was a recipient of a University of Waikato Doctoral Scholarship. Australian and hailing from Canberra, Mirrin's qualifications include a Master's in Training and Development from Griffith University, Queensland, and a Bachelor of Management (Employment Relations and Tourism) from the University of Canberra. She has lived in New Zealand for seven years, after having an extended working holiday in British Columbia, Canada. Mirrin is currently an academic staff member in the Centre for Events at Waikato Institute of Technology (Wintec) in Hamilton, New Zealand.

Michael Lück is Associate Professor and Head of Department (Tourism and Events) in the School of Hospitality and Tourism, and Associate Director for the coastal and marine tourism research programme area at the New Zealand Tourism Research Institute, both at the Auckland University of Technology. He received his PhD from the University of Otago in Dunedin. Michael has more than ten years' work experience in the tourism industry and has taught at universities in Germany, New Zealand, Scotland, and Canada. Michael's research interests lie in the areas of ecotourism, sustainable tourism, the impacts of tourism, marine tourism, and aviation. He has published in a number of international journals, is founding editor-in-chief of the academic journal *Tourism in Marine Environments*, and Associate Editor of the *Journal* *of Ecotourism*. Michael edited or co-edited two volumes on ecotourism, two on marine tourism, two on polar tourism, and the *Encyclopedia of Tourism and Recreation in Marine Environments* (CABI).

Omar Moufakkir is Director of the Tourism Management Institute, Group Sup de Co La Rochelle, La Rochelle Business School, France. He studied in Morocco, France, the Netherlands, and the United States where he earned a PhD in Park, Recreation and Tourism Resources at Michigan State University. He has published on gaming development, and more recently tourism and peace. His research interest centres around the impact of immigration-integration on travel propensity and destination choice. He is the founder of the International Center for Peace through Tourism Research, and editor of *The Journal of Tourism and Peace Research*, an open access journal (www.icptr.com).

Tomas Pernecky is a senior lecturer in the School of Hospitality and Tourism at the Auckland University of Technology. His research focuses mainly on knowledge production of and theoretical inquiries into tourism and events, sustainability, constructionist epistemology, hermeneutic phenomenology, and the critical exploration of issues surrounding peace. Recently, Tomas founded the EPTHE network which was created for researchers and students interested in critically exploring the issues of peace through tourism, hospitality, and events (www.epthe.net).

Brooke Porter is a PhD candidate at the Auckland University of Technology. Her research focuses on innovative approaches to marine conservation utilising participatory approaches. Brooke's primary research interest is developing access points into sustainable tourism markets for fishing communities in less-developed nations and understanding drivers behind resource dependencies. Her other areas of interests include fisheries management, ecotourism, interpretation in wildlife tourism, voluntourism, service learning, and community outreach.

Chris Preist is Reader in Sustainability and Computer Systems at the University of Bristol. He is principal investigator on the SYMPACT project, working with Guardian News and Media on how the digital transformation of the news and media sector will impact energy use, greenhouse gas emissions, and other sustainability factors. He is also an associate of the sustainability charity Forum for the Future, and a contributor to *Guardian Sustainable Business*. Prior to joining the University of Bristol, he was Head of Sustainable IT Research at HP Labs, Bristol from 2007 to 2009, where he led work on the strategic impact of climate change on business and technology development to exploit emerging opportunities. He joined HP Labs in 1987 following a degree in Pure Maths from the University of Warwick, and a PhD in logic programming from imperial College, London. In previous work at HP Labs, he conducted research in artificial intelligence, automated diagnosis, agent-mediated e-commerce, and the semantic web.

Peter Robinson is Principal Lecturer and Head of Leisure at the University of Wolverhampton, where he also oversees the management of the Arena Theatre, a University-owned event venue. Peter has a background in senior management positions in the public, private, and voluntary sectors, and has worked as a freelance consultant for a number of major tourism organisations in the UK. Peter is actively involved in a number of trade organisations and education associations, and is a member of the Executive Committee for The Association for Events Management Education and The National Council for the Tourism Management Institute. His research interests include human interactions at events, destination and operations management, and imagery and place construction in tourism. Peter has written a number of books around tourism and events management.

Nico Schulenkorf is a lecturer for Sport Management in the Business School, University of Technology, Sydney (UTS). His research focuses on the social, cultural, and psychological outcomes of sport and event projects, and in particular the role of sport in contributing to social development within and between disadvantaged communities. For several years, Nico has been involved in sport-for-development and health promotion programmes in countries such as Sri Lanka, Israel, and the Pacific Islands. He has been working with local and international NGOs, government agencies, sport associations, and ministries in developing capacities to implement, monitor, and evaluate development projects. Since 2011, Nico has been Deputy Editor of the *Journal of Sport for Development*.

Paul Shabajee is a multi-disciplinary research fellow based in the Department of Computer Science and also a visiting fellow at the Institute for Learning and Research Technologies (ILRT) at the University of Bristol. His broad research interests span three main areas: sustainability/sustainable development, applications of information and communications technologies (ICT), and education. His current foci are: developing approaches to assessing the systemic sustainability-related impacts of the use of ICT; and exploring the potentials and risks associated with the use of ICT innovations from a sustainability context. He is an advisor and analyst on the Greening Events project which is funded under the Joint Information Systems Committee (JISC), Greening ICT Programme based in the University of Bristol's operational Sustainability Unit and ILRT. The project is investigating the sustainability-related impacts of events and business travel in the higher and further education sectors in the UK.

Elisabeth Støle holds a Master's degree in Service Management from Copenhagen Business School and has more than seven years' experience in the meetings industry. She is currently International Sales Manager for the four-star hotel Bella Sky Comwell Copenhagen. Elisabeth has published a dissertation on 'The road to successful green destination branding', a multiple case study of six best-practice cities in the meetings industry. Elisabeth's interests in research are mainly sustainability, green marketing, and green destination branding in the meeting and event industry.

Sandy Strick, a graduate of Purdue University, has been on the faculty of the School of Hotel, Restaurant and Tourism at the University of South Carolina for over 20 years. For five of those years she served as department chair, and in June 2007 she took over as the Director of Graduate Studies. She teaches Wine and Spirits, Meeting and Event Planning, and Multicultural Human Resources Management courses at the graduate and undergraduate levels. Her publications include several co-authored chapters in the area of meeting and events and she wrote one of the first textbooks in this area.

Jing Tian wrote 'The 2008 Olympic Games: Leveraging a "Best Ever" Games to Benefit Beijing' (2006) for her Master's thesis at the Auckland University of Technology. She currently works in the private sector in Beijing.

Mark Rowell Wallin is an assistant professor in the Department of Journalism, Communication and New Media at Thompson Rivers University in Kamloops, British Columbia, Canada. His research interests run the gambit from technical and professional writing, through to visual semiotics and critical theory, to adaptation studies. Much of his work focuses on the intersections of representational modes: textual, visual, and auditory. Previous publications have addressed the relationship between film and video games, critical appraisals of marketing strategy, and the application of rhetorical and critical theory to mountain film. The work in his chapter arises out of his academic study of film, but also his work as Chair of the Kamloops Film Festival.

Christian Wittlich's research focuses on formal and non-formal environmental education, sustainability, tourism, and event management. He is currently a research assistant and junior lecturer to the Department of Geography at Johannes Gutenberg University in Mainz, Germany.

Heather Zeppel has conducted research on Indigenous cultural tourism in Australia, New Zealand, Canada, and Sarawak, Borneo. Her research interests include tourist interactions with Indigenous people, the marketing of Indigenous culture, presentations of Indigenous culture and history at museums and festivals, ecotourism, wildlife tourism, and Indigenous co-management of protected areas. She is the author of *Indigenous Ecotourism: Sustainable Development and Management* (CABI, 2006). Her other research interests are environmental sustainability, climate change and tourism, and carbon mitigation by tourism enterprises and local government.

Acknowledgements

An edited volume like this is always the joint effort of a number of individuals, and this book is no exception. We received enthusiastic support and would like to acknowledge a number of people. First, a big *thank you!* goes to the contributing authors for sharing their wisdom and for taking the time to write, edit, and amend the chapters making up this book: Alison Booth, Adriana Budeanu, Jenny Cave, Xin Chen, Don Clifton, Billy Collins, Deborah Edwards, George G. Fenich, Niki Harré, Debra Hiom, John S. Hull, Charles S. Johnston, Merrill Kaufman, Ian Kelly, Mirrin Locke, Omar Moufakkir, Brooke Porter, Chris Preist, Peter Robinson, Nico Schulenkorf, Paul Shabajee, Elisabeth Støle, Sandy Strick, Jing Tian, Mark Rowell Wallin, Christian Wittlich, and Heather Zeppel. Carol Barber and Emma Travis at Routledge have wonderfully supported us from the first proposal to the final production of this edited volume. It has been a pleasure working with such a friendly, helpful, and professional team. Our appreciation also goes to our colleagues at the School of Hospitality and Tourism at Auckland University of Technology – Linda O'Neill (Head of School) and Nigel Hemmington (Dean, Faculty of Culture and Society, and Pro Vice-Chancellor) for their support and encouragement to work on projects of this nature. Last, but certainly not least, we would like to thank our friends and families for their never-ending and unconditional support – Andrew and Neil in particular!

Tomas Pernecky and Michael Lück

Editors' introduction

Events in the age of sustainability

Tomas Pernecky and Michael Lück

> We are drowning in information, while starving for wisdom. The world hence-
> forth will be run by synthesizers, people able to put together the right information
> at the right time, think critically about it, and make important choices wisely.
>
> Edward O. Wilson (1998, p. 294)

Sustainability is high on the agenda of governmental institutions, it is on every
corporate radar and it has penetrated into people's daily lives. Its magnitude continues to shape societal directions, and it would appear that sustainability is a
wise orientation for humanity to follow. Data, information and knowledge on
sustainability abound, but so does confusion and ideological disorientation.
Whether seen as a concern, threat, problem, opportunity or non-issue, sustainability is here to remain our companion as we step further into the twenty-first
century. The next wave of sustainable discourse requires a critical synthesis of
information relating to the social, cultural, environmental, political, economic,
technological and psychological dimensions, all of which pervade the phenomenon under scrutiny in this book – events.

Events have always been an intrinsic part of people's lives and they continue
to feature even more prominently in our daily realities. They mark important
milestones and achievements, they are deployed to celebrate and engage communities, and they are an inherent aspect of many public occasions. Events now
have a place in government policies and increasingly feature in strategic documents for cities, regions and nations. The recognised promise of events as an
economic driver and their importance as a social and cultural nexus means that
we are witnessing tremendous growth in this sector.

The growth of any industry, however, brings with it issues of sustainable
management, the sharing of available resources, problems surrounding waste
and pollution, and also ensuring that people and places are not over-exploited.
Such concerns have been the primary focus of the sustainability discourse. This
is at a time when the world is still wrestling with making a distinction between
'growth' and 'development', neglecting to recognise that 'development' is more
aligned with sustainable thought and thus closer to improvement and transitioning to a better state, while 'growth' tends to refer to quantitative increase or

increase in size via assimilation of resources (Magis and Shinn, 2009). In the domain of Event Studies, information continues to emerge on what ought to change so that events can be declared 'sustainable', but with little critical thought and research. Equally limiting is the fixation on events as a business phenomenon, conceptualised mainly through a managerial lens. These two predicaments are the driving force behind this text, which strives to broaden and sharpen the discussions on events and sustainability.

Sustainability and events

The steady growth in titles that seek to advance knowledge on events is met with interest among students who are keen to learn more about the phenomenon; taking their part in driving the development of new programmes and expanding curricula. Not a long time ago, Getz (2008, p. 411) commented on the growth of event management education stating that it remained a 'hot growth area' around the world. If we were to take a look at the developments today, in the UK solely, there are at least sixty-eight colleges and universities that offer undergraduate events-related courses, and over twenty universities offering postgraduate masters (Bowdin *et al.* 2011). Similar trends can be observed internationally in the tertiary sector.

Thus far, the study of events has been overshadowed by managerial rhetoric and problem solving, and on the whole, the focus has tended towards the processes of event organisation and planning, production, design, budgeting, evaluation, policy making, measuring events' feasibility and economic impacts. Typically (see, for example Allen *et al.*, 2008; Getz, 2005; Goldblatt, 2002), events are differentiated by: (a) *size* and one can discern between mega, hallmark and major events; and (b) *type* or *form*, which allows us to make a distinction between sporting events, business events, political events and music events, to name a few. A common characteristic is that they are *temporal*, and can be *planned* or *unplanned* (Getz, 2007, 2012). These typologies are widely followed and adopted within the field (Baum *et al.*, 2009; Berridge, 2007), although they are not set in stone and small variations can be noted in the work of scholars such as Shone and Parry (2001) who organise events into four categories: leisure events (e.g. leisure, sport, recreation); personal events (e.g. weddings, birthdays, anniversaries), cultural events (e.g. ceremonial, sacred, art); and organisational events (e.g. commercial, political, sales). Other classifications vary further depending on a range of attributes and priority to various stakeholders, such as arranging events according to economic impacts (see for example UK sport classification in O'Toole, 2011, p. 49). This amounts to numerous definitions accompanied with a detailed list of typologies that fall under the broad umbrella term 'event management'.

It is not surprising then, that events have been largely an operational and managerial preoccupation. Bowdin *et al.* (2011) confirm that in the UK, the majority of courses which provide education and training for event professionals are generally built around a management core. Similar developments can be observed in Australia, Canada, Ireland, Germany, France, New Zealand and the USA. Notwithstanding that such contributions are certainly an important part of the accumulating knowledge, and we must emphasise that it is not our aim here to diminish the work of our colleagues, the downfall of this is that it has inevitable implications for the approaches to sustainability – shaping the extent as well as the direction towards which the discourse has been heading.

There is room for expanding the conceptual scaffolding of sustainability so that more balanced, informed and well-rounded perspectives can emerge. There is also scope for more theoretical and conceptual richness of the events phenomenon and the field in general. The academic initiatives driven by the sustainability discourse in Event Studies have been budding steadily but, in contrast to other fields, are lagging behind in both volume and breadth. This has been voiced by scholars such as Lawton (2011) in the *Special Issue on Sustainability in the Event Management Sector*, who introduces sustainability as a societal mega-trend, but at the same time acknowledges that there is a need for more scholarship.

The texts dominating the current market include *Sustainable Event Management: A Practical Guide* by Jones (2010), who offers hands-on practical solutions to festival organisers. The recently published book *The Complete Guide to Greener Meetings and Events* by Goldblatt (2012), is similar to Jones' in that it offers practical tips and solutions for event planners, including information on sustainable transportation, waste management and green venues, and delves into hands-on solutions to minimise environmental impacts (e.g. the use of beeswax instead of regular candles). On a similar footing is *Events and the Environment* by Case (2012) who focuses on implementing sustainable management practices; this work revolves largely around the environmental management of events. A more academically oriented book, in terms of conceptual and theoretical coverage, is Raj and Musgrave's (2009) edited text *Event Management and Sustainability*.

Other authors and editors who write more generically on event management tend to devote at least a few pages to discussing sustainability. In fact it is not uncommon to find sections on 'green' events and environmental issues in many of the popular introductory texts (see for example Allen *et al.*, 2011; Bladen *et al.*, 2012; Goldblatt, 2011; Wagen and White, 2010). The topics frequently covered include the environmental impacts of events, and pertain to specific areas such as event pollution, procurement, energy use, waste management, recycling, transport, water management and strategic partnerships. Overall, concerns over sustainability and the need to 'green up' the industry are no longer alien in the study of events. Perhaps this is a reflection of the fact that the push towards green and sustainable practices in the events sector is under way (Mair and Jago, 2010).

Established understandings of and approaches to sustainability: bridging tourism and events

There was little incentive to set an agenda for the book that would reiterate the already established models and replicate information on managing what may be wrong with the 'events industry'. However, it is important to at least briefly outline the prominent concepts and thoughts on sustainability, and also acknowledge the developments in its sister field of Tourism Studies. Events have had a presence under the wings of tourism as 'event tourism' since the 1980s (see for example the seminal work of Getz, 1989), and although there is now a push for a separate field of Event Studies, it is imperative to at least briefly address tourism's developments on the front of sustainability.

After the World Commission on Environment and Development (WCED) published the report 'Our Common Future', also commonly referred to as the 'Brundtland Report' in 1987, sustainable tourism became the lofty goal of many stakeholders in the tourism industry, including operators, RGOs and NGOs, as well as environmental and social pressure groups and various industry organisations (Lück, 1998; Lück *et al.*, 2010). Sustainability is defined as 'development that meets the needs of the present without compromising the ability of future generations to meet their own needs' (World Commission on Environment and Development, 1987, p. 43). With the launch of the Brundtland Report, the WCED set a major milestone in terms of the world's development. For the first time, sustainable development (SD) became a key issue in all parts of our daily lives, and tourism (including event tourism) is no exception. The goals of SD have subsequently been adapted for the tourism industry, and accordingly, sustainable tourism development (STD) should:

- meet the needs and wants of the local host community in terms of improved living standards and quality of life;
- satisfy the demands of tourists and the tourism industry, and continue to attract them in order to meet the first aim; and,
- safeguard the environmental resource base for tourism, encompassing natural, built and cultural components, in order to achieve both of the preceding aims (Hunter, 1995, pp. 155–156).

In the following years, many academics made an attempt to define sustainable tourism in many different ways. A closer look into the plethora of definitions shows all too clearly that even twenty-five years later, we are still far away from any all-encompassing definition. However, there are a few aspects that seem to be apparent and reoccurring in the STD goals, such as a sense for the host community, conservation of natural, built and cultural heritage and resources, and the generation of revenue. Later, these three main areas of development have commonly been referred to as the 'triple bottom line' (TBL), i.e. the need for social, economic and environmental sustainability. In the field of Event Studies, scholars have for example examined the use of TBL to leverage sport events (O'Brien and Chalip, 2008) and to assess the social impacts of events (Fredline *et al.*, 2003). Recently, it has been conceptualised into a framework for sustainable events by Musgrave and Raj (2009, p. 5) as the 'three pillar impacts' of events. Hede (2008, p. 14) further observes that a lot of current research focuses on 'amalgamating the economic, social, and environmental forms of evaluation into one framework', and has advocated for its use also in the planning of special events.

While it is the WCED's goal to have *all* forms of tourism developed sustainably – from mass tourism to special interest tourism, and including event tourism – Weaver (2008) notes that there is an area of contention with the inclusion of economic, environmental and social sustainability. There is no doubt that there are good intentions to include these three goals in development plans, however, problems become apparent when the implementation of tourism development provides the basis for conflicts between them. In fact, the complexity of the tourism industry makes it almost impossible to find a common ground for all components of the tourism sector. Similar problems arise in the study of events. All too often, the focus on one pillar of STD brings with it some negative developments of one or both of the other pillars. For example, the focus on environmental sustainability (such as the restriction of wildlife tour permits in the tourism sector, or holding an online conference as opposed to providing a traditional face-to-face interaction in the events sector) often causes economic hardship, and subsequently a decline in social sustainability.

Both tourism and events have been grappling with the issue of sustainability, giving rise to different conceptualisations and terminology. Sustainable tourism and ecotourism are two concepts that have occasionally been used interchangeably. It is important to note that while the goals of both are often very similar, sustainable tourism is a much wider umbrella concept. In fact, all forms of tourism should strive for sustainability, and ecotourism is often seen as a motor for sustainable development in the tourism sector. Similarly, some scholars make a distinction between 'sustainable' events and 'green' events. According to Goldblatt (2011) sustainable development does not necessarily imply environmental activism. Using the words *green* or *eco* suggests a 'concerted effort to reduce environmental impacts and conserve natural resources beyond the definition of sustainable development' (p. 192). In Goldblatt's view, greener events draw upon inputs of ecotourism, sustainable development, fair trade, renewable energy, corporate social sustainability and *outgreening* (green initiatives resulting in improved performance and competitive advantage).

It appears that most academics agree that there is a need for sustainable tourism development and increasingly for sustainable events development, but what it actually entails remains somewhat vague (Becker, 2012; Wheeller, 1994). When it comes to sustainability discourse in general, Becker (2012) states that there is no precise meaning of this concept. It can take different shapes and forms and, as he puts it:

> sustainability is a global concept that is used to discuss various societal fields, such as business or education and to discuss a range of crucial environmental, societal, and global issues, such as biodiversity loss, climate change, distribution and use of non-renewable resources, energy production and use, global equity and justice, and economic issues.

(Becker, 2012, p. 1)

This book strives to tackle sustainability in the broader context of societal issues and make further steps towards untangling the knotty relationship between sustainability and events. It has been acknowledged that events are a vital part of societies and cultures across the globe (Gibson and Connell, 2011). Events therefore ought not to be isolated from the actions of humans, which is one of the reasons an emphasis in this text is placed on people. This notion is broadly addressed in the title by the term 'society'. While environmental and economic sustainability has attracted a lot of attention in the past, the social aspect of sustainability has been neglected in social science and is by far the least developed (Dillard *et al.*, 2009). In contrast to other texts, this edited volume does not put as much weight on exploring events in relation to the natural environment, although it is inevitable that some contributions address these issues.

An important aspect that shaped this book arose from the need to critically engage in the debate on sustainability. This is something that is still lacking in the field, yet fundamental in progressing knowledge equitably and, as suggested in the quote opening this chapter, in making important choices wisely. The term 'sustainability' has much wider connotations and there is a sea of considerations that ought to be taken into account when speaking of events. This text brings together emerging critical perspectives, innovative conceptual frameworks and examples from the field to further advance knowledge in this area of discourse. Several of the contributing authors have been asked to put on their 'critical caps' so that students are exposed to a broader way of thinking about events and sustainability. This involves making informed decisions based on examining available information critically – a way of thinking and skill development that should be facilitated and cultivated by academia.

About the contributions and the structure of the book

We are grateful to be able to attract scholars to compile this edited volume, which is a challenging task when institutions and regulatory mechanisms, for example the Research Assessment Exercise (RAE) in the UK and the Performance-Based Research Fund (PBRF) in New Zealand, place researchers under pressure to publish exclusively in high-ranking peer-reviewed academic journals. The people who participate in this project are contemporary thinkers on the subject of sustainability and present voices from different parts of the world, including Australia, Canada, Denmark, France, Germany, New Zealand, the United Kingdom and the United States. Adding to the flavour of this book are also the varied academic backgrounds and experience of the authors.

Editing is a creative and subjective process, and several chapters in this text could be placed under multiple thematic headings. After much thinking and consideration, we have organised the book into five parts. The first segment is titled 'Thinking critically about events and sustainability' and focuses on critical and conceptual approaches to sustainability and events. The second part, headlined 'Events, sustainability and community', gathers works that accentuate the important function events have in a community setting. Part III, 'Strategic perspectives and the events sector' addresses the strategic dimensions of sustainability, covering topics such as governance, corporate social responsibility and the trends and challenges facing the meetings, incentives, conventions and exhibition (MICE) sector. Following, are three case studies positioned under the theme 'Insights from the field: case studies', leading to the last part of the book which is oriented towards the future as suggested by the heading 'Sustainable futures: visions of action and hope'.

Part I   Thinking critically about events and sustainability

The first chapter calls for broader conceptualisations of sustainability in Events Studies and offers five propositions to reinforce the importance of events in society and the significant role they play in the making of contemporary social, cultural, and political realities. The lack of sustainability, termed 'un-sustainability', is presented as a social problem which requires an element of critical thinking – necessary in evaluating the conditions upon which events are deemed (un)sustainable. A distinction is made between events that can be perceived as intentional agents promoting messages of sustainable practices, and a macro perspective which takes as its focus events at large. The chapter holds that sustainability is a promising area of research, in particular when attention is directed towards exploring sustainability in terms of fundamental relationships.

In the second chapter, Don Clifton questions why there has been so little progress with regard to transitioning to a sustainable world, given the amount of attention sustainable development has received over the past twenty years. He offers a critical assessment of the approaches adopted by businesses and governments, and discusses the current mainstream ways of thinking about sustainability: *reformism* and the *transformational approach*. On a quest to answer which system society should pursue, he argues that it is not the dominant sustainable world approach accepted widely by political and business communities of the West. Clifton warns against 'green' consumerism that does not solve the issue of consuming more and the 'business as usual' marketing strategies. A thought-provoking treatise, this chapter addresses the need for a societal change which inevitably pertains to the events industry.

Chapter 3 is a powerful example of the need to understand the contexts in which meanings are constructed, and demonstrates the importance of events in championing a diverse range of social changes. Johnston, Chen and Tian take the meaning of sustainability to a new level by offering a discourse analysis of the Beijing 2008 Olympic Games. This work not only challenges the dominant Western views and common understandings of what events 'do' and the extent to which they are intertwined with a society, it also shows that there is no one 'China' or 'Beijing'. Drawing on the concepts which date back to the *I Qing* (Book of Changes) and to Confucian principles, the authors reveal that the 'People's Olympics' is a living concept, one that continues to evolve and influence the public discourse concerning the nature of Chinese civic identity.

The use of information technology is often presented as a solution to reducing the impacts associated with travel to corporate and academic events, however, technology can also have its own limitations, be costly and not necessarily 'greener'. Shabajee, Hiom and Preist focus on higher and further education events such as academic conferences, workshops and symposia, and discuss their findings of the Greening Events Project in the UK. They argue for a systemic perspective which is presented as necessary to meaningfully assess and understand the impacts of events. This contribution highlights that taking sustainable measures comes with a range of challenges and that the use of information and communication technology is an area of research that is yet to be properly investigated.

Part II Events, sustainability and community

Sport events are an important part of the events industry and a prominent area of research in the field of Event Studies. Schulenkorf and Edwards recognise that not only can sporting events provide people and their communities with economic and social opportunities, they are also increasingly seen as a tool for community development, having the potential to deliver broader social outcomes. Chapter 5 thus investigates the ability of sporting events to contribute to sustainable social development by looking at disadvantaged communities. It discusses the opportunities as well as challenges that come with the planning and evaluation of these events. In bidding for sustainable community development and empowerment, the authors offer a Sport-for-Development Framework to emphasise the inevitability of active community participation and positive engagement.

In Chapter 6, Heather Zeppel turns the attention to socio-cultural benefits and impacts of Indigenous festivals. A very thorough and informative study, this overview of literature is based on hallmark Indigenous festivals in Australia, featuring examples of new urban Indigenous festivals. The chapter discusses the politics of Indigenous identity and cultural authenticity of events, and also addresses the diaspora of Indigenous people to urban centres. Zeppel's work adds to the vision of this book and expands the understandings of sustainability in the context of events, by covering topics such as *Indigenous well-being*, the process of de-territorialisation and re-territorialisation of Indigenous cultures.

Alison Booth continues the discussion of social sustainability in her study on Indian communities living in Auckland, New Zealand. Her research stems from a strong commitment to further develop knowledge on sustainable production processes of performance events networks and alliances. This seventh chapter is a window into the Auckland performing arts scene, and demonstrates through four case studies the ways producers of Indian events contribute to creating socially sustainable events.

Sustainability, offered through the lens of a just, equitable, and friendly world where events may play a role in bridging social and cultural gaps, is the premise of the work by Moufakkir and Kelly in Chapter 8. The authors ponder the place for events in development studies by specifically examining their role in contributing to peaceful relationships. They offer a SWOT analysis and suggest that while certain events create conditions conducive to interaction and sharing of experiences, the contribution of events to peaceful relationships as an element of sustainability is questionable or even counterproductive. To make their point, Moufakkir and Kelly look at an international music festival in Morocco to illustrate the controversial nature of the event. The extent to which events can be an agent of sustainable development with regards to the social-cultural-political meaning of the term is questioned.

Part III Strategic perspectives and the events sector

Cave, Robinson and Locke begin the third part of the book by asking whom sustainability is for. Adopting a critical stance, Chapter 9 looks at the stakeholder motivations and power complexities played out during the planning and implementation of events. Examples here include the use of sustainability concepts by governments as a platform to exhibit nationhood, and the discussion extends to issues such as corporate social responsibility and the motivation to adopt sustainable principles in the events sector.

In Chapter 10, Budeanu and Støle reflect on the challenges and success factors of sustainable events by examining the organisation of the fifteenth conference of the parties (COP15) for the United Nations Framework Convention on Climate Change (UNFCCC) in Copenhagen, Denmark in 2009. The centre of attention in this work is the need for sustainability to be implemented at a strategic level, and with sustainability criteria embedded into the different stages of events: including the bidding processes and the choice of destination in which events are held. The chapter looks closely at the persuasive power of multi-stakeholder alliances in promoting sustainability goals.

The meetings, incentives, convections and exhibitions industry, known under the acronym MICE, has witnessed an increase in events that are promoted as 'green' and 'sustainable'. Chapter 11 is an inquiry into the trends and challenges observable in the conference and conventions sector. Fenich and Strick are US-based scholars who bring under scrutiny four key themes: sustainability and greening in the MICE industry; the practical economics of sustainability; 'green-washing'; and the tension between service delivery and service perception when embracing 'greening'. Questions arise as to whether the current sustainability fixation in the industry is a trend or a fad, and the authors pose many questions that are likely to stimulate discussions in the classroom.

Part IV Insights from the field: case studies

The first case study by Porter and Kaufmann takes place in Hawaii and offers insights on a 'green' event – the Whale Day – which is part of the Maui Whale Festival. The growth and expansion from what used to be a small single-day event to a conservation-themed festival lasting an entire season, is perhaps the most compelling evidence of its success as presented by the authors. This twelfth chapter discusses the management of the interrelationships of the economic, social and ecological components of the event, and reveals the ongoing commitment and challenges which the organisation has to deal with.

Hawaii is also the locality for Chapter 13 and the second case study. Music events tend to be resource intensive not only when it comes to logistics, planning and organisation, but also in terms of the impact of the individual attendees. Christian Wittlich chooses the Kokua Festival and Jack Johnson World Tours as models for raising funds for environmental education, and as a way of encouraging positive actions of participants and the third parties. Of particular interest here are the initiatives that can be taken and demanded by performers. The chapter underscores that if sustainable measures are to be taken and implemented seriously, they ought to be embraced by all parties, including musicians and touring bands.

Chapter 14 is a reminder that events are perhaps even more important in smaller communities. Wallin, Collins and Hull examine sustainable community development and the application of the 'triple bottom line' approach in a hinterland destination. The authors look at the long-term sustainability of film-related events in small cities, and offer their research findings on a study of the Kamloops Film Festival in British Columbia, Canada. The chapter highlights the key issues facing the festival such as the changing demographic and economic pressures.

Part V Sustainable futures: visions of action and hope

The last part of this book is more contemplative and concentrates on the possibilities in the realm of sustainability and events. It is important to not only critique and question, but also to offer alternatives and possible directions. In Chapter 15, Don Clifton looks at organisational strategy from a sustainable business perspective and presents strategy concepts that can be applied to almost any organisation regardless of size, structure and industry sector. Consideration is given to what it means for a business to contribute to the achievement of a sustainable world, and Clifton critically explores various strategic approaches to how a business might pursue sustainability initiatives.

The books that call for the need to 'green up' the industry and to demonstrate sustainable practices often lack the persuasiveness to explain why and if at all, the few 'green' events, which are committed to such practices are likely to make a difference. Chapter 16 deals with the whys. Niki Harré tackles events as opportunities to showcase a sustainable society and presents convincing arguments based on psychological research. As proposed by the author, people are motivated to imitate each other but are also attracted to positive messages. Addressing the role of positive emotions and behaviours consistent with sustainability, this last chapter offers novel perspectives on how events can assist in promoting messages of sustainable futures.

References

Allen, J., O'Toole, W., Harris, R. and McDonnell, I. (2008). *Festival and Special Event Management* (4th edn). Milton, Qld: Wiley.

Allen, J., O'Toole, W., Harris, R. and McDonnell, I. (2011). *Festival and Special Event Management* (5th edn). Milton, Qld: Wiley.

Baum, T., Deery, M., Hanlon, C., Lockstone, L. and Smith, K. (2009). *People and Work in Events and Conventions: A Research Perspective*. Wallingford, UK: CABI.

Becker, C. U. (2012). *Sustainability Ethics and Sustainability Research*. London, UK: Springer.

Berridge, G. (2007). *Events Design and Experience*. Kidlington, UK: Butterworth-Heinemann.

Bladen, C., Kennell, J., Abson, E. and Wilde, N. (2012). *Events Management: An Introduction*. Abingdon, UK: Routledge.

Bowdin, G., Allen, J., O'Toole, W., Harris, R. and McDonnell, I. (2011). *Events Management* (3rd edn). Oxford, UK: Elsevier Butterworth-Heinemann.

Case, R. (2012). *Events and the Environment*. Abingdon, UK: Routledge.

Dillard, J., Dujon, V. and King, M. C. (2009). Introduction. In J. Dillard, V. Dujon and M. C. King (eds), *Understanding the Social Dimension of Sustainability* (pp. 1–14). New York: Routledge.

Fredline, L., Jago, L. and Deery, M. (2003). The development of a generic scale to measure the social impacts of events. *Event Management*, 8(1), 23–37. doi: 1525–9951/03.

Getz, D. (1989). Special events: Defining the product. *Tourism Management*, 10(2), 125–137. doi: 1261.5177169/020125–13.

Getz, D. (2005). *Event Management and Event Tourism* (2nd edn). New York: Cognizant Communication Corporation.

Getz, D. (2007). *Event Studies: Theory, Research and Policy for Planned Events*. Kidlington, UK: Butterworth-Heinemann.

Getz, D. (2008). Event tourism: Definition, evolution, and research. *Tourism Management*, 29(3), 403–428. doi: 10.1016/j.tourman.2007.07.017.

Getz, D. (2012). *Event Studies: Theory, Research and Policy for Planned Events* (2nd edn). Abingdon, UK: Routledge.

Gibson, C. and Connell, J. (2011). *Festival Places: Revitalising Rural Australia*. Bristol, UK: Channel View Publications.

Goldblatt, J. (2002). *Special Events: Twenty-first Century Global Event Management* (3rd edn). New York: Wiley.

Goldblatt, J. (2011). *Special Events: A New Generation and the Next Frontier* (6th edn). New York: Wiley.

Goldblatt, S. D. (2012). *The Complete Guide to Greener Meetings and Events*. Hoboken, NJ: John Wiley & Sons, Inc.

Hede, A.-M. (2008). Managing special events in the new era of the triple bottom line. *Event Management*, 11(1–2), 13–22. doi: 1525–9951/07.

Hunter, C. J. (1995). On the need to re-conceptualise sustainable tourism development. *Journal of Sustainable Tourism*, 3(3), 155–165.

Jones, M. (2010). *Sustainable Event Management: A Practical Guide*. London, UK: Earthscan.

Lawton, L. J. (2011). Introduction: Special issue on sustainability in the event management sector. *Event Management*, 15(4), 313–314. doi: 10.3727/152599511X13175676 722447.

Lück, M. (1998). Sustainable tourism: Do modern trends in tourism make a sustainable management more easy to achieve? *Tourismus Jahrbuch*, 2(2), 141–157.

Lück, M., Maher, P. T. and Stewart, E. (2010). Setting the scene: Polar cruise tourism in the 21st century. In M. Lück, P. T. Maher and E. Stewart (eds), *Cruise Tourism in the Polar Regions: Promoting Environmental and Social Sustainability?* (pp. 1–10). London, UK: Earthscan.

Magis, K. and Shinn, C. (2009). Emergent principles of social sustainability. In J. Dillard, V. Dujon and M. C. King (eds), *Understanding the Social Dimension of Sustainability* (pp. 15–44). New York: Routledge.

Mair, J. and Jago, L. (2010). The development of a conceptual model of greening in the business events tourism sector. *Journal of Sustainable Tourism*, 18(1), 77–94. doi: 10.1080/09669580903291007.

Musgrave, J. and Raj, R. (2009). Introduction to a conceptual framework for sustainable events. In R. Raj and J. Musgrave (eds), *Event Management and Sustainability* (pp. 1–12). Wallingford, UK: CABI.

O'Brien, D. and Chalip, L. (2008). Sport events and strategic leveraging: Pushing towards the triple bottom line. In A. Woodside and D. Martin (eds), *Tourism Management: Analysis, Behaviour and Strategy* (pp. 318–338). Wallingford, UK: CABI.

O'Toole, W. (2011). *Events Feasibility and Development: From Strategy to Operations*. Burlington, MA: Butterworth-Heinemann.

Raj, R. and Musgrave, J. (eds, 2009). *Event Management and Sustainability*. Wallingford, UK: CABI.

Shone, A. and Parry, B. (2001). *Successful Event Management: A Practical Handbook*. London, UK: Continuum.

Wagen, L. v. d. and White, L. (2010). *Event Management for Tourism, Cultural, Business and Sporting Events* (4th edn). French Forest, NSW: Pearson Australia.

Weaver, D. B. (2008). *Ecotourism* (2nd edn). Milton, Qld: John Wiley & Sons.

Wheeller, B. (1994). Egotourism, sustainable tourism and the environment – a symbiotic, symbolic or shambolic relationship. In A. V. Seaton (ed.), *Tourism: The State of the Art* (pp. 647–654). Chichester, UK: John Wiley & Sons.

Wilson, E. O. (1998). *Consilience: The Unity of Knowledge*. New York: Knopf.

World Commission on Environment and Development (1987). *Our Common Future*. Oxford, UK: Oxford University Press.

Part I

Thinking critically about events and sustainability

1 Events, society, and sustainability

Five propositions

Tomas Pernecky

Introduction

Events are important not only to individuals but also to civilisations. Many a sociologist, anthropologist, and historian would agree that events have always been a part of societies, although they may have taken on different forms, meanings, and significance. They serve specific functions in the ways we interact with one another, and play a part in the structuring and maintaining of societies. If we were to stop and think about all of the events commencing daily around the world – from festivals embedded in rich traditions, to religious events, conventions, and political rallies, we come to the realisation that this phenomenon is inseparable from the fabric of humanity. Events not only reflect the 'mood' of a people, they express community values, visions, and hopes, and speak of the environments in which they take place. Built into the socio-cultural systems, events are intertwined with many aspects of our lives, traversing the social, political, cultural, economic, historical, and psychological dimensions.

It is therefore appropriate to begin by stating that the term 'sustainability' ought to reflect the immensity of the events phenomenon. Sustainability and events research then should also extend to understanding the various roles and functions of events in societies. With the exception of a few scholars, the sustainability–events nexus has followed a single train-track, and mainly attended to environmental concerns, and less to the social and cultural aspects of events. If not deemed sustainable, events can be depicted as a 'problem' for the environment, which has led many authors to focus largely on management models and the impacts of events. The overarching aim of this chapter thus rests on a claim that there is a lot more to sustainability and events than is widely acknowledged. The following pages attempt to address the complex relationship between events, society, and sustainability beyond the prevailing environmental focus, and to explore how these intersect, so that new horizons of sustainability can emerge.

With regard to defining events for the purpose of this chapter, the operating presumption is that the vast majority of events have a cultural aspect, often require some level of organisation, and have an element of commonality which draws people together – whether motivated by particular interests, needs, cultural imperatives, or ideology. The character of the work presented is conceptual, and allows for events to be tackled broadly as temporal gatherings for a common purpose: as the 'coming together' of people. The term 'events' is therefore used in a broad sense to signify an aspect of human activity that pertains to modes of socio-cultural being, that is worthy of enquiry. Importantly, events are taken as a phenomenon that is inherent and significant to humans and society, a recognition that strengthens the field of Event Studies as a domain of important knowledge and experience.

How did we arrive at talking about sustainability?

> The present worry about sustainability is a consequence of man's capability to understand and manipulate the resources of earth.
>
> (Faber *et al.* (2010, p. 11))

Sustainability is not something that can be artificially divorced from the actions of individuals and the ways societies function. Sustainability, as we understand it today, is a contemporary issue, and the lack thereof, is closely linked with social problems for it implies undesirable outcomes. This opposite spectrum can be given the label 'unsustainability'. In other words there is something that at least some members of a society perceive as a problem. In this case, it is the lack of sustainable practices, careless decision making, and resource-intensive modes of operation that may pose a risk to society and its survival. Known as the *subjective element* of social problems, it is given a momentum when part of society believes that a certain condition will decrease the quality of human life – a belief that something is harmful and should therefore be changed (Mooney *et al.*, 2011). Much of the sustainability discourse arises out of such concerns, impacting many facets of our lives: from business, to politics, to increasing areas of science.

There is also the *objective element* in the study of social problems that refers to the existence of a social condition which we can for example experience, learn about, or be exposed to through media (Mooney *et al.*, 2011). Seeing children begging for food, being exposed to poverty, living in a neighbourhood with a high crime rate, witnessing inadequate housing – all of these are examples of the objectivity of social problems. This objective element in relation to sustainability, however, is a lot more problematic as there is no unified consensus on what counts as unsustainable behaviour or practice, and debates of this nature are met with great controversy and disagreement. Economic growth, for instance, is believed to be necessary for the reduction of poverty, but is not so welcome when speaking of environmental protection. This is one of the moot points in sustainable discourse (for greater insights see Verstegen and Hanekamp, 2005).

Loseke (1999, p. 25) further explains that 'constructing a successful social problem requires that audiences be convinced that a condition exists, that this condition is troublesome and widespread, that it can be changed, and that it should be changed'. She adds that, as used in social construction perspectives, 'a *claim* is any verbal, visual, or behavioural statement that tries to convince audiences to take a condition seriously' (p. 39) (original emphasis). A fitting generic example may be the well-known Al Gore documentary about climate in crisis *An Inconvenient Truth* (www.climatecrisis.net). Events-related claims driving the sustainability agenda are often underpinned by environmental concerns such as global warming, the rise of carbon dioxide, and pollution. The claims we are exposed to can take the form of a press article such as the case below:

> The ongoing 2010 World Cup has been in the design news for all the wrong reasons. Everybody's spent a lot of time griping about the design of the new ball, but more serious problems have emerged now. The whole event, it turns out, is an ecological disaster. According to a recent study undertaken by the Norwegian government (bless those Scandinavians!) the World Cup will have a carbon footprint of 2,753,251 tons of CO_2, equivalent to one year's emissions from one million cars.
>
> (Rajagopal, 2012)

Statements like this one are designed to make us think in certain ways. Many authors, academic or not, who write on the subject of sustainability, environmental issues, and the need to 'green up' the events industry tend to re-affirm that there is a problem that ought to be addressed. In the study of social problems, such claims serve the purpose of convincing audience members 'how to think about social problems and how to feel about these problems … to think and feel in particular ways' (Loseke, 1999, p. 27). While it is not the purpose of this chapter to examine whether any such claims are just or not, it is necessary to consider the process of constructing social problems and the possible implications in the context of events.

The field is in the process of evaluating, negotiating, and grappling with the complex issues of sustainability, leaving some looking for truth in the words and statements that surround us. Yet 'truth' doesn't necessarily matter in the social problems realm – what matters is what people believe is true and therefore all that matters is 'whether or not audiences evaluate the claims as true' (Loseke, 1999, p. 28). Put differently, it is knowledge versus popular belief. To a critical thinker, it would appear that the treatment of events depends on the constructed views on what it means to be sustainable and what falls out of the perimeters and is thus deemed as unsustainable. The first proposition therefore makes an argument for critical assessment of claims on sustainability in Events Studies.

Proposition 1 Sustainability is a concern closely related to social problems. It speaks of the contemporary action, behaviour, and attitudes of humans and society. Future events research ought to tackle sustainability critically in order to understand the forces, impacts, and consequences interconnected with sustainability discourse.

It is more important than ever for businesses to be 'good' and to demonstrate that they care about people and the environment. Events, which are largely seen as business entities, if not sustainable, fall under the category of unsustainable practices and behaviour. In this light, it is easy to understand the shift towards corporate sustainability and social responsibility, but on what counts are events (un)sustainable, and are we too accepting of the claims we are exposed to?

The need for criticality

Sustainability claims can be made on different levels, in varied contexts, and will differ depending on priorities and perspectives adopted. Larsen (2009, p. 65) stresses that in our pursuit of sustainability we will do well if we search for 'meaning and content in differing views of sustainability, rather than rushing to the conclusion of rightness or wrongness from a particular worldview'. In this regard, a critical enquiry doesn't take sides; it turns, reveals, and examines from different points of view so more informed choices and decisions can be made, and so that richer understandings can be derived. Critical thinking is also important when questioning claims of (un)sustainability and its supporting evidence, as well as the advantages, limitations, and contexts in which such claims are made. As proposed by Bowell and Kemp (2010, p. 4), 'critical thinkers should primarily be interested in arguments and whether they succeed in providing us with good reasons for acting or believing'.

The recent London Olympic Games were set to be the 'Greenest Games in modern times' (London 2012, 2007, cited in Hayes and Horne, 2011) and were also promoted as 'sustainable Games' – claims that have seen great controversy in recent months. Despite the pains of London 2012 to meet their vision, the sustainability aspect of this event has already been scrutinised. One of the leading UK newspapers, the *Guardian* (see the article by Boykoff, 2012), for example, questions the involvement of sponsors such as Dow Chemicals – a company responsible for the 1984 gas disaster in India, and British Petroleum (BP) whose environmental track record, the paper claims, is 'dodgy'. Hayes and Horne (2011) further argue that the 2012 London Olympics model for sustainability is 'a hollowed-out form of sustainable development' and explain that the approach is essentially a top-down approach with a limited civic engagement. This poses a problem if sustainability is to be about people and the environment which they are part of. Proclaiming the Games as a 'fundamentally unsustainable event' the authors conclude that:

> The lesson from London, as from other Games before it, is that sustainable development is conceptualized as 'best practice', 'best available technology', 'green growth' and so on; it is not a question of challenging the compatibility of economic growth with environmental remediation, nor of constituting environmental citizenship as democratic deliberation.
>
> (Hayes and Horne, 2011, p. 759)

Mega, major, and hallmark events are therefore more likely to reflect contemporary concerns and the shifting socio-economic-political realities. To some extent, Figure 1.1, following, portrays the human condition in relation to events. The predicament of mega events and the events industry as a whole, is that there is an ongoing competition to have better, bigger, and newer venues so that destinations can attract large events, international crowds, and worldwide publicity. Hence the trend seems to follow the path of building more and growing more, while employing the language of sustainability. This needs to be recognised and tackled critically along with other facts such as the necessity for thousands of people to fly, drive, buy, consume, and so forth. Furthermore, one must also take into account the corporate nature of events and the involvement of companies that are willing to invest millions of dollars worth of sponsorship. The reality is that commercial decisions by large corporations are less based on sustainability and well-being, and more on growth, access to new markets, branding, and awareness-related goals. In addition, sponsorship is a multi-billion-dollar business and sponsors are key stakeholders without which many events would cease to exist.

Figure 1.1 The human condition and events.

Sustainability is therefore a messy concept, operating across several dimensions. The multilevel approaches to sustainability do indeed acknowledge that while the economic dimension may focus on competitiveness, the ecological dimension is more concerned about habitability, the social dimension with community, the ethical dimension with moral legitimacy, and the legal dimension with legal legitimacy (M. G. Edwards, 2009). This polarity in sustainable thinking is problematic because economic growth, cost effectiveness, and profitability (e.g. the economic dimension of sustainability) is not the same as preserving the environment and biodiversity (e.g. the environmental dimension of sustainability). While the first might see 'growth' as a necessary pathway, the second is likely to perceive it as worrisome if not alarming. This tension is particularly troublesome in assessing events, and the three pillars of sustainability that dominate the current events literature (see for example Musgrave and Raj, 2009) demand a more critical treatment. There is no single and simple sustainable pathway. The fact that sustainability is a complex matter and that it can play out in different but not always complimentary ways is not yet fully recognised in Event Studies. The need for criticality expressed in this chapter therefore must include the ability to discern the contexts and dimensions in which claims take place. Only then can better assessments of sustainability-related arguments be made.

> **Proposition 2** The concept of sustainability traverses across different dimensions which do not necessarily rest on the same underlying premises. Events research ought to take into account that sustainability claims can be made on different levels, in varied contexts, and can differ based on the perspectives adopted.

Events and sustainability: different lenses

Following on from the previous section, it is important to acknowledge that scientific approaches to sustainability 'differ depending on the way a system, entity, or process is defined, the time horizon is chosen, and the parameters of study are determined' (Becker, 2012, p. 10). This chapter has already established that sustainability with regards to events tends to be largely underpinned by concerns about the natural environement. Faber *et al.* (2010) confirm that sustainability is often tackled from a technological and normative perspective with debate swinging towards ecological and environmental issues. Not surprisingly, there is a tendency to focus on managerial implications with editors of contemporary texts (e.g. Raj and Musgrave, 2009) motivated to illustrate sustainable management issues to be considered by managers. The conceptualisations of sustainability are often erected on the foundations of seeing events through an 'industry' lens (in this regard Smith-Christensen, 2009 offers useful insights), which has led to two predominant ways that the events phenomenon features in sustainability discourse. We ought to distinguish between events that are designed to promote, embrace, and communicate messages of sustainability, and a broader (managerial/industry) macro-perspective which tackles events in general.

With regard to the first, events are specifically organised to promote, debate, and demonstrate sustainable practices, and raise awareness of related issues such as global warming, the need for recycling, and so forth. This can take place by way of organising festivals, conferences, music events, symposiums, and also online events. Often motivated by environmentally focused policies, visions, and ideologies, the key term assigned to events of this nature is 'green events'. Harvey's (2009) work *Greening Live Earth UK*, for example, shows the importance of minimal environmental impact of the event to the organising body by way of reducing CO_2, offsetting emissions, and sustainability pledges from involved stakeholders. Wittlich (this volume) offers insights on how this can be requested and driven by invested performers such as the musician Jack Johnson. Gibson and Wong (2011) further argue that these events can send powerful place marketing messages to visitors about being forward-minded and aware of contemporary issues. One of the benefits, as they note, is that green festivals can 'promote environmental messages in ways that are fun, creative or experimental' and 'reach audiences otherwise rarely exposed to conservation or sustainability ideas' (p. 99). What this comes down to is the notion of some events becoming intentional agents of sustainability. Such events are charged by certain beliefs and principles which transpire though the planning, programming, organisation, design, promotion, and stakeholder management.

With regard to the second distinction, sustainability has been approached from a macro-perspective which takes as its focus events at large. This angle of vision is fortified by the need to address the industry, as events – major and hallmark events in particular, including related products, components, and operational aspects – pose a 'problem' for the environment. As a result, events need to be managed so that possible negative impacts are minimised. Developments on this front can be observed on a worldwide scale. The International Organisation for Standardisation (ISO), a network of the national standards institutes, for example developed ISO standard 20121:2012 which promotes sustainable management of events. This is a management system which specifically targets the events industry. It takes into account the fact that events cannot be divorced superficially from other business practices and that they rely on other professions, businesses, services, and the manufacturing of goods. Worth noting is also the recently developed standard ISO 26000:2010, which is designed to give guidance on social responsibility across a wide range of sectors and organisations. With regard to these developments, there is increasing concern about events due to perceived negative impacts. Under this rubric, sustainability inevitably becomes a managerial fixation.

Sustainability as continuance, orientation, and relationships

Apart from the above approaches, sustainability can also be understood by drawing on the discipline of ethics. In a recent book *Sustainability Ethics and*

Sustainability Research, Becker (2012) identifies three key characteristics which shape the contemporary meaning of the term sustainability. These are sustainability as *continuance*, sustainability as *orientation*, and sustainability as *fundamental relationships*.

Sustainability as *continuance* refers to maintaining or continuing the existence of something. Becker stresses that there are two possible interpretations of this term: first it can suggest the ability of a system, entity, or process to maintain itself (e.g. ecosystem), and second, it can refer to a human's ability to maintain a system, entity, or process. In this instance Becker gives an example of a forest which is an economically used ecosystem managed by humans. With regard to the first distinction, and given that events are socially constructed phenomena, we cannot speak of events sustaining themselves. However, by bringing natural and social sciences together, human actions and decisions can be included as part of the system (Becker, 2012). Mega sporting events and the rise of the events industry in general may have an impact on other systems, entities, and processes. Environmental damage, loss of local cultures, dislocated populations, and a possible impact of the events industry on Earth's ecosystems (known as ecological footprint) are just some examples. We can also speak of the continuance of events that have their functions and roles in society. Events are part of economic systems, political systems, traditions, education, knowledge, entertainment, and so on. This way of approaching sustainability (sustainability as continuance) has received attention mainly from scholars who write on event impacts.

The second meaning of the concept of sustainability, sustainability as *orientation*, refers to using the term in a normative and evaluative sense, as something positive – a norm towards which we ('we' being society, industry, organisations, and governments) should strive. Becker (2012) shows that the United Nations international agreement *Agenda 21*, for example, makes explicit statements about sustainable development becoming an international priority. In terms of events, the International Organisation for Standardisation (ISO), responsible for developing ISO 20121, is an example of taking into account long-term human actions and setting new aims. The vast majority of sustainable thinking in the domain of Event Studies falls into this category, and derives from normative approaches to sustainability. Consequently, there are many sustainable management models and solutions to reducing waste and pollution, and alternatives to minimise carbon footprint. Figure 1.2 suggests that sustainability as *orientation* has received most attention within the field.

The normative dimension of sustainability also asks questions such as: *What systems, processes, or entities ought to be maintained? For whom do we have to maintain them and for what reasons? Is there any responsibility or obligation to maintain a certain system, process, or entity?* (Becker, 2012, p. 17). As for events, we can similarly ponder: *What events and related processes shall be maintained? Why? For whom?* However, to be able to answer these questions it is fundamental to first understand the significance of the events phenomenon and

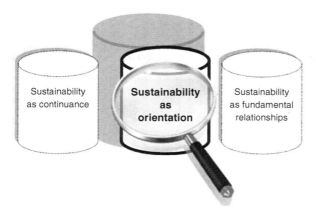

Figure 1.2 Becker's core characteristics shaping the contemporary meaning of the term sustainability.

its role in society. It is necessary to continue developing a field of studies that goes beyond management approaches, as only then can we fathom the value of events and respond to such queries. This area of research includes works that can demonstrate the worth of various events. Zeppel (this volume) does this rather well by bringing to our attention the socio-cultural benefits of Indigenous festivals in Australia.

The third meaning of the concept of sustainability, sustainability as *fundamental relationships*, refers to relationships between human beings and also between humans and nature. Becker (2012, p. 12) underscores that it is vital to not only see sustainability as continuance of something, but consider also the 'fundamental relationships of human beings'. This is notably the least explored area in the study of events, yet one that offers much promise for future research. It is encouraging to see that there are more innovative and broader concepts emerging, such as Richards and Palmer's book *Eventful Cities: Cultural Management and Urban Revitalisation* (Richards and Palmer, 2010, p. 383). The text promotes events as essential phenomena that are part of communities, traditions, practices, and places, and the authors analyse the ways in which events 'make' places. They set out on a journey of developing *eventfulness* and show the much needed shift in thought by contrasting between 'a city with events' and 'the eventful city'. Events become the core of the city, indissoluble with the city. The strong message here is of interconnectedness and relationships: if events are so important to the lives of peoples, in the functioning of societies and the ways we carry out our lives, they must then also be a significant player in the arena of sustainability. The following proposition underlines this prospect of the sustainability–events nexus.

Proposition 3 Sustainability is an orientation pertaining to the complex relationships among people, societies, and the natural world. Events are a phenomenon through which we can study such relationships.

Under this vision of sustainability, rather than seeing events in isolation as yet another industry that requires sustainable event management, events ought to be taken as a phenomenon that is deeply intertwined with human action and people's 'being in the world'. Positioning individual and collective human behaviour in the centre of the sustainability discourse is seen as vital also by others (Faber *et al.*, 2010). Dillard *et al.* (2009, p. 6) recognise sustainability in a similar fashion and put forward the view that 'sustainability and sustainable development are fundamentally about people, the choices they make, associated consequences, and the human learning that takes place'.

From social sustainability to civil society

Social sustainability is equally if not more important in the study of events, as without socially sustainable communities, it would be difficult to imagine that other forms of sustainability can flourish. The term *social sustainability* has been described as both 'a positive condition within societies that supports human well-being' and as 'a process within communities that can achieve that condition' (Dujon, 2009, p. 122). A number of authors (see for example Delamere, 2001; Lenskyj, 2002; Rollins and Delamere, 2007; Small *et al.*, 2005; Tassiopoulos and Johnson, 2009; Waitt, 2003) have written on social impacts of events, offering useful insights on related issues such as the importance of community participation (Rogers and Anastasiadou, 2011), social leverage of events (Chalip, 2006), and social capital building (Schulenkorf *et al.*, 2011). Although critical work is starting to emerge, social sustainability is yet to be firmly grounded within the field, for relatively little attention has been devoted to this important area of research (Smith, 2009). Studies by the likes of Minnaert (2012), which examines the non-infrastructural outcomes of the Olympic Games for socially excluded groups, begin to unveil that in many cases, social sustainability is neither part of the aims of the Olympic cities, nor of the organisation of the Games. Similar findings have been reached by Smith (2009) who offers a critical overview of social sustainability of major sporting events. He lists possible positive social effects which include: reinforcing collective identities, uniting people, improving self-esteem, increasing civic pride, raising awareness of disability, inspiring children, providing experience of work, encouraging volunteering, increasing participation in sport, and promoting well-being and healthy living. Smith (2009) is however quick to point out that these comprise potential social effects, and that research is yet to prove that this is the case, leading to the conclusion that the positive social effects of major events are short-lived and have a poor record.

Magis and Shinn (2009, p. 38) suggest that there are four conditions which are critical to social sustainability, or what they call 'primary constituents of social sustainability'. These are: (1) human well-being, (2) equity, (3) democratic government, and (4) democratic civil society. With regard to the first, human well-being is about ensuring that basic human needs are met. This includes guaranteed human rights, protection against violence and crime, and also having the opportunity to be creative and productive. The second constituent, equity, has to do with the reduction and eradication of inequalities. The third constituent, democratic government, suggests that governance needs to be oriented to the people. In Magis and Shinn's view, the government can be seen as the holder of the public trust and therefore must be not only responsive to the people but also accountable for the decisions made. The last of the constituents, democratic civil society, is a rather fuzzy concept, and as explained by M. Edwards (2009, p. 3), it can range from being a specific product of the nation-state and capitalism, to a universal expression of the collective life of individuals. To Tester (1992), the term civil society means the following:

> ...a coming together of private individuals, an edifice of those who are otherwise strange to one another. ... It involves all those relationships which go beyond the purely familial and yet are not of the state. Civil society is about our basic societal relationships and experiences; it is about what happens to us when we leave our family and go about our own lives. It is about the relationships I have with my colleagues and the person who crashed into my car.
>
> (Tester, 1992, p. 8)

The extent of social sustainability is therefore much broader than the focus on social impacts of some events – typically mega and major sporting events and prominent festivals. Examining social sustainability in New Zealand, Baehler (2007, p. 38) states that a comprehensive vision of social and political sustainability 'needs to include important bits of culture and behaviour that government cannot easily influence, such as day-to-day civilities among people, and social mixing across the ethnic, religious, and socioeconomic divides that so control our identities'. Events in their various shapes and forms offer a platform for many such activities. Fairs, festivals, symposiums, protests, business events, sporting events – all of these are important for the mixing, exposing, integrating, voicing, connecting, and relating of peoples. In this regard, not a great deal is known about the role of events in contributing to the dynamics of nationhood and identity, and research of this nature sits on the fringe of the field (apart from the few related works such as by Aitchison and Pritchard, 2007).

Related to social sustainability is also the problem of segregation. Semenza (2009) holds that isolation is socially unsustainable, eventually resulting in societal decay. To him civic engagement is an important building block towards developing sustainable communities. More events research therefore ought to be devoted to examining the extent to which events may be a bridge to overcoming isolation and to promoting inclusion, cross-cultural understanding, diversity, and tolerance. For some thinkers (Tassiopoulos and Johnson, 2009), events are believed to have an integrating effect when introduced into a social system. The hopeful and more optimistic prospect of events is that they can be part of a global civil society, something that is described by Magis as the 'endeavours of people engaged internationally to promote the public good' (Magis, 2009, p. 97). But there is of course the other side of the spectrum. Events have been deployed to manipulate, intimidate, distance, and alienate people. Furthermore, events (sporting events in particular) can be an arena for acts of violence and angst. The fourth proposition highlights the significance of events to social and cultural sustainability but warns against their self-righteous portrayal.

Proposition 4 Events are an important means of socio-cultural sustainability and have the potential to promote equality, cultural diversity, inclusion, good community relations, and human rights. However, events are not righteous in themselves, and an important aspect of the study of events must lead to the examination of the underlying meanings, messages, intentions, and ideologies.

On a final note, it is important to underscore the need to continue advancing knowledge of the events phenomenon which has been part of our existence for thousands of years. Events must be recognised as a medium through which societal relations and experiences are maintained, developed, and transformed. Events are intrinsic to how societies function, and it is the task of Event Studies to explore such wide ranging prospects critically. The final fifth proposition is indicative of the overall message in this chapter.

Proposition 5 Sustainability needs to be tackled not mainly through the prisms of event management but understood in a wider context of society. Events are the fabric of society, contributing to the complex socio-cultural-political worlds we live in. The acknowledgement of the significance of the events phenomenon is a fundamental requirement for moving the study of sustainability and events forward.

Concluding thoughts

The academic community is increasingly acknowledging the importance of events and there is now a concentrated effort to broaden our understanding of this phenomenon. As a consequence, we are at the verge of forming a new branch of knowledge under the name of Event Studies. This chapter has sought to stretch current thinking on sustainability in the field, and posits that there is a deeper and more profound way in which events feature in our lives. With regard to sustainability, it has been shown that it is a broad and multidimensional concept. Distinctions were made between events that can be perceived as intentional agents designed and organised to promote messages of sustainable and environmental practices, and a macro-perspective which takes as its focus events at large. Drawing on the discipline of ethics, sustainability was examined in relation to the core characteristics which shape the contemporary meaning of the term: as continuance, orientation, and as fundamental relationships. Research gaps have been identified and calls made for approaching sustainability not only critically, but seeing it in a broader context of society, and not only as a management initiative. This chapter holds that events are vital for the stability of social and cultural systems, taking a part in negotiating as well as the maintenance of existing and evolving cultures. The role events play by way of contributing to the making of societies and contemporary social, cultural, and political realities must not be overlooked.

An equally important issue that is interrelated with the discourse on sustainability, but only touched on in this chapter lightly, is the need for events to be fully recognised in the realm of academia. Events are beginning to be acknowledged as a legitimate and important domain of research. This is not an easy feat for a newcomer trying to grow and expand into new directions, with academics in different parts of the world actively contributing to a new branch of knowledge. There is no doubt that the field is ready for more theoretical and conceptual sophistication, which will lead to advances on the front of sustainability. The answers to the questions of how to approach sustainability in the context of events, and what can/ought to be done about it, depend on the constructed and negotiated understanding of sustainability (or the lack thereof), and the level of recognition of events as a noteworthy subject of study.

References

Aitchison, C. and Pritchard, A. (2007). *Festivals and Events: Culture and Identity in Leisure, Sport and Tourism*. Eastbourne, UK: Leisure Studies Association, University of Brighton.

Baehler, K. (2007). Social sustainability: New Zealand solutions for Tocqueville's problem. *Social Policy Journal of New Zealand*, July (31), 22–40.

Becker, C. U. (2012). *Sustainability Ethics and Sustainability Research*. London, UK: Springer.

Bowell, T. and Kemp, G. (2010). *Critical Thinking: A Concise Guide* (3rd edn). Abingdon, UK: Routledge.

Boykoff, J. (2012, 22 April). Has London 2012 been greenwashed? Sponsorship deals with Dow Chemical and BP threaten to derail the Olympics' sustainable aims. It's not too late to cancel them [electronic]. *Guardian*. Retrieved 23 May 2012 from: www.guardian.co.uk/commentisfree/2012/apr/22/has-london-2012-been-greenwashed.

Chalip, L. (2006). Towards social leverage of sport events. *Journal of Sport & Tourism*, 11(2), 109–127. doi: 10.1080/14775080601155126.

Delamere, T. A. (2001). Development of a scale to measure resident attitudes toward the social impacts of community festivals, Part II: Verification of the scale. *Event Management*, 7(1), 25–38. Retrieved 5 January 2012 from: www.ingentaconnect.com.ezproxy. aut.ac.nz.

Dillard, J., Dujon, V. and King, M. C. (2009). Introduction. In J. Dillard, V. Dujon and M. C. King (eds), *Understanding the Social Dimension of Sustainability* (pp. 1–14). New York: Routledge.

Dujon, V. (2009). In the absence of affluence: The struggle for social sustainability in the Third World. In J. Dillard, V. Dujon and M. C. King (eds), *Understanding the Social Dimension of Sustainability* (pp. 122–136). New York: Routledge.

Edwards, M. (2009). *Civil Society*. Malden, MA: Polity Press.

Edwards, M. G. (2009). Visions of sustainability: An integrative metatheory for management education. In C. Wankel and J. A. F. Stoner (eds), *Management Education for Global Sustainability* (pp. 51–92). Charlotte, NC: IAP-Information Age Publishing, Inc.

Faber, N. R., Peters, K., Maruster, L., Haren, R. v. and Jorna, R. (2010). Sense making of (social) sustainability: A behavioral and knowledge approach. *International Studies of Management and Organization*, 40(3), 8–22. doi: 10.2753/IMO0020–8825400301.

Gibson, C. and Wong, C. (2011). Greening rural festivals: Ecology, sustainability and human-nature relations. In C. Gibson and J. Connell (eds), *Festival Places: Revitalising Rural Australia*. Bristol, UK: Channel View Publications.

Harvey, E. (2009). Greening Live Earth UK. In R. Raj and J. Musgrave (eds), *Event Management and Sustainability* (pp. 195–205). Wallingford, UK: CABI.

Hayes, G. and Horne, J. (2011). Sustainable development, shock and awe? London 2012 and civil society. *Sociology*, 45(5), 749–764. doi: 10.1177/0038038511413424.

Larsen, G. L. (2009). An inquiry into the theoretical basis of sustainability: Ten propositions. In J. Dillard, V. Dujon and M. C. King (eds), *Understanding the Social Dimension of Sustainability* (pp. 45–82). New York: Routledge.

Lenskyj, H. J. (2002). *The Best Olympics Ever? Social impacts of Sydney 2000*. New York: State University of New York Press.

London 2012 (2007) *London 2012 – Sustainability Strategy Launched*. Retrieved 23 January 2007 from: www.london2012.com/press/media-releases/2007/01/london-2012-sustainability-trategylaunched.php.

Loseke, D. R. (1999). *Thinking About Social Problems: An Introduction to Constructionist Perspectives*. New York: Aldine de Gruyter.

Magis, K. (2009). Global civil society: Architect and agent of international democracy and sustainability. In J. Dillard, V. Dujon and M. C. King (eds), *Understanding the Social Dimension of Sustainability* (pp. 97–121). New York: Routledge.

Magis, K. and Shinn, C. (2009). Emergent principles of social sustainability. In J. Dillard, V. Dujon and M. C. King (eds), *Understanding the Social Dimension of Sustainability* (pp. 15–44). New York: Routledge.

Minnaert, L. (2012). An Olympic legacy for all? The non-infrastructural outcomes of the Olympic Games for socially excluded groups (Atlanta 1996–Beijing 2008). *Tourism Management*, 33(2), 361–370. doi: 10.1016/j.tourman.2011.04.005.

Mooney, L. A., Knox, D. and Schacht, C. (2011). *Understanding Social Problems* (7th edn). Belmont, CA: Wadsworth.

Musgrave, J. and Raj, R. (2009). Introduction to a conceptual framework for sustainable events. In R. Raj and J. Musgrave (eds), *Event Management and Sustainability* (pp. 1–12). Wallingford, UK: CABI.

Raj, R. and Musgrave, J. (2009). *Event Management and Sustainability*. Wallingford, UK: CABI.

Rajagopal, A. (2012). *Scoring Those Green Goals*. Retrieved 25 January 2011, from: www.metropolismag.com/pov/20100614/scoring-those-green-goals.

Richards, G. and Palmer, R. (2010). *Eventful Cities: Cultural Management and Urban Revitalisation*. Kidlington, UK: Butterworth-Heinemann.

Rogers, P. and Anastasiadou, C. (2011). Community involvement in festivals: Exploring ways of increasing local participation. *Event Management*, 15(4), 387–399. doi: 10.372 7/152599511X13175676722681.

Rollins, R. and Delamere, T. (2007). Measuring the social impact of festivals [Research Note]. *Annals of Tourism Research*, 34(3), 805–808. doi: 10.1016/j.annals.2007. 01.004.

Schulenkorf, N., Thomson, A. and Schlenker, K. (2011). Intercommunity sport events: Vehicles and catalysts for social capital in divided societies. *Event Management*, 15(2), 105–119. doi: 10.3727/152599511X13082349958316.

Semenza, J. C. (2009). Advancing social sustainability: An intervention approach. In J. Dillard, V. Dujon and M. C. King (eds), *Understanding the Social Dimension of Sustainability* (pp. 264–284). New York: Routledge.

Small, K., Edwards, D. and Sheridan, L. (2005). A flexible framework for evaluating the socio-cultural impacts of a (small) festival. *International Journal of Event Management Research*, 1(1), 66–76. Retrieved 22 April 2012 from: www.ijemr.org.ezproxy.aut. ac.nz.

Smith, A. (2009). Theorising the relationship between major sport events and social sustainability. *Journal of Sport and Tourism*, 14(2–3), 109–120. doi: 10.1080/147750 80902965033.

Smith-Christensen, C. (2009). Sustainability as a concept within events. In R. Raj and J. Musgrave (eds), *Event Management and Sustainability* (pp. 22–31). Wallingford, UK: CABI.

Tassiopoulos, D. and Johnson, D. (2009). Social impacts of events. In R. Raj and J. Musgrave (eds), *Event Management and Sustainability* (pp. 76–89). Wallingford, UK: CABI.

Tester, K. (1992). *Civil Society*. London, UK: Routledge.

Verstegen, S. W. and Hanekamp, J. C. (2005). The sustainability debate: Idealism versus conformism – the controversy over economic growth. *Globalizations*, 2(3), 349–362. doi: 10.1080=14747730500367843.

Waitt, G. (2003). Social impacts of the Sydney Olympics. *Annals of Tourism Research*, 30(1), 194–215. doi: http://dx.doi.org/10.1016/S0160–7383(02)00050–6.

2 Critical perspectives on sustainability

Don Clifton

The need for humanity to live sustainably – for there to be a 'sustainable world' – has roots dating back thousands of years in concerns at the environmental damage humans cause (Hughes, 2001). Contemporary sustainable world discourse is often dated from the 1880s and the response to environmental damage that paralleled the emergence of the Industrial Revolution. The 1987 World Commission on Environment and Development's report 'Our Common Future' (the 'Brundtland Report') (WCED 1987) and a series of follow-up international events saw the sustainable world concept, referred to as 'sustainable development', gain international prominence (Speth and Haas, 2006; Blewitt, 2008). Sustainable world narratives are now well embedded in national and international political circles, in the business sector, in the agendas of a broad range of NGOs, social groups, and research organisations, and in many academic and professional disciplines. Despite this, humanity is not living sustainably. Absolute and persistent poverty continues to affect hundreds of millions of people (Bell, 2009), the Earth's ecosystems continue to deteriorate (UNEP 2007), atmospheric greenhouse gas loads continue to rise (IPCC 2010), and humanity's use of Earth's renewable natural resources continues to exceed its rate of regeneration, with this unsustainable rate of use accelerating (Footprint Network 2010a).

Why is this happening? This chapter considers whether the dominant sustainable world approach, commonly tagged as sustainable development, is itself part of the problem such that, regardless of how aggressively it is pursued, it is by its nature unable, or highly unlikely, to deliver its promised outcomes. We begin by considering what it means for there to be a sustainable world, and describe two main sustainable world approaches: a 'reformist approach' and a 'transformational approach'. Reformism, which is the current dominant approach, is then assessed using Ecological Footprint Analysis ('Footprint Analysis') in conjunction with $I=PAT$ ($I=PAT$ presents human impact on the environment I, as a function of P: population, A: affluence, represented as consumption/production per capita, and T: technology, as the ecological impact per unit of consumption/production).

The analysis concludes that reformism is unlikely to progress humanity towards a sustainable world outcome. Further, rather than helping society achieve needed change, reformism can create a false sense of progress that acts as a barrier to the more decisive action necessary to address humanity's unsustainable behaviours. The chapter concludes by proposing that a more transformational approach is needed to see humanity successfully transition to a sustainable way of living.

A sustainable world

Despite general agreement that a sustainable world is something we need, the concept remains ambiguous, contested, and grounded in different value systems that defy efforts to find common ground beyond generalised motherhood slogans (Osorio *et al.*, 2005; Manderson, 2006). Two main streams of sustainable world thought, which we will refer to as a 'reformist approach' (or 'reformism') and a 'transformational approach', are however evident in the literature.

Reformism proposes that the current dominant socio-economic system – that of an economic growth model encompassing: (a) free trade; (b) globalisation; (c) a key role for multi-national corporations; (d) a focus on technological advance; and (e) human well-being progressed through increased personal income and consumption – is fundamentally sound and well capable of delivering the goal of continued human development or, more commonly, sustainable development. Under this approach, humanity's challenge is to pursue human development through global pursuit of the dominant socio-economic model in ways that address the ecological and social harms currently being experienced, i.e. make the current system more 'green and just' (Williams and Millington, 2004; Clifton, 2010a).

Alternatively, the transformational approach sees the current dominant socio-economic system as a root cause of current unsustainable behaviours and, to progress a sustainable world, transformational change is needed. Key features of this approach include: (a) human well-being as best progressed through consumptive sufficiency and a focus on well-being through life experiences; (b) continued consumptive growth as unsustainable and a primary cause of both ecological problems and poverty; (c) poverty as best resolved through resource reallocation not more global-level resource-throughput-growth with a key role for the rich, especially the industrialised North, to cease the exploitation of resources from the politically and economically weak; and (d) constraints placed on use of Earth's natural resources such that it remains within ecosystem limits (Williams and Millington, 2004; Clifton, 2010a).

Reformism is the current dominant sustainable world approach and is consistent with the sustainable development agenda promoted by the business sector, the UN, and by most, if not all, governments (Gould and Lewis, 2009; Clifton, 2010a). Some authors point out that reformism not only dominates, but is the only sustainability discourse granted legitimacy in political and commercial circles – to be heard politically or by business, any sustainable world pathway needs to fit the reformist model (Handmer and Dovers, 1996; Gould *et al.*, 2008). This has not prevented transformational narratives from being aired in other ways (through books, articles, interest group activities, and so on), but they rarely, if ever, find acceptance within political and business domains as a genuine and credible sustainable world approach.

So which sustainable world approach should society pursue? This is a challenging question but one that needs to be confronted. We do not have a second chance to live sustainably – we either transition to a sustainable world in an orderly way or face some form of imposed correction with consequences that may be far from desirable. One way to consider this 'which approach?' question is to use Footprint Analysis coupled with $I = PAT$, a task to which we now turn.

$I = PAT$ and Footprint Analysis

One way of looking at the reformist and transformational approaches is in terms of $I = PAT$ (Holdren *et al.*, 1995; York *et al.*, 2003), which presents human impact on the environment I, as a function of:

P: population;
A: affluence, represented as consumption/production per capita, usually as per capita GDP; and
T: technology, as the ecological impact per unit of consumption/production.

Table 2.1 on page 33 summarises the reformist and transformational approaches in $I = PAT$ terms.

We will apply $I = PAT$ to a critique of the reformist and transformational approaches in conjunction with Ecological Footprint Analysis ('Footprint Analysis') shortly, but first, an overview of Footprint Analysis.

In brief, Footprint Analysis involves (Kitzes, 2007; Footprint Network 2010a):

a   Calculating an 'Ecological Footprint' measure of human appropriation of the Earth's renewable natural resources, usually expressed as a standardised measure of global hectares per capita ('ghpc').
b   Calculating available 'biocapacity', that is, the regenerative capacity of the Earth's renewable natural resource base (also as ghpc).
c   Comparing these two measures to determine if humans are living in ecological credit or ecological deficit.

As such, Footprint Analysis seeks to determine a sustainability bottom line – the extent to which humans are living within the reproductive capacity of the Earth's renewable natural resource base as opposed to depleting it.

The most recent (2010 release) Footprint Analysis data show that, at a global level, humans have an average ecological footprint of about 2.7 ghpc compared to an available biocapacity of about 1.8 ghpc (Footprint Network 2010b). This means that we are using renewable natural resources at a rate of about 150 per cent of their regenerative capacity, i.e. we are systematically depleting this

Table 2.1 Sustainable world approaches in $I = PAT$ terms

$I = PAT$ element	Reformist	Transformational
I	Reduce renewable natural resource use to sustainable levels by focusing on T and using (mostly) market pricing systems that internalise social and ecological externalities. #	Set limits on renewable natural resource use to be well within regenerative limits. All of PAT are addressed to ensure limits are not breached.
P	Orientation to maximising the human population that can be supported within sustainable world criteria. Contain very high population growth rates in some (mostly developing) countries. Prevent population decline in some (mostly developed) countries. Otherwise allow population to settle to a 'natural' level.	Current human population is too high and unsustainable – is an issue for all countries to address. Long-term population reduction strategy is required through collective non-coercive and non-discriminatory choice.
A	Continued global GDP growth is necessary to progress human well-being and overcome poverty. Reducing consumption is, for the most, not viable and will harm society and fail to help the poor.	Increased consumption is needed for some where basic needs are not being met but this is achieved through equitable distribution, not more global GDP growth. Overall, and especially in the developed world and for the wealthy in developing nations, resource consumption needs to be reduced.
T	Technological progress to overcome the impacts of $P + A$ is the key to living sustainably and to reducing I to be within ecologically sustainable limits.	Technology is an important part of the overall sustainability solution but on its own will not achieve needed change. Technology to be progressed with caution.

Source: Clifton (2010b).

Note
#: Reformism does not ignore policy limits on renewable natural resource use – cap and trade systems (e.g. for carbon emissions) or quota limits (e.g. for fisheries) are examples of such policies. Reformism does however focus more on market pricing mechanisms than the strong scale-limiting strategies of the transformational approach.

Table 2.2 Projecting the ecological footprint

Factor	Reformist modelling inputs
I=PAT element: *I* (Ecological footprint)	• Current global average ecological footprint = 2.7 ghpc. • Projected 2050 biocapacity based on projected 2050 population and holding all else constant = 1.3 ghpc.
I=PAT element: *P*	• Current human population = approx. 7.0 billion (US Census Bureau, 2011). • Mid-range UN projection to 2050 = 9 billion (UN, 2007).
I=PAT element: *A*	• Assume real global average per capita GDP growth of 1.5% pa. Note: Global GDP per capita growth from 1961 to 2006 = 1.9% pa (WRI, 2010).
Decoupling rate between *P+A* and changes in *I*	• Assume that *I* grows at 75% of changes in *P+A*.

Note
The relationship between *I* and changes in *P* and *A* is not well researched. For a detailed analysis see Clifton (2010b). The 75% relationship used here is consistent with that observed in the European Union from 1971 to 2008 (WWF, 2007).

resource base. So what is the reformist answer to this problem? If we take *I* in *I=PAT* to equate to the Ecological Footprint measure, we can assess the reformist solution by plugging in the data shown in Table 2.2 to take us through to the year 2050 and observing what needs to be achieved:

The results of this *I=PAT* projection suggest that economic growth pressures (the *A* in *I=PAT*) will see a global average Ecological Footprint of about 4.1 ghpc by 2050: up from the current 2.7 ghpc. However, with a growing human population, the per capita biocapacity value reduces to about 1.3 ghpc by 2050 as compared to about 1.8 ghpc now: there are more people sharing a limited amount of biocapacity. This 1.3 ghpc of biocapacity is not all available for human use: some of it needs to be set aside for other species, some to ensure ecosystems remain resilient, and some to allow for the conservative nature of the Footprint Analysis data. How much is not safely available for human use is a debated issue but something in the order of 50 per cent or more may well be needed (for a discussion on this, see Clifton (2010b)). Using this 50 per cent value, available biocapacity for human use by 2050 is more in the order of 0.7 ghpc, not the 1.3 ghpc shown.

What does all of this mean? Put simply, reformism proposes that for humans to live within biocapacity limits by 2050 (if this time frame was adopted as a worthy target), we would need to rely on *T* (technology) to reduce the impact of *P+A* (population and consumption growth) to pull the projected 2050 global average ecological footprint of about 4.1 ghpc down to about 0.7 ghpc, more than a five-fold (over 80 per cent) reduction. To put the magnitude of this challenge into perspective, of the 152 nations listed in the most recent Footprint Analysis accounts (Footprint Network, 2010b), only 6 have an ecological footprint value of 0.7 ghpc or less, all of which are in the category of least developed nations.

Only 23 have a current ecological footprint of 1 ghpc or less. In comparison, on average, the developed nations have a current ecological footprint of about 6.1 ghpc.

We can debate whether the Footprint Analysis numbers are plus or minus some level of error margin, how much *I* goes up based on changes in *P* + *A*, and how much biocapacity should be set aside for other species, but this is more a distraction than something of substance – the numbers are substantial even allowing for uncertainty in the values quoted. It is also true that humans living within biocapacity limits is only one condition we need to meet in order for a sustainable world to be realised, but it is a necessary condition (Kitzes, 2007; Footprint Network, 2010a). The harsh reality is that despite sustainable development having been prominent on the world stage for over 25 years since the publication of the Brundtland Report, natural resource use is increasing, the global aggregate Ecological Footprint is increasing, and ecological degradation continues at an alarming pace. Yet we continue to beat the reformist drum in the hope that a series of technology breakthroughs will somehow transport us to a sustainable world.

Would we tolerate this approach in other settings? Consider a business situation. Imagine for a moment that you are a board member of an event management company. The firm has plenty of capital and is a hive of activity with new staff being added, employees well paid, and a constantly growing stream of contracts to fulfil. The problem is that the business is burning capital – costs exceed revenues, the gap is increasing, and there is no end to this in sight. The board quizzes the CEO on a strategy to address this problem. The CEO's answer is 'have faith in our R&D and market development departments – I'm convinced, as is the entire management team, that we will find the technology breakthroughs and new service packages to give us the winning edge we need!' You protest and demand a restructure to reduce costs, wind back staff numbers, and pull costs within revenue limits, and do so in a clear and rapid time frame. The CEO responds by accusing you of being a pessimist, lacking imagination, failing to show faith and confidence in the management team, and rejects your view as being worthy of discussion. What would you do? The first step would probably be to dismiss the CEO and make the needed changes. But without stretching the analogy too far, this scenario is basically what is happening in the sustainable world space – we are burning renewable natural capital, continuing to push the underlying drivers of resource consumption that are causing the problem, living in hope of technology-based solutions, and dismissing as nay-saying pessimists or extremists those who say the current reformist approach is unrealistic, highly risky, and showing no meaningful signs of working.

Before moving on, one last comment on the growth agenda that is a key plank of reformism. It is well documented that GDP growth and consumption of material goods are limited in their ability to improve human well-being. Above a certain level of personal income, a level which the industrialised world has long exceeded, rising incomes have little impact on improved human well-being and can instead detract from it (Daly, 2005; Cato, 2009). The point is that regardless of the challenges in addressing the impacts of $P+A$ via a focus on T, the pursuit of more A is itself limited in its ability to deliver continued improvements in human well-being.

The collective message here is simple. Reformism presents a road map that is challenging to accept as able to deliver on a key and necessary condition for a sustainable world – that humans live within biocapacity limits. Further, reformism is based on an economic growth premise that has been shown to fail to deliver the continued gains in human well-being that it professes to do. Despite these contradictions, business and government still advocate reformism as the way forward, but surely we must start to openly question the merits of this stance.

Unpacking the T in $I=PAT$

Despite the concerns discussed above, does a focus on T as advocated by reformism offer a meaningful sustainable world pathway regardless of the challenges involved? There are a number of themes that can be identified in unpacking T's components to help answer this question; however, the three we will consider are:

a   improving renewable natural resource productivity.
b   improving resource use efficiency in the production process.
c   Adopting less harmful behaviours in the production and consumption process.

Resource productivity

Applying new technologies to increase renewable natural resource productivity is an important part of the reformist agenda and includes things such as the use of industrialised agricultural practices, genetic engineering of plant and animal species, and so on. Debates continue as to whether these technologies have genuinely increased resource productivity in a sustainable way. Some claim they have while others are far from convinced and propose that this is only apparent if all negative externalities (use of fossil fuels, chemical and fertiliser pollution, soil degradation, biodiversity loss, destruction of cultures) are excluded from the analysis (Shiva, 2005). Beyond this debate is the issue of ecosystem resilience.

Resilience is discussed in two main ways in the literature (Walker and Salt, 2006; Gunderson et al., 2010):

a   engineering resilience, which has to do with the ability of a system to bounce back to its pre-disturbance state following some form of disturbance – such as a personal illness and our ability to overcome it and get back to normal health; and
b   socio-ecological (or 'ecological') resilience, which has to do with the ability of a system to continue to function despite exposure to disturbance, with

this form of resilience enhanced through a range of factors including diversity within a system, maintaining of spare capacity and keeping well away from system tipping points, and a system's ability to adapt to change, evolve, and self-organise.

It is socio-ecological resilience that is of key importance for a sustainable world, and has to do with continuing to meet key sustainable world criteria regardless of what changes might occur to ecological and social systems over time. The key point is that in the sustainable world context, an approach that seeks to maximise renewable natural resource productivity to underpin a quest for continued economic growth as a means of achieving human well-being for as many people as can optimistically be accommodated – as does reformism – undermines the resilience of the very system on which it depends. Pursuit of the goal is its own undoing. This occurs for many reasons including the removal of spare capacity as all natural resources are pulled into the field of production maximisation, the imposition of change at a faster rate than ecosystem feedback mechanisms can provide information concerning the consequences of this change, and, in general, pushing ecosystems close to or beyond undesirable tipping points without society necessarily even knowing this may be happening (Meadows *et al.*, 2004; Walker and Salt, 2006).

Resource use efficiency

One of the main business case arguments to pursue a sustainability agenda is the claimed win-win result that can come from more efficient use of resource inputs in the production process. This is a more-from-less argument claiming that the environment wins through less pressure on resource use, and the firm wins by improvements to the bottom line (Hargroves and Smith, 2006). But if we assume a win for the firm, is there a corresponding win for a sustainable world?

Efficiency gains have long been recognised as a key means by which firms improve productivity, reduce costs, and increase wealth (Princen, 2005; Gould *et al.*, 2008). It is also well known that production-based gains in resource efficiency can, and often do, lead to an increase in output and consumption that negate some or all of the resource use gains (rebound), or result in greater overall resource use (backfire) (Polimeni *et al.*, 2009). The extent of rebound or backfire varies from case to case and could benefit from greater research; however, it is a well-understood and recognised phenomenon.

This does not mean that using resources efficiently in the production process or, more specifically for the issues covered in this book, in the management of events, is not important – it clearly is. The problem is that unless this is coupled with a means to prevent efficiency gains being spent on more resource-consuming production and consumption that negates the gains achieved, then we are deluding ourselves into thinking that progress is being made (think for example of an events management firm reducing resource use, power for instance, saving money in the process, and using that money to expand its business by staging of more and bigger events that themselves use more power). This has major implications for reformism when looked at in $I = PAT$ terms, as if an important component of T is efficiency gains, then the more this is pursued in the absence of some mechanism to control how the gains are spent, the more it will drive increases in A, putting further pressure on I (the Ecological Footprint), and making the needed offsetting impact of T even harder to achieve.

Less harmful production and consumption

Less harmful behaviours in the production and consumption process can cover a multitude of issues including less harmful ways of extracting resources (e.g. fishing practices that reduce by-catch and the killing of non-target species), less polluting technologies, products manufactured for ease of recycling, and so on. All of these practices are again important for businesses and society to pursue. The business sector in particular has a key role to play as, for the most, it is business that determines which resource extraction technologies are used, what the product design and manufacturing technologies are, what set of options the public has to select from in its consumption decisions, what information members of the public have in relation to the impacts of their consumptive choices, and whether consumptive waste can be recycled in a meaningful way (Bruno and Karliner, 2002; Gould *et al.*, 2008). But do we have a similar problem here as for resource use efficiency? In some respects, yes. One reason is that the more we feel our activities are less harmful (less polluting, less resource intensive), the more we may feel inclined to consume, or be convinced by marketing departments that we can consume, and believe we can do so sustainably. One way to explore this issue is to look at the idea of green consumerism, something that is actively promoted in the business sector as one aspect of the business sustainability agenda.

Green consumerism refers to the development, packaging, and marketing of products claimed to be 'environmentally friendly' (in an absolute or relative sense) – 'green events' is a case in point. The marketing message is simple – you can save the world through your consumption choices, and can consume with a clear conscience (Beder, 2002; Bell, 2009). The business message is that green products (including 'green events') and green marketing can provide opportunities to increase sales and profits. All up so the claim goes, everyone wins – business, the consumer, and the environment. This strategy is not difficult to see through. For one thing, green consumerism continues to push humanity down the resource consumption path which has been shown earlier to be running at unsustainable rates – consuming more does not solve this problem regardless of the 'green' nature of what is consumed (Beder, 2002). In addition, green consumerism continues the business-as-usual marketing strategies of need creation through the deliberate engineering of feelings of dissatisfaction and deprivation in people's lives, offering the solution to this dissatisfaction through consuming a particular product (in this case, a 'green' product), and cycling the dissatisfaction-consume-dissatisfaction-consume routine indefinitely to drive continued consumptive demand and economic growth. This need-creating-and-consuming process is however ecologically damaging, undermines human well-being, and offers no durable well-being solution (Hamilton and Denniss, 2005; Cato, 2009).

Another stream of thought connected to this less-harmful-production-and-consumption issue relates to the claimed shift in production and consumption activities to less-resource-intensive service and information industries as economies continue to industrialise. The claim is that increased industrialisation moves a society to becoming less resource intensive and hence contributes to the delivery of less harmful production and consumption behaviours. But is this really something of any significance in addressing sustainable world problems?

The claim that the service sector becomes an increasing part of the economic system of industrialised nations is not as clear-cut as it may seem (for more on this, see Victor (2008) and Douthwaite (1999)); however, one way to look at this issue is through the Footprint Analysis data. A strength of the Ecological Footprint is that it is consumption based – what matters is what is consumed regardless of where in the world goods or services are produced (Footprint Network, 2010a). The Footprint Analysis data show that it is the high-income industrialised nations that, as a collective, have the highest ecological footprint at 6.1 ghpc compared to middle-income nations at 2.0 ghpc and low-income nations at 1.2 ghpc (Footprint Network, 2010b). In this sense the services transition argument comes up as meaningless. The industrialised countries that presumably have transitioned to a higher proportion of service industries in their economic mix have per capita Ecological Footprint measures well above what is sustainable on a global level.

Conclusion

Although only scratching the surface of a few themes by which reformism can be assessed, the critique offered in this chapter suggests that despite its dominance, reformism is challenging to believe as a viable pathway forward for humanity. Instead, it is structured around population, economic, and consumption strategies that place increased pressures on already over-taxed ecological systems, and places a level of faith in human technological advance that is challenging to believe. Further, some advocated technology strategies, although important for society to pursue (resource use efficiency at the production level, less polluting products) can, when coupled with the broader reformist agenda, actively work against the very human and ecological well-being objectives reformism seeks to achieve.

What should we do about this? One response is to say 'well, pursuing mainstream sustainable development will probably not work so why bother – let's just give up on sustainability and hope something will sort itself out in the future'. This is not an acceptable option. We owe it to those of the current generation on whom our activities impact, and to generations that follow, to solve our unsustainable world problems.

Alternately, we could continue to push the reformist line in the hope that, despite its problems, it will somehow get us into sustainable world territory. But this something-is-better-than-nothing approach is not necessarily helpful. As Handmer and Dovers (1996) have put it, an approach to a sustainable world that is based on reformist principles:

> [is] likely to simply put off the needed changes to a time when options will have narrowed ... [it] is possibly the most dangerous path: a relief valve that gives the appearance of change and alleviates symptoms for a time.
>
> (pp. 505–506)

Should society adopt the transformational approach? The claim of this chapter is 'yes' and a few concluding comments may help support this view beyond what has already been presented. First, the transformational approach offers pathways that go beyond the technical fix solutions of reformism and the problems these create. It instead presents alternatives that reformism is unwilling to entertain, such as reformism's unwillingness to pursue strategies that challenge the core tenets of the current dominant socio-economic system. As such, the transformational approach offers society broader options and freedoms to pursue sustainable world objectives rather than, as does reformism, expect that sustainability actions can be engineered to fit a pre-existing socio-economic ideology. But the transformational approach is still no guarantee of sustainable world success. The challenges ahead remain substantial and many of the questions of how to transition to a sustainable society have yet to be identified let alone answered.

Next is the issue of social capacity to change. Robinson (2004) discusses the need for a society that is facing fundamental change to have 'an alternative to the existing order that is viable and that is seen as viable and preferable by a majority of society' (p. 172). The point is that reformism not only dominates current sustainable world discourse but, as mentioned earlier, is the only sustainability discourse that is granted legitimacy in the political and commercial realm. The effect is that society is being consistently groomed by business and government to have no credible and accepted alternate – humanity's future is being wagered on a single sustainability model that is itself challenging to accept as likely to ever deliver needed outcomes. The key point to make here is that progress down a transformational sustainable world path requires broad social change that goes well beyond 'greening' activities within individual firms and industries – events management included. Here lies a key role for business and government – to grant legitimacy to transformational narratives and encourage others in the broad public sphere to do the same. Perhaps then society can meaningfully direct its energies to more creative solutions to the sustainability problems we are facing and be more open and accepting of needed change.

References

Beder, S. (2002). *Global Spin: The Corporate Assault on Environmentalism*. Devon, UK: Green Books Ltd.

Bell, M. M. (2009). *An Invitation to Environmental Sociology*. California: Pine Forage Press.

Blewitt, J. (2008). *Understanding Sustainable Development*. London, UK: Earthscan.

Bruno, K. and Karliner, J. (2002). *Earthsummit.biz: The Corporate Takeover of Sustainable Development*. Oakland, CA: Food First Books.

Cato, M. S. (2009). *Green Economics*. London, UK: Earthscan.

Clifton, D. (2010a). Representing a sustainable world – a typology approach. *Journal of Sustainable Development*, 3(2), 40–57.

Clifton, D. (2010b). A sustainable world – an ecological footprint and I=PAT perspective. *Journal of the Asia-Pacific Centre for Environmental Accountability*, 16(2), 3–26.

Daly, H. E. (2005). Economics in a full world. *Scientific American*, 293(3), 78–85.

Douthwaite, R. (1999). *The Growth Illusion*. Dublin, Ireland: The Lilliput Press.

Footprint Network. (2010a). *Ecological Footprint*. Retrieved 25 November 2011 from www.footprintnetwork.org/.

Footprint Network. (2010b). *Ecological Footprint and Biocapacity – 2010 release*. Retrieved 25 November 2011 from www.footprintnetwork.org/.

Gould, K. A. and Lewis, T. L. (2009). The paradoxes of sustainable development. In K. A. Gould and T. L. Lewis (eds), *Twenty Lessons in Environmental Sociology* (pp. 269–289). New York: Oxford University Press.

Gould, K. A., Pellow, D. N. and Schnaiberg, A. (2008). *The Treadmill of Production*. Boulder, CO: Paradigm Publishers.

Gunderson, L., Allen, C. R. and Holliday, C. (2010). Commentary on Part One articles. In L. Gunderson, C. R. Allen and C. Holliday (eds), *Foundations of Ecological Resilience*, (pp. 3–18). Washington, DC: Island Press.

Hamilton, C. and Denniss, R. (2005). *Affluenza: When Too Much is Never Enough*. Crows Nest, NSW: Allen & Unwin.

Handmer, J. W. and Dovers, S. R. (1996). A typology of resilience: Rethinking institutions for sustainable development. *Industrial and Environmental Crisis Quarterly*, 9(4), 482–511.

Hargroves, K. and Smith, M. H. (2006). *The Natural Advantage of Nations*. London, UK: Earthscan.

Holdren, J. P., Daily, G. C. and Ehrlich, P. R. (1995). *The Meaning of Sustainability: Biogeophysical Aspects*. Washington, DC: United Nations University and The World Bank.

Hughes, J. D. (2001). *An Environmental History of the World*. New York: Routledge.

IPCC. (2010). *Intergovernmental Panel on Climate Change*. Retrieved 18 November 2011 from www.ipcc.ch/.

Kitzes, J. (2007, 8–10 May). *A Research Agenda for improving National Ecological Footprint Accounts*, paper presented at the International Ecological Footprint Conference: Stepping Up the Pace – New Developments in Ecological Footprint Methodology, Policy and Practice, Cardiff.

Manderson, A. K. (2006). A systems based framework to examine the multi-contextual application of the sustainability concept. *Environment, Development and Sustainability*, 8, 85–97.

Meadows, D. H., Randers, J. and Meadows, D. (2004). *Limits to Growth: The 30-Year Update*. White River Junction, VT: Chelsea Green Publishing Company.

Osorio, L. A., Lobato, M. O. and Castillo, X. (2005). Debates on sustainable development: Towards a holistic view of reality. *Environment, Development and Sustainability*, 7, 501–518.

Polimeni, J. M., Mayumi, K., Giampietro, M. and Alcott, B. (2009). *The Myth of Resource Efficiency*. London, UK: Earthscan.

Princen, T. (2005). *The Logic of Sufficiency*. Cambridge, MA: MIT Press.

Robinson, W. I. (2004). *A Theory of Global Capitalism*. Baltimore, MD: The John Hopkins University Press.

Shiva, V. (2005). *Earth Democracy*. Cambridge, MA: South End Press.

Speth, J. G. and Haas, P. M. (2006). *Global Environmental Governance*. Washington, DC: Island Press.

UN. (2007). *World Population Prospects – 2006 Revision*, United Nations – Department of Economic and Social Affairs, Population Division, New York.

UNEP. (2007). *Global Environmental Outlook 4*, United Nations Environmental Programme, Nairobi, Kenya.

US Census Bureau. (2011). *World Population Clock*. Retrieved 18 November 2011 from www.census.gov/main/www/popclock.html.

Victor, P. A. (2008). *Managing Without Growth*. Cheltenham, UK: Edward Elgar Publishing Limited.

Walker, B. and Salt, D. (2006). *Resilience Thinking: Sustaining Ecosystems and People in a Changing World*. Washington, DC: Island Press.

WCED. (1987). *Our Common Future: World Commission on Environment and Development*. Oxford, UK: Oxford University Press.

Williams, C. C. and Millington, A. C. (2004). The diverse and contested meanings of sustainable development. *Geographical Journal*, 170(2), 99–104.

WRI. (2010). *Earth Trends – Economics, Business and the Environment*, World Resources Institute. Retrieved 9 March 2010 from http://earthtrends.wri.org/searchable_db/index.php?theme=5.

WWF. (2007). *Europe 2007: Gross Domestic Product and Ecological Footprint*. Brussels: World Wide Fund for Nature.

York, R., Rosa, E. A. and Dietz, T. (2003). STIRPAT, IPAT and impACT: Analytic tools for unpacking the driving forces of environmental impacts. *Ecological Economics*, 46(3), 351–365.

3 Beijing's 'People's Olympics'

From slogan to sustainability

Charles S. Johnston, Xin Chen, and Jing Tian

Winning the bid

Events begin, occur, and end. To speak of the sustainability of an event can only mean addressing tangible and intangible associated aspects, not the event itself. These aspects are generally considered to be legacies. Tangible legacies of hosting sporting events such as the Olympic Games include the set of stadiums and ancillary buildings required for hosting. Intangible legacies refer to the sense of status granted by peers to the hosts and the sense of pride that arises. Sustaining these legacies requires something more – further effort. In other words, while the Olympic Games may be readily sustainable because they are held every four years, post-Olympics activity is needed for the hosting city to sustain the Olympics DNA and continue leveraging the glory. This is challenging as the direction of the world's spotlight shifts to newer stadiums housing the next Games and the associated status is bestowed upon the latest proud hosts.

This chapter examines sustainability aspects of the XXIX Olympiad Games held in Beijing in 2008. As we write, the London Games are fast approaching. We realise a fuller sustainability analysis could be done two or three years from now, when Beijing becomes the-Olympics-before-last. Yet there is also justification for the present analysis: post-Games trends indicate Olympics impacts continue to play a role in Beijing's urban development.

We begin by considering what return the International Olympic Committee (IOC) and the host city get from hosting the Olympic Games. The two are bound together for seven years between the time when the bidding city is chosen among competitors and its staging of the Games. What the IOC wants is to spread the message about the Olympics. The Olympics is in fact a 'movement' with its own philosophy. The IOC cannot keep the message alive without a live demonstration – the Games – that Olympics values are worthwhile. It cannot do this without designating a proper venue – a host city. The bidding city wants recognition and status from the world and other cities. Many Olympics are coming-of-age parties and successful hosting gives a city bragging rights. Internally, the city wants the civic pride of having successfully hosted the most prestigious event humans hold.

To win the right to host, a city must bid. The submitted bid document is a contract. It is akin to a vow to be in a partnership with the IOC that will produce a result that will give both partners what they need. This partnership is not two-way. The IOC does not have to adjust. To win the bid, a city must commit to hosting the IOC's way. Candidate cities are suitors; they come calling with their bids, and the IOC chooses the city which best demonstrates it will adhere to the Olympics philosophy.

Within the Candidate city, many people are involved in assembling the bid. The act of assembly can require an extensive cultural transformation. To win, the bid must be sincere, and hence people who put the bid together must believe in, or convert to, Olympics values. Further, they must be willing to act. Bid-believers must do what is required after the city has been chosen. The Games need to be successfully staged. This is, however, not the end. The believers assembling the bid must, to fully satisfy the IOC, deliver the environment of the city AND its residents. The IOC tests this in the bidding process, by requiring information about the environment and the level of enthusiasm among the citizenry. IOC representatives visit the candidate city before announcing the winner; it is vital to display the proper environment and the proper enthusiasm of the residents. Only when the IOC is convinced that the candidate city can best deliver the Games in a desirable urban environment with the full support of the residents that maximally fulfils the philosophy of the Olympics will it bestow hosting rights.

Delivering the environment and the residents is not easy but is an absolute necessity above and beyond winning the bid. The bidders want to bask in the full glory of being the host city. They want the status, the recognition, the pride. A city will be in the spotlight for seven years as it prepares for hosting. For 16 days, while the Games are held, and to a lesser extent a month later during the hosting of the Paralympics, the whole world will be watching and evaluating. Nothing must go wrong. The city itself, and its residents, must pass muster with the world.

When the Games are over the city is left with a legacy. The main tangible component is the athletics infrastructure. The intangible component is the memory of the Games, with the accompanying status and recognition, and pride. When one speaks of the sustainability of an Olympic Games these legacy aspects are what usually come to mind. For the Beijing Olympics, these occurred as per normal. Yet, for the XXIX Olympiad held in Beijing, something else happened. Some may think this merely notable, others remarkable, still others amazing. It was certainly unique. What differed initially was that the bidders had to make promises to the IOC that involved far more extensive modification of both the physical environment and Beijing residents, themselves. Getting Beijing ready for prime time involved far more work than anywhere else. It involved sloganeering, hence Beijing's Games were the 'Green, Hi-tech and People's Olympics'. The hard part was making the slogan a reality so that the city and its residents passed muster when the time came.

The amazing factor, to the authors at least, is that the slogan and the subsequent efforts completely worked. By this we mean that the residents of Beijing embraced the suggestions for change. By August, 2008, Beijing was ready: the

Games were ready; the environment was ready; the people were ready. The Games were held and nothing went wrong. What differed after this has been that the people did not want Beijing to go back to the way it had been. For the Olympics, Beijing had become a better, more liveable city. For the Olympics, Beijingers had become people with a higher level of civic literacy. In this one Olympiad instance, the residents have refused to allow life to return to normal. The substance of the sustainability of the 'People's Olympics' is thus much different and more profound than is typical – it is to be found in the transformed consciousness of the people who live there. The proof is that the slogan 'People's Olympics' evolved after the Games to become 'People's Beijing'. How long will this transformation last? For now, we can say that the 'development' of Beijing that occurred between receiving the bid in 2001 and hosting in 2008 will be sustained because the People demand it.

Delivering the games: concerns of the Beijing organisers

A city that wishes to host the Olympics must conform to an established tradition that is enforced by the IOC. The Olympics of ancient Greece were revived during the late nineteenth century, and the first modern Olympiad was held in Athens in 1904. The founding father, Pierre de Coubertin, believed Olympism was a 'religion of energy' (Torres, 2010, p. 4) that, through competitive sports, would lead to an enhanced way of life for individuals and societies. Fundamental Principle #2 of the Olympic Charter notes that 'the goal … is to place sport at the service of the harmonious development of man, with a view to promoting a peaceful society…' (IOC, 2011, p. 10). Olympism thus contains a higher moral purpose that forms the basis for a type of education-through-sports that, in turn, reaps rewards for all of humanity. Any city expecting to be a host must believe it is doing this.

China, from early days, had a desire to be a part of this humanistic event. In her book *Beijing's Games: What the Olympics Mean to China*, Brownell (2008, p. 19) established that the desire to host an Olympics dates back an entire century, when 'patriots in the Chinese YMCA' posed three questions:

1   When will China be able to send a winning athlete to the Olympic contests?
2   When will China be able to send a winning team to the Olympic contests?
3   When will China be able to invite all the world to come to Peking for an International Olympic contest, alternating with those at Athens?

The answers, she notes, were the 1980 Winter Olympics when China made its Olympic debut; the 1984 Summer Olympics at which Chinese shooter Xu Haifeng won the first gold medal to be awarded at that Games and first-ever medal won by China; and finally, the XXIX Olympiad in 2008. China's hosting of the Games thus represents a cross-generational dream that was finally achieved.

By 2001, with the winning of the bid, China had demonstrated to the IOC that it would produce the Games most in line with the philosophy of the Olympic movement. Having given the bid to Beijing, the IOC's main role was of enforcement and support – both having the purpose of ensuring that Beijing would do what it said it would do in its bid document. The onus was now on Beijing, and to a great extent China as a whole, to host the flawless Games. In 2004, Wang Qishan, mayor of Beijing, told this story:

> When the Olympic Flag was passed to me in Athens on 29 August this year, I was very emotional. I said to journalists present: 'we have now taken over the crushing responsibility for hosting the next Olympic Games. The whole world will be watching Beijing.'
>
> (cited in Lu, 2005, p. 25)

There could be no doubt the residents of Beijing were willing and enthusiastic about the 2008 Games. A poll, taken by Gallup before the pre-decision visit of the IOC in early 2001, showed that 94 per cent of the residents in Beijing favoured hosting (Brownell, 2009, p. 189). Shortly afterwards, an article in *The Spokesman Review* (2001, p. C6) noted that the celebration in Beijing for winning the bid was 'laden with meaning that went beyond the awarding of a sports event'. As might have been the case with countries such as Mexico, Japan, or South Korea, the choice of Beijing could very well represent 'China's coming out party' (deLisle, 2009, p. 181). But were Beijingers able to rise to the occasion? There could be no reassurance that the Games they were to put on would impress the world and bring the desired recognition and status. Many feared world derision might be the result. Another story from Mayor Wang is revealing:

> Not too long ago, I attended the China–Japan Soccer Asian Cup final. I was arranged to sit next to the Japanese Ambassador.... In the stadium, I was most worried that the audience would not stand up when the Japanese anthem was played. After all, Japan is a country with which China has diplomatic relations. To my relief, the spectators all stood up. Yet many of them booed and hissed. We could not even hear the anthem.
>
> (cited in Lu, 2005, p. 27)

Five months after being chosen, the Beijing Organising Committee for the Olympic Games (BOCOG) was formed, taking over from the bidding committee (BOBICO) (Tian, 2006). Riding on the sense of pride and public enthusiasm, BOCOG announced Beijing would host the 'best ever games in history'. At this time, the three themes, Green, Hi-tech and People's, were established.

'Hi-tech' as a theme focused on developing the technical ability to host. According to the *Manual for the Candidate City of the Games* (n.d.) this includes factors such as 'computer equipment, telephony, communications and telecommunications systems, timing, public address systems, copying machines and photographic equipment for accreditation [that] requires major financial resources of up to US$400,000,000'.

In the *Manual*, the theme 'Environmental Protection and Meteorology' notes that the Olympic movement is fully committed to sustainable development and endeavours to contribute to the protection of the natural environment: 'all measures should be taken to minimise or eliminate impact on the environment and to contribute to the harmonious integration of the Olympic Games into the natural surrounding'. Above and beyond a commitment to sustainability, the *Manual* notes: 'Environmental protection is an area where Candidates Cities often experience tough public scrutiny...'. For meteorology, the *Manual* has specific requirements on when the Summer Games should be held. The bidding city is also obliged to provide 10 years worth of data on temperature and humidity and precipitation for the year and during this specific period. Beijing Mayor Wang Qishan did not hide his worries about the dates and weather during the 2008 Games, when he addressed the 2004 China Science and Humanities Forum:

> The 2008 Olympic Games are required to begin in late July or early August. But that is the hottest time in Beijing. It also rains a lot then. Good weather in Beijing begins in late August. I thought maybe we could negotiate with the IOC for a later date.... But the IOC did not accept our suggestion.
>
> Why cannot we postpone the games for half a month? The IOC's explanation goes: Europe and North America have their summer holidays in late July and early August. If we have the Games after the holidays, few people in those continents would stay up late to watch the matches. If nobody in the West watches the Games at night, who would buy TV commercials?
>
> (cited in Lu, 2005, p. 26)

For the Green theme, Beijing's hopes were riding on a wing and a prayer. Drastic measures, such as relocating factories well outside the city limits, moving ahead with eliminating coal as a source of residential heating, and limiting automobile access to every other day would be necessary to deliver on the 'Green' promise. Yet these measures did not entirely eliminate Beijing Games organisers' anxiety about the physical environment during the show. Professor Jin Yuanpu, a leading scholar on the Beijing Olympics from Renmin University of China, for example, warned the Chinese public right before the 2008 Games against overestimating or becoming complacent about Beijing's environmental efforts and improvements:

> Of the three concepts, the 'green Olympics' means to create a harmonious ecological environment so as to provide a good foundation for the event.... China is not the first one to propose a 'green Olympics'. Sydney was. Beijing's 'green' can, however, hardly hold a candle to Sydney's. There are deserts 100 kilometres outside of Beijing. We are doing better now, but we cannot compare with Sydney or many other cities in natural conditions. Among the three concepts, 'green' is not our strength. It is our goal and our commitment.
>
> (Jin, 2008, p. 6)

The third theme, People's Olympics, touches upon the relationship between the Games and the philosophy of Olympism. Here again, the *Manual for the Candidate City of the Games* specifies its requirements. As a hosting city, Beijing had to put in place a detailed cultural programme that focused both on national and international culture. It was required to hold multiple ceremonies: the Olympic flame relay; Opening and Closing Ceremonies; the welcoming ceremony at the Olympic Village; the medal presentation ceremonies. These components, however, were just the top layers for the theme of People's Olympics. The bottom layers were numerous and interwoven but ultimately boiled down to two challenging tasks. On the one hand, the Olympics had to be for the Chinese people. On the other, the Chinese people had to be good hosts. The 2008 Games organisers by no means took for granted that the ecstatic crowds cheering in Beijing's streets for the city's successful Olympic bid in 2001 would automatically stand up to the rigorous scrutiny of the world as good hosts in 2008. Their qualms and lack of confidence in this regard were exhibited by the *Beijing Olympic Action Plan* (n.d.), which noted in innumerable places that Beijingers would have to be educated into the role of hosts. The *Plan* announced activities that, according to deLisle (2009, p. 185) promised to bring 'transformative and internationalising effects on China's citizenry'.

'People's Olympics': discursive articulations

When bidding for hosting the 2008 Olympic Games, Beijing promised that 'if the world gives us the 16 days, we will return the world 5000 years' (Jin, 2010). The declaration immediately became an appealing slogan among Chinese. Yet how would Beijing display China's 'extensive', 'rich' and 'splendid' culture in 16 days? 'Through its people', answered the then Chinese Olympic Committee Chair, He Zhenliang (cited by Xia, 2008, p. 3) in 2006. He's reply was further elaborated to mean that 'Beijing will present the world in 2008 an ancient and modern, warm and smiling, civilised and enterprising city' (Jin, 2006, p. 1). Fulfilling such an ambition would clearly have to 'take a village', and hence the 'People's Olympics'.

Arguably the modern Olympic movement has at all times in the past century been pushing for greater involvement of people across the world. The Beijing Games organisers, however, made it public from very early on that they intended to set a record in this regard by hosting an 'all-people's Olympics'. They boasted,

> If for one moment in the Olympic history, there are 1.3 billion more people involved in the event, that will be China's significant contribution to the Olympic movement.... The 'all-people' participation has introduced a new concept into the Olympic movement: the Chinese are hosting a common people's Games in which ordinary folks can all participate.
>
> (cited in Jin, 2008, p. 10)

Yet, practically in the same breath, they admitted that cultivating the 'social software' of or, more precisely, *for* the Beijing Games would be extremely challenging and demanding, much more so than building the 'Hi-tech' facilities, or meeting the 'Green' pledge (He, 2010, p. 12).

The Beijing Games organisers never seemed to have many qualms that the average Chinese would, in one way or another, participate in the Games for fun. Their concern was always about how Beijingers, and Chinese for that matter, would present themselves to the world in the lead-up to and during the 2008 Olympics. The People's Olympics was thus implemented, first and foremost, as a social reconstruction project to help the locals become conscious hosts of the Beijing Games and to become walking 'windows' to both Chinese ancient civilisation and China's present-day drive for modernisation (Lu, 2005, p. 27). Likewise, the 'all-people's Games' were defined as '1.3 billion Chinese ... learning about the Olympic movement, from its history and development trends to the specifics of the sport items included in the Games' (Jin, 2008, p. 9). For justification, de Coubertin was widely quoted in China as having said that his purpose to revive the Games was not only to popularise competitive sports, but more importantly to incorporate it into education. Furthermore, de Coubertin was interpreted to have meant educating both athletes and spectators. Accordingly, the People's Olympics would be an education process for the entire Chinese population (Feng *et al.*, 2010).

The Olympics are, nevertheless, a Western concept. How could they be related to a 'People's Olympics with Chinese characteristics' and conveyed to the Chinese public? The late Professor Ji Xianlin from Peking University, who was dubbed in China as 'Master of Chinese Culture', suggested that Confucius 'should be invited out' to help (Bian, 2007, p. 2). Yet there were also openly expressed concerns that while Chinese Cultural Studies were being revived in various forms across China, only a few in China had adequate knowledge of Confucianism. For most Chinese, Confucius remained little more than a cultural symbol, and their reverence for him was more like icon worship, superstition, or trend-chasing than real appreciation of his doctrines (Zhou, 2008, p. 4). These concerns, however, only fuelled Beijing organisers' attempt to reinvigorate the Chinese culture and anchor it to the identification and engagement of the average Chinese with the Olympics, a sports tradition that originated in the West.

In late 2000, the Renmin University People's Olympics Research Centre was set up, and the People's Olympics website was launched. The Centre carried out a large number of Beijing Olympics-focused research projects (Hu, 2010). Its research findings were both published and presented at public lectures and seminars, and online discussion websites. In 2004, BOCOG published the *Olympic Knowledge Reader for Secondary Students*, which was distributed nationwide through the school system. The book was later put online for free download. Also in 2004, the People's Sports Press published the *Olympic Children's Series* for primary school students and younger readers. In 2006, Professor Jin Yuanpu, Director of the Renmin University People's Olympics Research Centre, published *University Tutorial on the Olympic Culture*. In addition to the mass distribution of these publications, public activities were organised by and in schools, public and private institutions, commercial organisations, professional communities, neighbourhoods, associations, and clubs to publicise and popularise Olympics knowledge. Among the most popular functions were public prize-giving Olympic knowledge competitions, which were held throughout China. Brownell (2009, p. 44) argues that those efforts enabled China to 'carry out the largest 'Olympic education' programme ever implemented by an Olympic host country'.

China's social marketing of the Olympic movement devoted special attention to the potential of integrating the Olympic philosophy and the Chinese culture to bring forth an 'all-people's' Games. The Olympic motto 'higher, faster, stronger' was, for example, advocated as being admirable as it encouraged athletes to press forward with an indomitable will and, in the spirit of fighting, surmount difficulties, hardships, and sufferings often unimaginable by people outside professional sports circles (Jin, 2008). Yet it was often publicised in comparison with the Confucian principle of the 'golden mean', which reportedly underscored the unity of the opposites, and implied that 'too much is as bad as too little', and 'going beyond is as wrong as falling short' (Jin, 2008, p. 9). The relevance of the 'golden mean' to the Olympics movement was said to lie in its 'one-many' continuum notion, in which the 'one' resided in the mass of the 'many', while the 'many' in the universe were interconnected. Not distinguishing between 'one' and 'many', in other words, meant 'you are in me, and I am in you'. The focus was thus placed on 'relationship' and 'harmony' (Chen and Meng, 2010, p. 122).

Here, the message for Beijingers and the Chinese public as a whole was that China would remain fully engaged in international sporting competitions, yet people should not be obsessed with how many gold medals China would win at the Olympics. They were particularly urged to abandon the 'weak-state' (Jin, 2008, p. 11) mentality that was often blamed for China's having been given the cold shoulder, blockaded, and even humiliated for the past two centuries. They were also constantly reminded that there were after all only 300-something gold medals, and that there were no eternal champions in Olympics arenas. In past contests, the potential for failure and loss had haunted literally every Chinese athlete. What the Olympic movement advocated was courage, dedication, perseverance, commitment, and determination to spare no efforts in reaching a goal. Hoping to bring home the message that winning gold medals, important as it might be, was not the be-all-and-end-all of the Olympics movement, China Central Television (CCTV) launched *My Olympics Series* in 2006. According to Zhang (2008, p. 26) this programme focused on the human drama of athletes themselves and told stories of more than 500 'medal winners, losers, and athletes who longed to compete in the Games, but have never made it'. The programme was an immediate success, making its way onto the top-10-rated programmes list of CCTV1 in the first year it was put on air.

These efforts were believed to have translated into social practice the Chinese cultural concepts of 'universal love', 'impartial caring', and 'harmony' (Feng *et al.*, 2010, p. 39). The effect was supposedly best illustrated by the incident of sportsman Liu Xiang, who bore high national expectations to win gold in the 100-metre hurdle in the 2008 Games, but had to withdraw from the qualifying round because of a heel injury. When it happened:

> The Chinese people did not sink into a national depression or bombard Liu Xiang with complaints and ridicule. Instead, they demonstrated a great deal of tolerance, understanding, and care.... The public care about athletes shows that our civic literacy is increasing.... We are more understanding and aware that when we burden our athletes with duties and responsibilities of winning honours for the nation, we should also recognise and respect their rights, and think about their health.
>
> (Feng *et al.*, 2010, p. 39)

To bridge 'higher, faster, stronger' with 'all-people's participation' in the Beijing Games, the Olympic motto was also publicised in China in connection with the traditional Chinese concept that sports should enable longevity. The People's Olympics was thus defined as 'my involvement, my health, my happiness, and my better quality of life', and was linked to the 'National Fitness' initiative, which had been initiated in 1995 (Jin, 2008, p. 10). The Chinese public was persuaded that mass participation in sports and physical exercises would help create a healthy, civilised, and harmonious societal environment for a 'higher, faster, stronger' Beijing Games (Qin, 2010, p. 20). Around the time when the Beijing Olympic theme song, emblem, and mascots were made public in 2006, the national initiative – 'Public Participation in Fitness Exercises Going Hand-in-Hand with the Olympic Games' – was also launched. Incited by the Hi-tech Olympics concept and intended to help the public develop an 'informed' healthy way of life, the Beijing Sports Bureau and the Beijing Science and Technology Association jointly published a four-volume *National Fitness General Knowledge Handbook* and distributed two million sets in the capital in 2008 (Qin, 2010, p. 16).

Actualising each other, the 'National Fitness' programme and the People's Olympics slogan brought forth a multitude and variety of public sports events across China. In Beijing, public single sports events at the municipal, district, and county levels were increased from 216 in 2001 to 784 in 2008 (Qin, 2010). Community and neighbourhood public single sport events went from 681 events drawing a total of 612,000 spectators in 2001 to over 10,000 events and 6.8 million total spectators in 2008. The percentage of people in Beijing who exercised regularly increased from 42 per cent in 2001 to 52 per cent in 2008. At the time the 2008 Olympic Games were held, 'there has never been a moment in Chinese history when ordinary people were as conscious and concerned as today about their personal physical fitness and general quality of life' (Jin, 2008, p. 7).

Invoking Confucianism in the public Olympic education, the People's Olympics was meant to improve Chinese behaviour and etiquette to 'present a refined image to visiting foreigners' (Wang, 2011, p. 27). The task was a huge effort in vernacular social engineering. In the years leading up to the 2008 Olympic

Games, the Beijing Government put out millions of copies of the *General Text-book on Civility and Propriety* (112 pages) that combined etiquette practices from both China and the West, on 'nearly all aspects of human behaviour' (*Daily Times*, 2006). In 2005, the government also launched a series of city-wide etiquette advocacy activities under the general theme 'Polite Beijing, People's Olympics' (Feng *et al.*, 2010, p. 39) The ensuing 'Welcoming the Olympics, improving Manners, and Fostering New Attitude' campaign perhaps set the world record for the scale of public etiquette advocacy and awareness activities. The public behaviour education efforts especially pushed for 'riding public transit in a civilised manner', 'civilised taxis', 'civilised sports grounds', 'integrity and trust in businesses and services', 'no spitting', 'no littering', and 'no barbecuing in the street' (Song, 2006; Xinhuanet, 2008). The result was that the Beijing Public Civic Behaviour Index rose from 65.21 out of 100 in 2005, the first year when the data were collected and calculated, to 82.68 in 2008 (Wang, 2012).

Beijing's public etiquette and behaviour education for the 2008 Olympics Games was thorough. A good example was the effort to cultivate civic manners for 'civilised sports grounds'. A key component of this attempt was to raise the level of Beijingers' awareness on polished audiences' behaviours at different sport events. This point was made clear and simple by Mayor Wang Qishan:

> I have been invited to present the trophy to the men's and women's single winners at the recent China Tennis Opens. Chinese audiences' knowledge of tennis is obviously inadequate. For example,... some of our audience including government officials go in and out at will. They also make noises when they shouldn't, and stay silent when they should cheer.
>
> Beijing residents should be aware that different sports have different rules and different underlying cultures. We want the Olympic to help us realise our dreams ... we want to demonstrate to the world that we have accomplished a lot in a short period of time. Yet the most important sign and symbol of modernisation is the modernisation of our people. That is what we mean by 'People's Olympics'.
>
> (cited in Lu, 2005, p. 27)

The essence of the People's Olympics was perhaps best articulated by the slogan of the Beijing Games volunteers: 'my participation, my contribution, my fun' (Liu, 2008). The *Manual* specifies that the host city must develop a programme for volunteers. Beijing 'created the largest volunteers' participation in the history of the Olympic Movement' (Zhuang and Girginov, 2012, p. 252). According to Huang (2008, p. 4), in the three years leading up to the hosting, BOCOG 'recruited and vetted more than two million applicants'. By August, 2008, the totals were: 100,000 venue volunteers, 200,000 cheerleading volunteers, 400,000 city volunteers, and 1,000,000 society volunteers. The huge group of blue uniformed volunteers brought the presence of the Olympics literally to all corners of the Beijing city (CRI Online, 2008). They exemplified to Beijingers that the

Olympic Games were not merely for competition or individual achievements, but were social efforts to advance the common good.

Mass participation at the scale intended for and mobilised by the People's Olympics also understandably created embarrassment. Innocent foreign language translation mistakes were perhaps the least harmful but most humorous. The authors of this chapter noticed that, in the years leading up to the 2008 Games, most restaurants in Beijing had their menus translated into English, serving such dishes as 'bean paste exploding meat nails' (stir-fry diced pork in bean paste), or 'staggering body' (sashimi). When asked who translated the menus, wait-staff often replied 'computer auto translation'. The authors also learned about a popular joke in China: to answer the call for public foreign language proficiency, a restaurant's owners Googled the Chinese characters for an English translation of its name and proudly had the result printed on the door in English: 'Zero results found'.

Sustaining the People's Olympics legacies

'Longing for a decade, and waiting for 7 years, the Chinese welcomed the Olympics. After 16 days of festivities, the gala event was over, and the Olympics left' (Ji, 2008). When the Olympic song, 'Difficult to say good-bye' was still ringing at the Closing Ceremony, Liu Qi, Deputy Mayor of Beijing and President of BOCOG, noted that the dying Olympic flame would spread sparks of new dreams and hopes among Beijingers, which would forever keep the Olympic spirit in the city and allow its residents to benefit from the Olympic wealth (cited in Li, 2009). As we write in 2012, the Olympic wealth being sustained has two main dimensions – sports participation and civil society.

The education and training programme undertaken to fulfil the Olympic mandate to educate the population about Olympic sports, and to increase sports participation as an educational means to healthy living, was the most ambitious ever attempted. At a general level, the IOC (2010, p. 18) considered Beijing's efforts to have been very successful, noting: 'In terms of human legacies, the Beijing 2008 Games provided an unparalleled platform from which to promote healthy living through participation in sport and the inclusion of individuals with disabilities'. He (2010, p. 183) further noted that: 'the spiritual legacy, characterised by the competitive drive of the athletes, and the concepts of fair competition and harmonious interaction ... have extended beyond the sports arenas to influence people-to-people and people-society engagements'. The related IOC goal of creating a public sports culture was also fulfilled. Qin (2010, p. 13) has asserted that bidding for and hosting the Games effectively 'transformed' public sports development in Beijing through a significant increase in the role of sports organisations rather than government, with the result that public sports participation at the community level increased dramatically during the seven-year preparation period. A new slogan emerged – 'sports for fitness, and fitness for rejuvenating the Chinese nation' – suggesting to Qin that public sports participation was now a 'key component of the Beijing culture'.

Yet government participation in sports development also remains high. The Beijing Government has put in place plans and mechanisms for maintaining the momentum created during the Olympic Games. Eight new sports and fitness areas had been constructed by 2009 (Li, 2009), forming a city-wide network of sports theme parks. Further, in working with the public for fitness improvement, Beijing's government has developed policies and mechanisms paying special attention to promoting sports activities among youth. For example, the 'Hundreds-of-Millions-Students Sunshine Sports' programme enlists the participation of all primary and secondary schools in the city. The *Olympic Knowledge Reader for Secondary Students* and the *Olympic Children's Series* remain incorporated into the curriculum of regular physical education classes. These programmes encourage students to appreciate not only superb athletic skills, but also good sportsmanship and the charismatic personalities demonstrated by Olympics athletes (Li, 2009). Qin (2010, p. 20) has asserted that, holistically: 'The broad masses of the people may thus share the latest achievements of economic development through being able to more easily enjoy and appreciate sports.'

Regarding civil society, after winning the bid to host the Games, China and Beijing spent seven years preparing 'the people' for the People's Olympics. The people responded so enthusiastically that, as the Games were ending, Deputy Mayor Liu announced that the Olympics themes would be transformed into ongoing development themes for the city: 'Green Beijing', 'Hi-tech Beijing', and 'People's Beijing' (cited in Li, 2009). While these themes were co-equal before the Games, in the post-Olympics period 'People's Beijing' is both the foundation and the pinnacle. Huang (2010, pp. 172–176) has noted that 'Hi-tech' and 'Green' will improve technology and the physical environment but both of these are being continued for the benefit of the people. Thus, People's Beijing will signify the overall level of the city's urban development.

Beijing's People's Olympics was different because of the degree that Beijingers themselves were required to shape up for a world audience. Feng *et al.* (2010, p. 38) believe the Beijing Games were a 'citizen-oriented Grand Lecture' when 'rights and duties were illustrated at all times'. This was particularly true due to the 'sense of participation,' epitomised by the increase in volunteerism. Citing Deputy Mayor Liu Qi, Li (2009) notes that 'People's Beijing' will continue to develop the organisational structure of the volunteer services. Since 2009, volunteerism has officially been included in the curricula of all primary and secondary schools in Beijing. Further, all 1.7 million Olympic volunteers recruited and all the 500 volunteer stations established for the 2008 Games have been retained.

Having been heavily engaged in the deliberations about and implementation of the People's Olympics, the Beijing public now want People's Beijing to maintain and raise the quality levels of life in the city. For them, the People's Olympics was not merely a noble, aspirational concept. It was more importantly a highly applicable strategy concerning core features of human existence and balanced development (Feng *et al.*, 2010). Emerging from Olympics requirements,

Beijing and the central government issued over 4,000 standards, covering such areas as food safety, environmental protection, transport management, public security, hygiene, and public health. Since 2008, Beijing has maintained all these regulations as guidelines for city operation and management (Li, 2009). Sticking to the Olympic standards for environmental and air qualities, for example, Beijing has updated the 'odd-even licence plate tail number alternating system' for cars during the 2008 Olympics to a 'one no-driving day per week per car' scheme (Li, 2009).

Similarly, People's Beijing conceptually underscores that humanistic concerns will be stressed throughout Beijing's urban construction and growth. According to Lu (2011, pp. 67–72), economic growth should be accompanied by the co-development of social fairness and justice, in order that the growth be translated into social welfare and enjoyed by the people. For Beijing residents, People's Beijing means applying 'people-oriented' principles to education, social security, employment, medical services, income/wealth distribution, and social management. As a phrase, 'People's Beijing' is a slogan for creating a humanistic, harmonious, and most-liveable city, so as to provide a favourable social environment for its residents to develop in a dignified and all-rounded way.

Satisfying IOC requirements for the bid to host the Games necessitated that BOBICO bidders imagine a Western-based programme of socio-cultural change. Such was the eagerness to host, to show off Beijing to the world, that Chinese – a people well known for subsuming individual needs into the collective good – embraced and endorsed this mostly culturally alien programme as the march to the Games proceeded. Such public approval enabled literally thousands of changes, small and large, to be implemented in an apolitical manner. Ordinarily, when an event concludes, life returns to what it was. Even for Olympic host cities, by the next Games the legacy sustained is mostly infrastructural. Not so for Beijing. The interim between the XXIX and XXX Olympiads has been a time when Beijing's people have refused to let go of the Olympics. Life has not returned to normal. The people continue to invoke Olympics concepts in daily life and, in turn, Beijing's government continues to implement a multitude of aspects that sustain the favourable changes in city life that came to exist by 2008. Will this still be the case in 2016, when Rio de Janeiro has its coming out party? We can only say that it seems very unlikely that Beijing will ever return to what it was the day before winning the bid in 2001. Hosting the Olympics has created a cultural climate that has translated into sustained improvements that the people have come to take for granted. Beijing's People's Olympics will thus be sustainable as long as the people retain these internalised expectations for humanistic progress.

References

Beijing Olympic Action Plan. (n.d.). Lausanne, Switzerland. Retrieved 23 June 2012, from http://en.beijing2008.cn/59/80/column211718059.shtml.

Beijing Organising Committee for the Games of the XXIX Olympiad (BOCOG). (2004). *Olympic Knowledge Reader for Secondary Students.* Beijing: Beijing Publishing House.

Bian, Y. (2007, 28 July). Prof Ji Xianlin talking about Olympics on his 96 birthday: I suggest we 'carry out' Confucius at the Opening Ceremony. *People's Daily Overseas Edition,* p. 2.

Brownell, S. (2008). *Beijing's Games: What the Olympics Mean to China.* Plymouth, UK: Rowman & Littlefield.

Brownell, S. (2009, March). Beijing's Olympic education programme: Re-thinking *suzhi* education, re-imagining an international China. *The China Quarterly* 197, pp. 44–63. doi: 10.1017/x0305741009000034.

Chen, A. and Meng, L. (2010). On 'People's Olympics'. *Journal of Shanxi University Philosophy and Social Sciences Edition* 33 (5), pp. 121–124.

CRI Online. (2008, 29 August). Volunteers: My participation, my contribution, my fun. Retrieved on 23 June 2012, from http://gb.cri.cn/17844/2008/08/29/1945s2217597.htm.

Daily Times. (2006, 2 March). China publishes etiquette guide for a polite 2008 Olympics, p. 2.

deLisle, J. (2009, Spring). After the gold rush: the Beijing Olympics and China's evolving international roles. *Orbis,* pp. 179–204.

Feng, X., Zheng, W., and Wu, M. (2010). Universal value of 'People's Olympic' concept to building civil society. *Journal of Nanjing Institute of Physical Education Social Sciences Edition* 24 (3), pp. 37–39.

He, N. (2010). On China's sports and social construction in the post-Olympic era. *Internet Fortune* 7, pp. 183–184.

Hu, R. (2010). Research on the development of the Olympic culture in China. *Sports World Scholarly* 6, pp. 102–103.

Huang, C. (2008, 16 July). For Beijing's Olympic volunteers, the rules are many. *The Christian Science Monitor,* p. 4.

Huang, D. (2010). 'People's, Hi-tech, Green Beijing' and development of creative cultural and service industries, in *Collected Works on 'People's, Hi-tech, Green Beijing'* Academy of Beijing Social Sciences (ed.), Beijing: Beijing Press, pp. 172–176.

International Olympic Committee (IOC). (2010). Final report of the IOC Coordination Commission: Games of the XXIX Olympiad, Beijing 2008. Lausanne, Switzerland.

International Olympic Committee (IOC). (2011). Olympic Charter. Lausanne, Switzerland. Retrieved 23 June 2012, from www.olympic.org/Documents/olympic_charter_en.pdf.

Ji, X. (2008, 24 August). Farewell the Olympics but it is difficult to say good-by. [Web log comment]. Retrieved 24 May 2012, from http://blog.cntv.cn/13930947–144903.html

Jin, Y. (2006). *University Tutorial on the Olympic Culture.* Beijing: Higher Education Press.

Jin, Y. (2008). Chinese cultural contents and People's Olympics concept. *Research and Practice* 4, pp. 6–9.

Jin, Y. (2010, August). Beijing: from 'People's Olympics' to a world-class city. *Scientific Chinese* 8, pp. 28–29.

Li, H. (2009, 7 August). Liu Qi on legacies and wealth of the Beijing Olympic Games. *Sohu Sport.* Retrieved 19 May 2012, from http://sports.sohu.com/20090807/n265786599.shtml.

Liu, Q. (2008). Volunteers: my participation, my contribution, my fun. CRI Online. Retrieved on 23 June 2012, from http://gb.cri.cn/17844/2008/08/29/1945s2217597. htm.

Lu, R. (2005). Beijing Mayor Wang Qishan speaking frankly about 6 major problems in hosting the Olympics at the China Sciences and Humanities Forum, Beijing, 4 November 2004. *Information Guide* 7, pp. 24–27.

Lu, Y. (2011). 'People's Beijing': from concept to practice. *Studies on Socialism with Chinese Characteristics*, 5, pp. 67–74.

Manual for the Candidate City of the Games. (n.d.). Retrieved 23 June 2012, from www. olympic.org/Documents/Reports/EN/en_report_297.pdf.

Qin, M. (2010). impact of the Beijing Olympic Games on public sports in Beijing. *Sports Culture Guide* 2, pp. 13–24.

Song, Y. (2006, 20 November). Four projects in 2008 to implement People's Olympics. *Beijing Evening News*, p. 26.

The Spokesman-Review (2001, 14 July). Chinese ecstatic over successful bid, p. C6. Retrieved 23 June 2012, from http://news.google.com/newspapers?nid=1314&dat=200 10714&id=RGVWAAAAIBAJ&sjid=bvIDAAAAIBAJ&pg=6946,1894567.

Tian, J. (2006). The 2008 Olympic Games: leveraging a 'best ever' games to benefit Beijing. Master's thesis. Auckland University of Technology, New Zealand.

Torres, C. (2010). The Youth Olympic Games, their programs, and Olympism. International Olympic Committee web. Retrieved 19 May 2012, from http://doc.rero.ch/record/22125.

Wang, Q. (2012, 16 May). Beijing's public civic behaviour index has risen to 83.05. *Beijing Evening*, p. 6.

Wang, W. (2011, 15 February). Getting a lesson in manners. *China Daily*, p. 27.

Xia, W. (2008). What parts of the Beijing Olympics touch people the most? *Bimonthly Selected Readings* 7, pp. 3–5.

Xinhuanet. (2008, February 29). No spit: Beijing's latest etiquette campaign draws mixed reaction. Official website of the Beijing Olympic Games. Retrieved 19 May 2012, from http://en.beijing2008.cn/news/olympiccities/beijing/n214259657.shtml.

Zhang, C. (2008). People-centred concept, international outlook, and CCTV My Olympics Programme: Sports TV broadcasting in the Olympic Era. *South China Television Journal* 2, pp. 25–29.

Zhou, Z. (2008, 12 May). Is it necessary for Confucius to participate in the Olympics Games? *Honghe Daily*, p. 4.

Zhuang, J. and Girginov, V. (2012). Volunteer selection and social, human and political capital: a case of the Beijing 2008 Olympic Games. *Managing Leisure* 17 (2–3), pp. 239–256.

4 Rethinking events in higher and further education

A systemic sustainability perspective

Paul Shabajee, Debra Hiom and Chris Preist

...academic conferences, weekly team meetings, research funding briefings, departmental away-days, project review meetings, exam moderation, training and professional development events, board meetings, policy development meetings, grant assessment meetings, union negotiations, fieldwork meetings, professional association AGMs, vendor pitches, award ceremonies, consultations, event planning meetings, brainstorming sessions, employment interviews, symposia, trade shows, budget allocation meetings, steering group meetings...

Planned events,[1] such as those listed above, pervade the lives of those who work within universities and colleges. They are embedded into the fabric of the way that virtually every aspect of higher and further education (HE and FE) operate; spanning *teaching and learning*, *research*, *operations* and *administration*.

If we spend more than a few minutes browsing any governance or operational document of a large institution, planned meetings and other kinds of events are

> *"The University is a chartered corporation ... objects, powers and framework of governance ... four separate bodies – Court, Council, Senate and Convocation, ... Council is the University's 32-strong governing body. It normally meets six times a year and is responsible for policy, financial affairs ... It includes members of the academic and support staff, students and lay people.... Senate is the University's principal academic body, ... has more than 100 members ..."*

'Governance: how the University is run'
(University of Bristol)

Figure 4.1 Example of content of governance document.

likely to tumble out. See Figure 4.1 as an illustration from the authors' own institution, the University of Bristol. This was found as the first result by typing 'governance university of bristol' into Google [18-Nov-2011].

Precisely because planned events are integral to the fabric of our organisations, we can sometimes forget just how pervasive and significant they are. We may also not notice that they have some significant negative consequences. Within the last few years there has been an increasing awareness of anthropogenic climate change that has led to discussion pieces and editorials in academic and professional journals about the 'carbon footprint' of events, with titles such as (Shabajee and Curtis, 2012):

- 'The need for sustainable conferences' (Bonnett, 2006)
- 'Rethinking scientific meetings: an imperative in an era of climate change' (Young, 2009)
- 'Why do we fly? Ecologists' sins of emission' (Fox *et al.*, 2009)
- 'Are international medical conferences an outdated luxury the planet can't afford? Yes' (Green, 2008) [and 'No' (Drife, 2008)]

It is in the context of the kinds of debates and questioning reflected in those journal articles that this chapter sits. It is based on the work and findings of the Greening Events Project, which was a short exploratory project (February– November 2010), funded as part of the Greening ICT (Information and Communication Technology) Programme of the UK Joint Information Systems Committee (JISC). The Greening ICT Programme aims to '...support UK colleges and universities in reducing their energy use, plan for more sustainable use of ICT for the future and help chart the course to new technology enabled paradigms for the university and college of the future' (JISC, 2011). The Greening Events Project investigated the potential sustainability benefits and issues that arise from the use of information and communications technologies in the contexts of organised events.

This chapter draws on the findings and issues that arose during the Greening Events Project to help meet the goals of this book; that is to prompt reflective and critical perspectives of events in the context of sustainability. Our focus here is to highlight some of the novel perspectives taken by the project, for example looking at events as systems and as part of larger systems, a focus on changes driven by ICT innovations, and some of the more problematic and interesting questions that arise.

The changing nature of events

The sustainability imperatives implicit in the titles of the journal articles listed above, and much more extensively discussed in this volume, are a significant driver of current changes in the nature and use of events by all kinds of organisations. However, this imperative is one driver of many that make up the wider dynamic cultural, socio-economic and technological environment in which 'events' exist.

We say 'events' to emphasise an important point. Colloquially the term 'event' is applied to a vast set or class of things. In the context of Greening Events, these span from small internal business meetings in a room the size of a large cupboard that lasts 20 minutes, to conferences and tradeshows with 10,000+ attendees spread over multiple locations over a number of days. Not only is the term 'event' ambiguous because there are many *kinds* of event, but also because the very nature of what an event is, has changed over time and necessarily continues to do so.

Events and the way we use them have co-evolved with wider human culture, including socio-cultural structures, cultural traditions and technologies, throughout human history. To take a simple technology-focused example, the nature of events taking place in the evening has co-evolved with the development of lighting technologies, ranging from controlled fire of the early stone age (Bowman *et al.*, 2009) to modern floodlit stadiums seating tens of thousands of people.

Equally, as our social structures change so the events associated with them change in response; for example large-scale funding of research activities worldwide over the last century, has played a significant part in the existence of international academic and professional conferences with over 10,000 delegates, with all of the associated complexity. Without large-scale funding, such events would not take place. More generally, such conferences are also only possible because of many thousands of *other* enabling structures: social, physical, political and technological.

Significantly their nature is also constrained by the limitations of those very structures. These range from political structures (for example, immigration controls restrict who can physically attend certain events), through to limitations in transport technologies: it might be useful to hold a conference on Martian atmospheric chemistry on the surface of Mars; however, that is not yet practical.

We argue that in this present age, the advent of networked digital technologies is enabling and driving a very rapid phase of co-evolution and dramatically changing what we think of as constituting an event. And, importantly for this volume, that the sustainability implications of these changes are likely to be highly significant. We will return to the theme of the impacts of networked digital technologies later; however, first we delve more into the nature of events in order to put that theme into context and provide a conceptual framework in which the sustainability impacts of events can be placed.

Events as systems and part of systems

Events are not isolated in time or space

From an attendee's point of view a planned event can feel that it is something that happens at a given place and time. However, a moment or two's reflection makes it clear that events are actually spread out in time. For example, by definition a 'planned event' must be planned prior to it happening; venue(s) booked, catering organised, invitations sent and registration forms completed.

When we look from a sustainability perspective the temporal spread of an event is even more evident. A very common approach to assessing the sustainability-related impacts of products (goods and services) is Life Cycle Assessment (LCA) (Baumann and Tillman, 2004). This approach seeks to provide an estimation or assessment of the impacts of a product by adding up all of the impacts of the components of that product over the whole life cycle of the product. This is from resource extraction through to disposal and/or recycling, as illustrated in Figure 4.2.

In a comprehensive formal LCA study, every component of the final product is traced back (and forward) through its life cycle. Inventories of all material and energy inputs and output are measured or estimated. This list is called a Life Cycle Inventory (LCI). Each lifecycle stage will consist of tens, hundreds or even tens of thousands of sub-processes, each with its own sub-processes, etc. From the LCI the material and energy flows of the whole product system can be estimated. Figure 4.2 illustrates the kinds of input and output that make up an inventory for a single sub-process.

If we know the environmental impacts of each of those flows, e.g. CO_2, methane and chlorofluorocarbon (CFC) will impact global warming; sulphur and nitrogen oxide gases are linked to acid rain, this can then lead to a measure of the overall environmental impacts of a product life cycle across various impact categories such as climate change, human health, resource depletion, acidification potential and eutrophication potential (Baumann and Tillman, 2004). The

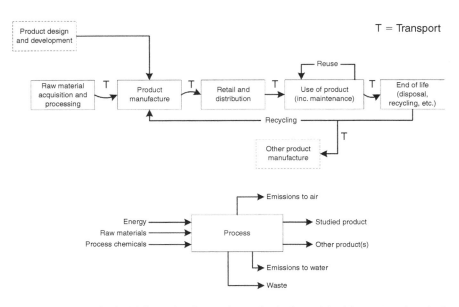

Figure 4.2 Hypothetical life cycle of a product (physical good in this case) and typical types of input and outputs to a life cycle process (source: adapted from Baumann and Tillman, 2004, p. 103).

LCA approach has also been adapted to include social impact categories, called social LCA (UNEP/SETAC Life Cycle Initiative, 2009).

The LCA methodology is the basis of existing carbon footprinting standards such as the Greenhouse Gas Protocol (WRI and WBCSD, 2011) and PAS2050 (BSI Group and Carbon Trust, 2008). Conducting a comprehensive LCA is a complex task, even for simple goods. There are many intricacies in producing LCAs that make issues such as the comparability of study results, e.g. from one event to another, problematic (Deloitte, 2010). Baumann and Tillman (2004) provide a good introduction to LCA for those who wish to know more; the *International Reference Life Cycle Data System (ILCD) Handbook* (European Commission – Joint Research Centre, 2010) provides more detail on methodological issues.

Even a small planned event consists of thousands of components, from a share of the impacts of building a venue itself, the emissions due to travel of attendees and catering, to the supply chain impacts of all of the goods used.

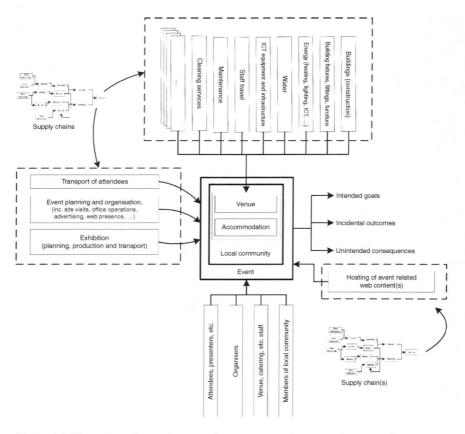

Figure 4.3 Illustration of some inputs and outcomes to a larger conference style event.

Many of the service and material components themselves are sophisticated products with complex and complicated supply chains. Figure 4.3 illustrates some of the components that make up the overall impact of an event. As De Camillis *et al.* (2010) point out, there have been few significant LCA studies in tourism (leisure or business) related areas, in large part because of this complexity.

Figure 4.3 also shows that an event is not a single thing, but is a dynamic combination of people (organisers, venue staff, attendees, exhibition staff, third-party suppliers, members of local communities), venue and accommodation facilities and local infrastructure such as utilities, transport, telecommunications and internet.

What an LCA approach makes very clear is that the environmental (and socio-economic) impacts of events are significantly spread out in time. The supply and value chains that enable events to happen are both wide (many kinds of components come together to make an event) and deep (there are many layers of subsidiary supply chains), for example, the computer at a venue has many layers of supply chains and associated impacts. These impacts began possibly years before any particular event-on-the-day: the fertiliser manufactured and spread on the land to enable the growing of the cattle feed, to feed the animals whose meat is used in the catering, may have taken place years before. The sustainability-related impacts of events will also go on into the future, for example at an environmental level waste will be managed and the impacts of that may remain for decades or even centuries.

Wider systemic impacts of events

The environmental and social impacts (defined by an LCA) of the consumption of goods and services due to the occurrence of a single event are but one – perhaps quite small – set of impacts associated with an event. We began the chapter by listing a range of types of events each of which itself sits within a sub-system of the operations of an HE/FE institution. That sub-system might be academic research, procurement, teaching, student recruitment or employment.

Events happen within and between organisations and between individuals because they are intended to have a, generally positive, impact as part of those larger systems: decisions made, knowledge/learning disseminated, careers progressed or effective policies developed. The criteria for 'positive' will depend on the specific context and value base of the organisations and individuals involved. In Figure 4.3 these are represented by 'Intended Goals'. However, there are other outcomes and consequences of events. In Figure 4.3 we call them 'Incidental Outcomes' and 'Unintended Consequences'.

We use the term incidental outcomes to describe outcomes that are generally implicit and sometimes so embedded in the nature of a particular type of event that they can be virtually invisible. However, they can be very important. Examples include the benefits of networking at conferences and meetings, including collecting business intelligence (for example funding opportunities, up and coming policy changes and business 'gossip'), catching up with old friends, hearing of new ideas, trends or technologies. The impacts of these, while they may have a low profile at an event, may be very significant overall and we return to them later.

What we call unintended consequences in Figure 4.3 may include the positive and negative environmental and socio-economic impacts of events. At least in the case of an academic context, events are not generally organised, explicitly or implicitly, to benefit local businesses or communities. Of course, while many local and national government and community organised and facilitated events do have the primary and intended goals to have positive impacts on local communities, this is not generally the case for academic or business events.

Equally, in general, the organisers do not intend their events to have negative impacts on the environment or play a part in causing social ills. However, indirectly, social and economic hardship for the individuals and communities in the supply chains may occur.

In addition some kinds of outcome cannot be intended as such, for example, serendipitous meetings or insights.

Even if we only focus on the intended outcomes of an event, that is, planned or hoped for outcomes, we can follow the knock-on impacts of those outcomes. These may have very significant sustainability consequences. For example, a meeting to develop and improve an institution's sustainability policy and practices might, one hopes, have a significant positive impact on the sustainability-related performance of the institution as a whole.

In such a case the direct impacts of the event itself such as resources consumed, waste produced and trade involved in procurement ('fair' or not), are likely to be insignificant in comparison to the overall organisational impact of the event. If we include incidental and unintended consequences the range of knock-on impacts is very much larger. Figure 4.4 (adapted from Coyle, 2004) generalises the idea of knock-on impacts by representing how these impacts propagate and illustrates, in a simplified way, that different sets of impacts have consequences for environmental, socio-economic and economic issues – clearly in most cases any single impact will have consequences in all three.

Taking this simplified representation of cause and effect of events we can see that the net impacts or consequences of any event are the cumulative impacts of both the primary (direct) and secondary impacts.

What Figure 4.4 does not illustrate are feedback loops. That is, making a change not only feeds forward to have effects on other parts of a system but can *feed back* to those parts of the system making the change.

Figure 4.5 gives a simplistic example of such feedback. An organisation may decide to make an investment into video conferencing equipment and services, perhaps as a means to reduce the travel footprint of holding events within the organisation. As employees use the facility, the perceived benefit on the part of management may rise so driving more investment and on around the loop again – so called positive feedback.

This is simplistic because, for example, even if increased perceived benefit does drive more investment, the loop must stop at some point. More sophisticated

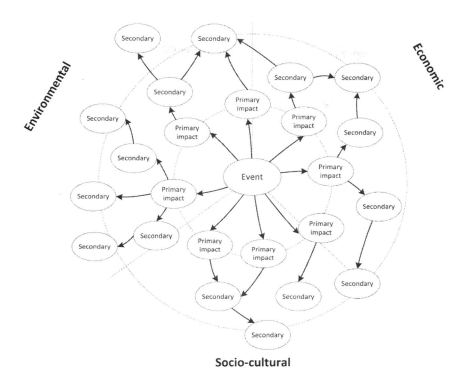

Figure 4.4 Simple illustration of knock-on impacts (source: adapted from Coyle, 2004).

models would include other factors that would balance the positive feedback with negative (controlling) feedback and represent the interactions of this small sub-system with others. In this case a negative feedback factor would be the fact that the number of events for which substitution by video conferencing was appropriate would reduce, eventually to zero, and so the positive feedback would stop.

More widely in that example, there are many other internal and external factors that would be part of the system as a whole, such as the capacity and capability of other organisations to have video conferencing calls (e.g. collaborators), costs of travel and video conference equipment, attitudes of staff to video conferencing and travel, financial state of the organisation itself and the political importance of 'being seen' at an event.

The important point here is not that these factors need to be taken into account – as they almost certainly would be in the decision making process of the management in this case – but that knock-on impacts and feedback loops change the system itself recursively and generally in ways that cannot easily be predicted. For example it is unlikely to be possible to predict the actual uptake of video conferencing facilities within an organisation or whether holding video

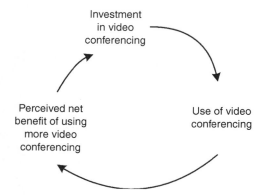

Figure 4.5 Simplistic example of feedback.

conferences may actually stimulate more net face-to-face events, perhaps because they enable more successful collaborative working. Even more difficult is predicting the knock-on impacts of the loss of informal networking opportunities if face-to-face meeting events are replaced by video conferencing events.

Systems thinking and events

The term 'systems thinking' describes a wide range of ways of looking at systems that enable them to be understood in terms of the interactions of their parts. As illustrated in Figures 4.4 and 4.5, this perspective includes aspects often missed when a non-systemic perspective is taken. They encourage the analysis of knock-on or secondary/tertiary impacts rather than simply direct impacts. For example, so-called rebound effects, in which a planned change with an intended consequence may lead to unintended consequences that can reduce or even have the opposite consequence to that intended.

A hypothetical illustration of a rebound effect might be an organisation that introduces video conferencing in order to reduce greenhouse gas (GHG) emissions enables financial savings by reducing travel and event attendance. The 'savings' may be spent elsewhere in GHG intensive ways, thus offsetting some (potentially all) of the original savings. The impacts of this spending may not appear directly or quickly and so may not be attributed to the original change. Once the financial savings have been reallocated it may be very difficult to undo changes later. These are examples of consequences of the more basic systems concepts such as delay, lock-in and displaced or secondary effects.

Other concepts that are explained, and can often be identified, by systems thinking approaches include: wider rebound phenomena, that can be positive as well as negative (Hertwich, 2005), perverse incentives (through which policies can cause the opposite of their intentions), the Mathew effect (by which benefit breeds benefit and disadvantage breeds disadvantage), the more general law of unintended consequences (Merton, 1936), emergence and the behaviours of complex adaptive systems.

The Greening Events project explored potential sustainability impacts of information technology-based innovation on the nature and use of events by higher and further education. The disruptions (Christensen, 1997) to the events industry, and use of events more generally, caused by the introductions of networked, multimedia and increasingly, mobile, communications technologies are already dramatic (see 'Event Evolution, ICT and Sustainability' below). No less dramatic are the potential sustainability impacts of these changes. As they take place there will be rebound effects and unintended consequences, both positive and negative, there will be new structures, even new types of companies emerging, while other practices and organisations disappear.

Systems thinking methodologies (scenario planning, soft systems methodology, systems dynamics modelling, agent-based modelling) and more recently ideas from complexity science seem to offer great potential, and indeed we argue may be essential for, understanding not only sustainability impacts of events, but also how we can develop the ways in which events are used effectively, and how events may themselves be impacted by wider systemic behaviours.

If we acknowledge that the world – including events and their sustainability impacts – is indeed systemic in nature and so behaves in complex ways, critical questions arise, including: do current impact assessment methods take sufficient account of effects such as secondary impacts, feedback and consequent rebound effects? If not, are such simplifications appropriate, and what kinds of methods are most appropriate for enabling effective assessment that includes these factors.

There is a well-known illuminating story:

> Walking along the street a woman finds a man on his hands and knees, it is dark, he is searching the ground in the light under a lamppost. He had lost his keys. Where had he dropped them? He points along a dark lane, somewhere along there. Why then is he searching under the lamppost? Because it is light under the lamppost.

Understanding the systemic impacts of events is highly problematic, quantifying them even more so. However, if the deeper and more significant impacts of events are largely systemic, and cannot be seen by looking at events individually or in isolation, then we probably need to look there for some of the answers we need.

If we are to take this wider perspective, one helpful change is to shift focus from the event to the wider system in which the event is situated. From a systemic perspective there is simply no such thing as an isolated event. It is a meaningless concept, a thing that could never exist and so it is not really very meaningful to think of the event in isolation.

One necessary step in understanding the systemic context of an event is to begin to answer the question, what exactly are the roles of an event in the wider system or systems within which it sits? The next section explores this question in the context of Greening Events and the role of events within higher and further education.

Multiple purposes: what do events really do?

We began this chapter with a list of types of event that pervade the operations of higher and further education organisations. Much of our initial work focused on academic conferences, seminars, workshops and colloquia. The Greening Events project identified over 50 distinct roles fulfilled by organising and/or attending conferences, beyond the more obvious (primary explicit) goals such as disseminating research findings or sharing best practice. For example:

> gather business intelligence (who's doing what, funding opportunities), find new project partners, provide a 'safe' place for interdisciplinary gathering, support job seeking & recruitment, escape the 'daily grind' and have time to reflect, debate new ideas, enculturate new researchers, signal the importance of topic, be (re)inspired, meet personal performance metrics...
>
> (Shabajee and Hiom, 2011, p. 16)

During our Greening Event case studies we found through interviews and observation, that for some attendees the actual content and planned sessions of a conference were peripheral, indeed they may not attend a single programmed presentation. The event acted as a valuable place for networking, meeting colleagues, finding out what was going on in the community, identifying funding opportunities, checking out potential collaborators, but also, spotting talented junior researchers and doctoral students, 'being seen' and ensuring that their research topic was visible and making sure that their doctoral students were introduced to key people were all examples of what we came to call incidental roles of attending or organising events.

Anecdotally, we found similar examples for other types of event. Many purposes seem to be common to many kinds of events, e.g. sharing gossip/business intelligence, building trust in partners, collaborators and suppliers, opportunities to discuss peripheral (off topic) issues with key people and getting a sense of the mood/morale of a team or community. Others are much more specific, for example face-to-face academic conferences seem to provide a primary means of introducing/enculturating new researchers into a research community.

We also found some incidental purposes whose role may be significant but at present are largely hidden or invisible. These will require more systematic study to understand. An example of this is that events provide opportunities for serendipitous meetings and inspiration. See Merton and Barber (2004) for an exploration of the wider roles of serendipity. In our interviews we heard many examples of the significant consequences of chance meetings at face-to-face events.

If we look at these multiple purposes from a systemic perspective we see that in order to understand the overall impacts of events and in particular changes in the way that we organise, run or use events, that we need to take account not only for the primary explicit goals of events but also the implicit and incidental roles that they play.

One of the greatest surprises of the Greening Events project has been the apparent lack of systematic study of academic events (and professional association events attended by academics) such as conferences and symposia. We had assumed that there would be a large body of literature and work on the nature, workings and implications of such events, because of their apparently central roles in enabling effective intra- and inter-disciplinary communication, their role in peer review and many other explicit and implicit roles as noted above. Blumen and Bar-Gal (2006, p. 341) reflect our surprise in the apparent lack of systematic study of academic events:

> The conference is an important arena of academic life, a meeting place where people present and receive knowledge; ... Its neglect as an arena in the study of academic life is reflected by the fact that Pierre Bourdieu in his nearly 300-page study of academic life acknowledges briefly the important contribution of participation in conferences for the professional capital of academics, but does not develop the issue further (Bourdieu, 1988, 46, 235, 241) ... The conference is also mentioned fleetingly by others, who seemingly take it as given that its significance is well understood ... In practice consensus apparently exists about the importance of conferences, as organizations and scholars put much effort into supporting and attending them.

It is difficult to see how effective decisions can be made regarding how to make best use of events and/or change the way we use events unless we have a grounded and clear understanding of exactly what it is that events actually do. Our, albeit very time constrained, research found no detailed systematic analysis of even core event purposes such as networking. Networking was consistently listed by event attendees in post-event surveys as valuable; however, it is not clear exactly what networking means or what its consequences are. It seems highly likely (hypothesis), in an academic event context, that many new projects are initiated, new collaborations begun, research careers changed in direction or jobs obtained, and yet it seems there has been no systematic study to test that kind of hypothesis; what there is appears to be anecdotal.

We have focused here on the implicit and incidental roles of events from the perspective of organisers and attendees as this is generally less well explored as an issue in work related to the sustainability impacts of events. More widely explored is the fact that each set of wider stakeholders (sponsors, venue hosts, other service providers, event organisers, local businesses, local authorities) will have different interests and motivations, and be impacted differently by events. Once again a comprehensive and systemic assessment of impacts would need to take these factors into account.

In our review of existing guidelines (Greening Events bibliography, Shabajee and Curtis 2011) we felt that there is a risk in current approaches to assessing or providing guidelines for planning sustainability of events – often based on lists of good practice in particular areas of sustainability impacts – that the systemic impacts of the inter-relationships between these factors is hidden.

Perhaps the most difficult to deal with insight that such a systems perspective brings is that it is, in general, simply not possible to optimise the sustainability outcomes associated with an event in all areas of sustainability. Changes that reduce the carbon footprint may also reduce opportunities for economic development in event host communities; choosing to host an event for optimum participation may very significantly increase its carbon footprint. A narrow focus on creating positive impacts in one type of problem area runs significant risks of negative impacts in others, and because of systemic phenomena in that situation, may well risk unforeseen and undesirable outcomes on the very problem that was the focus of the effort.

Event evolution, ICT and sustainability

In the last two sections we have argued for the need to understand events and their impacts systemically as they are at present. However, sustainability is inherently and fundamentally about the future. While it is necessary and vital to be capable of assessing sustainability impacts of activities in the present, it is not sufficient to ensure a sustainable future. To recast Hartley's famous quote about the past, 'The future is a foreign country: they will do things differently there'. (Hartley, 1953, p. 3), and the choices we make today deeply affect the paths that the future make take.

We have already noted that the nature of events has changed significantly over time, co-evolving with socio-cultural and technical innovations and contexts. The last few decades since the introduction of networked and multimedia information and communications technology (ICT) have seen dramatic changes in the nature of the way that planned (and unplanned) events have evolved. The technologies involved include:

> Presentation software, data projectors, teleconferencing (PSTN and IP), video conferencing (suites, desktop and mobile), telepresence (high end video conferencing), online meeting tools (inc. webinar tools), live video streaming, pre-recorded video, sub-titling services, integrated conferencing software/services, interactive voting systems, virtual community services (e.g. Facebook, Ning, Lanyrd,...), wireless (WiFi) networking, websites (and their many associated media and interactive technologies), virtual learning environments, blogging, micro-blogging (e.g. Twitter), instant messaging/IRC (Internet Relay Chat), media sharing services (e.g. YouTube and Flickr), podcasting, active badges (e.g. based on RFID), personal area networks, slide sharing, mobile devices (laptops, smartphones,...), location based services (network and GPS enabled), translation services, e-Readers, digital recording of physical and virtual events, event mobile apps (e.g. for iPhone/Android smartphones), 3D virtual environments (such as Second Life), asynchronous collaboration environments...
>
> (Shabajee and Hiom, 2011, pp. 9–10)

These and other technologies and more importantly the abilities (affordances) that they provide have changed and continue to change the way we plan, organise and use events. For example, events now take many forms along a spectrum of purely face-to-face to fully virtual/remote where all attendees are in different physical locations such as those held in Second Life (e.g. Leong *et al.*, 2008). So-called hybrid events where some attendees are physically co-located while others attend individually and remotely are increasingly common.

Networked ICT and the new services layered on top of those can be thought of as fundamentally changing the concepts of place and presence implicit in non-networked technology-enabled events and redefine the mechanisms of communication during events (e.g. Urry, 2007). They enable and provide many additional ways in which people can interact in relation to events, including prior to, during and after events as well as being physically remote. Back-channel technologies, such as instant messaging, allow multiple conversations to take place simultaneously and even multiple events to be attended simultaneously. They also change the power dynamics of traditional events (Jacobs and McFarlane, 2005; Brumfiel, 2009).

The term event amplification (Kelly, 2008) can be used to describe the way in which such technologies and the social software services that they enable, can be used to enhance the value of events for a wide range of stakeholders. The changes that take place as part of the interplay of technologies, the new abilities (affordances) that they offer and other changes in practice, all have significant implications for the way we use events. The positive potentials of amplification bring with them challenges and risks as well as opportunities.

As new technologies arise they will continue to disrupt the nature of events and the way we use them and may fundamentally alter even the very basic conceptions related to events. For example, already the concept of meeting has fundamentally been altered with mobile communications technologies creating a world in which it is now possible to be in constant touch (by voice and now video) with family, friends and colleagues. If or as holographic display technologies develop along with very high bandwidth mobile networks the meaning of meeting will continue to morph. From an events perspective we are likely to need to continually and critically re-evaluate what an event is.

Sustainability implications of networked ICT-enabled events

The previous section has highlighted the fact that digital networked technologies are already changing the way events take place and the very nature and definition of events. These innovations and changes have not by and large been driven by any sustainability-related goals. However, as widely reported, information and communications technologies do appear to have the potential to have a positive role in helping to find solutions to many sustainability-related issues. See for example the Smart2020 report by the Climate Group (The Climate Group, 2008) that illustrates and attempts to begin to quantify the potential enabling effect that ICT can have in reducing GHG emissions across the whole economy. For example, this can be through dematerialisation, i.e. the shifting from physical to digital goods and services and subsequently from physical to digital 'transport', by using digital technologies to manage buildings and physical transport logistics more efficiently (see also Intellect, 2008 and Pamlin, 2008).

In the context of events, the most obvious is the potential for the reduced travel, and subsequent energy and carbon reductions, through the use of virtual presence technologies of various kinds. However, as is the case in other sectors of the economy, ICT brings other opportunities to reduce negative and enable positive impacts, for example dematerialisation and associated reduction in use of material and energy resources such as replacement of paper by online digital materials. It also brings with it potential to improve access, participation and inclusiveness though enabling remote participation, e.g. reducing (in principle) issues with the cost of attendance or removing the need to obtain visas.

In this chapter we cannot explore the many potential systemic impacts that technologies may bring in the context of events; however, ICT has the potential to create demand for goods or services not previously available (recent examples being mobile phones, mp3 players). Such new or increased demand may potentially drive negative environmental impacts (such as use of non-renewable resources, energy and carbon emissions), that outweigh net savings from, for example, reduced travel, or may induce negative social impacts such as 'resource wars' associated with rare raw materials required by the electronics industry, and the drive to keep costs down may lead to poor treatment of workers in the electronics industry supply chain. Of course the longer-term and wider implications for society as a whole of what might be called information revolution associated with ICT are unknown.

There are however new and developing approaches and standards for assessing ICT's negative and positive impacts, for example GeSI's (Global e-Sustainability Initiative) document 'Evaluating the Carbon-Reducing impacts of ICT' (GeSI, 2010). These are in their relative infancy and much work needs to be done to evaluate the approaches themselves. As yet existing approaches do not include extensive inclusion of more complex systemic impacts of ICT-based interventions.

Current and developing event sustainability assessment standards and guidelines are also in their infancy – the BS8901 was developed in 2007 (revised in 2009), the subsequent international standard (ISO, 20121) is due to be published in 2012. The Global Reporting Initiative's (GRI) Event Organizers Sector Supplement is due to be published in 2012. None of these in their final or draft stages include any extensive guidance on the use of ICT as part of or as the primary meeting space. We assume this is largely for historical reasons as the events industry has traditionally been built around physical face-to-face events. In general neither the ICT assessment or event assessment methodologies, standards or guidelines include the wider-ranging systemic impacts described above.

Conclusions – rethinking events

Events pervade all aspects of higher and further education and indeed most large organisations. Their socio-cultural and economic importance can hardly be over-emphasised. Events are highly complex systems themselves – in sustainability terms they are not the localised things that they can appear; their impacts spread out widely in time and space beyond the event-on-the-day. They are systems within systems; integral parts of larger systems. Indeed they happen *because* they are part of larger systems.

This means that studying or assessing the sustainability-related impacts of an event or set of events in isolation can only ever be part of a much bigger picture – assessing or understanding the net impacts; personal, organisational, socio-cultural, economic and environmental impacts of any event (or events in the abstract) can only make sense by taking into account the multi-level roles and interactions that events have with the wider world.

This chapter has argued that a systemic perspective is necessary if we are to make effective and socially and environmentally responsible decisions about how we use and organise events – decisions that acknowledge the many systemic roles of events in the wider world, decisions that account for the impacts of events far beyond the-event-on-the-day.

Finally we argue that what we mean by an event is itself continually evolving and that today's digital networked technologies such as broadband internet and mobile technologies and the services that are layered on top of them, are driving profound changes in the nature of events. These disruptions bring with them opportunities and risks. Opportunities to, for example, reduce negative impacts of resource consumptions due to events and, for example, expand participation and representation. Risks include potential negative unintended business and socio-economic consequences and of increased resource consumption.

The final report of the Greening Events project was entitled 'Rethinking Events' (Shabajee and Hiom, 2011). It argued that if the goal of that project was to help understand how to make events more sustainable, then it appeared that the most fruitful answer may not lay in focusing on how to reduce the negative sustainability impacts of any particular event (although that is important) but rather to rethink the way that we 'do' events:

- rethink why we have them and what purposes they fulfil;
- rethink what they are and how we 'do' them;
- rethink where and when we have them;
- rethink who is involved and who they are for;
- rethink how we can learn to meet the underlying needs currently met by events more effectively.

Sustainability is inherently about the future. Developing sustainability policies and practice require that we include future scenarios in our (re)thinking and do so continuously. Thus rethinking is not, and cannot be, a onetime process after which we will know what a sustainable event is and how to organise and run one. Nor is it possible to have, once and for all, a single set of policies in place to ensure that they happen. As the contexts of our use of events change, and as the nature of events continue to co-evolve with those contexts, such rethinking is a continuous process.

Note

1 There are many ways to define 'event' (Getz, 2007). Here we choose a broad working definition: three or more people who agree to gather together (see for example Urry, 2007).

References

Bauman, Henrikke and Tillman, Anne-Marie. (2004). *The hitch hiker's guide to LCA*. Lund: Studentlitteratur.

Blumen, Orna and Bar-Gal, Yoram. (2006). The academic conference and the status of women: the annual meetings of the Israeli Geographical Society. *The Professional Geographer* 58(3), 341–355.

Bonnett, Alastair. (2006). The need for sustainable conferences. *Area* 38(3) (September), 229–230.

Bourdieu, P. (1988). *Homo academicus* (1st edn) (P. Collier, Trans.). Stanford: Stanford University Press.

Bowman, David M. J. S., Balch, Jennifer K., Artaxo, Paulo *et al.* (2009). Fire in the earth system. *Science* 324(5926), 481–484.

Brumfiel, Geoff. (2009). Breaking the convention. *Nature* 459(25), 1050–1051.

BSI Group. (2009). *BS 8901 – Sustainability management systems for events*. Milton Keynes: BSI.

BSI Group and Carbon Trust. (2008). *PAS 2050:2008: specification for the assessment of the life cycle greenhouse gas emissions of goods and services*. BSI British Standards Institution. Retrieved 1 March 2011 from: www.bsigroup.com/Standards-and-Publications/How-we-can-help-you/Professional-Standards-Service/PAS-2050.

Christensen, Clayton M. (1997). *The innovator's dilemma: when new technologies cause great firms to fail*. Boston: Harvard Business School Press.

The Climate Group. (2008). *SMART 2020: Enabling the low carbon economy in the information age*. The Climate Group. Retrieved 2 May 2011 from www.smart2020.org/_assets/files/02_Smart2020Report.pdf.

Coyle, R. G. (2004). *Practical strategy: structured tools and techniques*. Harlow: Financial Times Prentice Hall.

De Camillis, C., Raggi, A. and Petti, L. (2010). Tourism LCA: state-of-the-art and perspectives. *The International Journal of Life Cycle Assessment* 15(2), 148–155.

Deloitte. (2010). *COP15 carbon footprint: approach and methodology*. Retrieved 2 May 2011 from: www.e-pages.dk/visitdenmark/472/fullpdf/full4c08d200cd6e5.pdf.

Drife, J. O. (2008). Are international medical conferences an outdated luxury the planet can't afford? No. *BMJ*, 336(7659).

European Commission – Joint Research Centre – Institute for Environment and Sustainability. (2010) *International Reference Life Cycle Data System (ILCD) Handbook* (1st edn). Luxembourg: Publications Office of the European Union.

Fox, H. E., Kareiva, P., Silliman, B. *et al.* (2009). Why do we fly? Ecologists' sins of emission. *Frontiers in Ecology and the Environment* 7(6), 294–296.

GeSI (Global e-Sustainability Initiative). (2010). *Evaluating the carbon-reducing impacts of ICT.* GeSI. Retrieved 2 May 2011 from www.gesi.org/ReportsPublications/AssessmentMethodology.aspx.

Getz, D. (2007). *Event studies: theory, research and policy for planned events (Events Management),* London: Butterworth-Heinemann.

Green, M. (2008). Are international medical conferences an outdated luxury the planet can't afford? Yes. *BMJ,* 336 (7659).

Hartely, L.P. (1953). *The go-between,* Hamilton: London.

Hertwich, E.G. (2005). Consumption and the rebound effect: an industrial ecology perspective. *Journal of Industrial Ecology* 9, 85–98.

Intellect. (2008). *High tech: low carbon the role of technology in tackling climate change.* Retrieved from 2 May 2011 www.intellectuk.org/hightechlowcarbon.

Jacobs, N. and McFarlane, A. (2005). Conferences as learning communities: some early lessons in using 'back-channel' technologies at an academic conference – distributed intelligence or divided attention? *Journal of Computer Assisted Learning* 21(5), 317–329.

JISC. (2011). *Overview of green ICT.* Retrieved 2 May 2012 from www.jisc.ac.uk/whatwedo/topics/greenict/overview.aspx.

Kelly, Brian. (2008). *Defining an 'amplified conference'.* Retrieved 2 May 2012 from http://ukwebfocus.wordpress.com/2008/08/28/defining-an-amplified-conference/.

Leong, Julian J., Kinross, James, Taylor, David and Purkayastha, Sanjay. (2008). Surgeons have held conferences in Second Life. *BMJ* 337(7661).

Merton, R. K. and Barber, E. G. (2004). *The travels and adventures of serendipity: a study in historical semantics and the sociology of science.* Princeton: Princeton University Press.

Merton, R. K. (1936). The unanticipated consequences of purposive social action. *American Sociological Review* 1(6), 894–904.

Pamlin, Dennis. (2008). *Outline for the first global IT strategy for CO2 reductions (Report): A billion tonnes of CO2 reductions and beyond through transformative change.* WWF. Retrieved 2 May 2012 from http://assets.panda.org/downloads/global_strategy_for_the_1st_billion_tonnes_with_ict_by_wwf.pdf.

Shabajee, Paul and Curtis, Heppie. (2012). *Updated Greening Events bibliography.* Institute for Learning and Research Technology (ILRT), University of Bristol. Retrieved 9 July 2011 from http://greeningevents.ilrt.bris.ac.uk/2011/07/05/greening-events-bib/.

Shabajee, Paul and Hiom, Debra. (2011). *Rethinking events, Greening Events in higher and further education.* Institute for Learning and Research Technology (ILRT), University of Bristol. Retrieved 9 July 2011 from http://greeningevents.ilrt.bris.ac.uk/files/2011/06/Rethinking-Events.pdf.

UNEP/SETAC Life Cycle Initiative. (2009). *Guidelines for social life cycle assessment of products* (C. Benoit and B. Mazjin, eds). Retrieved 2 May 2011 from www.unep.fr/shared/publications/pdf/DTIx1164xPA-guidelines_sLCA.pdf.

Urry, J. (2007). *Mobilities.* Cambridge: Polity.

WRI (World Resources Institute) and WBCSD (World and Business Council for Sustainable Development). (2011). *Product life cycle accounting and reporting standard, September 2011.* WRI and WBCSD. Retrieved 14 December 2011 from www.ghgprotocol.org/standards/product-standard.

Young, S. N. (2009). Rethinking scientific meetings: an imperative in an era of climate change. *Journal of Psychiatry & Neuroscience* 34(5), 341–342.

Part II

Events, sustainability and community

5 Planning and evaluating sport events for sustainable development in disadvantaged communities

Nico Schulenkorf and Deborah Edwards

Introduction

Sport events of all forms and sizes have been growing in volume and importance over the past century. Sport events can vary in scale and type and represent a temporary drawing together of resources to provide structured sport activities for participants, spectators and other stakeholders. These activities can feature either informal or formal competition between organised individuals and teams of athletes. Their duration can range from a single day to multiple days, and include local, national and international participants. Sport events are popular in many societies as they can provide people and their communities with both economic and social opportunities such as entertainment, socialisation and the establishment of contacts and networks between people and groups. A growing awareness of the social opportunities by government agencies and community groups has led to sport events being used as a method for fostering community development and delivering broader social benefits. Thus, while the actual sport event is often the key focus for organisers and participants, there is an opportunity for sport events to contribute to wider community development efforts.

This chapter illustrates the significance of sport events in our society and examines their ability to contribute to sustainable development in disadvantaged communities. The chapter discusses opportunities and challenges in the areas of sport event planning and evaluation. Moreover, it introduces the Sport-for-Development (S4D) Framework that can be used to guide and facilitate the creation of sport event activities designed to benefit people in (disadvantaged) communities.

Community sport events

The term community comes from the Latin *communis*, which means common, public, shared by all or many. Williams (1976, p. 76), in his famous *Keywords*, describes community as a 'warmly persuasive word', which can be applied either to an existing set of relationships or alternatively a new set which may be realised in the future. Similarly, Elias (1974, p. xiii) points out that 'the use of the term community has remained to some extent associated with the hope and the wish of reviving once more the closer, warmer, more harmonious type of bonds between people vaguely attributed to past ages'. Nisbet (1969) explains community as a fusion of feeling, tradition, commitment, membership and psychological strength, which leads to a shared feeling of togetherness and a sense of belonging. A community is seen as a place where solidarity, participation and coherence can be found (Purdue *et al.*, 2000; Taylor, 2003) and may be described as a network of social relations marked by mutuality and emotional bonds among its members.

Communities can include people from different local regions or geographical areas, and can therefore be described as dispersed interest groups. What is shared in such collective ensembles is a combination of 'interest' and specific characteristics such as ethnicity, religion, political ideology, occupation, sexuality or leisure pursuit (Ife, 1995; Willmott, 1988). To be a functional and dynamic community, Shaffer and Anundsen (1993) argue that community members have to engage and make decisions in cooperation with each other. Commitment and active participation are the preconditions for any type of sustainable community development.

So what, then, are community sport events? Building on the discussion above, community sport events can be described as planned sporting activities that aim to generate particular social, cultural and/or economic benefits for stakeholders and the host community. The host community can either be a geographical community (e.g. a certain village, town or neighbourhood) or an interest community (e.g. a sports club or running group). In both cases, community sport events are organised *by* a community *for* their community. Communities come together around sport and event activities such as training sessions, match-day games, tournaments and national and international sporting competitions (Figure 5.1).

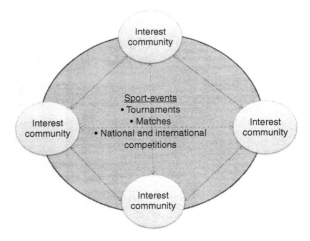

Figure 5.1 Intersect between community and sport events.

Local governments often support sport events as part of their community development strategy, because they can produce a range of benefits including tourism activation, engendering pride in the community, strengthening a feeling of belonging, exposing people to new ideas and experiences, and encouraging tolerance, diversity and participation in sports (Allen *et al.*, 2011; Preuss, 2006). Furthermore, Schulenkorf (2010b) suggests that community sport events have the capacity to function as active and exciting vehicles for stimulating positive social changes and reconciliation between divided and disadvantaged communities.

Sport events in disadvantaged communities

A disadvantaged group is defined by a particular pattern of denied resources and barriers that it faces which can be a result of factors such as race, poverty or gender. Meyer (2003, p. 3) argues that 'barriers are the ways in which people are denied access to needed tools, and include unavailability of resources, inaccessibility to resources, the society's regard for a group, government and corporate practices, and certain conditions of the group itself'. Disadvantaged groups can face more than one barrier, some of which may be more easily overcome than others. There are numerous examples of disadvantaged groups in both the developing and developed world. However, for the purposes of this chapter disadvantaged communities are considered to be groups of people who live in a developing world context and are resource deficient and face difficult socio-economic and political circumstances such as poverty, social exclusion and/or political turmoil in their country. Sport events can provide such communities with an opportunity for overcoming these barriers through tourism and economic benefit, as well as the creation of positive social and cultural outcomes.

People's contribution to and participation in sporting events can for example lead to improvements in people's physical and mental health; an enhancement of education and life-long learning; the promotion of active citizenship; and programmes aimed at combating crime and anti-social behaviour, which can lead to an increase in perceived well-being (Coalter, 2005; Kay, 2009; Kunz, 2009). For disadvantaged communities, sport events may provide a liberating escape from their daily struggles, or they can function as bridge builders when dealing with issues such as social exclusion and/or intergroup conflict (Schulenkorf and Sugden, 2011; Stidder and Haasner, 2007; Sugden, 2006).

Sport events that are designed to make a positive difference in disadvantaged communities can be referred to as sport-for-development (S4D) activities. S4D is a relatively new stream within the field of international development: it utilises sport (incl. sport events) as a development tool, in divided societies and/or seriously underprivileged communities (Kidd, 2008). S4D evolved out of the common belief that well-designed, sport-based initiatives incorporating appropriate values from within sport can be powerful, practical and cost-effective tools to achieve specific development goals (Coalter, 2010; Sugden, 2010; Schulenkorf, 2010b; Schulenkorf and Sugden, 2011). S4D utilises and builds on the potential of sport events to bring communities and disparate groups together to contribute to inclusive social change. According to advocates, when people are engaged in appropriately organised sport and event projects, they are provided with opportunities to interact in an environment that promotes intergroup trust and cultivates respect (Misener and Mason, 2006; Schulenkorf *et al.*, 2011; Sugden, 2006).

Chalip (2006) contends that sport events have the potential to promote dialogue, solidarity, understanding, integration and teamwork, even in conflict-ridden contexts where other forms of social and political negotiation have been unsuccessful. For a long time these perspectives were largely anecdotal and, according to critics, therefore idealistic (Coalter, 2010). It was, indeed, hard to find practical evidence of S4D projects that demonstrated sustainable outcomes in terms of reconciling or re-uniting disparate communities. However, over the past ten years the number of grassroots initiatives has risen and different sport event projects are now starting to flourish all over the world. Most of these projects are listed on the web portal of the Swiss Academy for Development (SAD) (www.sportanddev.org) which provides practitioners, researchers and students interested in S4D with a great opportunity to browse, learn, connect and network.

The variety of S4D programmes and the contexts in which they operate have led to the formulation of a number of specific objectives that can realise positive community outcomes. These objectives have included:

- reduced sense of social isolation and strengthened social networks;
- increased self-esteem and confidence in one's own abilities;
- increased trust and a sense of communal responsibility;
- new and improved social skills (e.g. comfortable meeting new people, willing to seek and accept advice, can work cooperatively; understands impact of behaviour on others);
- improved life skills (e.g. sportsmanship);
- greater understanding of other cultures;
- increased commitment to education and school;
- understanding of, and commitment to, gender equity;
- positive attitudes to the future and improved aspirations.

(Adapted from Coalter (2005))

With the ever increasing number of sport events, there have been growing calls by funding bodies for these S4D projects to engage in programme evaluations that can provide evidence that goals and objectives have been met. In other words, the projects now need to demonstrate their operational effectiveness and sustainable contribution to overall development efforts.

Planning sport events in disadvantaged communities

To achieve sustainable community development, strategic planning and active community participation are required (Coalter, 2005; Midgley, 1986; Orjuela, 2003; United Nations, 2006). However, disadvantaged communities are often challenged when trying to organise and stage sport events independently, as they lack the skills, knowledge and expertise to conduct them. Therefore, external 'change agents' plan and manage S4D projects to support local activities under the principle of 'guided self-help'. Change agents act as anchormen or mediators between groups and are defined as 'external parties who help [communities] establish contact, open negotiations and develop projects for cooperation and sustainable development' (Schulenkorf, 2010a, p. 119). Change agents are supposed to guide and teach communities how to use their capacities and to cooperate effectively (Ife, 1995; Lawson, 2005; Uruena, 2004). External knowledge can thus be combined with local input, in the hope that communities and change agents will benefit in a reciprocal process of knowledge creation and cultural exchange.

When sport events are initiated or guided by external agencies there is, however, the danger that they may employ a dominant paternalistic approach to management (Botes and van Rensburg, 2000; Stiglitz, 2002). The change agent may unconsciously or consciously have the feeling of 'knowing what's best' for communities, which may result in local input being undervalued (Midgley, 1986; Willmott, 1988). A potential to misuse power and drift from a 'bottom up' towards a 'top-down' approach may prohibit communities from realising their own potential, which can lead to community alienation and resistance. This problem often arises when international change agents employ a 'Western approach' to leadership and management, and focus on using human capital and the commitment of workers to a predetermined plan (Kay, 2009; Skinner *et al.*, 2008; Vail, 2007). Furthermore, change agents do not always have the requisite 'cultural' skills to work within or among given communities which means that their work can benefit substantially from local input and participation.

Another challenge in the planning stage for both the change agent and communities is to utilise the *momentum* of sport events to strategically plan for lasting outcomes for the wider population (Chalip, 2004, 2006; Kellett *et al.*, 2008; O'Brien, 2007; O'Brien and Chalip, 2008). This phenomenon is referred to as 'event leverage'. Significant opportunities to leverage a sport event exist in economic and social areas. For example, before, during, or after a sport match, side-events can be used to attract, capture and motivate spectators to spend extra time and money in the community. In the area of economic leverage, event organisers can employ strategies that encourage repeat visitation by event participants and attendees as future tourists to the host region (Chalip and Leyns, 2002; Chalip and McGuirty, 2004; Costa and Chalip, 2005; O'Brien, 2006). At the same time, sport events can be used to foster long-term business relationships between the community and sponsors by encouraging future trade, investment and employment.

From a social perspective, the areas of sport and entertainment have been blurred due to the proliferation of event-related entertainment such as half-time music shows or post-game fireworks (Goldblatt, 2011). Often, these social opportunities result in a sense of celebration and social camaraderie that can enhance the enjoyment of sport events. The key, then, is to leverage these experiences with a sense of togetherness to achieve lasting social benefits for the community (Chalip, 2004, 2006). Organisers can further use the positive atmosphere that is generated at sport events as a platform to highlight community issues, or to change people's perception regarding social problems.

The Sport-for-Development Framework

In order to understand the processes towards social change and sustainable community development through sport events, this chapter refers to the Sport-for-Development (S4D) Framework (see Schulenkorf, 2012). The framework draws together the previously described areas of Community Participation, Sport-for-Development and Sport and Event Management, and describes an *ex ante* approach towards understanding and guiding the strategic planning, investigation and evaluation of sport and event development projects (Figure 5.2) The S4D Framework should be understood as a loose frame towards sustainable community and/or inter-community empowerment.

The starting point of the S4D Framework is a change agent who identifies (disparate) communities as needing activities that can improve their status quo. These communities have to decide whether they participate in a S4D project, e.g. a community sporting event. If they decide to participate, they engage with each other and the change agent in a cooperative strategic planning exercise. Through active and reciprocal engagement, local knowledge is joined with external expert

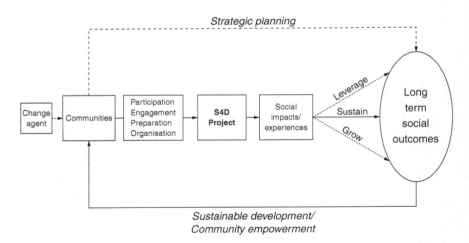

Figure 5.2 Schulenkorf's (2012) S4D Framework.

input, which is the recipe for staging culturally appropriate and professionally managed sport and event projects (Stidder and Haasner, 2007; Sugden, 2006). importantly, the strategic planning phase also includes a strategic discussion on leverage strategies that are implemented to maximise event benefits and long-term outcomes for the wider community.

The actual participation at the sport event project leads to various socio-cultural impacts and experiences including socialising, celebration or the enhancement of skills and capabilities. From an inter-community perspective, sport projects may bridge social gaps between groups, for example by encouraging teamwork, intergroup learning and reciprocal skill development (Gasser and Levinsen, 2004; Schulenkorf *et al.*, 2011; Sugden, 2006). The leisure atmosphere prevailing before, during and after S4D projects is seen as conducive of new contacts to be made and relationships to be established. However, it needs to be acknowledged that there is an opportunity for negative social impacts to occur, especially if communities are not properly included in the management of projects. Negative impacts may, for example, result in a revival of historical and prejudicial stereotypes, which can undermine intergroup development efforts.

As a final step, direct social impacts ought to be sustained, grown or leveraged into long-term social outcomes. In other words, the different social experiences made at an event can be maximised to achieve lasting social consequences, such as the creation and development of (inter-)community capacities and/or the establishment of social cohesion (Moscardo, 2007). For example, first contacts made at an event could be developed into trustful friendships or inter-community networks, which have the power to make a considerable change in intergroup relations. To grow and leverage social impacts beyond event borders, strategic cooperation between participating groups and links with key players in the community need to be sought, for example with the government, the educational sector and/or the media (Chalip, 2004, 2006). If these stakeholders have a clear idea about the desired long-term outcomes of sport events, they can plan, manage and support accordingly. They could for example engage in, contribute to or report about event-related activities such as street festivals, community workshops, cultural shows or social/educational marketing campaigns. Such event-related socio-cultural activities are likely to lead to additional positive outcomes such as an increase in (inter-) community capacities and the communities' quality of life (see e.g. O'Brien, 2007; O'Brien and Chalip, 2008).

Within the S4D Framework, the long-term social outcomes are embedded in a cyclical process towards sustainable development and community empowerment. This means that the outcomes of a project will influence (inter-) community relations and people's attitudes and intentions to a) participate at the next project, and b) engage in further community activities. Overall, the S4D Framework highlights that active community participation and positive engagement are central to achieve sustainable development and community empowerment. Only if people are committed to achieve social development can sport event projects play an enabling role in bringing (disparate) groups together and contribute to capacity building and empowerment in an integrated way. For this to happen, sport-for-development initiatives have to be strategically planned, managed, leveraged and evaluated to achieve the desired long-term outcomes.

Evaluation of sport events for sustainable development

The evaluation of event impacts and long-term outcomes is necessary to provide evidence of the longevity and profundity of projects. Indeed, if the goal of a sport event initiative is to advance social development within or between communities, then the sustainability of relationships, community partnerships and social networks beyond the project provide key areas for ongoing assessment. Evaluation is therefore a process in which the sport event is critically observed, measured and monitored to accurately assess its outcomes (Allen *et al.*, 2011). Evaluation further determines how well the sport event was conducted in terms of the impact on the economic, social and cultural considerations (Presbury and Edwards, 2010).

Evaluation should be undertaken from the perspective of the change agent, government agencies, staff, volunteers, sponsors, spectators, participants, host community and the media. These stakeholders have a right to know what the sport event has achieved. For example, from an economic perspective funding bodies need to know if their investment has created the promised results in terms of the economic or social impact. Evaluation of the community can help to assess if social cohesion has improved, or if the sport event was able to contribute to people's overall well-being or quality of life. An environmental evaluation may clarify what impact the sport event has had on the natural resources and environmental quality of the destination. Overall, reporting back to stakeholders is an important part of the sport event's ongoing success. Evaluation aids in:

- identifying the economic, environmental and social effectiveness of the sport event;
- providing information to assist with accountability and transparency;
- providing information for sensitive marketing and interpretation;
- gaining acceptance/credibility/support;
- incorporating changes that may occur and from which others can learn for the future;
- encouraging and facilitating informed dialogue between the organisation and its stakeholders as part of a reflective process;
- facilitating a self-critical and self-improving organisation.

(adapted from Presbury and Edwards, 2010)

Presbury and Edwards (2010) explain that evaluation can measure the proposed goals and objectives against the actual outcomes or results by answering questions about: what was done?; who did it?; how was it done?; and what worked, what did not and what is recommended for next time? These questions can be applied to the whole sport event as well as to various elements of the sport event.

When choosing an evaluation method consideration should be given to the capabilities and resources available to the change agent and the community. Generally, a range of quantitative and qualitative methods can be used to evaluate sport events. Quantitative methods allow for the precise assessment and measurement of the sport event's performance, while qualitative methods provide an in-depth way to understand the 'why' and 'how' of people's experiences. Data analysis can be supported by professional software such as PASW (a statistical program), or qualitative software packages such as NVivo or Microsoft OneNote. Methods for evaluation include:

- Surveys that provide information on demographics, and spending and revenue patterns, not only at the sport event but within the broader community. These may include spectator entry and exit surveys, participant and sponsor satisfaction surveys. Surveys can be either self-completed or interviewer completed.
- Surveys to gauge the feelings and attitudes of various stakeholders, especially the social factors, that is, those that affect the quality of life and well-being of the individuals or groups within the community.
- Observation including visual inspections of the outcome of an activity, observation of performance and working methods, discussion of work practices and the generation of information on quality performance, spectator reaction, crowd flow and behaviour, infrastructure and services capacity, effects on the community, as well as observed impacts on the environment.
- De-briefings with various stakeholders to discuss issues, initiatives, problems and possible solutions. This allows for the generation of new ideas, provides valuable feedback from different perspectives and enables stakeholders to have a sense of ownership of the process.
- Semi-structured discussions with participants to understand their attitudes, experiences and benefits gained.
- Small group discussions or focus groups that can provide an in-depth understanding of participants' perceptions and experiences which is not always possible through quantitative survey data.
- Financial control measures, including scrutinising the expenditure and reviewing the use of the resources that have been consumed in achieving set activities. Expenditure can then be compared to the budget, which was planned at the outset.
- Recording of both positive and negative media coverage. Keeping a file of newspaper articles and summaries of radio interviews can offer important lessons for the future.
- Benchmarking, that involves identifying those projects that exemplify best practice and then comparing the sport event's performance to them.

(adapted from Presbury and Edwards, 2010)

The nature of the evaluation will be determined by the purpose and size of the sport event. In any case, the newly gained knowledge can and should contribute to the future planning, management and development of sport event initiatives. This way, evaluation links back to the planning stage which facilitates continuous improvement (Presbury and Edwards, 2010).

Issues and challenges

Communities and change agents that use sport and event activities to make a difference in disadvantaged communities face a number of issues and challenges. In addition to obvious financial limitations there are other significant obstacles to be overcome during the planning, managing, monitoring and evaluation stages of projects. From our own experiences, the following areas are key aspects for further consideration.

Achieving participation

In a developing world context, individuals and groups often do not possess the resources to take over time-intensive community roles, as they are primarily concerned with their own survival (Orjuela, 2003). This restriction leads to a significant problem that arises in community development work, namely the lack of participation of lower socio-economic groups in the organisation and implementation of projects (Campbell and McLean, 2002; Gittell, 1980; Skinner *et al.*, 2008). When disadvantaged groups cannot or do not participate, this results in a skewed representation of stakeholders in development initiatives. Botes and van Rensburg (2000) therefore consider the integration and empowerment of people who initially do not have the capacity to participate, as one of the biggest challenges in the community development process.

Setting realistic expectations

When planning events in disadvantaged communities, it is important to be pragmatic in regards to expected outcomes avoiding an 'eyes wide shut' approach. For example, the steady increase of S4D projects and the reliance on volunteers in the organisation and delivery of projects often results in a situation that can be described as 'optimism of the will, pessimism of the intellect'. In other words, while the involvement of volunteers and their willingness to 'do good' in disadvantaged communities is commendable, it needs to be remembered that a) volunteers are no development experts, b) volunteers often have an incomplete understanding of the local culture, customs and traditions, and c) development processes such as social change and reconciliation need a lot of time and strong local commitment. To avoid disappointment and frustration it is therefore essential to set realistic expectations and to inform stakeholders of the best and worst case scenarios. This is especially important in situations where events are staged for the first time and comparisons to similar events are unavailable.

Unfortunately, a realistic 'step by step' approach is often not accepted by local communities who tend to expect miracles from S4D projects. Their high expectations and excitement paired with limited organisational skills, management knowledge and planning abilities is likely to result in frustration or wider community tensions. For example, at a sport event project in rural Sri Lanka, tensions arose during the event planning stages because external change agents and local stakeholders had different views on how to organise and structure the event project (see Schulenkorf *et al.*, 2011). Ineffective cooperation and varying degrees of commitment resulted in poorly coordinated advertising, marketing and promotional campaigns. A lower than expected number of event participants was the consequence, which had flow-on effects on people's satisfaction levels and reduced confidence in the event organising team.

Managing differences

When trying to implement sport events in disadvantaged communities, attitudes – described by Zimbardo *et al.* (1977) as 'mental readiness' towards a particular idea or project – can differ among individuals and groups. In other words, the mindset, proactivity and enthusiasm to engage with a sport event, its theme and other people can vary between event participants and other stakeholders. At times, these differences can lead to disagreement and tension between groups. For example, at a 'sport for peace' event some dedicated peace-activists may be frustrated with participants who focus on the physical aspect of the sport event instead of the sport event's peace objectives. Incompatible attitudes may thus result in intergroup frustration and/or disappointment.

A similar situation may occur when local community members interfere with a sport event's mission and objectives. For example, if parts of the local community are not convinced of the wider benefits of an event, they may react with pessimistic and judgemental comments about the organisers and participants. In divided communities some members may reject the idea of a Western change agent, or may not accept the idea of inter-community celebration. In the previously described reconciliation event in the ethnically divided Sri Lanka it was found that in some cases, locals intimidated and even threatened the international organisers, participants and spectators with words and gestures (Schulenkorf *et al.*, 2011). These behaviours can undermine the actual intention of events, and demonstrate the challenges of working with divided communities.

Maintaining objectivity

During the evaluation stage, open and honest feedback increases the likelihood of events improving their performance in the future. However, it is not always easy for sport event managers and researchers to generate unbiased responses from sport event stakeholders or to access 'independent voices' in the sport event community. This is particularly relevant when sport event projects are dependent on external funding. Sport events in disadvantaged communities that receive financial support from aid organisations are particularly difficult to research, as organisers and local communities fear that any critical/negative feedback may impact on future funding or political support. As a result, researchers are confronted with largely 'evangelistic' or 'romanticised' comments that glorify the impact of sport-for-development or event-for-development projects (Coalter, 2010). Negative outcomes often remain unreported.

Achieving participation, setting realistic expectations, managing differences and maintaining objectivity are indeed significant challenges. The challenges discussed above as well as the suggestions for overcoming them are represented in Table 5.1.

Table 5.1 Issues and challenges around sport and event projects in disadvantaged community settings

Issue/challenge	Addressing challenges
Achieving participation	• Include participation of lower socio-economic groups in the organisation and implementation of projects • Integrate and empower those who do not have capacity to participate • Build in autonomy, non-dependence and self-sufficiency • Allow the community to contribute their principles, ideals and capacities • Provide opportunities for the community to participate in decision-making • Provide meaningful employment where possible
Setting realistic expectations	• Be pragmatic in regards to expected outcomes • Allow time for development processes and reconciliation • Seek strong local commitment • Inform stakeholders of best and worst scenarios and avoid an 'eyes wide shut' approach • Manage and monitor community expectations to avoid community tensions • Seek cooperation between external change agents and local stakeholders
Managing differences	• Understand the perspectives of the local community, event participants and stakeholders • Provide education that enhances understanding of differences • Avoid 'top down' and encourage 'bottom up' approach • Understand your role as facilitator and mediator
Maintaining objectivity	• Include wide range of stakeholders into evaluation • Obtain open and honest feedback • Engage independent researchers into monitoring and evaluation • Avoid misrepresenting negative feedback • Report negative outcomes and opportunities for improvement

Although the strategies are considered as generally applicable for meeting the needs of a disadvantaged community in which the sport event is staged they are by no means exhaustive. They should be used to form the basis for the development of other strategies to suit the context of the sport event and disadvantaged community in which a person may be working.

Conclusion

The staging of sport events that contribute to the sustainable development of disadvantaged communities requires the balancing of competing needs, expectations and interests of a diverse range of stakeholders. This chapter has discussed the way in which organisers can effectively plan and evaluate sport events with a focus on providing positive outcomes for disadvantaged communities. Within this context, change agents are required to work with the community to maximise the sport event's potential, and to ensure that positive event impacts develop into lasting event outcomes.

The chapter has introduced the Sport-for-Development (S4D) Framework which can help understand and guide the strategic planning and evaluation of sport event projects. The S4D Framework is based on salient theory and research from the areas of community participation, social development and sport event management. It demonstrates the importance of culturally informed change agents that act as partners, mediators or anchormen particularly in the opening stages of development initiatives. Over time, their influence should reduce and local communities are required to take up roles and responsibilities in managing and sustaining sport event projects.

For any sport event project, the goals and objectives should meet the needs of the community in which it is to be staged. This chapter has suggested a variety of qualitative and quantitative methods that can be used to evaluate sport event success and to identify areas for improvement; the choice of methods should be guided by the specific sport event's objectives and the capacities available in the community. In the future we can and should expect more sport events to use the synergy between sport and social issues to maximise awareness and positive social outcomes for the wider community. Moreover, future research should empirically test and validate the S4D Framework to determine its suitability in providing a basis from which sport-for-development initiatives can build.

References

Allen, J., O'Toole, W., Harris, R. and McDonnell, I. (2011). *Festival and Special Event Management* (5th edn). Milton, Qld: John Wiley & Sons.

Botes, L. and van Rensburg, D. (2000). Community participation in development: nine plagues and twelve commandments. *Community Development Journal*, 35(1), 41–58.

Campbell, C. and McLean, C. (2002). Ethnic identity, social capital and health inequalities: Factors shaping African-Caribbean participation in local community networks. *Social Science and Medicine*, 55(4), 643–657.

Chalip, L. (2004). Beyond impact: A general model for host community event leverage. In B. Ritchie and D. Adair (eds), *Sport Tourism: Interrelationships, impacts and Issues* (pp. 226–252). Clevedon, UK: Channel View.

Chalip, L. (2006). Towards social leverage of sport events. *Journal of Sport and Tourism*, 11(2), 109–127.

Chalip, L. and Leyns, A. (2002). Local business leveraging of a sport event: Managing an event for economic benefit. *Journal of Sport Management*, 16(2), 132–158.

Chalip, L. and McGuirty, J. (2004). Bundling sport events with the host destination. *Journal of Sport Tourism*, 9(3), 267–282.

Coalter, F. (2005). The social benefits of sport: An overview to inform the community planning process. Research Report no 98. Edinburgh: sportscotland.

Coalter, F. (2010). The politics of sport-for-development: Limited focus programmes and broad gauge problems? *International Review for the Sociology of Sport*, 45(3), 295–314. doi: 10.1177/1012690210366791.

Costa, C. A. and Chalip, L. (2005). Adventure sport tourism in rural revitalisation – an ethnographic evaluation. *European Sport Management Quarterly*, 5(3), 257–279.

Elias, N. (1974). Foreword. In C. Bell and H. Newby (eds), *The Sociology of Community* (pp. ix–xli), London: Routledge & Kegan Paul.

Gasser, P. K. and Levinsen, A. (2004). Breaking post-war ice: Open fun football schools in Bosnia and Herzegovina. *Sport in Society*, 7(3), 457–472.

Gittell, M. (1980). *Limits to Citizen Participation: The Decline of Community Organizations*. Beverly Hills, CA: Sage Publications.

Goldblatt, J. J. (2011). *Special Events: A New Generation and the Next Frontier* (6th edn). Hoboken, NJ: John Wiley & Sons.

Ife, J. W. (1995). *Community Development: Creating Community Alternatives – Vision, Analysis and Practice*. Melbourne: Longman Australia.

Kay, T. (2009). Developing through sport: Evidencing sport impacts on young people. *Sport in Society*, 12(9), 1177–1191.

Kellett, P., Hede, A.-M. and Chalip, L. (2008). Social policy for sport events: Leveraging (relationships with) teams from other nations for community benefit. *European Sport Management Quarterly*, 8(2), 101–122.

Kidd, B. (2008). A new social movement: Sport for development and peace. *Sport in Society*, 11(4), 370–380.

Kunz, V. (2009). Sport as a post-disaster psychosocial intervention in Bam, Iran. *Sport in Society*, 12(9), 1147–1157.

Lawson, H. A. (2005). Empowering people, facilitating community development, and contributing to sustainable development: The social work of sport, exercise, and physical education programs. *Sport, Education and Society*, 10(1), 135–160.

Meyer, S. (2003). What is a 'disadvantaged group'? *Effective Communities Project*. Retrieved 10 April 2012, from www.effectivecommunities.com/pdfs/ECP_DisadvantagedGroup.pdf.

Midgley, J. (1986). *Community Participation, Social Development and the State*. New York: Methuen.

Misener, L. and Mason, D. S. (2006). Creating community networks: Can sporting events offer meaningful sources of social capital? *Managing Leisure*, 11(1), 39–56.

Moscardo, G. (2007). Analyzing the role of festivals and events in regional development. *Event Management*, 11(1–2), 23–32.

Nisbet, R. A. (1969). *The Quest for Community*. New York: Oxford University Press.

O'Brien, D. (2006). Event business leveraging: The Sydney 2000 Olympic Games. *Annals of Tourism Research*, 33(1), 240–261.

O'Brien, D. (2007). Points of leverage: Maximising host community benefit from a regional surfing festival. *European Sport Management Quarterly*, 7(2), 141–165.

O'Brien, D. and Chalip, L. (2008). Sport events and strategic leveraging: Pushing towards the triple bottom line. In A. Woodside and D. Martin (eds), *Tourism Management: Analysis, Behaviour and Strategy* (pp. 318–338). Wallingford, UK; Cambridge, MA: CABI.

Orjuela, C. (2003). Building peace in Sri Lanka: A role for civil society? *Journal of Peace Research*, 40(2), 195–212.

Purdue, D., Razzaque, K., Hambleton, R., Stewart, M., Huxham, C. and Vangen, S. (2000). *Community Leadership in Area Regeneration*. Bristol: The Policy Press.

Presbury, R. and Edwards, D. (2010). Managing sustainable festivals, meetings and events. In J. Liburd and D. Edwards (eds), *Understanding the Sustainable Development of Tourism*. London: Goodfellow Publishers.

Preuss, H. (2006). impact and evaluation of major sporting events. *European Sport Management Quarterly*, 6(4), 313–316.

Schulenkorf, N. (2010a). The roles and responsibilities of a change agent in sport event development projects. *Sport Management Review*, 13(2), 118–128.

Schulenkorf, N. (2010b). Sport events and ethnic reconciliation: Attempting to create social change between Sinhalese, Tamil and Muslim sportspeople in war-torn Sri Lanka. *International Review for the Sociology of Sport*, 45(3), 273–294.

Schulenkorf, N. (2012). Sustainable community development through sport and events: A conceptual framework for Sport-for-Development projects. *Sport Management Review*, 15(1), 1–12.

Schulenkorf, N. and Sugden, J. (2011). Sport for development and peace in divided societies – cooperating for inter-community empowerment in Israel. *European Journal for Sport and Society*, 8(4), 235–256.

Schulenkorf, N., Thomson, A. and Schlenker, K. (2011). Intercommunity sport events: Vehicles and catalysts for social capital in divided societies. *Event Management*, 15(2), 105–119.

Shaffer, C. and Anundsen, K. (1993). *Creating Community Anywhere: Finding Support and Connection in a Fragmented World*. New York: Putnam Pub. Group.

Skinner, J., Zakus, D. and Cowell, J. (2008). Development through sport: Building social capital in disadvantaged communities. *Sport Management Review*, 11(3), 253–275.

Stidder, G. and Haasner, A. (2007). Developing outdoor and adventurous activities for co-existence and reconciliation in Israel: An Anglo-German approach. *Journal of Adventure Education and Outdoor Learning*, 7(2), 131–140.

Stiglitz, J. E. (2002). Participation and development: Perspectives from the comprehensive development paradigm. *Review of Development Economics*, 6(2), 163–182.

Sugden, J. (2006). Teaching and playing sport for conflict resolution and co-existence in Israel. *International Review for the Sociology of Sport*, 41(2), 221–240.

Sugden, J. (2010). Critical left-realism and sport interventions in divided societies. *International Review for the Sociology of Sport*, 45(3), 258–272. doi: 10.1177/1012690210374525.

Taylor, M. (2003). *Public Policy in the Community*. Houndmills, Basingstoke (England): Palgrave Macmillan.

United Nations. (2006). Sport for development and peace: The way forward. Sixty-first session, Agenda item 49, A/61/373, United Nations General Assembly.

Uruena, N. (2004). *Citizen Participation as a Means of Controlling Corruption at the Local Level in Colombia.* M.Sc., Oxford University, Oxford.

Vail, S. (2007). Community development and sports participation. *Journal of Sport Management*, 21(4), 571–596.

Williams, R. (1976). *Keywords: A Vocabulary of Culture and Society.* London: Fontana.

Willmott, P. (1988). *Community Initiatives: Patterns and Prospects.* London: Policy Studies Institute.

Zimbardo, P. G., Ebbesen, E. B. and Maslach, C. (1977). *Influencing Attitudes and Changing Behavior: An Introduction to Method, Theory, and Applications of Social Control and Personal Power* (2nd edn). Reading, MA: Addison-Wesley Pub. Co.

6 Reclaiming identity and territory

Events and Indigenous culture

Heather Zeppel

Introduction

This chapter reviews the socio-cultural benefits and impacts of Indigenous festivals, along with the politics of Indigenous identity and cultural authenticity at events. It begins by reviewing research on the socio-cultural, economic and political impacts of hallmark Indigenous festivals in Mexico, Sweden, Canada, New Zealand, Papua New Guinea and Australia. The chapter then focuses on Indigenous cultural festivals in Australia, including community festivals (Heydon, 2007), the Garma Festival (Phipps, 2010a, 2010b, 2011; Borthwick, 2011; Pearson, 2011), Laura Aboriginal Dance Festival (Henry, 2000a, 2002, 2010; Thompson and Connolly, 2006; Slater, 2010a; Finch, 2011), The Dreaming Festival (Hanna, 2000; Slater 2007) and the Yalukit Willam Ngargee People Place Gathering in Melbourne (Svoronos, 2010). Case studies then focus on new urban Indigenous festivals attended by the author in Queensland, Australia: the Cairns Indigenous Art Fair (2009, 2010 and 2011) in Cairns; The Torres Strait Islands: A Celebration (2011) and the Reconciliation Beats Concert (2011) both in the capital city of Brisbane. The objectives, sponsorship, cultural programme and social or economic outcomes are compared for each urban Indigenous festival. This chapter analyses how these Indigenous festivals contribute to the process of re-territorialisation (Elias-Varotsis, 2006) of Indigenous culture in their original homelands or in new urban locations. The authenticity and sustainability of Indigenous cultural festivals in these new spaces and contexts is also examined.

Indigenous cultural events

Cultural events are integral to Indigenous rituals, spirituality, kinship and social interaction. These traditional cultural celebrations encompass dance performances, music, feasting, life stage events (i.e. births, weddings and funerals), skill contests and trading of produce or artefacts. Community-based traditional cultural celebrations have evolved into contemporary cultural festivals and events targeting both Indigenous and non-Indigenous audiences. These include Indigenous cultural events still held within Indigenous communities/homelands and new Indigenous cultural festivals held within urban areas involving diverse Indigenous groups. Major hallmark sporting events (i.e. summer Olympic Games, Sydney 2000; winter Olympic Games, Vancouver, 2010) now include Indigenous cultures in ceremonies. Indigenous festivals reflect the ongoing diaspora or migration of Indigenous people to urban centres. The socio-cultural benefits of these Indigenous festivals include the revival or maintenance of Indigenous cultural practices, particularly for Indigenous youth; the validation or reaffirmation of Indigenous cultural identity; and the political assertion of Indigenous territorial occupation or claims. Hence Indigenous festivals are culturally situated performance events that allow Aboriginal people a means of political and economic engagement in both local and international arenas (Henry, 2000b, 2008). Despite the prevalence of traditional and contemporary Indigenous festivals, there has been little research on the socio-cultural impacts, relations and values embodied in these trans-cultural spaces.

The sustainable management of Indigenous festivals involves the negotiation and presentation of cultural performances, funding support from government agencies and commercial sponsors, along with promotion by tourism, cultural or Indigenous organisations. The multiple goals of Indigenous festivals are reflected in their key statements or objectives. These include sharing Indigenous culture; promoting Indigenous music, film, art or dance; selling Indigenous products; and more recent aims of improving Indigenous health and well-being. There are tensions between Indigenous cultural festivals held as local community celebrations or as tourist events, dependent on external funding and re-oriented to non-Indigenous audiences. The main economic benefits of Indigenous festivals may also accrue to non-Indigenous owners of tourist accommodation or services and event staging companies. There are conflicts and compromises in expressing Indigenous cultural identity or independence due to financial limitations in staging events and reliance on government grants or agencies. The broader context of social, political and financial issues thus influences the delivery of these Indigenous events. Indigenous groups and individuals are both shaped by and responding to these sociopolitical factors when involved in organising, promoting and staging Indigenous cultural festivals. Key trends include Indigenous culture as part of place promotion and the political identity of nation states or regions. Indigenous events thus reflect new cultural representations of territorial landscapes and tribal identity. Ethno-commodification of cultures in 'spectacles of ethnicity' (Bankston and Henry, 2000) is part of the capitalist process shaping groups in an 'identity economy' (Comaroff and Comaroff, 2009).

Reclaiming Indigenous cultural identity and territory

A diverse range of local Indigenous groups perform at cultural festivals along with Indigenous performers from other regions or countries. Indigenous festivals thus reflect the globalised nature of cultural production and consumption (Stewart-Harawira, 2005; Comaroff and Comaroff, 2009). New elements are incorporated in cultural performances such as plastic items in 'traditional' costumes, and African-American hip-hop music, rapping or break dancing by Indigenous youth (Svoronos, 2010; Warren and Evitt, 2010). This raises the issue of what constitutes 'authentic' Indigenous culture for host communities, performers and spectators. Many Indigenous cultural performances are now amplified on sound stages or with microphones, with photographers and video or film cameras often on stages or dance arenas. Festivals also present a wide range of new, hybrid or blended Indigenous cultural art forms, reflecting the evolving and dynamic nature of Indigenous cultural production and representation. They transmit or consolidate cultural identity by building awareness and reshaping perceptions of others. They also reflect the global process of de-territorialisation and re-territorialisation through mobility of people, ideas, images and cultural practices (Elias-Varotsis, 2006). De-territorialisation and re-territorialisation mainly refer to 'the deconstruction and reconstruction of territorial borders as a result of economic and political change' (Elias-Varotsis, 2006, p. 25). In this chapter it refers to reshaping of spatial and cultural borders, through Indigenous festivals (Table 6.1). Many festivals are now less connected to the place where they began, moved to urban areas or purpose-built festival sites, and integrated or linked with alternative lifestyles and social or environmental concerns. Hence many events, including Indigenous festivals, are now de-contextualised either spatially or culturally from their origins and reconstituted in new settings. The ensuing process of re-contextualisation impacts on representations of cultural identity at festivals.

Table 6.1 De-territorialisation and re-territorialisation of Indigenous culture

De-territorialisation: *Colonisation: Invasion & Dispossession*
People: Forced removal of Indigenous peoples from their homelands
Territories: Appropriation of Indigenous homelands by colonisers
Knowledge: Banning and suppression of Indigenous culture, religion and language
Culture: Constraints on Indigenous cultural practices, rituals and art forms
Festivals: **Indigenous festivals banned or suppressed**

Re-territorialisation (homelands) *Activism: Indigenous Legal & Political Rights*
People: Indigenous people stay on or return to traditional homelands
Territories: Treaties, Land claims, Native Title legally recognised
Knowledge/Culture: Revival of 'traditional' culture, new hybrid cultural forms emerge:
Reviving and recording 'traditional' Indigenous knowledge
Festivals: **Local Indigenous cultural festivals**

Re-territorialisation (urban areas) *Globalisation: Reassertion of Indigenous Identity & Culture*
People: Mix of traditional owners and Indigenous peoples from other areas
Territories: Indigenous land claims; Indigenous migrant links to other tribal areas
Knowledge: Reviving and recording 'traditional' knowledge, copyright protection
Culture: Revival of 'traditional' culture, new hybrid cultural forms, youth culture
Festivals: **New urban Indigenous festivals**

Indigenous cultural festivals as tourism attractions

Research on Indigenous cultural events includes market segmentation of domestic tourists visiting an Aboriginal cultural festival in the Rukai tribal area of
Taiwan (Chang, 2006), and tourists' perceptions about the impacts of a tribal
festival (Wu, 2002). Rukai Day in Taiwan is a 3–4 day cultural festival, based
on the main ceremony of the Rukai tribe's harvest festival. All participants,
including tourists, have to wear traditional Rukai outfits (sold in local shops) to
be admitted to the festival (Chang, 2006). Similar case studies of hallmark or
regionally significant Indigenous events include the Naadam festival in Ulaanba-
tar, Mongolia (O'Gorman and Thompson, 2007), the 400-year-old Sami winter
festival in Jokkmokk, northern Sweden (Pettersson, 2003; Petterson and Viken,
2007), the Festival of Pacific Arts held every four years in the Pacific Islands/
Oceania region (Zeppel, 1992) and the Guelaguetza Festival in Oaxaca, Mexico
(Whitford, 2009). Other nationally significant hallmark events involving Indi-
genous cultures are more recent community celebrations and tourism attractions.
These include the Hibiscus Festival in Suva, Fiji (Bossen, 2000), the Merrie
Monarch Festival in Hawaii (Phipps, 2010a), the Pasifika Festival in Auckland,
New Zealand (Buch *et al.*, 2011), the Aotearoa Maori Performing Arts Festival
(Richards and Ryan, 2004), the Papua New Guinea Mask Festival (Martin, 2008,
2010), the Osogbo Festival in Nigeria (Cousin and Martineau, 2009) and the
Smithsonian Institution's Festival of American Folklife (Mato, 1998). In Aus-
tralia, hallmark Indigenous events include the Laura Aboriginal Dance Festival
on the Cape York Peninsula (Henry, 2000a, 2002, 2008, 2010; Thompson and
Connolly, 2006; Slater, 2010a; Waanta, 2011), the Garma Festival in Arnhem
Land (Phipps, 2010a, 2010b, 2011; Borthwick, 2011) and The Dreaming Festival in Sydney (2000) and Woodford, Queensland, since 2005 (Hanna, 2000;
Slater, 2007, 2010b). These festivals, based on Indigenous traditions and events,
have been re-contextualised in terms of their location, purpose, participants, performances or audience.

Hinch and Delamere (1993) reviewed key issues and challenges in developing First Nation festivals as tourism attractions in Canada. Native cultural festivals and celebrations were originally suppressed or tightly controlled by
government regulations, with native ceremonies and dancing restricted to rodeos
and wild-west shows. The inaugural Dreamspeakers Festival was held in 1992 in
Edmonton, Alberta, by the Aboriginal Film Makers Association of Alberta. The
festival promoted Aboriginal cultural achievements and history through concerts, performances and films. A financial deficit, and lower than expected audiences, saw the 1993 festival moved to late August near the end of the high
tourism season, reduced municipal funding support and a shorter festival programme. The tourist aspect of this new event affected Indigenous control of
planning, management, authenticity and cultural ties. Festivals and powwows
now represent mass-mediated Aboriginal cultural products (Buddle, 2004).

Whitford (2009) reviewed socio-cultural, economic and political impacts of
the Guelaguetza Festival, held annually in Oaxaca City, Mexico. 'Guelaguetza'

is a Zapotec word referring to the exchange of gifts and services among Indigenous people, mainly for agricultural work, also honouring Indigenous gods. Held over two Mondays in July, the Guelaguetza began in the 1930s, and has been a festival since 1953. It combines Indigenous traditions such as parades, dancers, music and re-enactments of Zapotec legends with contemporary events such as the Queen of the Guelaguetza. In 2006, the Gualagetza was cancelled following a teacher's union strike and protests that blocked city streets and damaged the main amphitheatre. The teacher's union claimed the state-sponsored Guelaguetza only benefitted tourism enterprises and big business, and organised an 'Alternative Guelaguetza of the People' in 2006 attended by 20,000 people (Denham, 2006). The 2007 state Guelaguetza Festival was marred by riots and protestors with heavy security. It still attracted over 26,000 visitors (with 5,700 international tourists) and generated US$9 million in economic benefits. The 2005 Guelaguetza Festival, however, attracted 48,000 more visitors with a downturn in Oaxaca tourism in 2006/07. Local people felt the Indigenous dances at Guelaguetza were now folkloric tourist presentations, not a celebration. The commercialised and commodified state Guelaguetza Festival was mainly held to attract tourists. In Oaxaca, Indigenous cultural traditions were being exploited for economic and political purposes.

In Nigeria, the Osogbo Festival was promoted by local authorities following UNESCO's declaration of the Sacred Grove of Osogbo as a World Heritage site in 2005 (Cousin and Martineau, 2009). To advance their own cultural and political ambitions, the elected officials and local king leveraged the tourist value of Osogbo's World Heritage designation. This included promoting the Osogbo Festival and rewriting local history to elevate the significance of the sacred grove. Tourism also assisted local Osogbo ambitions to play a leading regional role in elevating Yoruba ethnic identity within Nigeria. In Peru, the Inti Raymi Festival of the Sun created in 1944 reinforces Inca cultural identity along with the political and economic importance of Cusco as a tourist destination (Arceneaux and Zhang, 2009).

In contrast, the annual Sami winter festival has been held for the last four hundred years in Jokkmokk, northern Sweden. The festival started as a trading place for the Indigenous Sami people of northern Scandinavia, a reindeer herding culture. The winter festival presents Sami culture and traditional practices, and has undergone significant tourism development over the past few decades with added attractions. The Sami winter festival has remained popular despite being located at the Arctic Circle (Petterson, 2003). The tourism focus of the Sami winter festival also coincides with political recognition of the Sami as Indigenous people and the growing engagement of Sami people with Indigenous tourism (Muller and Huuva, 2009), raising issues about tourist presentations of Sami culture (Petterson and Viken, 2007). Martin (2008, 2010) also reviewed economic and cultural conflicts with the Papua New Guinea Mask Festival, held annually in the town of Rabaul on the island of New Britain. The festival features masked performances by the Tolai people, including the *tabuan* masked dancing figures linking clans. The festival is organised by the Papua New Guinea government to preserve Tolai culture and to attract tourists. Some Tolai people think the *tabuan* dancing figures should only be used in rituals, and not in tourist displays. Tolai women were not allowed to approach male *tabuan* dancers, yet female tourists took close-up photos. *Tabuan* performances have featured in a Tolai popular music festival since the 1970s. Local business elites in Rabaul also opposed moving the mask festival to the new provincial capital of Kokopo, following the volcanic eruption in 1994 that damaged Rabaul. Village Tolai people felt that local elites were commercialising customs such as the masked dancing figures for economic gain. A local Tolai Big Man prevented Australian hotel owners in Rabaul from using images of *tabuan* masks, yet used customary power to put *tabuan* images on the brochures for his own tourism business.

Richards and Ryan (2004) reviewed the development of the Aotearoa Traditional Maori Performing Arts Festival from 1972 to 2000. The festival was originally launched by a Polynesian entertainment sub-committee of the New Zealand Tourism Development Council (Kawai and Zemke-White, 2004). Held biennially, this major national festival (renamed Te Matatini) features Maori groups from throughout New Zealand performing *waiata* (songs), along with *haka, poi* and other dances. This Maori festival is a significant hallmark tourism event, attracting a growing number of Maori participants and spectators, along with other tourists. It is a dynamic part of contemporary Maori culture although the event is still largely outside mainstream New Zealand tourism. Key Maori personalities have played a major role in the success of this Maori arts festival. Similar to Canada, the colonial government of New Zealand previously suppressed Maori cultural practices, *haka* performances and beliefs. Maori cultural revival from the 1920s supported Maori performances at public events to express Maori identity, while Maori dance performance styles were increasingly standardised in festivals and tourism displays (Condevaux, 2009). However, there are tensions at this Maori Performing Arts Festival between traditional and contemporary performances, and expressing Maori independence and cultural identity versus dependency on New Zealand government grants and financial limitations in holding a large cultural festival. This Maori arts festival displays and reaffirms the cultural and political status of Maori people in New Zealand.

The Pasifika Festival, held annually in Auckland, showcases and celebrates Pacific Island cultures. It strengthens Pacific Islander identity and provides a signature cultural attraction for Auckland, with the city having the largest Polynesian community in the Pacific region (Buch *et al.*, 2011). Samoan and Maori cultural groups also participate in a high school cultural festival in Auckland. The migrant Samoan students use nostalgic performances aligned to their Samoan homeland, while Maori students critique New Zealand government policies in their cultural performances. Both the Samoan and Maori students express their marginality in the New Zealand nation through dance shows (Gershon and Collins, 2007). Maori people also engage in protests at the annual Waitangi Day celebrations of New Zealand's founding treaty.

Other festivals, such as the Hibiscus Festival in Fiji, were developed as part of national culture and to be a tourist attraction. In Fiji, these new festivals incorporating native Fijian culture developed prior to independence in 1970 due to growth in tourism, urbanisation and for national identity (Bossen, 2000). The Merrie Monarch Festival in Hawaii (Phipps, 2010a) also reaffirms Polynesian cultural identity and history. Hence, these new urban events presented by migrant or resident Indigenous groups represent the re-territorialism of Indigenous culture and identity within new urban and political settings.

Indigenous cultural festivals in Australia

There are more than a hundred Indigenous festivals held annually across Australia, ranging from community celebrations and sports events (Zeppel, 1999; Henry, 2000b; Heydon, 2007; Slater, 2011) to hallmark arts and cultural festivals in regional areas (Table 6.2). Major Indigenous festivals include the Laura Aboriginal Dance and Cultural Festival (Cape York, Queensland) held since 1986; Garma Festival (Arnhem Land, Northern Territory) from 1999; and The Dreaming Festival (Woodford, Queensland) since 2005. The 2011 Laura Aboriginal Dance Festival involved 20 Aboriginal communities and 5,000 attendees (Finch, 2011; Waanta, 2011). Regional Indigenous festivals include the Barunga Sports and Cultural Festival, Merrepen Arts Festival and Walking with Spirits festivals (Northern Territory); Law and Culture Festival (Kimberley, Western Australia); and Zenadth Cultural Festival (Thursday Island, Queensland). Indigenous youth festivals include the Croc Festival (1995–2008) held in regional towns across Australia, and Blak Nite, part of the Come Out Youth Arts Festival (Adelaide, South Australia). Aboriginal dance festivals have been funded across northern Australia since the 1970s, while urban Indigenous festivals have developed since the late 1990s. The Festival of the Dreaming was staged in Sydney in 1997 as the first Olympic Arts Festival and celebration of contemporary Aboriginal culture (Hanna, 2000). The Indigenous director then developed The Dreaming Festival in South East Queensland held annually since 2005 (Slater, 2010b), but incorporated with the larger Woodford Folk Festival in 2011. The Yabun Festival in Sydney is the largest single-day Indigenous music festival held in Australia. Indigenous cultural events are also part of the programme at other festivals such as the Bush Bands Bash for Aboriginal musicians at the Alice Desert Festival (Northern Territory), while the Island Vibe Festival on North Stradbroke Island (Queensland) features Quandamooka culture. Indigenous rights are profiled at events including NAIDOC Week, National Reconciliation Week and National Sorry Day held across Australia, Survival Day Concert (on Australia Day) and Mabo Day. The Coalition of Aboriginal and Torres Strait Islander Festivals was formed in 2010 and advocated for the cultural and economic interests of 12 hallmark Indigenous events in a submission on Australia's *National Cultural Policy* (Office for the Arts, 2011).

Indigenous music, dance, arts and crafts, history, ceremonies, film, theatre, workshops and forums are featured at these festivals. These Indigenous events contribute to cultural maintenance and attract tourists and local visitors to regional areas of Australia. Indigenous people also attend these regional cultural

Table 6.2 Selected Indigenous cultural festivals in Australia

Festival (year began/held)	Location(s)	Host organisation
Barunga Sports and Culture Festival (1985)	Barunga, NT	Barunga community
Blak Nite Youth Arts Festival#	Adelaide, SA	Carclew Youth Arts
Cairns Indigenous Art Fair# (2009)	Cairns, QLD	Arts Queensland
Croc Festival (1998–2007)	Regional towns – six states	
The Dreaming Festival# (2005)	Woodford, SE QLD	Qld Folk Federation
Garma Festival# (1999)	Arnhem Land, NT	Yothu Yindi Foundation
Indigenous Arts and Culture Festival (2012)	Melbourne, VIC	Melbourne Council
Laura Aboriginal Dance Festival# (1986)	Laura, Cape York, QLD	Quinkan & Regional Cultural Centre
Law and Culture Festival	Kimberley, WA	Kimberley Ab. Law & Cultural Centre
The Long Walk Festival (2007)	Melbourne, VIC	The Long Walk
Merrepen Arts & Sports Festival (1989)	Daly River, NT	Nauiyu community
Mornington Island Gulf Festival (1979)	Mornington Is, QLD	Mirndiyan Gununa Ab. Corporation
Nurlu Arts and Cultural Festival	Broome, WA	Goolarri Media
Share the Spirit Festival (2003)	Melbourne, VIC	Songlines Ab. Music
Spirit Festival	Adelaide, SA	Tandanya National Aboriginal Cultural Institute
Walking with Spirits Festival# (2003)	Beswick, NT	Wugularr community
Yabun Festival (2003)	Sydney, NSW	Gadigal Information Service
Yalukit Willam Ngargee: People Place Gathering# (2006)	St Kilda, Melbourne, VIC	City of Port Philip
Yugambeh Corroboree (2009)	Gold Coast, QLD	Kombumerri Ab. Corporation
Winds of Zenadth Cultural Festival# (1987)	Thursday Island, QLD	Torres Shire Council

Sources: Festival websites; Heydon, 2007; *Arts Yarn Up*, 2010; Phipps and Slater, 2010.

Notes

NSW = New South Wales; NT = Northern Territory; QLD = Queensland; SA = South Australia; VIC = Victoria; WA = Western Australia.
# Indigenous directors: *Blak Nite* (Lee-Ann Buckskin, 2005–11); *Cairns Indigenous Art Fair* (Avrill Quaill, 2011–12); *Festival of the Dreaming* (1997, Rhoda Roberts and Lydia Miller); *The Dreaming*: (Rhoda Roberts, 2005–09); *Garma*: (Rhoda Roberts, 2010–11); *Laura*: (Jeremy Geia, since 2003); *Walking with Spirits*: (Tom E. Lewis); *Yalukit Willam Ngargee* (Bo Svonoros, 2006–10); *Zenadth* (Frank Cook, 2010).

events as performers, participants and spectators. The Dreaming Festival attracted 8,593 visitors in 2009 including an Indigenous audience of 14–20 per cent (Slater, 2010b). These festivals play a crucial role in supporting Indigenous actors, artists, dancers and musicians, and traditional crafts. The Dreaming Festival provides a national showcase for Indigenous performers along with public forums about Indigenous rights and government policies for Indigenous education and welfare (Slater 2007, 2010b). The Garma Festival includes policy discussions on Indigenous issues along with Yolngu performances (Phipps, 2010a, 2010b). Festivals also contribute to Indigenous well-being, pride, self-esteem, cultural confidence and social connection with family and friends, young people and elders (Slater, 2010a; Waanta, 2011). Apart from youth festivals, the Indigenous festival 'sector is under-recognised and under-utilised by governments in advancing the policy aims of social inclusion, closing the gap [education, health, employment], cultural maintenance and fostering creative industries' (Phipps and Slater, 2010, p. 9).

Indigenous people are now involved in event management as staff, coordinators, producers and festival directors, thus enhancing local leadership and skills in event coordination and performance. However, the viability and sustainability of these biennial and annual Indigenous cultural festivals is a key issue. Few have full-time staff, most generate no profits and they rely on government grants to fund event infrastructure, transport, materials, event staff and performers. Indigenous festivals depend on government agencies, industry partners and corporate or philanthropic support (Arts Yarn Up, 2010). The infrastructure, product and service needs in staging short-term events burdens local Indigenous organisations with limited funding and resources, for minimal economic returns (Heydon, 2007). The success of Indigenous festivals is measured by Indigenous participation and economic benefits, size, durability, income generation (e.g. art sales), sponsorship, audience satisfaction, and media coverage. For festival sustainability, Indigenous event producers require funding and mentoring of Indigenous events staff, corporate sponsorship and government partnerships, and festival linkages to support artists (Arts Yarn Up, 2010). This would enable longer-term event planning and expanded cultural investment for Indigenous festivals. The Telstra Foundation funds the Indigenous youth programme at The Dreaming Festival (Slater, 2010b), with a mining company, Santos, the controversial main sponsor for this festival (Nolan, 2011). The Aboriginal and Torres Strait Islander Arts Board provided triennial funding support for festival administration by nine larger Indigenous festivals such as Garma and The Dreaming Festival. Other federal funding for community festivals and cultural development is sourced through the Indigenous Culture Support programme and the Community Festivals for Education Engagement programme. State and local government arts and event funding supports other local Indigenous festivals (Phipps and Slater, 2010). However, this funding is short-term and targeted to Indigenous cultural events of interest to visitors or contemporary music with mainstream appeal. The Coalition of Aboriginal and Torres Strait Islander Festivals sought five-year funding of key cultural events (Office for the Arts, 2011).

The Melbourne Council allocated AU$500,000 for its new Indigenous Arts and Culture Festival in 2012 (Price, 2011).

Garma Festival, Arnhem Land

The Garma Festival, held annually since 1999 and organised by the Yothu Yindi Foundation, takes place on the homelands of the Yolngu Aboriginal people in north-east Arnhem Land. The Yothu Yindi band derives from this area, with the lead singer Mandawuy Yunupingu taking a lead role in Garma along with his brother Galarrwuy Yunupingu, an influential political leader of the Northern Land Council. The Garma Festival profiles Yolngu *bunggul* ritual ceremonies and traditional dances along with Indigenous healing programmes, didjeridoo workshops and the Garma forum on national Indigenous policy issues. The Yothu Yindi Foundation provides Indigenous training in cultural tourism, event security, musical performance and recording at Garma. The festival employs over 130 Yolngu people in cultural and event services (Phipps, 2010a, 2010b). In 2007, the Telstra Foundation funded a training programme in film making and new digital media for Yolngu high school students. Garma attracts some 2,000 participants including actors, musicians, politicians and Indigenous academics. It also generates sales of Yolngu art from the Buku-Larrngay Mulka Art Centre in Yirrkala. The festival educates non-Indigenous people about Yolngu culture while supporting education, training and alternative income opportunities for Yolngu people in their homeland. A bauxite mine dominates the area, while government agencies control delivery of education, welfare and health services to the 5,000 Yolngu. Overtly political acts at Garma include the negotiation of education and development agreements, while a hybrid Australian/Aboriginal flag was flown over the Garma site by a clan helicopter in 2007. The ritual performances at Garma thus reassert Yolngu cultural practices and sovereignty, providing a locus for Indigenous cultural activism and negotiation of Indigenous rights (Phipps, 2011). The Garma festival represents re-territorialisation and reaffirmation of Yolngu homelands and culture.

Yalukit Willam Ngargee: People Place Gathering, Melbourne

This Indigenous festival in St Kilda, Melbourne, held since 2006 on traditional Boon Wurrung country, is organised by the Indigenous arts officer at the City of Port Philip Bay (Svoronos, 2010). The festival began as a two-day Indigenous and Polynesian music festival linked with the 2006 Commonwealth Games. The expanded festival includes Indigenous music, visual arts, theatre, forums and a Koori Night Market for selling Aboriginal arts and crafts, books and toys. It has revived Victorian Aboriginal art forms and practices, such as a contemporary dance performance based on a traditional Boon Wurrung creation story. Aboriginal elders with the Boon Wurrung Foundation suggested the Indigenous name for the festival translated as People Place Gathering. This increased recognition of the local Boon Wurrung people at the festival and by the City of Port Philip

Bay. Local Indigenous people were paid for organising event marshalling and security at the 2009/10 festivals. Festival organisers partnered with community cultural development agencies to foster contemporary dancing by Indigenous male dancers and youth dance groups in Melbourne (Svoronos, 2010). This festival represents re-territorialisation and reconstruction of Boon Wurrung culture in an urban area.

Urban Indigenous festivals in Queensland

This section discusses new urban Indigenous festivals attended by the author in Queensland: the Cairns Indigenous Art Fair (2009, 2010 and 2011) in Cairns; The Torres Strait Islands: A Celebration (2011) and the Reconciliation Beats Concert (2011) in Brisbane. These festivals focus respectively on promoting and selling Queensland Indigenous art; showcasing Torres Strait Islander art, cultural practices, music, dance and history; and contemporary Indigenous music. The objectives, sponsorship, cultural programme and socio-economic outcomes are assessed for each Indigenous cultural festival.

Cairns Indigenous Art Fair

The Cairns Indigenous Art Fair (CIAF) promotes and sells Aboriginal and Torres Strait Island art from around Queensland. It is held in the northern tropical city of Cairns, a major tourist gateway to the Great Barrier Reef and thriving hub for Indigenous arts practitioners. CIAF is a key part of the Queensland Government's *Backing Indigenous Arts Strategy*, which focuses on supporting and marketing Indigenous artists and art centres with AU$2.2 million to hold CIAF over the first four years. The strategy originally allocated AU$1 million to CIAF but the success of CIAF in 2009 saw the Premier allocate an additional AU$1.2 million to host CIAF in 2010 and 2011 as part of the Cairns Economic Future Plan. Additional building skills and opportunities grants were disbursed under this strategy (AU$303,287 in 2009) for Indigenous artists to produce work and attend CIAF (Arts Queensland, 2011a). The idea for CIAF arose from a 2007 report on the feasibility of hosting an Indigenous art fair in Cairns, with artists advocating for the promotion of Queensland Indigenous art based on successful Indigenous art programmes in the Northern Territory including a Darwin Aboriginal Art Fair established in 2007 (Martin-Chew and Snelling, 2009; Arts Queensland, 2010). CIAF includes invited Queensland Indigenous art centres and key art dealers, arts magazines and artist collectives (e.g. proppaNow, Brisbane). The fair includes talks and demonstrations by Indigenous artists, a children's art station and Aboriginal women weaving ghost nets (fishing nets) into artworks. CIAF has free performances by Indigenous dance groups from Cairns, Cape York and the Torres Strait in front of the venue, and Indigenous music nights. The fair also includes an Indigenous art symposium, other Indigenous art exhibitions at Cairns galleries, theatre and dance forums, and films (Musa, 2010). Indigenous people provide security, marshalling, media and catering services at CIAF.

Evaluation reports of Indigenous participants and CIAF visitors for CIAF 2009 and 2010 assessed the artistic, social, industry, economic and organisational outcomes of this hallmark arts event (Arts Queensland, 2010, 2011b, 2011c). The 2009 CIAF had 10,000 visitors and AU$523,897 in Indigenous art sales, while CIAF 2010 had 10,500 visitors and Indigenous art sales over AU$732,000. Visitor attendance at CIAF satellite Indigenous events in Cairns increased from 1,800 in 2009 to 9,000 in 2010. In 2009–10, CIAF generated an economic benefit of AU$2.45 million to Cairns from tourism expenditure, with AU$908,798 spent on local business contracts. CIAF programme partners in 2009–10 also contributed AU$1.51 million in cash and in-kind support, including event sponsorships with businesses, media groups and a university (12 in 2009 and 18 in 2010). CIAF 2010 involved 266 Indigenous artists and performers with 18 Indigenous people employed in event delivery. The economic benefits of CIAF 2010 were equal to 71 per cent of the event's cost with other benefits including post-CIAF art sales, tourism promotion and enhanced market integrity of Queensland Indigenous art. Some 21 per cent of attendees at CIAF 2010 purchased Indigenous artwork (up from 14 per cent in 2009) with 41 per cent of non-local visitors stating CIAF was the main reason for visiting Cairns (Arts Queensland, 2011b). CIAF mainly attracts Cairns and North Queensland visitors, art collectors and other tourists. The event is now promoted as 'Australia's premier Indigenous art fair' (Arts Queensland, 2011d).

An Indigenous artistic director managed the CIAF 2011 programme that featured the work of over 150 Queensland Indigenous artists from 8 galleries and 13 art centres (Anderson, 2011; CIAF, 2011a; Cumming, 2011). Some 13,000 people attended CIAF 2011 at the Cairns Cruise Liner Terminal, including North Queenslanders (67 per cent), other Queenslanders (11 per cent), interstate (15 per cent) and international (6 per cent) visitors (CIAF, 2011c). The fair received funding of AU$600,000 from the Queensland Government and AU$320,000 from the federal government, while it cost art galleries AU$15,000-$25,000 to attend. The Lockhart River Arts group sold 66 artworks for AU$60,000 in 2011 compared to just 4 paintings sold in 2010. Urban Aboriginal art was featured in a *Be Deadly* installation and keynote talk by proppaNow artists. One contemporary Indigenous artist challenged the arts trading at CIAF by non-Indigenous dealers that kept artists separate from selling their artwork (Boland, 2011; CIAF, 2011b, 2011d). However, at the exhibition space for CIAF 2011 the author heard a non-Indigenous art centre manager exhorting the Indigenous artist to 'sell, sell, sell'. The author also purchased a painting and met the young artist who signed a Certificate of Authenticity. Cairns residents and other visitors attend CIAF to buy artwork directly from Indigenous art centres. CIAF represents re-territorialisation and reconstruction of Aboriginal and Torres Strait Islander visual and performing arts and Indigenous cultural identity within the tourism economy of Cairns.

CIAF has publicly recognised the traditional Yidinji Aboriginal owners of the Cairns region, with CIAF 2011 featuring a historical exhibition about the life of Queebalem Henry Fourmile (1930–2010), a Gimuy Walubara Yidinji elder and community leader from Yarrabah near Cairns (Stephens, 2011). A public memorial outside the venue marked the final bronze sculpture of deceased CIAF patron Tapich Gloria Fletcher. The Umi Arts Centre in partnership with CIAF and the Cairns Festival also hosted a satellite 'Big Talk One Fire' Indigenous cultural festival on the Cairns Esplanade with Indigenous music and crafts. Staff at 'Big Talk One Fire' emphasised their local Indigenous event over the commercialised CIAF. There is some concern over the longer-term funding and sustainability of CIAF. Indigenous art centres prefer an annual CIAF event to interact with buyers, while some commercial galleries prefer a biennial event or a wider focus on Indigenous arts from the Asia-Pacific region. The 2011 Indigenous artistic director wanted to expand CIAF to include Asia-Pacific art dealers and contemporary artists (Boland, 2011). The previous artistic director felt the Australian Indigenous arts arena may not be able to sustain both CIAF and the Darwin Aboriginal Art Fair as events (Martin-Chew and Snelling, 2009). It is unlikely the AU$920,000 in direct public funding for CIAF 2011 was matched by equivalent art sales. Events Queensland, however, has provided AU$350,000 in funding support for CIAF 2012, a major increase on the AU$50,000 provided in 2011 (CIAF, 2012).

The Torres Strait Islands: a celebration

This celebration of Torres Strait Islander (TSI) culture and history was held in the capital city of Brisbane from 1 July–23 October 2011. This event coincided with the 140th anniversary of the Coming of the Light when Christianity was introduced to the Torres Strait Islands, located between Cape York and Papua New Guinea. The celebration involved a major exhibition of contemporary TSI art by 40 artists (*Land, Sea, and Sky*); ceremonial masks and historical films (*Awakening: Stories from the Torres Strait*), TSI stories (*Strait Home*) and performances across all four arts venues in the main cultural precinct (i.e. library, gallery, museum and theatre). An opening weekend celebration was held over 2–3 July 2011 with performances by TSI dance groups and musicians from Brisbane, Cairns and other groups from the TSI (i.e. Boigu, Poruma, Erub, Mer, Mabuiag, Moa and Saibai). The opening weekend also included free dance workshops, artist and curator talks and public forums on TSI history and cultural issues (Queensland Government, 2011). The Mabo Oration 2011 talk was delivered by Terri Janke on Indigenous intellectual property rights (Noonan, 2011). A world premiere performance of *Belong* by Bangarra Dance Theatre was also held, featuring a work choreographed by a TSI dancer. A major arts publication profiled the geography and history of the TSI, along with exhibitions, artists and performances at this celebration of TSI culture (Arts Queensland, 2011e). This event, funded by the Queensland state government, was the largest official celebration of TSI culture ever held in the state. It raised urban awareness of TSI culture, art, and history (Cooper, 2011). The TSIs have gained prominence since the 1992 Mabo case recognised Native Title, won by Eddie Koiki Mabo from Meriam (Murray Island). However, the majority of TSI people now live in mainland Australia. The TSI arts staff and performers from Brisbane at the opening weekend repeatedly expressed their appreciation for TSI groups from Cairns and the islands attending this major celebration. It reaffirmed the importance of urban TSIs continuing their cultural traditions through dance and contemporary art. This event represents re-territorialisation and reconstruction of TSI culture in Brisbane and other urban areas by TSI people.

Reconciliation Beats Concert

Reconciliation Beats was a new Indigenous music festival held in Musgrave Park, South Brisbane on 9 July 2011. Targeting young people, it featured Indigenous musicians with a hip-hop showcase, along with folk, rock and funk acts. Hosted by the Musgrave Park Cultural Centre, this concert followed the free Musgrave Park family fun day celebrations for the 20th anniversary NAIDOC week on the same site. Musgrave Park is a well-known Aboriginal site in South Brisbane often used for public events. This Indigenous music event was supported by the Triple J radio station, the Australian and Queensland Governments, Queensland Aboriginal and Islander Health Council, State Library of Queensland, Brisbane City Council and City Church. It was an alcohol-free event with an AUD$25 admission. There were Indigenous food, clothing and craft stalls, and Indigenous event or security staff at this concert. Reconciliation Beats was sparsely attended by Indigenous people and older non-Indigenous people. There were complaints from Indigenous attendees about the admission fee for the concert while one Indigenous performer asked the Indigenous audience to 'bring along their white friends next time'. This Reconciliation Beats concert tried to involve Indigenous youth in the re-territorialisation of Musgrave Park as an Aboriginal site, limited by admission fees.

Sustainability of Indigenous cultural events

Indigenous cultural events and festivals are held for cultural, social, economic and tourism reasons. They contribute to cultural maintenance and Indigenous well-being and increase public awareness of Indigenous cultural identity. The ongoing impacts of globalisation also lead to the reassertion of Indigenous identity and culture, whereby Indigenous groups engage with a capitalist economy through arts and cultural products. Historically, Indigenous festivals and ceremonies were banned or suppressed and Indigenous people controlled and/or removed from homelands in the colonial process of de-territorialisation. Indigenous festivals thus contribute to the process of re-territorialisation (Elias-Varotsis, 2006) of Indigenous cultures in their original homelands or in new urban locations. Re-territorialisation refers to the reconstruction of territorial borders and the reshaping of spatial and cultural boundaries. Many events, including Indigenous festivals, are de-contextualised spatially or culturally from their origins and reconstituted in new urban or regional settings. This chapter demonstrates the ensuing process of re-contextualisation impacts on Indigenous representations of cultural identity at events and festivals.

Indigenous festivals contribute to the cultural maintenance and transmission of traditions to younger Indigenous people. They also mark the emergence of individual Indigenous artists rather than community-based rituals where songs, dances and ceremonial objects are linked to creation stories and clan groups (Glaskin, 2010).

The sustainability of Indigenous cultural events and festivals depends on funding, staff and resources. Community-based cultural festivals are mainly delivered by Indigenous organisations and volunteers. Most festival funding is short-term and targeted to Indigenous cultural events of interest to visitors. There is a heavy reliance on funding from government agencies and grant programmes (i.e. arts, education, community development, health and welfare) to hold Indigenous festivals. Hence, there is limited criticism of government policies at these cultural events in contrast to prior political activism. There is some corporate sponsorship and philanthropic funding for hallmark Indigenous events such as The Dreaming Festival, marketed as 'Australia's International Indigenous Arts Festival'.

Indigenous festivals have developed the institutional status and recognition that guarantees funding (Getz and Anderson, 2009). Exceptions include the Laura Aboriginal Dance Festival, held since 1986, and the Cairns Indigenous Art Fair for its economic impact in selling Queensland Indigenous art. Regional events and cultural festivals contribute significantly to economic development in regional areas (Gibson and Stewart, 2009; Gibson and Connell, 2011; Gibson *et al.*, 2010) and Indigenous cultural festivals also support and stimulate 'traditional' and contemporary arts production and performances.

Conclusions

Contemporary Indigenous festivals represent the ethno-commodification of Indigenous cultural practices within traditional homelands and urban areas. In this process, Indigenous groups are part of an identity economy where Indigenous cultural presentations also fulfil economic and political goals. Hence, Indigenous festivals are part of the ongoing global process of de-territorialisation and re-territorialisation through mobility of people, ideas, images and cultural practices (Elias-Varotsis, 2006). This chapter reviewed the process of de-territorialisation and re-territorialisation of Indigenous cultures whereby spatial and cultural borders are reshaped through Indigenous festivals. Many Indigenous festivals now take place in urban areas or at dedicated event sites, and may be linked to other environmental concerns or social issues. Urban Indigenous festivals and performers are now de-contextualised either spatially or culturally from their origins and reconstituted in new settings. The ensuing process of re-contextualisation thus impacts on representations of Indigenous cultural identity at festivals.

Indigenous people are involved in festivals as performers, participants, event managers and attendees. This chapter demonstrated how the process of re-territorialisation operates through Indigenous festivals, and highlighted key issues for organisers in the sustainability of Indigenous cultural events. This includes securing ongoing funding for Indigenous festivals while meeting local cultural needs. Indigenous festivals provide a trans-cultural space that facilitates cultural exchange within a market economy, while maintaining and reshaping Indigenous identity and enhancing well-being. They also reaffirm the ongoing presence of Indigenous peoples and territorial links to tribal lands. Indigenous festivals on traditional lands reassert sovereignty and revitalise cultural practices. Metropolitan festivals also assert the cultural and political presence of Indigenous people in urban areas, but their focus on entertaining or marketable products often obscures racism and social disadvantage. Urban Indigenous festivals are being used by cities to boost their cultural and tourism profile while community festivals in rural and regional areas strive to maintain core Indigenous arts and rituals.

The sustainable management of Indigenous festivals thus involves the negotiation and presentation of cultural performances, funding support from government agencies and commercial sponsors, along with promotion by tourism, cultural or Indigenous organisations. The multiple goals of Indigenous festivals include sharing Indigenous culture; promoting Indigenous music, film, art or dance; selling Indigenous products; and improving Indigenous health and well-being. There are social tensions between Indigenous festivals held as local community celebrations or as tourist events, dependent on external funding and non-Indigenous audiences. Hence there are conflicts and compromises in expressing Indigenous cultural identity or independence due to financial limitations in staging events and reliance on government grants. Hallmark Indigenous festivals also reflect broader social and political forces where Indigenous culture is used as a part of place promotion and the political identity of nation states or regions. Indigenous events are thus shaped by new cultural representations of territorial landscapes and tribal identity.

References

Anderson, S. (2011) 'Introducing artistic director Avril Quaill', *CairnsLife*, 5 (August): 24.

Arceneaux, C. and Zhang, N. (2009) 'Cultural tourism as a political dilemma: A comparative study of Cusco, Peru and Xi'an, China', 2009 Congress of the Latin American Studies Association, Rio de Janeiro, Brazil, 11–14 June 2009. Online. Available at: www.lasa.international.pitt.edu (accessed 30 January 2012).

Arts Hub (2011) 'Qld determined to support indigenous art'. *Arts Hub*, 12 August. Online. Available at: www.artshub.com.au/news-article/opinions/arts/qld-determined-to-support-indigenous-art (accessed 30 January 2012).

Arts Queensland (2010) *Cairns Indigenous Art Fair 2009 Evaluation Report*, Brisbane: Arts Qld. Online. Available at: http://esvc000174.wic046u.server-web.com/aboutaq/eval-ciaf.html (accessed 30 January 2012).

Arts Queensland (2011a) *Backing Indigenous Arts Evaluation Report*, Brisbane: Arts Qld. Online. Available at: www.arts.qld.gov.au/aboutaq/bia-evaluation-report.html (accessed 30 January 2012).

Arts Queensland (2011b) *Cairns Indigenous Art Fair 2010 Evaluation Report*, Brisbane: Arts Qld. Online. Available at: http://esvc000174.wic046u.server-web.com/aboutaq/eval-ciaf.html (accessed 30 January 2012).

Arts Queensland (2011c) *Cairns Indigenous Art Fair 2010 Partners Report*, Brisbane: Arts Qld.

Arts Queensland (2011d) *Cairns Indigenous Art Fair*. Online. Available at: www.arts.qld.gov.au/funding/cairns-indig-art-mktp.html (accessed 30 January 2012).

Arts Queensland (2011e) *Torres Strait Islands*, Brisbane: Arts Qld.

Arts Yarn Up (2010) 'Special feature Indigenous festivals: Indigenous cultural festivals unite communities', *Arts Yarn Up*, Summer: 9–18. Online. Available at: www.australiacouncil.gov.au/__data/assets/pdf_file/0004/84982/Arts_YarnUp_Summer_2010.pdf (accessed 30 January 2012).

Bankston, C.L. and Henry, J. (2000) 'Spectacles of ethnicity: Festivals and the commodification of ethnic culture among Louisiana Cajuns', *Sociological Spectrum*, 20(4): 377–407.

Bester, C. (2011) 'Talent and traditions draw thousands to Cairns Indigenous Art Fair 2011', *The Cairns Post*, 22 August.

Boland, M. (2011) 'Fears for bumper festival', *The Australian*, 22 August: 17.

Borthwick, J. (2011) 'Bridging the gulf', *The Weekend Australian*, Travel, 28–29 January: 3.

Bossen, C. (2000) 'Festival mania, tourism and nation building in Fiji: The case of the Hibiscus Festival, 1956–1970', *The Contemporary Pacific*, 12(1): 123–154.

Buch, T., Milne, S. and Dickson, G. (2011) 'Multiple stakeholder perspectives on cultural events: Auckland's Pasifika Festival', *Journal of Hospitality Marketing and Management*, 20(3–4): 311–328.

Buddle, K. (2004) 'Media, markets and powwows: Matrices of aboriginal cultural mediation in Canada', *Cultural Dynamics*, 16(1): 29–69.

Cairns Indigenous Art Fair (CIAF) (2011a) *Cairns Indigenous Art Fair 2011 Program*, Arts Queensland.

Cairns Indigenous Art Fair (CIAF) (2011b) *Cairns Indigenous Art Fair 2011 Symposium Program*, CIAF. Online. Available at: www.ciaf.com.au/images/2012/Programs%20 and%20info/symposium%20prog.pdf (accessed 30 January 2012).

Cairns Indigenous Art Fair (CIAF) (2011c) 'CIAF 2011 – what you guys thought'. *CIAF Newsletter*, December 2011. Online. Available at: www.ciaf.com.au/plugins/Announce/default.asp?articleId=750&name=CIAF+2011+-+WHAT+YOU+GUYS+ THOUGHT (accessed 30 January 2012).

Cairns Indigenous Art Fair (CIAF) (2011d) 'Listen to the CIAF symposium keynotes'. *CIAF Newsletter*, December 2011. Online. Available at: www.ciaf.com.au/plugins/Announce/default.asp?articleId=757&name=LISTEN+TO+THE+CIAF+SYMPOSIU M+KEYNOTES (accessed 30 January 2012).

Cairns Indigenous Art Fair (CIAF) (2012) '$350,000 funding boost secures CIAF's future'. *CIAF Newsletter*, January 2012. Online. Available at: www.ciaf.com.au/plugins/Announce/default.asp?articleId=763&name=%24350%2C000+FUNDING+B OOST+SECURES+CIAF%27S+FUTURE (accessed 30 January 2012).

Chang, J. (2006) 'Segmenting tourists to aboriginal cultural festivals: An example in the Rukai tribal area, Taiwan', *Tourism Management*, 27(6): 1224–1234.

Comaroff, J.L. and Comaroff, J. (2009) *Ethnicity Inc.*, Chicago: University of Chicago Press.

Condevaux, A. (2009) 'Maori culture on stage: Authenticity and identity in tourist interactions', *Anthropological Forum*, 19(2): 143–161.

Cooper, N. (2011) 'We get Strait to the point', *The Courier Mail*, etc, 2 July: 16.

Cousin, S. and Martineau, J.L. (2009) 'The festival, the sacred grove and the UNESCO', *Cahiers d'Etudes Africaines*, 49(1–2): 337–364.

Cumming, G. (2011) 'North shows of its talent pool', *The Courier Mail*, 13–14 July: 10.

Denham, D. (2006) 'State-sponsored Guelaguetza cancelled', *News Oaxaca*, 38. Online. Available at: www.casacollective.org/en/node/288 (accessed 30 January 2012).

Elias-Varotsis, S. (2006) 'Festivals and events – (re)interpreting cultural identity', *Tourism Review*, 61(2), 24–29.

Finch, C. (2011) 'Dance festival gathers the mob', *The Courier Mail*, Escape, 13–14 August: 26–27.

Gershon, I. and Collins, S. (2007) 'Outspoken indigenes and nostalgic migrants: Maori and Samoan educating performances in an Aotearoa New Zealand cultural festival', *Teachers College Record*, 109(7): 1797–1819.

Getz, D. and Andersson, T.D. (2009) 'Sustainable festivals: On becoming an institution', *Event Management*, 12(1): 1–17.

Gibson, C and Connell, J. (eds) (2011) *Festival Places: Revitalising Rural Australia*, Clevedon, UK: Channel View.

Gibson, C. and Stewart, A. (2009) *Reinventing Rural Places: The Extent and Significance of Rural and Regional Festivals in Australia*, Wollongong, NSW: University of Wollongong.

Gibson, C., Waitt, G., Walmsley, J. and Connell, J. (2010) 'Cultural festivals and economic development in nonmetropolitan Australia', *Journal of Planning Education and Research*, 29(3): 280–293.

Glaskin, K. (2010) 'On dreams, innovation and the emerging genre of the individual artist', *Anthropological Forum*, 20(3): 251–267.

Hanna, M. (2000) 'Reconciliation and Olympism: The Sydney 2000 Olympic Games and Australia's indigenous people', in T. Taylor (ed.) *How You Play the Game: Papers from the First International Conference on Sport and Human Rights* (pp. 148–151). Sydney: University of Technology Sydney.

Henry, R. (2000a) 'Dancing into being: The Tjapukai Aboriginal Cultural Park and the Laura Dance Festival', *The Australian Journal of Anthropology*, 11(2): 322–332.

Henry, R. (2000b) 'Festivals,' in M. Neale, S. Kleinert and R. Bancroft (eds) *Oxford Companion to Aboriginal Art and Culture*, Melbourne: Oxford University Press.

Henry, R. (2002) 'Dancing into connection: The Laura Aboriginal Dance and Cultural Festival', *Poligrafi*, 27–28(7): 31–48.

Henry, R. (2008) 'Engaging with history by performing tradition: The poetic politics of Indigenous Australian festivals', in J. Kapferer (ed.) *The State and the Arts: Articulating Power and Subversion* (pp. 52–69), New York: Berghahn Books.

Henry, R. (2010) 'Landscapes of memory: Tjapukai Dance Theatre and Laura Festival', *Queensland Historical Atlas*, 1. Online. Available at: www.qhatlas.com.au/content/landscapes-memory-tjapukai-dance-theatre-and-laura-festival (accessed 30 January 2012).

Heydon, J. (2007) *Indigenous Community Festivals – Top End: An Evaluation using Encore Event Evaluation Kit*, Gold Coast: Sustainable Tourism CRC.

Hinch, T.D. and Delamere, T.A. (1993) 'Native festivals as tourism attractions: A community challenge', *Journal of Applied Recreation Research*, 18(2): 131–142.

Kaiai, H. and Zemke-White, K. (2004) 'Kapa haka as a web of "cultural meanings"', in C. Bell and S. Matthewman (eds) *Cultural Studies in Aotearoa New Zealand: Identity, Space and Place* (pp. 139–160), South Melbourne: Oxford University Press.

Martin, K. (2008) 'The work of tourism and the fight for a new economy: The case of the Papua New Guinea Mask Festival', *Tourism, Culture and Communication*, 8(2): 97–107.

Martin, K. (2010). 'Living pasts: Contested tourism authenticities', *Annals of Tourism Research*, 37(2): 537–554.

Martin-Chew, L. and Snelling, M. (2009) 'CIAF in focus', *Art Monthly Australia*, 222 (August): 5–6.

Mato, D. (1998) 'The transnational making of representations of gender, ethnicity and culture: Indigenous peoples' organizations at the Smithsonian Institution's festival', *Cultural Studies*, 12(2): 193–209.

Muller, D.K. and Huuva, S.K. (2009) 'Limits to Sami tourism development: The case of Jokkmokk, Sweden', *Journal of Ecotourism*, 8(2): 115–127.

Musa, O. (2010) 'Kai-eye for CIAF', *Art Monthly Australia*, 235 (November): 50–51.

Nolan, A. (2011) 'A message to our readers', Greenhouse Special, *Eco*, December 2011/ January 2012: 14.

Noonan, K. (2011) 'Warrior of culture', *The Courier Mail*, etc, 2 July: 36.

Office for the Arts (2011). National Cultural Policy Discussion Paper Submission. Online. Available at: http://culture.arts.gov.au/sites/default/files/submissions/Submission%20 329_Redacted.pdf (accessed 30 January 2012).

O'Gorman, K. and Thompson, K. (2007) 'Tourism and culture in Mongolia: The case of the Ulaanbaatar Naadam', in R. Butler and T. Hinch (eds) *Tourism and Indigenous Peoples: Issues and implications* (pp. 161–175), Oxford, UK: Elsevier.

Pearson, N. (2011) 'Yolngu inspire us to pursue all our ambitions', *The Weekend Australian*, 13–14 August: 14.

Pettersson, R. (2003) 'Indigenous cultural events: The development of a Sami winter festival in northern Sweden', *Tourism*, 51(3): 319–332.

Petterson, R. and Viken, A. (2007) 'Sami perspectives on indigenous tourism in northern Europe: Commerce or cultural development?', in R. Butler and T. Hinch (eds) *Tourism and Indigenous Peoples: Issues and implications* (pp. 176–187), Oxford, UK: Elsevier.

Phipps, P. (2010a) 'Performances of power: Indigenous cultural festivals as globally engaged cultural strategy', *Alternatives*, 35(3): 217–240.

Phipps, P. (2010b) 'Garma Festival North East Arnhem Land', in P. Phipps and L. Slater (eds) *Indigenous Cultural Festivals: Evaluating impact on Community Health and Wellbeing* (pp. 63–75), Melbourne: Globalism Research Centre, RMIT University. Online. Available at: http://mams.rmit.edu.au/ufwg124fk6adz.pdf (accessed 30 January 2012).

Phipps, P. (2010c) 'Indigenous festivals in Australia: Introduction and methods', in P. Phipps and L. Slater (eds) *Indigenous Cultural Festivals: Evaluating impact on Community Health and Wellbeing* (pp. 10–19), Melbourne: Globalism Research Centre, RMIT University.

Phipps, P. (2011) 'Performing culture as political strategy: The Garma Festival, Northeast Arnhem Land', in C. Gibson and J. Connell (eds) *Festival Places: Revitalising Rural Australia* (pp. 109–122), Clevedon, UK: Channel View.

Phipps, P. and Slater, L. (2010) *Indigenous Cultural Festivals: Evaluating impact on Community Health and Wellbeing*. A report to the Telstra Foundation on research on Indigenous festivals, 2007–2010, Melbourne: Globalism Research Centre, RMIT University. Online. Available at: http://mams.rmit.edu.au/ufwg124fk6adz.pdf (accessed 30 January 2012).

Price, N. (2011) 'Melbourne to become indigenous culture capital', *Melbourne Leader*, 2

May 2011. Online. Available at: http://melbourne-leader.whereilive.com.au/news/story/culture-capital/ (accessed 30 January 2012).

Queensland Government. (2011) 'The Torres Strait Islands: A Celebration'. Online. Available at: www.tsi.org.au/opening-weekend.html (accessed 30 January 2012).

Richards, P. and Ryan, C. (2004) 'The Aotearoa Maori Performing Arts Festival 1992–2000: A case study of cultural event maturation', *Journal of Tourism and Cultural Change*, 2(2): 94–117.

Slater, L. (2007) 'My island home is waiting for me: The Dreaming Festival and archipelago Australia', *Cultural Studies*, 21(4): 571–581.

Slater, L. (2010a) '"Calling our spirits home": Indigenous cultural festivals and the making of a good life', *Cultural Studies Review*, 16(1): 143–154.

Slater, L. (2010b) 'The Dreaming Festival Woodford' in P. Phipps and L. Slater (eds) *Indigenous Cultural Festivals: Evaluating impact on Community Health and Wellbeing* (pp. 48–62), Melbourne: Globalism Research Centre, RMIT University. Online. Available at: http://mams.rmit.edu.au/ufwg124fk6adz.pdf (accessed 30 January 2012).

Slater, L. (2010c) 'Croc Festival Cape York, Torres Strait, Derby and Shepparton' in P. Phipps and L. Slater (eds) *Indigenous Cultural Festivals: Evaluating impact on Community Health and Wellbeing* (pp. 30–47), Melbourne: Globalism Research Centre, RMIT University.

Slater, L. (2011) '"Our spirit rises from the ashes": Mapoon Festival and history's shadow', in C. Gibson and J. Connell (eds) *Festival Places: Revitalising Rural Australia* (pp. 123–135), Clevedon, UK: Channel View.

Stevens, A. (2011) 'Doors opening', *The Weekend Post*, Weekender, 20 August: 8–10.

Stewart-Harawira, M. (2005) *The New imperial Order: Indigenous Responses to Globalization*, London: Zed Books.

Svoronos, B. (2010) 'Yalukit William Ngargee People Place Gathering City of Port Philip, Melbourne', in P. Phipps and L. Slater (eds) *Indigenous Cultural Festivals: Evaluating impact on Community Health and Wellbeing* (pp. 76–83), Melbourne: Globalism Research Centre, RMIT University. Online. Available at: http://mams.rmit.edu.au/ufwg124fk6adz.pdf (accessed 30 January 2012).

Thompson, D. and Connolly, M. (2006) 'Clapsticks and karaoke: The melting pot of indigenous identity', *Pacifica*, 19(3): 344–355.

Waanta (2011) Laura Aboriginal Dance Festival 2011. *Waanta: Lockhart River Aboriginal Shire Council Newsletter*. Online. Available at: www.lockhart.qld.gov.au/sites/default/files/Joseph/Waanta_Lockhart_Festival_2011.pdf (accessed 30 January 2012).

Warren, A. and Evitt, R. (2010) 'Indigenous hip-hop: Overcoming marginality, encountering constraints', *Australian Geographer*, 41(1): 141–158.

Whitford, M. (2009) 'Oaxaca's indigenous Guelaguetza Festival: Not all that glistens is gold', *Event Management*, 12(3–4): 143–161.

Wu, T.C. (2002) 'Tourists' perceptions of tribe festival impacts', *Tourism Management Research*, 2(2): 39–56 (in Chinese).

Zeppel, H. (1992) 'The Festival of Pacific Arts: An emerging special interest tourism event', in B. Weiler and C.M. Hall (eds) *Special Interest Tourism* (pp. 69–82), London: Belhaven Press.

Zeppel, H. (1999) 'Aboriginal festivals and special events', in H. Zeppel (comp.) *Aboriginal Tourism in Australia: A Research Bibliography* (pp. 211–226). CRC Tourism Research Report Series Report 2, Gold Coast, Qld: CRC Tourism. Online. Available at: www.crctourism.com.au/wms/upload/Resources/bookshop/Aboriginal%20Tourism%20in%20Australia.PDF (accessed 30 January 2012).

7 Sustainability and community networks

The case of the Indian diaspora

Alison Booth

Introduction

> Social Sustainability is: a positive condition within communities, and a process within communities that can achieve that condition.
>
> (McKenzie, 2004, p. 40)

This chapter explores how producers of live performance events representing Auckland's Indian communities create networks and alliances in order to produce sustainable events. Community events create opportunities to showcase cultural diversity, build networks and showcase alternative voices to the wider public. Socially sustainable events play an important role in creating and maintaining a quality of life for individuals as well as the health of communities (Caistor-Arendar *et al.*, 2011, p. 31). It is argued in this chapter that sustainable events in a social context must demonstrate meeting specific tangible and intangible objectives. First, a sustainable event must be economically feasible by achieving set-out objectives that typically involve attracting audience, gaining media attention and meeting the budget parameters. Second, less tangible objectives are met such as having the ability to grow the producer's and/or the performer's reputations or build production networks that share expertise and resources. Third, tangible resources are created such as production manuals and other management tools for knowledge transfer and the easy replication of similar events in the future.

There has been much debate on notions of sustainability focusing on events and their economic, environmental and social impacts on host communities and tourism (Getz, 1997; McDonnell *et al.*, 2008; Raj and Musgrove, 2009; Richards, 2007; Yeoman *et al.*, 2004). Little attention has been paid to the sustainable production processes of performance events involving specific ethnic communities and how this contributes to social sustainability. Social sustainability can be defined as creating formal and informal processes, systems, structures and relationships that actively support the capacity of current and future generations to create healthy and liveable communities. Socially sustainable communities are equitable, diverse, connected and democratic and provide a good quality of life (McKenzie, 2004, p. 18).

Social sustainability plays a paramount role in the continuous journey toward sustainability, because it is, ultimately, the human beings, individually and in collectives, that will determine economic and environmental well-being (Magis and Shinn, 2009, p. 38). As the process of formulating and discussing cultural meanings can be quite complex this chapter demonstrates through four case studies how sustainable live performance events are negotiated involving Auckland's diverse Indian communities.

Event types and production networks

Annually, in Auckland, New Zealand, hundreds of events are produced featuring Indian culture. The variety includes a wide offering including Bollywood themed events, classical and semi-classical performances that reflect the cultural diversity within the Indian community. Events include fashion shows, popular youth culture including DJ mix, jazz, rock and fusion, large annual religious festivals like Diwali and Navaratri and smaller events produced by cultural groups or private house concerts featuring friends, family and overseas entertainers. Music and the performing arts provide a context for the formulation and negotiation of cultural meaning and identity (Seeger, 1987, pp. 128–131). Performances representing specific cultural communities can act as sights for cultural advocacy by creating public visibility, highlighting the positive and colourful features of the community to the wider public.

As with any event, a successful event is one that achieves set objectives and nothing untoward happens on the day. The success depends on meticulous planning and the producer's ability to access a range of resources including administration and marketing skills, access to venues and media, technical teams, artists and adequate funds. Access to these resources is often negotiated through personal relationships that event production networks. Without strong networks events may fail or the producer may lose control over the production process. Event production networks are resources in themselves and key to sustainable events as they build local as well as potentially larger global communities.

Production networks take different forms by creating alliances and partnerships dependent on the type of event, the producer's cultural perspective and the resources required for the successful event delivery. Networks may involve a specific cultural identity, community representatives of other identities, as well as diasporic communities. Partnerships are formed within community groups, local governments as well as with international agencies to gain access to grants, sponsorships, international performers and other required production resources. When producing events representing specific communities, the formation of production networks and alliances may be affected by complex relationships within specific cultural sectors or develop across cultural sectors (Roy, 2001, p. 252). Conflicts sometimes arise between 'local established' members of the community and 'new' migrants creating 'insider-outsider' positionality and issues of power involved in securing sponsorship and/or funding, venues and access to audience.

While the New Zealand national identity is being keenly contested in a multicultural context, the Indian-New Zealand migrant story is culturally significant (Bandyopadhyay, 2010; Friesen, 2008a; Johnson, 2010b). The unfolding of this story is intertwined with the way in which Auckland's Indian communities produce sustainable events and how such events reflect the changing nature of twenty-first century Indian diasporic communities. As social sustainability involves formal and informal processes, systems, structures and relationships that actively support community endeavours, the manner in which cultures construct, use, rearrange and maintain event production networks and alliances affects issues of social cohesion and accessibility allowing communities the ability to thrive.

The cultural context

New Zealand's colonial and postcolonial heritage

Like many other countries in the world, New Zealand's colonial past and postcolonial history has created a rich tapestry of cultural diversity. What makes New Zealand unique is the New Zealand government's official recognition of the indigenous Māori population who settled the land hundreds of years before the European settlers' arrival in the eighteenth and nineteenth century. The New Zealand government's policy of biculturalism negotiated between Maori and Pakeha (those of European heritage), has resulted in New Zealand not adopting multicultural policies as practiced in comparative nations including Canada and Australia (Bendrups, 2010). The increasing diverse multicultural identity of New Zealand's population plays a role in the larger debates that are currently changing the definition of New Zealand's national identity, multiculturalism and issues of transnational linkages (Bandyopadhyay, 2010; Friesen, 2008b).

Asia has an important historical and contemporary place in the making of New Zealand (Johnson, 2010b). The culturally diverse, quickly growing Indian community is the third largest ethnic minority in New Zealand's cultural melting pot. Since the immigration reforms that started in 1987, the Indian population has increased dramatically in size and cultural diversity reflecting trends in the rapidly evolving global Indian diaspora (Friesen, 2008b). The Indians in New Zealand are represented by diverse languages, religions and migratory histories. What appears from the outside to be a homogenous community, from within includes differentiated and diversified identities (Bandyopadhyay, 2010). Indian identity in New Zealand is framed in a cultural interplay that exists between British and Indian cultures in a postcolonial environment. The historical interconnections between past and present serve to contribute to the cultural enrichment of New Zealand through the contribution of diverse musical, religious and cultural traditions for more than a century (Johnson, 2010a).

Population growth

Indian migrants are one of New Zealand's fastest growing populations. Auckland's ethnically and culturally diverse Indian communities include recently arrived professionals to fifth generation agricultural workers related to the early settlers from India's Northwest or anything in between (Bandyopadhyay, 2010; Friesen, 2008b; Leckie, 2010). The growing size and changing demographics of Auckland's Indian communities are transforming the content, practice and place of Indian cultural production in Auckland. Event production practices are placed in the context of this rapid demographic change within Auckland's Indian population and those with postcolonial or the more modern global eyes of twenty-first century transnational global India.

Until 1996, the majority of those identifying themselves as from India were in fact Indo-Fijians with slightly smaller Indian populations from the north-western regions of Gujarat and the Panjab making up most of the remainder. In recent years, the majority of Indians arriving in New Zealand have come directly from India and represent a wide variety of regions. Significant numbers are also arriving from other countries. New Zealanders of Indian descent have increased from 6.6 per cent of the total New Zealand population recorded in 2001 to 9.6 per cent recorded in the latest complete census in 2006 (Friesen, 2008a, p. 7). If the perceptible increase in the Indian presence in Auckland is any indication, the next census can be expected to return a percentage higher than 10 per cent.

These developments reflect the 2003 changes in immigration policy introducing New Zealand's Skilled Migration Category (SMC) that allows migrants with specific valued skills and qualifications to qualify for New Zealand residency or a permit to work. The government's aim from this time was to shift immigration policy from the passive acceptance of residence applications to the active selection of skilled migrants with priority to applicants with an offer of skilled employment or current skilled work in New Zealand. International students are awarded bonus points and may be eligible to migrate on course completion. This change in policy and the resulting changes to the demographic makeup of New Zealand's Indian immigrants have resulted in changes in the nature of events and the socially sustainable production practices of events representing New Zealand's Indian communities.

Diasporic identities and globalisation

The way in which an event is represented and perceived by the community is dependent on an individual's personal experiences with India. The producer's age, culture and education as well as migration history will affect personal concepts of what is India, what it means to be Indian and many ideas of 'Indianness'. Culturally identifying with India does not indicate a producer has actually lived in or in fact ever visited India. Cultural identities created are situational, negotiated individually, locally, regional as well as globally (Bandyopadhyay, 2010). The India of postcolonial history is complex combining diverse cultural identities that include various religions, languages and cultural practices of the South Asian diasporas.

Diaspora networks also come into play as they reflect the twin concerns of transnational process abroad and ethnic identity politics at home (Dietrich, 1999; Maira, 2002; Turino and Lea, 2004). Globalisation can be viewed as a liberating process, characterised by increasingly mobile flows of people rooted in a diasporic identity. Diaspora refers to ethnic populations that have become dispersed due to a variety of 'push' (floods, disease, social unrest) and 'pull' (jobs, climate, cultural resources) factors. Globalisation is characterised by an increasingly mobile flow of people and affects how the historically rooted notion of diaspora is perceived; internal as well as external to the specific cultural group (Hopper, 2007). The diasporic cultural picture is shaded by a multitude of hues.

Diaspora communities may identify with a picture that centres on cultural essence or purity, but it is essential to recognise the conception of 'identity' which lives with and through, not despite, difference; by hybridity and the influence of globalisation. In this way the concept of diaspora encompasses the twin concerns of transnational process abroad and ethnic identity politics at home (Turino and Lea, 2004). Diaspora identities are constantly producing and reproducing themselves anew; adjusting, transforming and differentiating within their cultural community as well as being part of the host community (Hall, 1996, p. 223). When diasporic cultures are hybrid (consisting of different languages, histories, religions and migratory histories) identity differences can be used as persuasive marketing positioning when promoting and branding 'ethnic' cultural communities through small as well as high profile events (Carnegie and Smith, 2006, p. 255).

Cultural diversity and cultural representation are contrasted and illustrated by two recent Auckland socially sustainable events. Falguni Pathak is Mumbai based with strong affinity towards the traditional music of the Indian state of Gujarat. In Figure 7.1 Falguni Pathak is performing 'Dandiya' at an annual Hindu Navaratri festival event. This is in strong contrast to a pop/rock performance by the Pakistani singer, Atif Aslam, performing to a less traditional audience in Figure 7.2.

These examples also illustrate how events create differing notions of cultural representation depending on how producers and their corresponding audiences place value on the differing cultural perspectives that are imbedded in the history of the Indian diaspora. Both events created positive event experiences offering audiences and performers an opportunity to engage in cultural and historical shared values. This factor is important when considering the issue of social sustainability and community events as how events invoke identity affects the success of an event and the effectiveness of the producer's ability to attract audience support as well as attract the attention of the wider community.

Auckland's performing arts scene

Indian performing arts have had a community profile in New Zealand since the formation of Indian cultural associations in the 1950s. The religious diversity of

Figure 7.1 Falguni Pathak, Telstra Clear Pacific Events Centre, Auckland, New Zealand (4 September 2011) (source: Agastya Pesara, unpublished photograph, 2011).

Figure 7.2 Atif Aslam performing at the Logan Campbell Centre, Auckland, New Zealand (21 January 2011) (source: Agastya Pesara, unpublished photograph, 2011).

the Indian populations introduces an extra dimension to the complexity of defining ethnic identity within the Indian community. In some cases Hinduism has been promoted as the epitome of 'Indian' culture with the prominence of large religious based celebrations such as the Diwali festivals in Auckland (Johnson, 2007). However, significant Sikh, Muslim, Christian and other religious sectors of the Indian population are not adequately incorporated within this representation of 'Indianness', but even within the Hindu population, regional and linguistic groups are increasingly celebrating their own festivals elevating the growing South Asian population representing their 'Indian' cultural identities through the performing arts as a visible and public voice.

Auckland's Indian communities actively support live performance events with specific themes that are based on regional and religious cultural affiliations as well as musical preferences whether classical, film, music or other popular genres such as fusion. Events are produced by individual producers, cultural associations, as well as through government affiliated agencies. The performance may be an amateur, community or professional production. The event may involve local, overseas performers or in combination as part of a festival, a one-off performance or part of a larger national or international tour. Typically, live performance genres will include Indian classical music and dance with regional variations, DJ mix, Bollywood dance and songs, community cultural shows and fusion concerts.

The popular songs of the Hindi cinema are at the heart of popular culture in India and the Indian diaspora. Currently Bollywood is the popular global genre and found in a variety of event experiences including the Diwali festivals and large venue events like Asha Bhosle and Jagjit Singh, annual religious based events, such as Navaratri and Holi as well as local school and community Bollywood performances and amateur shows (Gopal and Moorti, 2008; Johnson and Figgins, 2005; Rajadhyaksha, 2008). New Zealand's Indian communities create film-song events that are designed to enact a common diaspora-homeland identity (Johnson, 2007; Lavezzoli, 2006; Rajadhyaksha, 2008; Tomlinson, 1999). The use of the term Bollywood as it is applied to the products and culture of the global Hindi cinema industry has been problematised by some Indian scholars (Gopal and Moorti, 2008; Prasad, 2008; Rajadhyaksha, 2008). Nevertheless, Bollywood is a term central to the marketing of the events globally and specifically in Auckland.

The diversity of the Auckland Indian communities' cultural heritage is presented through a wide range of events appealing to various types of audiences from within the specific culture heritage as well as the wider population. Annually hundreds of events are produced ranging from arts festivals, large commercial shows, religious and cultural functions to house concerts. Some events (run by community groups, individuals, trusts and councils) have been more successful than others. Some producers have made small fortunes while others have lost their homes by creating unfeasible business practices. New migrants, without event experience, recently arrived from large global cities in India, the United Kingdom, South Africa, the Middle East, etc., are especially vulnerable as they have not built the relationships and networks required to produce sustainable events.

Auckland with a population of 1.2 million people in a country of 4.5 million creates unique challenges for creating feasible events. The influx of new skilled migrants and students from India is increasing the numbers of productions and types of commercial events occurring in Auckland. This in turn is increasing commercial event competition for audience, venue and media attention. In the increasingly competitive battleground that has become the Indian production scene successful producers are those who can form sustainable alliances.

Historically, producers of Indian events have been individuals who created their own events within a closed business partner circle. The dominant producers relied on a one-off event business model, involving existing sponsors and media partnerships from within specific cultural and language groups. This production model proved possible in a community that was dominated by a single Indian radio station and a relatively small, homogeneous Indian population. In this situation conventional promotion campaigns within the Indian community were sufficient to make many of these events successful.

This type of production model is similar to the production models that dominated much of the cultural event production in India during India's postcolonial period. The postcolonial period presents the cultural representation of India before 1985 and India's economic liberalisation. The performers as well as the producers experienced India when it was a postcolonial country. This shared cultural outlook creates a common ground on which producers are able to promote artists, attract audience and create production networks. The 'old is gold' concept is also regularly produced by local community performers imitating these large events at local school halls and in house concerts.

This production model is in stark contrast to the newer younger migrants arriving with twenty-first century global eyes who are forming alliances with second generation members of the Auckland Indian communities. Many of these producers are young, educated and globally oriented individuals who are in the social world of live events as well as in the virtual world. Global performances utilise the twenty-first century world of internet, cell phones, global film distribution and other digital means of information transfer. This is a cross-border, international approach that includes Indi hip hop DJ mix fusion and world music acts that feature in clubs, concert halls and festivals. Performers include local DJs as well as performers from Europe, the Middle East, India or any other transnational localities.

Case studies: cultural societies, festival, postcolonial and transnational networks

Socially sustainable events create opportunities to showcase cultural diversity, build networks, showcase alternative voices and build healthy communities. How producers of Indian events in Auckland create socially sustainable events is demonstrated though four diverse case studies. Sustainable events are produced

differently according to the type of event as well as the production team formation and the role and cultural affiliation of the producer. In this context, to be
sustainable, the ideal model meets budget objectives and creates networks with
ongoing alliances, as well as developing opportunities and resources for future
events. Events produced by cultural societies, government negotiated festivals,
Bollywood concerts featuring overseas stars and the popular youth oriented
events highlight contrasting critical success factors indicating how the producers
achieved their objectives and goals.

Cultural Society Productions: Auckland's Carnatic Society

In a consideration of producing sustainable performing art events, I suggest that
the identity of the producer, relative to that of the community or culture
involved, is crucial to how events represent cultural identities to the wider
public. In the case of cultural societies, there is little need to have access to the
power structures of the society in which they operate. This is because the production networks and alliances are located within a single cultural context.
Although this creates a strong internally focused production network the producers may have weaker network relationships within the broader society in which
they are located. What this means is that members of the local cultural community are directly involved in designing, producing and managing the event
production process. Local government provides event funds for cultural societies
in recognition of the importance of supporting the social sustainability of the
local multicultural diversity.

The Auckland Carnatic Society is one of the most active and offers a classic
example of the many Indian societies that are involved in producing events that
promote classical Indian cultures. Over the past couple of decades, this group
has produced concerts and workshops of classical South Indian music, featuring
local and international artists. The Society produces annually at least two classical vocal and/or instrumental concerts involving overseas artists as well as religious festivals involving local musicians and their students. They own their own
sound system allowing them to produce adequate concerts in local school halls.
The society members are very active and willing to contribute time and resources
when required to ensure the sustainability of their cultural activities and events.
The audience is almost exclusively members of Auckland's South Indian community. This production structure is similar to the highly organised South Indian
classical music groups in Britain (Farrell *et al.*, 2000). The events are designed
to reinforce notions of religious and regional identity and less importantly to
gain representation of their local or diaspora community to the wider New
Zealand public.

Concerts that feature overseas musicians are linked into 'sister' societies in
Australia creating networks to reduce airfares and performance fees. Expenses
are kept low by using community halls and promoting events through word of
mouth, inexpensive posters and website marketing. The concerts attract a full
house with an audience that is composed of 95 per cent of South Indian cultural

identity. The Carnatic Society's performance events are also assisted by annual government arts funding contributing to the airfares required to bring international artists who are touring Australia from South India. This demonstrates how the Carnatic Society creates events to promote a specific cultural affiliation. By creating strong, culturally specific networks and sourcing government funding opportunities specifically for community representation, the Carnatic Society is able to create socially sustainable events that can be easily replicated annually over the long term and that build networks within the local South Indian and the wider diaspora. The Carnatic Society plays an important role in creating and maintaining the musical lives of performers and showcasing this cultural identity to the society members as well as preparing for performances in larger city produced events such the next case study, Diwali (Festival of Lights).

Auckland's Diwali (Festival of Lights)

Ethnic cultural festivals are typically sponsored and funded by the government as they offer the hegemonic culture a window into 'other' cultures and identities. Auckland's Diwali (Festival of Lights) started as a community based religious event that for the past 11 years has been produced in partnership with the local city council and private/public sponsors. The Diwali Festival celebrations epitomise this phenomenon by offering the non-Indian population a window into Indian culture, which is identified by specific key cultural signifiers including food, crafts and Bollywood dancing. At the same time, the Indian communities create a united ethnic Indian identity based on cultural patriotism binding differences across regional and linguistic differences (Johnson, 2010b).

For Auckland Council to create a feasible event, complex networks of local as well as international alliances are required. The strong commercial business and cultural identity interests have been built over a ten-year period producing a strong production network. The model is underpinned by alliances between Asia New Zealand Foundation and Auckland Council in partnership as the host organisers. Asia New Zealand Foundation attracts sponsors and support from other government agencies and corporations with interests in business development with India and/or the Indian community. The host community includes religious, cultural and community groups who provide co-workers including stall holders, performers and volunteers as well as audience and a major Indian radio station as a sponsor. The local government provides the infrastructure for local communities to participate in an event without taking on the high risks associated with running large festivals. The audience of 100,000 plus is traditionally represented by 50 per cent Indian and 50 per cent European in the daytime for the dance competitions and classical performers, increasing to a much younger crowd of 90 per cent Indian for the popular performance genres: Bollywood and Bhangra in the evening.

Every year the value of programming, how Indian cultural identity is represented and who controls the decision-making process is publically debated with the diverse cultural perspectives coming into play. The festival has two producers with teams placed outside of the culture and multiple stakeholders from various factions within the culture. The format that the programming takes is never to the liking of all involved, with varying opinions of how India should be represented by the festival. The non-Indian producers carefully negotiate the traditional Indian and unconventional cultural viewpoints and funding negotiations with sponsors and international funding agents. For city councils and government agencies large cultural events are important as they are used as destination tourism marketing tools and international business development (Jago *et al.*, 2003).

The longevity and sustainability of Diwali (Festival of Lights) is dependent on complex networks and alliances that are local, national and transnational. In this way Diwali acts as a means to the social sustainability of the Indian community in Auckland by showcasing culture to within as well as outside of the Indian communities. The festival acts as a cultural interface by building stakeholder relationships and showcasing the diversity of the local Indian cultural communities and their variety of cultural identities. The festival model remains socially sustainable as long as the government agencies are able to maintain strong Indian community links and deliver events that appeal to a broad audience attracting audiences within and outside the festival cultural identity.

Asha Bhosle Concert (postcolonial Bollywood)

The Asha Bhosle concert demonstrates how an independent producer is able to produce nostalgic, postcolonial performances for personal prestige. The producer has built strategic alliances with the local Indian media, local sponsors and an airline that he has maintained over a several-year period. Postcolonial performances have been historically predominant in Auckland's Indian music event scene including the late Jagjit Singh and Asha Bhosle who both built careers from 1950 through the mid 1980s in India. Recent successful tours were organised by independent producers (outside of festival management and cultural group structures) bringing overseas artists to Auckland. Although Singh worked largely outside of the film industry, both careers existed in relation to film songs' overwhelming popularity in this period. Their more recent performances have offered nostalgic glimpses of an older India to large Indian audiences in Auckland.

These were events produced by the Indian community for the Indian community linking Auckland into the Australian tour management networks with secured local sponsorship support. Members of the local Indian community spent a year organising the concert starring the legendary Bollywood playback singer Asha Bhosle, Amit Kumar and 18 Bollywood musicians from India. The 5,000 seat stadium attracted an audience of more than 3,500 people and many sponsors from the local community. The producer of this show holds a unique position having successfully delivering several concerts in the past several years as well as being an experienced Bollywood singer.

Asha Bhosle pitched her songs to the diverse cultural make-up of the Indian communities by singing in a variety of Indian languages. A high ticket price and less than prestigious venue did not deter buyers. This concert was, in effect, a sharing of cultural memory which interacts and is ideologically aligned with nostalgia (Wilson, 2005). It has also been shown that underlying motivations behind many Indian events are linked to matters of socio-musical positioning and prestige (Farrell, 1997; Lavezzoli, 2006).

This type of individual produced event has become difficult to sustain in twenty-first century Auckland as independent producers typically are competing with arts festivals and other government subsidised events. In addition, a growing and heterogeneous population, increasing number of media platforms and evermore diverse cultural content all create obstacles for those pursuing the traditional individual producer model. The Asha Bhosle concert was economically viable as well as creating strong community networks and attracting the Indian media. This has not been the case for many other individual producers as the economic risk of Bollywood productions is high. Annually producers lose significant amounts of money attempting to produce events that are not financially feasible. The key to sustainable commercial events is to choose acts that have genuine appeal to a targeted audience, a realistic budget as well as a carefully selected venue.

Imran Khan (transnational DJ mix)

Many recent successful events are the result of production alliances between young producers with twenty-first century global culture perspectives. The emerging young producers are highly educated and work in teams. They have developed skills useful in the event industry including DJs, marketers, IT experts and strong global networks. These production teams include international students and skilled migrants who arrived after 2003 while others came to Auckland with their parents between 15 and 20 years ago. This production model is a cooperative one that does not have one person controlling the production practice but a team configuration.

They produce events targeted at the 'Desi' youth market. Desi is a popular term derived from Sanskrit meaning a 'national' as opposed to a 'foreigner'. For the youth of the Indian diaspora, Desi has become a term that identifies a person with South Asian origins. The producers use the term to describe themselves as well as using the term in branding their event company. The difference between their events and the previous examples is the transnational nature of the production networks and alliances and how Indian identity is represented. Their events are not about nostalgia as they present events that represent the international world of twenty-first century global India.

The Imran Khan Unforgettable Music Festival was the most successful Indian youth oriented event of 2011. The event sold out through a targeted Facebook viral marketing campaign. The event was designed to feature local talent alongside international performers residing in Holland and the Middle East. This event was carefully designed to promote a quality event based on delivering an event that the target market would consider an amazing experience. The goal was to create an experience that ticket buyers were talking about before they got there and walk out still talking about it. The producers stressed the importance for the event to look good and sound good. Extra effort was put into the quality of the performers, the run sheet line-up and the technical requirements for the stage being high quality equipment. This extra effort raised the producers' reputations within the local community as well as through their transnational production networks.

The initially offered 700 tickets sold out three weeks before, resulting in a viral marketing frenzy. The producers doubled their expected ticket sales selling to maximum venue capacity. They offered an alcohol free zone aimed at an audience of 15–17 years of age. This strategy captured a market that usually is not able to attend such events. The drinking age in New Zealand is 18 and the drinking laws are strictly enforced in clubs. This marketing strategy captured profiles of an emerging target audience that will grow with their business in the future. The audience was mainly aged under 25 and represented the diasporic diversity of Desi cultural identity but also included an audience of East Asian and European cultural backgrounds.

This event featured overseas musicians linked into an Australian tour. The main acts were members of the Indian diaspora based in Europe and the Middle East. Local musicians were also given a chance to perform, turning the event in a festival format as opposed to a concert. The economic success of the event helped grow the producers' reputations and has opened further event opportunities. The event attracted a sell-out crowd hitting venue capacity. The growing youth market had not been tapped into outside of small DJ mix clubs. The key to sustainable transnational events is to create events that appeal to the growing target market and tap into their excitement and strong networks through the virtual world.

This example demonstrates key social sustainability factors including opportunities to showcase cultural diversity, build networks and showcase alternative voices to the wider public. The event provided a platform for these producers to create larger shows involving overseas artists that have been financially viable as well as showcasing new performers to an eager Auckland audience. The events that they are featuring have strong international brands with global marketing. The success factors of such events reflect the changing nature of twenty-first century Indian diasporic communities.

Conclusion

This chapter discussed how event sustainability is a balance between private and public partnerships that are internal and external to the producer's cultural identity and orientation. The four case studies illustrate a variety of events that represent the cultural diversity of Auckland's Indian communities. The first example, the Carnatic Society, produces events for and by a specific cultural community. The internally focused model relies on the South Indian cultural community networks to create a unified cultural identity through events. The Diwali (Festival of Lights) format promotes multiple images of Indian culture targeting the Indian communities as well as the wider Auckland community. Alliances are created between government agencies external to the culture, and the local Indian business and cultural interests providing resources necessary to produce large free festivals. This contrasts with the entrepreneurial concert that presented the Bollywood star Asha Bhosle. The hiring of a large arena, production costs and promotion rely on a large audience willing to pay high ticket prices. The final example, The Imran Khan Unforgettable Music Festival, represents the international world of twenty-first century global India and the emerging youth voice.

The social sustainability of cultural community events depends on a balance of private and public partnerships internal and external to the producer's cultural identity and orientation. It is the strength of the production networks and their ability to evolve and grow, as well as the formal and informal processes, systems, structures and relationships that deserve to be recognised in academic discourse. Socially sustainable events are powerful as they have the capacity to showcase communities inside and outside of the specific cultural identities adding quality of life to local individuals and diasporic communities.

References

Bandyopadhyay, S. (ed.). (2010). *India in New Zealand: Local identities, global relations*. Dunedin: Otago University Press.

Bendrups, D. (2010). Migrant issues in New Zealand: Issues and concepts. In H. Johnson (ed.), *Many voices* (pp. 30–38). Newcastle on Tyne: Cambridge Scholars.

Caistor-Arendar, L., Woodcraft, S. and Hackett, T. (2011). *Design for social sustainability: A framework for creating thriving communities*. London: Young Foundation.

Carnegie, E. and Smith, M. (2006). Mobility, diaspora and the hybridisation of festivity: The case of the Edinburgh Mela. In D. Picard and M. Robinson (eds), *Festivals, tourism and social change: Remaking worlds* (pp. 255–268). Clevedon, UK: Channel View.

Dietrich, G. (1999). Desi music vibes: The performance of Indian youth culture in Chicago. *Asian Music*, 31(1), 35–61.

Farrell, G. (1997). Indian music and the West. Oxford: Oxford University Press.

Farrell, G., Welch, G. and Bhowmick, J. (2000). South Asian music and music education in Britain. *Bulletin of the Council for Research in Music Education*, 147 (Winter, 2000/2001), 51–60.

Friesen, W. (2008a). *Diverse Auckland: The face of New Zealand in the 21st century*. Wellington: Asia New Zealand Foundation.

Friesen, W. (2008b). The evolution of 'Indian' identity and transnationalism in New Zealand. *Australian Geographer*, 39(1), 45–61.

Getz, D. (1997). *Event management and event tourism*. New York: Cognizant Communication Corp.

Gopal, S. and Moorti, S. (2008). Introduction. In S. Gopal and S. Moort (eds), *Global Bollywood: Travels of Hindi song and dance* (pp. 1–62). Minneapolis: University of Minnesota Press.

Hall, S. (1996). Introduction: Who needs identity? In S. Hall and P. du Gay (eds), *Questions of cultural identity*. London: Sage.

Hopper, P. (2007). *Understanding cultural globalisation*. Cambridge: Polity Press.

Jago, L., Chalip, L., Brown, G., Mules, T. and Ali, S. (2003). Building events into destination branding: Insights from experts. *Event Management*, 8(1), 3–14.

Johnson, H. (2007). Happy Diwali! Performance, multicultural soundscape and intervention in Aotearoa/New Zealand. *Ethnomusicology Forum*, 16(1), 71–94.

Johnson, H. (2010a). Introduction. In H. Johnson (ed.), *Many voices* (pp. 1–19). Newcastle on Tyne: Cambridge Scholars.

Johnson, H. (2010b). Lighting up Aotearoa: Presenting Diwali to a multicultural nation. In S. Bandyopadhyay (ed.), *India in New Zealand* (pp. 149–163). Dunedin: Otago University Press.

Johnson, H. and Figgins, G. (2005). Diwali downunder: Transforming and performing Indian tradition in Aotearoa/New Zealand. *New Zealand Journal of Media Studies*, 9(1), 25–35.

Lavezzoli, P. (2006). *The dawn of Indian music in the West: Bhairavi*. New York: Continuum.

Leckie, J. (2010). A long diaspora. In S. Bandyopadhyay (ed.), *India in New Zealand* (pp. 43–63). Dunedin: Otago University Press.

Magis, K. and Shinn, C. (2009). Emergent principles of social sustainability. In J. Dillard, V. Dujon and M. C. King (eds), *Understanding the social dimension of sustainability* (pp. 15–44). New York: Routledge.

Maira, S. (2002). *Desis in the house: Indian American youth culture in New York City*. Philadelphia, PA: Temple University Press.

McDonnell, I., Allen, J., O'Toole, W. and Harris, R. (2008). *Festival and special event management*. Milton, Qld: John Wiley and Sons Australia.

McKenzie, S. (2004). *Social sustainability: Towards some definitions*. University of South Australia, Magill: Hawke Research Institute Working Paper Series. Retrieved from www.sapo.org.au/pub/pub241.html (last accessed 20 March 2012).

Prasad, M. M. (2008). Surviving Bollywood. In A. P. Kavoori and A. Punathambekar (eds), *Global Bollywood* (pp. 41–51). New York: New York University Press.

Raj, R., and Musgrove, J. (eds). (2009). *Event management and sustainability*. Wallingford, UK: CABI.

Rajadhyaksha, A. (2008). The 'Bollywoodization' of the Indian cinema: Cultural nationalism in a global arena. In A. Punathambekar and A. P. Kavoori (eds), *Global Bollywood* (pp. 17–40). New York: New York University Press.

Richards, G. (2007). *Cultural tourism: Global and local perspectives*. Binghamton, NY: Haworth Hospitality Press.

Roy, A. (2001). 'The reverse side of the world'; Identity, space and power. In N. Al-Sayyad (ed.), *Hybrid urbanism*. Westport, CT: Praeger.

Seeger, A. (1987). *Why Suyá sing: A musical anthropology of an Amazonian people*. Cambridge: Cambridge University Press.

Tomlinson, J. (1999). *Globalisation and culture*. Cambridge, UK: Blackwell.

Turino, T. and Lea, J. (2004). *Indentity and the arts in diaspora communities* (Vol. 40). Warren, MI: Harmonie Park Press.

Wilson, J. L. (2005). *Nostalgia: Sanctuary of meaning*. Lewisburg, PA: Bucknell University Press.

Yeoman, I., Martin, J. A.-K., Drummond, S. and McMahon-Beattie, U. (2004). *Festival and events management: An international arts and culture perspective*. Oxford: Elsevier.

8 Peace through tourism

A sustainable development role for events

Omar Moufakkir and Ian Kelly

Introduction

> One of the most significant challenges facing citizens of the world in these early decades of the 21st century is the challenge to live and work together peacefully with others in all arenas of personal and public life.
>
> (Haessly, 2010, p. 1)

Getz' (2010) systematic review of the relevant English-language research literature revealed important research trends, themes and gaps in the study of festivals and events. He provides a comprehensive framework for 'understanding and creating knowledge about events' (p. 1) to help develop event studies generically. The areas most frequently covered in earlier literature (1970–96) were economic and financial impacts, marketing, profiles of festivals or events, sponsorship, management, trends and forecasts (Getz, 2010). A more recent review of the literature found topics to be more related to economic development, sponsorship and event marketing, with studies of community impacts mainly focusing on resident attitudes and perceptions, mostly related to sport events. Hede and Deery (2003) reviewed 13 tourism, hospitality and leisure journals and conference proceedings and identified more than 150 publications focused on special events during the period 1990–2001. Community impacts and sporting events were more frequently examined than commercial, political or religious events.

Certainly, the field of events is not limited to meetings, conventions, festivals, expositions, sport and other special events, but also encompasses the work of government agencies and not-for-profit organisations in pursuit of a variety of goals, including fund-raising, community development and the fostering of causes (Hede and Deery, 2003). This chapter extends the debate on the place of events in development studies, by specifically examining their role in contributing to peaceful relationships as an element of sustainability. A general SWOT analysis (strengths, weaknesses, opportunities and threats) suggests that many events contribute nothing or are even counterproductive in this context, but that certain events create conditions conducive to interaction and sharing of experiences. A specific SWOT analysis based on the case of an international annual music festival in Morocco is discussed, in relation to its accompanying controversies as another window to further our understanding about events and the role they play in bridging social and cultural gaps.

There is more to events than their development, planning and outcomes. Planned events, especially social events that have the purpose of fostering a cause, demand much attention from decision- and policy-makers. A policy is deemed policy not by virtue of its impact on the public, but by virtue of its source (Pal, 1993). The complexity of an event lies not only in the purpose and selection, but also in its reception by the community. If sustainability, ingrained in the peace proposition, means preserving our past heritage, making our present a past meaningful to and enjoyable in our future, then events are a strong contributor to the repertoire of human heritage.

Human heritage is controversial, contested and can be painful in its negativities. In the sustainability discourse, in its relation to peace, the focus of attention is more on the positive side of heritage and the optimistic side of history and the future. Events, as contributors to our lives, help us celebrate the past, enjoy the present and dream about our future. Owusu-Frempong (2005) argues that the celebration of events and festivals in communities 'must not be seen merely as an annual congregation of street and food vendors, marching bands, and musicians but also as a tool of cultural reconstruction and transmission of knowledge to the younger generation' (p. 730).

Since events are entrenched in the past, present and future, they are as much about power, control and showcasing a cause than mere entertainment and fleeting amusement moments. Debates about the function and role of festivals and events in relation to leisure go as far back as ancient Greece and Rome, exemplified in the leisure ideal of the ancient Greeks and the gladiatorial spectacles of the ancient Romans (see for example, Arnold, 1999 on modern leisure scholarship). Fund-raising events are a means to an end; tools to promote, sustain and promote a social, cultural, environmental or political agenda or idea.

It is apparent that events are an important theme in policymaking. For example, amid debates over cultural and political issues, such as identity, exclusion and elitism, in relation to events the question is: who decides on the legitimacy of an event or a festival? Since many stakeholders are involved in their production and consumption, the events discourse cannot exist outside stakeholder theory. Getz and Andersson (2010, p. 533) argue that: 'Stakeholder theory relates to the wide environment of people or entities that can affect, or be affected by an organization's actions.' Stakeholder theory stresses the interactions of power, legitimacy and urgency in creating overall salience (Mitchell *et al.*, 1997), and these authors argued that a party in a relationship has 'power to the extent that it has or can gain access to coercive, utilitarian, or normative means to impose its will in the relationship' (p. 865).

Although the authors' focus was on events tourism, this argument also holds for cultural community events or festivals. In various ways, local social tensions may be refracted through festivals (Gibson and Davidson, 2004). Planned events do not exist in a vacuum, nor is an event an end in itself. Inclusion, exclusion and promotion of some values over others are policies that are attached to ideology. Who decides the what, why, when and how of an event or festival must be critically examined for the role of ideology, policy and politics in event studies.

Sustainable development

The term *sustainability* is derived from the Latin *sustinere* (*tenere*, to hold; *sus*, up), and dictionaries provide more than ten meanings for *sustain*, including 'maintain', 'support' or 'endure'. The etymology of the word *sustainable* has continued to evolve with the progress of sustainability studies and practices.

In the Brundtland Commission report for the World Commission on Environment and Development (WCED, 1987), sustainable development is defined as measures to meet the needs of the present while ensuring access to the same level of resources by future generations. While most studies use the Brundtland definition of sustainability as their basis, it is important to note that events studies concerned with sustainability have moved away from a focus on 'green' issues to include factors relating to social and economic sustainability (Raj and Musgrave, 2009). For a comprehensive account of the types of action (referred to as the 'science of sustainability') relating to energy/power, transport, waste management, waste reduction and resource recovery, materials purchasing and procurements, see Jones (2010).

Researchers focusing on festivals and events conceive sustainability not only as an environmental concern, but also as a matter of festival and event survival (Gration *et al.*, 2011). According to these and other authors (e.g. Ensor *et al.*, 2011), sustainability has broadened to incorporate new elements such as risk management planning practices, event managers' perceptions and attitudes, investment limitations, levels of expertise, areas of responsibility and socio-cultural norms. Significantly, sustainability is also seen as the capacity to endure and sustain benefits equitably distributed among stakeholders. Moreover, 'events are explicitly linked to fundamentals of the human race – social and cultural values, and the more basic ladders of social inclusion, as sense of belonging and a sense of identity' (Raj and Musgrave, 2009, p. 4).

It is clear that these authors regard events as presenting opportunities to contribute to societal values. Events are assessed not only in terms of their negative impacts but also on the environmental, economic, social and cultural benefits that they can bring to the community. Given the importance of events in modern society, there is need for a sustainable event management framework that is not embedded only in corporate or environmental strategic thinking but which encourages such outcomes as attitude change, poverty alleviation and crisis management. Hediger (2000) suggests that a component of the sustainability principle is to induce cultural change within society, change in attitudes, civic pride, social capital, quality of life, social cohesion and health (see also Foley *et al.*, 2009; Raj and Musgrave, 2009). These authors argue for a development mindset that moves towards means-end management under which events are not only concerned with short-term business profits but also with ethical practices and behaviour. As stated by Getz (2009, p. 62), the 'new sustainable and responsible events paradigm' concerns not only the evaluation of the impacts of the event but also the worth of the event.

Some events seek to raise awareness about world issues, such as poverty, racism, bigotry, xenophobia, disease, crime, genocide, human trafficking and prostitution and war crimes. According to Foley and his colleagues (2009) the value of events as social happenings resides in their capacity to bring people together and cement neighbourhoods and communities. In this chapter we support the call by Chalip (2006) to consider the 'social leverage' of events by incorporating a SWOT analysis assessing the ability of events to contribute to peaceful communities.

Sustainability and peace through events

There is widespread recognition of peace as an appropriate theme for festivals and events. For example, the planners for the 2012 Olympic Games incorporated peace as a central focus. In addition, a scan of Google Alerts for peace and tourism during the year 2011–12 identified events dedicated to peace in a range of categories. These included a Peace Marathon in Israel and week-long athletic and team competitions in the Philippines; music festivals in Belfast (Northern Ireland), Ghana, Seoul (South Korea) and Kashmir (India); a peace carnival and cultural festivals in Nigeria (featuring a children's parade and performances); a flower show (London); a commemoration in Belfast of the *Titanic* sinking; a tea festival in Darjeeling (India); a food festival in Sagayan (the Philippines); and an exhibition in Istanbul (Turkey). A number of peace-oriented festivals were associated with Christmas celebrations, and the Rotary International Peace Summit was held in Bangkok and Phuket (Thailand).

A major sustainability objective is the development of concern for communities and their environments, forming an alliance for the common good of all forms of life. The pursuit of sustainability is an acknowledgement that harmonious relationships and global peace are possible. From this perspective, sustainability discourse and practice is the essence of humanity, incorporating a comprehensive vision of a just, equitable and friendly world in a vision of and for peace (Haessly, 2010). According to Haessly (2010, p. 6), peace is 'an image of the world where women and men share equally in creating and sustaining a world of justice and peace ... and care for the ecosystem'.

On the other hand, a failure to clearly link development to social, cultural, economic and environmental objectives will leave it vulnerable to abuses such as false 'green' labelling, corporate window dressing, masked transparency and veiled interests. While the premise of sustainability is to care for each other and all of creation, unsustainable development and practices may lead to injustice, conflict and violence. In short, a culture of sustainability is synonymous with a culture of peace. Nussbaum (1997, p. 38) explains:

> Citizens who cultivate their humanity need ... an ability to see themselves as not simply citizens of some local region or group, but also, and above all, as human beings bound to all others by ties of recognition and concern.

The objective implicit in the above quotation was confirmed by a number of speakers at the Third Global Conference of the International Institute for Peace through Tourism (IIPT) (held in Glasgow in October 1999) which was directed to initiating a '21st Century Agenda for Peace through Tourism'. It was suggested at the conference that the creation of such an agenda must be preceded by a SWOT analysis, a procedure generally carried out before the development of a business plan (Kelly, 1999). It involves a detailed examination of the strengths and weaknesses of the business organisation, and the opportunities and threats in the environment within which it operates. The 'business' to be examined in the analysis was the ability of tourism to contribute to 'a harmonious relationship' (Var *et al.*, 1994, p. 30) among the peoples of the world.

It is recognised by a number of commentators (e.g. Tomljenovic and Faulkner, 2000) that, despite serious shortcomings, tourism has the potential to facilitate contacts of the desired nature. It is also recognised that there are other forces such as aid organisations and institutions for conflict resolution which are more clearly directed to working for peaceful relationships at various levels. In discussions of the role tourism might play, the potential of events to contribute to the peace objective has not received much attention. Of the 135 papers and reports presented at the above conference, only one was concerned with events. Janson (1999) outlined problems which developed as the Central Pennsylvania Festival of the Arts grew over the years from its commencement in 1967. These problems stemmed primarily from local community resentment over increasing out-of-state involvement, rising prices for exhibitors' products and an orientation favouring higher-spending visitors. However, since 1993, the People's Choice Festival, featuring locally crafted, reasonably priced products, has been run in parallel with the Central Festival, and this appears to have met the concerns of the community, increased the number of visitors and enhanced the economic benefits generated (Janson, 1999).

The mission statements associated with some events imply peace-related goals, but these usually have a specific focus, for example on women's rights or revolutionary literature. In Australia, events such as the Sydney Harbour Bridge Walk in 2001 have been directed to encouraging reconciliation with the indigenous peoples, but these have little or no tourism significance. There are numerous references to social and cultural impacts in journal articles and textbooks on events (e.g. Walsh-Heron and Stevens, 1990; Getz, 1991; McDonnell *et al.*, 1999; Van Der Wagen, 2001) but they tend to focus primarily on economic advantage, management and marketing. A conference held in Sydney, Australia in July 2000 ('Events Beyond 2000: Setting the Agenda') included papers on similar issues, with a few touching on cultural and environmental impacts, education and training, and measuring customer satisfaction. None of the listed texts or conference papers makes specific mention of peace as an event objective. However, the above authors note that festivals and events have been elements of community tradition for a long time, are growing in number and variety, and are increasingly linked with tourism. It is, therefore, appropriate to examine the extent to which events might contribute to the peace objective, defined for the purposes of this chapter, as a state of harmonious relationship among the people of the world. Although events attracting international visitors are deemed of major importance, there is recognition of the role played by local events in contributing to harmonious relationships among people of differing backgrounds within a country.

It should be noted that, in the following analysis, the term 'event' is used for attractions which attract visitors to a destination, are staged infrequently and are of short duration. According to Getz (1991) events are distinguished by openness to the public, a central theme, infrequent occurrence and predetermined opening and closing dates. They may make use of permanent structures, comprise a number of activities and be associated with a particular district or region. Events are commonly based on sporting activities (racing, tournaments and sports carnivals), festivals (commemorative, entertainment, cultural, religious and special themes), business and community interests (conventions, exhibitions and agricultural shows) and political affairs (state and government special occasions).

The SWOT analysis

The SWOT analysis examines the strengths, weaknesses, opportunities and threats pertaining to the ability of events to contribute to more peaceful intergroup relationships. McDonnell *et al.* (1999) provide a comprehensive list of impacts pertaining to events and a number of these are at least partially relevant to the SWOT analysis. Positive impacts include opportunities for shared experiences, maintenance of traditions, expression of community pride and enhanced prestige. Among the negative impacts identified are community alienation, behavioural problems and loss of authenticity. These are recognised in the following analysis, a summary of which is provided in Table 8.1.

Strengths

The strengths are those attributes of events which bring people together in circumstances conducive to goodwill and improved understanding among them. Mega-events such as the Olympic Games attract many thousands of visitors and command the attention of billions through media broadcasts and reports. Contact between host community and visitors is not confined to those attending an event, but usually extends throughout the destination area as visitors make use of accommodation and other facilities, and indulge in sightseeing and shopping.

Unlike mainstream tourist attractions, some events have the advantage of being 'footloose', in the sense that they need not be tied to a particular location. Dance, musical and theatre groups are taken on tour, and provide audiences around the world with a taste of a culture different from their own. For example, in 1997 Australians gained an insight into Japanese culture through a Sumo Wrestling Championship held in Melbourne and Sydney. There are also those, such as the Edinburgh Festival (Scotland), which demonstrate how a cohesive

Table 8.1 A peace through events SWOT analysis

STRENGTHS:	OPPORTUNITIES:
Event attributes which bring people together in non-adversarial circumstances	*External developments which can contribute to the desired event outcomes*
Growth in numbers and variety	Media support/publicity
Cultural elements	Globalisation
Associated economic benefits	Multiculturalism
Locational and temporal flexibility	Advances in technology
Community involvement	Growing sophistication of tourists
Perception of authenticity	Sustainability concerns
	Tourism education
WEAKNESSES:	THREATS:
Attributes which hinder or restrict events in achieving the desired outcomes	*Developments likely to increase hostility or contribute to a decline in event effectiveness*
Controversial themes	Terrorism
Poor visitor behaviour	Focus on war/atrocity themes
Community disruption	Tourist demands – volume and nature
Ethnocentrism/competition	Rejection of sustainability measures
Limited time span	Dismissal of peace objective

programme can be developed in one location by involving participants from a range of countries.

Events can also be freed from temporal restraints, and are widely used to reduce seasonal fluctuations in visitation levels, extend the tourist season or encourage visitation by market segments such as retirees who are not bound by work commitments. The goodwill of the general public in affluent societies is sometimes called upon in the form of events mounted to raise funds for specific causes such as disaster relief and refugee support.

In recent times, the attractive power of events has been greatly enhanced by the growth of an 'events industry' (McDonnell *et al.*, 1999) comprising individuals and organisations devoted to the development of facilities (often with government funding) and the promotion of destinations as sites for events. Professionalism in the industry is encouraged by the provision of courses in educational institutions and representation and supervision by industry associations.

However, the contributory ability of events cannot be measured merely by the numbers of visitors or the expertise with which they are organised. Are there event attributes which help people from different social and cultural backgrounds to understand and empathise with each other?

It is argued (e.g. Weaver and Opperman, 2000) that community pride and internal relationships may be strengthened through involvement in mounting an event, and visitors may acquire greater understanding and appreciation of the community traditions and way of life. Small-scale events such as village festivals draw visitors from surrounding districts and may help give visitors from urban areas a more accurate perception of rural life. This aspect of events may best be seen in local wine and food festivals, usually heavily dependent on voluntary inputs, and providing a means by which communities can confirm and communicate pride in their local products.

An illustrative example at the local level is South Australia's Barossa Vintage Festival. This is Australia's oldest wine festival, an event which has been mounted every second year since 1947. It is presented as a commemoration of the region's heritage, expressed in fine wine, food, music and art and is organised by a committee, with the support of over one thousand volunteers from the local community. Visitors are attracted from overseas, interstate and the nearby urban area of Adelaide. The success of the Festival is attributed to the partnership of winegrowers, tourism interests and the general community, and to the quality of the experience offered to visitors (Salter, 1998).

Another strength of some events is the perception of authenticity attached to them. There are many events – such as those involving local foods, wines and craftwork – at which a visitor can see or even participate in a genuine manifestation of the local community way of life. Although they are obviously staged, historical re-enactments, if faithfully rendered, can contribute to a visitor's understanding of a community's formative influences.

In short, the strengths of events in the current context lie in their ability to bring large numbers of people together in circumstances where they can share experiences with and learn to look at the world through the eyes of others. However, it must be emphasised that, in the current context, these attributes can be deemed strengths only insofar as they contribute to the goal of a more harmonious world. Unfortunately, the strengths may be insufficient or may not always work in the desired direction.

Weaknesses

Weaknesses relate to those attributes of events which hinder the achievement of the desired outcomes and may even contribute to hostility and division among people. In late 2001, those responsible for the planning and promotion of the 2002 Adelaide Festival of the Arts invited the general public to consider the arts as a civilising influence with the power to create a better world. Promotion was developed around the question: What difference would it have made if Adolf Hitler had not been rejected by the art college in which he had attempted to enrol as a student? To their surprise, the organisers were accused of glorifying Hitler, government figures expressed concern and the major sponsor threatened to withdraw support. The festival director resigned, a new one was appointed and a less challenging advertising theme was adopted.

This was not Adelaide's first experience of event-generated community division. Before the event was lost to Melbourne, Adelaide hosted the Formula One Grand Prix, presented by the State Government as a major revenue raiser, and supported by a large proportion of the city population. However, there was opposition from those who condemned the event as noisy, wasteful, polluting and responsible for the 'hoon effect' among young drivers, and from residents who were disadvantaged by noise and the interruption to normal traffic movement during the race period. In Melbourne, too, the race organisers have been faced with strident protests from residents seeking to protect the park area in which the event is held.

These examples demonstrate that some events divide rather than unite a community, and may be tolerated only because of their economic input. Indeed, it may be that events dedicated to attracting large numbers of visitors and generating substantial revenues – that is, those most valued by governments and the events industry – are least likely to contribute to harmony within and among communities. It is apparent that some mega-events such as the Olympic Games encourage individual ethnocentrism and competition among nations rather than a world view and a spirit of cooperation. Furthermore, it is likely that some potential visitors interested in acquiring a better understanding of the host community will be discouraged by the crowding and increased costs associated with such events (de Souto, 1993).

However, even events of a more positive nature are limited in their impact for a number of reasons. Although attendance at an event may provide visitors with intercultural contacts, the experience is fleeting and still relatively superficial. In addition, certain events, particularly festivals, are valued because they emphasise the differences, rather than the commonality, between hosts and visitors, a generally divisive process referred to as 'othering' (Hollinshead, 1998). Events may also share with mainstream tourism a condition of inequality between host and visitor – a condition not conducive to the kind of relationship desired.

It appears, then, that while events may be a major factor in the success of a destination's tourism industry, there are many which contribute only economic advantage, and which may even create division and reinforce pre-existing prejudices.

Opportunities

Opportunities are elements of the wider environment which may serve to enhance the strengths of events as contributors to harmonious relationships. The Snowy Mountains, a regional tourism area in New South Wales, is a well-known destination for winter sports. However, the local tourism authority has been seeking to promote the area to spring, summer and autumn visitors on the basis of its varied and scenic natural environment. An association spokesperson (Last, 2001) reported on plans to mount a hallmark event – the Snowy Mountains Muster – based on the theme of the Banjo Paterson poem, 'The Man From Snowy River' and taking advantage of the popular television series of the same name. The goal was to create a feeling of regional cohesion and ownership among the tourism operators and the wider community, and establish the region as an Australian 'icon'.

The report demonstrated how event developers may draw inspiration and support from apparently unconnected occurrences in other fields such as the media, entertainment and literature. These opportunities are likely to increase with globalisation. Although it is claimed by some that globalisation is bringing about 'a shrinking world', the reality is that for many the world is opening up as information and transport technology increase the reach of regional promoters and reduce the friction of distance. Increasing multiculturalism in many countries is reflected in ethnic festivals, and even where this is not occurring, events can provide a means by which the distinctiveness of a region can be protected and displayed in a world moving towards standardisation and homogenisation.

It is claimed that as travel becomes a more popular leisure activity, travellers become more confident and sophisticated (Pearce, 1988; Ross, 1994), and are likely to seek more meaningful travel experiences, involving the deeper and more extended interaction with host communities which events offer. In conjunction with this is the widespread promotion of sustainability as an objective in all areas of human activity, and a corresponding increase in adoption of the ecotourism ethic, with its emphases on conservation, education and host community well-being. Another development which may offer opportunities is the expansion of tourism education in colleges and universities, providing a channel for the encouragement of enlightened attitudes and appropriate skills in travellers and event managers.

It is submitted, therefore, that there are trends in the wider environment which favour the expansion and diversification of tourism event offerings, and the inclusion of more events dedicated to the development in individuals of positive attitudes towards people from other societies and cultures.

Threats

Threats, too, lie in the external environment, present and future. They include elements which are likely to increase hostility among different social groups or contribute to a decline in event offerings or attendance. In early 2002, admission prices to major golf and tennis events in Australia and New Zealand were increased to cover the costs of additional security necessitated by fears of terrorist activity against the venues or key participants. Similar precautions were being taken in a number of other countries.

Although she is not referring specifically to event tourism, Brown's (1998) arguments suggest a firm negative to the question: Is event tourism able to bring about or facilitate peace? She cites apparently insoluble problems in the Middle East, the use of tourists as targets or hostages for terrorist groups, the disintegration of countries such as Yugoslavia, the imposition of politics in mega-events such as the Olympic Games and the continuing use of war as a solution to problems despite improved living standards. She does, however, recognise the potential for tourism to change the attitudes of individuals.

There is even a danger that tourism – and event tourism in particular – may be widely regarded as a beneficiary of war and violence. Seaton (1999), in referring to thanatourism (travel to a location for actual or symbolic encounters with death), reminds us of the crowds who flocked to gladiatorial contests in ancient Rome, who visit the sites of massacres and crimes, and enjoy re-enactments of battles. Smith (1998) also notes the value to tourism of sites commemorating violent historical events.

Even where peaceful conditions prevail, it is apparent that a major threat to event tourism as an instrument of peace is the volume and nature of the demand it generates (Muller, 1997), and this is not confined to numbers of visitors. Event visitors, like other tourists, may demand a hedonistic, self-indulgent lifestyle which contrasts sharply with the community conditions in which these expectations are met. Can event tourists be persuaded to accept the less luxurious conditions and operators the reduced returns likely to result from more modest demands?

Furthermore, reliance on education and the sustainability ethic to assist in the development of more appropriate events may be misplaced. Stabler (1997) claims that sustainability management tends to focus on viability and resource protection rather than community welfare, and suggests that it may be an industrialised nation concept foisted on developing countries. Wheeler (1997) reminds us that the more educated people are, the more they travel; that the numbers involved are too large for any sensitisation programme to have effect; and that host communities desperate for economic benefits have little bargaining power and will not impose environmental and growth controls. Questions raised by this review of threats include the following. Will the objective of peaceful conditions be devalued by a widespread reliance on events commemorating war? Will greater numbers of events provide a larger and more widespread target for terrorists seeking international exposure for their causes? Will events be regarded as just another form of tourism, with all its problems of inequality and exploitation? Will the ability of events to make a positive contribution be lost or restricted by the growth in environmentalism? Will proponents of peace through events be dismissed as idealists for whom there is no place in the real world?

It may be inappropriate to anticipate the findings of a more complete SWOT analysis, and those involved in tourism, events, peace studies and other relevant fields are invited to identify shortcomings to be corrected, propose additional items for inclusion and suggest solutions to the problems raised. However, it is suggested that the following conclusions will be widely accepted.

There are few, if any, alternatives to match tourism as a generator of intercultural contact, and events are an important and growing element of that attribute. Many events contribute nothing to or even hinder the pursuit of a peace objective. Peace-related event objectives will only be achieved by purposeful management directed to enhancing intercultural contacts. Responsibilities for purposeful event management lie at all levels, from individual travellers and members of the host community to national governments.

Although this SWOT analysis is incomplete, it indicates that there are major difficulties to be overcome if events are to contribute to the peace objective. The view that there is a need to bring people together is supported by reports in other areas of investigation. For example, a summary of findings related to racial integration in the United States (Kelly, 1987) noted that, in initial interactions between groups of differing race, existing attitudes (positive and negative) are intensified. However, over time and with increasing familiarity, attitudes tend to become generally more favourable, especially if the groups share similar, non-conflicting goals and beliefs on many issues. There is also some relevance in factors identified as facilitating political integration (Kelly, 1987). Despite abundant evidence that it does not preclude hostilities, spatial proximity (bringing people together) is seen as a contributor to mutual understanding. The likelihood of this is enhanced if there is also social homogeneity (common culture elements), high levels of interaction, mutual knowledge and shared functional interests.

These findings may be seen to confirm the view that the superficial contacts offered in most host-visitor interactions can be counterproductive, but that events involving more substantial exchanges (referred to by Goldblatt, 2001, as 'high touch' experiences) are likely to be more effective in the effort to promote harmonious relationships. Efforts, therefore, should be directed to providing host-visitor exchanges which emphasise the universality of the problems faced by all societies, encourage understanding of the different ways in which these problems are addressed and facilitate appreciation of the alternative solutions thereby offered.

While it is likely that a proportion of event attendees are not interested in learning about the culture of their hosts, there are many who wish to be regarded as travellers rather than tourists and who take pleasure in demonstrating their knowledge of how to behave in alien environments. Reisinger (1997) outlines the difficulties commonly encountered in intercultural contacts and suggests that such problems may be alleviated by educational programmes for those involved in international tourism, an emphasis on the service attributes of potential hosts and greater use of intermediaries.

It is submitted here that large-scale events are least likely to provide the required type of contact, and that there is a need to recognise the value of small, everyday events in informing visitors about the essential character of a community (Kelly, 1991). These provide opportunities to mingle with parents and children at sports meetings for children, to discuss gardening with fellow enthusiasts at a local garden show, to see a school concert, to judge a children's art competition or perhaps attend a special church service, all of which could constitute particularly memorable experiences, valued all the more because of their non-touristic nature.

It is further submitted that positive impacts are more likely to occur if those involved, both hosts and guests, are open-minded, free from prejudice and inclined towards goodwill (Kelly, 1998). This is recognised by schoolteachers in Cyprus who have sought to counter the suspicion and hostility prevalent among the adult populations by arranging events involving the exchange of school concert parties across the line which has divided the island since 1974. Similar approaches have been tried in the difficult environments of Northern Ireland and Israel/Palestine.

It is recognised that small-scale events of the type proposed are unlikely to receive support from the 'events industry' because of their non-commercial orientation. However, this does not necessarily preclude sponsorship support from organisations pursuing or likely to benefit from association with the peace objective. In addition, the Internet now provides a means whereby people can identify others with whom they share a common interest, exchange information and lay the groundwork for subsequent face-to-face contact, thereby reducing the need for expensive promotion campaigns (Getz, 2000).

A case study in event controversy: the Mawazine Music Festival

There is more to peace than the absence of arms. Peace commentators talk about the presence of peacelessness in our communities. In this context, cultural events are sustained and new ones created to fulfil certain purposes. The role of cultural events, such as street festivals, is to bring communities together to celebrate cultural commonalities as well as differences. However, cultural events can also be controversial.

For example, at its inception in 2006 The Stockholm Culture festival was the object of a political debate, with reports stating that if the conservatives were to seize power in Stockholm in the 2007 elections, the new festival would be discarded because there were more pressing issues on which to spend taxpayers' money (Brandel, 2006).

To illustrate the controversial nature of certain cultural events in relation to its role as culture broker and a contributing agent to peaceful relations in communities, the example of Morocco's 'Mawazine Music Festival' (or 'Rhythms of the World' is discussed. The question is to what extent does such a planned event contribute to peace? An event will affect people in different ways (Dickinson and Shipway, 2007). Some authors have argued that the decision to hold an event, especially a large-scale event, is essentially a political decision (e.g. Hall, 1989; Hall, 1992, 1994; Bowdin *et al.*, 2006; Reid, 2006), to either showcase a desired political agenda, divert the attention of the public from an ongoing social-political issue to a focus on 'entertainment', or to protest against an 'undesired' social-political agenda or protest.

Controversy emerges in the form of arguments concerning issues (Moufakkir and Burns, 2011). The argument for and against the hosting of the Mawazine Festival (Figure 8.1) are presented below. These argumentations may shed more light on our understanding of the social impacts of events, not in the sense of a 'classic' impacts analysis but from an events leverage perspective (Chalip, 2006).

Ten years ago, Mawazine was a small festival that had trouble finding financiers for its sound-and-lights show, but it has quickly grown in size, dwarfing all the other musical events in the country. Its current budget is reportedly as high as US$12 million. Perhaps not coincidentally, scandals and controversy have dogged it. The festival began as an opportunity to expose people to music from

Figure 8.1 The Mawazine Festival poster.

around the world. Currently, it has turned into a mega-production featuring international stars with hefty price tags. The festival features Arab pop stars, as well
as several big African acts. International artists such as Kanye West, Cat
Stevens, Earth Wind and Fire, Lionel Ritchie and Quincy Jones have participated in the festival. The 2012 festival features about 112 artists. These include
international names such as Pitbull, Scorpions, Jimmy Cliff, Lenny Kravitz,
Mariah Carey and Gloria Gaynor.

The growing popularity of the Mawazine music festival has received the
attention of both religious and secular Moroccan citizens. On the one hand, it
has been criticised by the diehard religious for its perceived amorality and promotion of associated libertine values. This objection is no different from
responses to similar westernised festivals in Islamic countries. On the other
hand, there is a secular citizens' objection which relates to the festival's

perceived grotesque spending relative to the poor economic condition of the majority of citizens.

The festival received more attention and generated more debate after the *occupy movement* of the Arab Spring took place in Tunisia and Egypt. The social uprising of the Arab streets resonated among the Moroccan community, who took to the streets in peaceful demonstrations calling for attention and economic change. Moroccan citizens took the opportunity of the festival's promotion to promote their economic and political grievances. To some Moroccans, it was undeniably wrong to spend an exorbitant amount of money on bringing in an international performer to the festival while the cry of the Moroccans about food and a decent living condition went unheard.

These controversies surrounding this festival relate to its Strengths, Weaknesses, Opportunities and Threats as presented here. Our search on the Internet for the key term 'Mawazine festival' identified the following statements from the social media (see box below). These quotes were thus literally taken from different Internet sources to serve as our data and further inform our understanding. Subsequently, a SWOT analysis of the Mawazine music festival has been developed in Table 8.2.

- For Morocco's would-be revolutionaries, a popular music festival is a corrupt symbol of the country's misplaced priorities.
- Protesters against the festival gathered last week in downtown Rabat before they were dispersed by truncheon-wielding policemen.
- The festival comes at a delicate time for the February 20 movement, which through demonstrations around the country pushed Morocco's all-powerful king, Mohammed VI, to start a process of constitutional reform.
- Moroccan Activists Slam Music Festival as Corrupt
- With Shakira and other top international artists performing in open air venues around Morocco's capital – often for free – the annual Mawazine world music festival doesn't at first seem like something anyone could dislike.
- Activists from Morocco's pro-reform February 20 movement, however, tried to get it canceled, describing it as a symptom of the country's corruption and cronyism.
- Imagine if, like 15 percent of Moroccans, you and your family lived on less than $2 per day. Three loaves of bread and a bottle of milk cost about as much as that – never mind housing, health care, or education. Imagine if, like a large majority of working Moroccans, you were paid the standard minimum wage of 10.64 dirhams per hour; that's almost exactly the price of a liter of gasoline. (Assuming, of course, you've saved up the tens of thousands of dirhams it takes to buy a car.) Imagine, now, if you found out that Shakira were paid 6.5 million dirhams to perform – nearly a million dollars.

- The large sums of money allocated to Mawazine, the statement said, would be better spent on schools, hospitals – or arts infrastructure that would contribute to sustainable cultural growth for all Moroccans. Slogans repeated during street marches throughout the kingdom in the last few months have included some directed at the festival: 'Where is the people's money? In Mawazine and celebrations.' (This rhymes in Arabic.) Facebook groups with names such as 'Tous Contre Mawazine' or 'stop mawazine' have cropped up.
- With the money you pay Shakira to shake her body, you can provide a whole neighborhood with decent living conditions.
- According to a member of the festival's organizing committee, the event cost around $7.8 million – a hefty price tag in a country lacking the oil of its North African neighbors and with at least 30 percent unemployment, especially among urban youth.
- Moroccan youngsters are asking for more freedom, better living condition, more democracy, equal opportunities and less corruption. One slogan that the protesters at the impoverished district of Sbata, Casablanca shouted was 'we don't need Shakira, we need a loaf of bread', denouncing the official insistence on organizing extravagant festivals while poverty is omnipresent and democracy is a more urgent need.
- Our Tourism Industry suffered a huge blow with the recent Marrakesh bombing. Having an International Icon sing in Morocco would certainly help reassure and lure more tourists, who play a huge role in our economy. The message was simple and clear: 'Morocco is still safe – So come on down and join the party'.
- The million dirham's paid to Shakira is a small investment in restoring our badly damaged tourism industry. If the naysayers get out of the way, this investment would pay huge dividends in the immediate future.
- In the past, religious conservatives have criticized the eight-day extravaganza for being decadent, and last year they were angered that it featured openly gay performer Elton John. This year, however, the attacks are coming from Facebook-savvy youth who would normally be found in the audience of such celebrations of international music.
- 'That's what Morocco is, its roots are Arab with influences of Africa and links to the West,' said festival organizer. 'That's what we want to express through the festival.'
- He explained that with artists from 60 different countries, the festival's creed has always been to promote values of diversity, exchange and cultural tolerance, and this year's 10th anniversary show is the biggest yet.
- In the wake of the April 28 bombing at a Marrakech cafe that killed 17, many of them foreigners, it was even more important to keep the festival going.

- '(The cancellation) is what those people, the terrorists are looking for, this has never been considered,' he said.
- By all accounts, the festival is popular, especially with a certain number of seats kept free at every venue. According to the organizer, 2.2 million are expected to attend with another 16 million Moroccans, in a country of just 30 million, watching it on television.
- Last year, for instance, there were calls by members of the PJD, a religious party in Parliament, to ban Elton John because his appearance would be 'promoting homosexuality' (In the end, Elton John performed to sold-out crowds, and there have been no reports of Moroccan men suddenly turning gay as a result of their attendance.)
- In an interview with *TelQuel* magazine, spokesperson and artistic director for Mawazine, said that those who oppose Mawazine are 'demagogues' who keep an 'obscurantist discourse.' And, just as there are anti-Mawazine groups on Facebook, there are pro-Mawazine groups as well.
- 'The struggle against the Mawazine is the struggle for democracy,' said a freelance journalist heading the National Campaign to Cancel the Mawazine, a Facebook group with more than 30,000 members.
- 'The festival Mawazine (or Rhythms of the World) is an event that celebrates cultural diversity, openness, tolerance and discovery of chants and music, coming from far cultures and geographies. This event is riveted not only in joyful communicative character, but also positions Rabat as a city open to the world. Mawazine, is also a date that inscribes Morocco in the calendar of great rendezvous of music in the world. And more importantly in our opinion: this festival constitutes a model for the youth who believe in the chance of success and the virtues of work for personal improvement' (author's translation of excerpt from *Mot du Committe Executive, 2012*).
- In artistes testimonies, Elton John explained: 'I have always had the conviction that music is situated in a world independent from politics, religious differences or all kinds of prejudice; that, effectively, music is an international language for all ... music is and will always be a universal language, without frontiers. It can and it inspires unity and constructs bridges between peoples....' (author's translation of excerpt from *Témoignages artiste, 2012*).

If the nature of this festival and its transformation from a small national music festival to a mega event music festival were not controversial, there would be no rationale for studying its impacts on people. However, it offers another opportunity to study the political, social and cultural impacts of events. The festival is contested from cultural, social, economic and political perspectives. For such a festival to contribute to the peace proposition, the organizers need to comprehensively examine its potential impacts – cost and benefits (Table 8.2).

Table 8.2 A peace through events SWOT analysis: the case of the Mawazine music street festival in Morocco

STRENGTHS	OPPORTUNITIES
Bringing citizens together to celebrate, regardless of social, political and economic backgrounds	Revival of traditional music
	Promotion of traditional music
	Bringing in international artists
Promoting unity	
Promoting country image as a safe country	
Promoting Western and Eastern values	
Attracting tourists, sharing values	
WEAKNESSES	THREATS
Controversial themes	Loss of festival's grounding spirit
Creating tension among citizens	Loss of festival's authenticity
Religious	Commercialisation of the festival
Moral	Split community based on values
Political	Loss of tradition
Economic	Discontinuity of the festival

Conclusion

It is recognised that events can be controversial, that they do not exist outside the social, cultural, political, biophysical and economic environments, and that these must be taken into account in pursuing peaceful relationships as an inseparable element of event sustainability.

It is also recognised that events are important social and cultural strategies, often incorporating entertainment with awareness-raising about serious societal issues. They can be contributors to relationship building and the development of social capital and networks. A major ingredient in this process is the element of trust. As argued by Putnam (2000, p. 21), 'Trustworthiness lubricates social life. Frequent interaction among a diverse set of people tends to produce a norm of generalized reciprocity.'

There is relevance also in Putnam's (2000, p. 22) crucial distinction between 'bonding' and 'bridging' social capital. Bonding activities are 'inward looking and tend to reinforce exclusive identities and homogeneous groups', while bridging activities are 'outward looking and encompass people across diverse social cleavages'. In this sense, events have a potential for bonding members of a community (by facilitating intra- and inter-group relationships) and for bridging with others in the world community (by facilitating supra-group relationships).

A number of recommendations stem from this review. Event organisers should conduct a SWOT analysis of a proposed event in consultation with its stakeholders, including the community. Certain events should be encouraged as major contributors to the objective of bringing people together, and tourism and event educators should work in conjunction with those involved in peace and conflict resolution. Educators should also help identify the types of events likely to encourage appropriate attitude change, conduct research on how the contribution of events to the peace objective might be optimised and devise measures for evaluation of their effectiveness. Educational and training courses in event management should be designed to recognise peace objectives along with commercial, management, political and environmental objectives. Support should be provided for events, no matter how small, which encourage participants to share knowledge and skills and cooperate in problem solving, and efforts should be directed to ensuring that event hosts and guests are provided with information about each other, and/or that contacts are carefully mediated to avoid conflict.

The argument here is that a SWOT analysis of an event can contribute to its sustainability and its role in developing social and cultural capital through bridging and bonding processes. As the world becomes more globalised and cultures increasingly transparent and fluid, the role of events in sustaining understanding among and between world communities will be even more important. Therefore, it is imperative to study the contribution of events and festivals, including those held in developing and non-Western countries, and of their impacts on the local, national and world communities.

References

Arnold, S. (1999) 'The Dilemma of Meaning', in T.L. Goodale and P.A. Witt (eds) *Recreation and Leisure: Issues in an Era of Change*, Chelsea, MI: BookCrafters, pp. 47–54.

Bowdin, G., Allen, J., O'Toole, W., Harris, R. and McDonnell, I. (2006) *Events Management*, Oxford: Elsevier.

Brandel, M. (2006) 'The NEW Project Manager', *Computerworld*, 40(15): 43–45.

Brown, F. (1998) *Tourism Reassessed: Blight or Blessing?*, Oxford: Butterworth-Heinemann.

Chalip, L. (2006) 'Towards Social Leverage of Sport Events', *Journal of Sport & Tourism*, 11: 109–127.

de Souto, M.S. (1993) *Group Travel*, 2nd edn, Albany, NY: Delmar.

Dickinson, J. and Shipway, R. (2007) *The impact of Events: A Resource Guide on the impacts of Events*. Higher Education Academy [On-line]. HLST: Oxford.

Ensor, J., Robertson, M. and Ali-Knight, J. (2011) 'Eliciting the Dynamics of Leading a Sustainable Event: Key Informant Responses', *Event Management*, 15: 315–327.

Foley, M., McGillivary, D. and McPherson, G. (2009) 'Policy, Politics and Sustainable Events', in M.J. Stabler (ed.) *Tourism and Sustainability: Principles to Practice*, New York: CAB International, pp. 13–21.

Freeman, R.E. (1984) *Strategic Management: A Stakeholder Approach*, Boston: Pitman.

Getz, D. (1991) *Festivals, Special Events and Tourism*, New York: Van Nostrand Reinhold.

Getz, D. (2000) 'Developing a Research Agenda for the Event Management Field', in J. Allen, R. Harris, L.K. Jago and A.J. Veal (eds), *Events Beyond 2000: Setting the Agenda, Proceedings of Conference on Events Evaluation, Research and Education*, Sydney, Australian Centre for Event Management, University of Technology, pp. 10–21.

Getz, D. (2009) 'Policy for Sustainable and Responsible Festivals and Events: Institutionalization of a New Paradigm', *Journal of Policy Research in Tourism, Leisure and Events*, 1(1): 61–78.

Getz, D. (2010) 'The Nature and Score of Festival Studies', *International Journal of Events Management Research*, 5(1): 1–47.

Getz, D. and Andersson, T. (2010) 'Festival Stakeholders: Exploring Relationships and Dependency Through a Four-Country Comparison', *Journal of Hospitality & Tourism Research*, 34(4): 531–556.

Gibson, C. and Davidson, D. (2004) 'Tamworth, Australia's Country Music Capital: Place Marketing, Rurality, and Resident Reactions', *Journal of Rural Studies*, 20(4): 387–404.

Goldblatt, J.J. (2001) *Special Events: Twenty First Century Global Event Management*, New York: John Wiley and Sons.

Gration, D., Arcodia, C., Raciti, M. and Stokes, R. (2011) 'The Blended Festivalscape and its Sustainability at NonUrban Festivals', *Event Management*, 15: 343–359.

Haessly, J. (2010) 'Tourism and a Culture of Peace', in O. Moufakkir and I. Kelly (eds) *Tourism, Progress and Peace*, Oxfordshire, UK: CABI, pp. 1–16.

Hall, C. (1992) *Olympic Politics*, Manchester: Manchester University Press.

Hall, C. (1994) *Tourism and Politics: Policy, Power and Place*, Chichester: John Wiley & Sons.

Hall, S. (1989) 'Ethnicity: Identity and Difference', *Radical America*, 23: 9–20.

Hede, J.A.L. and Deery, M. (2003) 'An Agenda for Special Event Research: Lessons From the Past and Directions for the Future', *Journal of Hospitality and Tourism Management*, 10: 1–14.

Hediger, W. (2000) 'Sustainable Development and Social Welfare', *Ecological Economics*, 32(3): 481–492.

Hollinshead, K. (1998) 'Tourism and the Restless Peoples: A Dialectical Inspection of Bhabba's Halfway Populations', *Tourism, Culture & Communication*, 1(1): 49–77.

Janson, J. (1999) 'Why Did One Successful Festival Become Two? Arts and Crafts Festivals in Central Pennsylvania', Paper Presented at the International Institute for Peace Through Tourism Third Global Conference, Glasgow, Scotland, 17–21 October 1999.

Jones, M. (2010) *Sustainable Event Management: A Practical Guide*, London: Earthscan.

Kelly, I. (1987) *Hong Kong: A Political-Geographic Analysis*, London: Macmillan.

Kelly, I. (1991) 'Sideline Tourism', *The Journal of Tourism Studies*, 2(1): 21–28.

Kelly, I. (1998) 'Tourism and the Peace Proposition, The Role of Tourism: National and Regional Perspectives', Proceedings of the Fourth Asia Pacific Tourism Association Conference, Tanyang, Korea, 18–21 August 1998.

Kelly, I. (1999) 'Peace and Tourism: A SWOT Analysis', Paper Presented to the International Institute for Peace through Tourism Third Global Conference, Glasgow, Scotland, 17–21 October 1999.

Last, D. (2001) *There Was Movement in the Mountains*, an Address to the Australian Regional Tourism Convention, Port Macquarie, NSW, 6–8 September.

McDonnell, I., Allen, J. and O'Toole, W. (1999) *Festival and Special Event Management*, Wiley: Brisbane.

Mitchell, R.K., Agle, B.R. and Wood, D.J. (1997) 'Toward a Theory of Stakeholder Identification and Salience: Defining the Principle of Who and What Really Counts', *Academy of Management Review (Academy of Management)*, 22(4): 853–886.

Mot du Committé Exécutif (2012) Festival Mawazine-Rythme du Mondes, www.festival-mawazine.ma/fr/le-festival/mot-du-president.html, accessed 12 June 2012.

Moufakkir, O. and Burns, P. (2011) *Controversies in Tourism*, Wallingford, UK: CABI.

Muller, H. (1997) 'The Theory Path to Sustainable Tourism Development', in L. France (ed.) *Sustainable Tourism*, London: Earthscan, pp. 29–35.

Nussbaum, M. (1997) 'Democracy's Wake-up Call, Higher Education', *The Australian*, 5: 38–39.

Owusu-Frempong, N. (2005) 'An Evaluation of the impact of Tourism Development on the Economy of Ghana', in S. Greenland (ed.) *Contemporary Issues in Marketing*, London: London Metropolitan University.

Pal, L.A. (1993) *Interests of State: The Politics of Language, Multiculturalism, and Feminism in Canada*, Montreal and Kingston: McGill-Queen's University Press.

Pearce, P.L. (1988) *The Ulysses Factor*, New York: Springer-Verlag.

Putnam, R.D. (2000) *Bowling Alone: The Collapse and Revival of American Community*, New York: Simon and Schuster.

Raj, R. and Musgrave, J. (2009) 'Introduction to a Conceptual Framework for Sustainable Events', in R. Raj and J. Musgrave (eds) *Events Management and Sustainability*, Oxfordshire, UK: CABI, pp. 1–12.

Reid, G. (2006) 'The Politics of City Imaging: A Case Study of the MTV Europe Music Awards in Edinburgh 03', *Event Management*, 10(1): 35–46.

Reisinger, Y. (1997) 'Social Contacts Between Tourists and Hosts of Different Cultural Backgrounds', in L. France (ed.) *Sustainable Tourism*, London: Earthscan, pp. 129–134.

Ross, G.F. (1994) *The Psychology of Tourism*, Melbourne: Hospitality Press.

Salter, B. (1998) 'The Synergy of Wine, Tourism and Events, in Wine Tourism: Perfect Partners', Proceedings of the First Australian Wine Tourism Conference, Margaret River.

Seaton, A.V. (1999) 'War and Thanatourism: Waterloo 1815–1914', *Annals of Tourism Research*, 26(1): 130–158.

Smith, V. (1998) 'War and Tourism: An American Ethnography', *Annals of Tourism Research*, 25(1): 202–227.

Stabler, M.J. (1997) 'An Overview of the Sustainable Tourism Debate and the Scope and Content of the Book', in M.J. Stabler (ed.) *Tourism and Sustainability: Principles to Practice*, New York: CAB International, pp. 1–22.

Témoignages artiste, 'Artistes,' www.festivalmawazine.ma/fr/le-festival/temoignages. html, accessed 12 June 2012.

Tomljenovic, R. and Faulkner, B. (2000) 'Tourism and World Peace: A Conundrum for the Twenty-First Century', in B. Faulkner, G. Moscardo and E. Laws (eds) *Tourism in the Twenty-First Century: Reflections on Experience*, London: Continuum, pp. 18–33.

Van Der Wagen, L. (2001) *Event Management*, Melbourne: Hospitality Press.

Var, T., Ap, J. and Van Doren, C. (1994) 'Tourism and World Peace', in W. Theobald (ed.) *Global Tourism: The Next Decade*, Oxford: Butterworth-Heinemann.

Walsh-Heron, J. and Stevens, T. (1990) *The Management of Visitor Attractions and Events*, Englewood Cliffs, NJ: Prentice Hall.

WCED (1987) *Our Common Future*, Oxford: Oxford University Press.

Weaver, D. and Oppermann, M. (2000) *Tourism Management*, Brisbane: Wiley.

Wheeler, B. (1997) 'Tourism's Troubled Times: Responsible Tourism is not the Answer', in L. France (ed.) *Sustainable Tourism*, London: Earthscan, pp. 61–67.

Part III

Strategic perspectives and the events sector

9   Sustainability, for whom?

Jenny Cave, Peter Robinson and Mirrin Locke

This chapter considers the concept of sustainability in the context of events. We explore the motivations behind the adoption of the principles of sustainability for venue managers and event organisers, asking what is sustainability and who is it for?

Methodically we adopt a critical stance drawing on post-modern and social constructionism to illustrate the respective perspectives, roles and implied power complexities played out during the planning and implementation of events.

The chapter starts by introducing the concepts of sustainability and Corporate Social Responsibility (CSR), and their emergence within the event sector. We then explore event stakeholder motivations, such as politics or mitigation of event impacts, offering examples for instance of government use of sustainability concepts within events as a platform to exhibit nationhood, ethical considerations for venue managers and illustrating implicit social constructionism among event organisers. We look too at the growing interest from consumers and accreditation agencies in driving and responding to demand, and we conclude with a focus on future challenges and current trends that may shape the environmental concerns and morals of the event industry in the future.

Sustainability

A core issue for this chapter is the definition of sustainability, and how it can be enacted in the event industry. Perhaps the notion of 'a sustainable event' is an oxymoron since events are singular by nature, and maybe it is legacy that we should focus upon.

Sustainability implies commitment to local actions over time that cumulatively makes a difference to local and (ideally) global contexts. The developmental role of sustainability has become increasingly important to tourism economies in recent years and presents the event industry with many opportunities and challenges.

The World Commission on Environment and Development (WCED, 1987) defines sustainable development as that which meets current needs while not compromising the ability to meet the needs of future generations. While the development of sustainability from a tourism perspective has been recognised for some time, for example the impact of airline flights on local ecosystems and people, and an up to 3.6 per cent impact on global warming (Owen *et al.*, 2010), these concerns were not considered in the events context until after the signing of the Agenda 21 document at the Earth Summit in Rio de Janeiro in 1992. The adoption of Agenda 21, and the subsequent Local Agenda 21, which calls for and commits the public sector to local action, is a driving force for the 'greening' of the event industry. However, it was the International Olympic Committee who, although criticised for being slow on the uptake (Allen *et al.*, 2006), first adopted the principles of environmental concerns during the 1994 Lillehammer Winter Olympic Games.

In the events sector, the challenge has been taken up by organisations such as the Sustainable Events Alliance which offers a virtual network for ideas exchange, resources and current international programmes, seeks to engage new participants and encourages adoption of management systems such as ISO 20121 and public sustainability reporting; for example, the Global Reporting Initiative (GRI) (Sustainable Event Alliance, 2012).

Sustainability however extends beyond environmental concerns, to include local community well-being and business success. In an events context this means a strategic development approach and local management practices within national, regional and local governmental contexts to: minimise negative impacts while enhancing positive impacts; assure economic viability for the event organisation or government; safeguard local culture and heritage; protect natural environments and provide residents and visitors with an enjoyable experience (Heitmann and Lóránt, 2010). Businesses generate the wealth that supports communities and their prosperity, in even the most sensitive of natural environments. As a result many organisations today measure their medium-term performance using the 'triple bottom line' where profitability and financial growth (the bottom line) are measured alongside socio-cultural contributions and environmental protection.

Commercial adoption of the principles of sustainability is embodied in Corporate Social Responsibility (CSR). Many businesses now possess a CSR strategy, which should, ideally, focus on the triple bottom line as a key measure of performance to meet the needs of the organisation's stakeholders and shareholders. But, CSR has now been 'widened to incorporate social and corporate governance issues such as supporting charity work, outreach programmes, employee well-being, etc' (Heitmann and Lóránt, 2010, p. 191). Early concerns about the utility of CSR focussed on its incompatibility with profitability, its perception as costly and burdensome and the fact that managers did not possess the necessary skills to manage CSR. However, a number of factors have now led to its adoption including cost savings, improved reputation, sponsorship endorsements to extend the audience or replace costs, and consumer awareness. Cost savings arise for example from waste and energy minimisation, paperless technology strategies, emissions control and reusable supplies. Poor environmental behaviours impact negatively on businesses and events. Organisations should promote their CSR philosophy and demonstrate their legislative compliance.

Although little is known about the importance of environmental practice in the context of consumer decision making, it is important to explain environmental activities to consumers (Allen *et al.*, 2006).

Long-term event legacies must be planned. While an event may leave an unplanned legacy, the importance of planning is linked to the value and impact of the legacy. Unplanned legacies may be positive, negative or, as is most common, a combination of both, but without a plan there is no process through which to maximise the benefits. A legacy is not just about the impacts of the event either, but about the long-term benefits it brings. Generally, the bigger the event, the more impactful the legacy, but not all events will leave any legacy. The legacy for London 2012 has arguably begun before the event has taken place, as facilities have to be designed to still have a purpose after the event, and many regions of the UK have planned and delivered Olympics-relevant events before the actual Olympic event.

Part of the idea of legacy relates to leveraging activities around an event to maximise its long-term benefits (Chalip, 2004) and to be proactive in creating specific benefits for the host community (O'Brien and Chalip, 2007). However, event legacies can also be negative, for example the doubts that surrounded belief in Greece's ability to progress timely construction work of new Olympic venues in 2004 (Dickson, 2010).

The relatively late adoption of sustainability within the events sector means that there is, as yet, little in the way of published research, much of which has focussed on the impacts of sporting events (e.g. Collins *et al.*, 2009; Hiller, 1998; Orams, 2007; Smith, 2009). Despite this lack there are many examples of sustainable practices at events; one example can be found in the preparation for London 2012, which was planned to be the first truly sustainable Olympic Games and aimed to be the first to leave a strong environmental legacy by addressing the themes of climate change, waste, biodiversity, inclusion and healthy living (London Organising Committee of the Olympic Games and Paralympic Games, 2007). These may however be difficult to measure. The sector is also aided by well-articulated policy documents such as Guidelines for the Environmentally Sound Organisation of Events (BMU, 2008) and number of online forums (A Greener Festival, 2011).

Events can then be located in the wider context of sustainability but this depends on the adoption of the principles of sustainability, CSR and legacy in a social constructionist vein for venue design and management, breadth of engagement and event implementation.

However, the motivations to adopt the principles of sustainability for venue managers and event organisers can include politics and economic motives, as well as mitigation of socio-cultural and environmental effects. Market forces theory suggests that supply is responsive to demand, but tourism, in which events and festivals play a major role, is an exception and can also create demand, especially if imaginatively conceived, high quality and hedonistic. Thus venue managers and organisers have dual roles in responding to changing consumer attitudes and in structuring the physical and business platforms on which sustainability, CSR and legacy can be enacted by negotiations with governments, the construction industry, like-minded sponsors (including NGOs) and accreditation agencies. This leads to the central question of this chapter – sustainability, for whom?

Motivation

Politics is a major motivator when it comes to large scale events with international impact, accompanied by international prestige, high profile television coverage and potentially greater political influence on the world stage. This is illustrated by the desire of regions and nations to host major events such as the Olympic Games, European Capitals of Culture, Commonwealth Games or the Rugby World Cup. Many destinations build their tourism product on the reputation and legacy of annual events. Edinburgh has established itself as the Festival City through the Edinburgh Fringe Festival, The Edinburgh Tattoo and Hogmanay (Scottish New Year Celebrations). But events can also change and legitimise ideology and political views by 'the cognitive validation of an entity as desirable, proper and appropriate in a widely shared system of beliefs and norms' (Berger and Luckman, 1966). An event organising entity is more likely to be considered for funding and endorsement by politicians and sponsors when reputation and legitimacy coexist, especially if the event is expected to provide a long-term boost to a host city/nation (Dickson, 2010). However, legitimacy may be misused for propaganda, may not reflect the country's true politics or may hide issues of poverty, bribery and deprivation. Other negative impacts include the risk of event failure, or the perceived inability of a nation to prepare effectively (for example, the XIX Commonwealth Games in Delhi in 2010, when the venues and facilities were partially incomplete at the start of the event), the misallocation of funds, budgetary shortfall or private deals for preferred seats with a wealthy business club to allow the club to secure the best seats for its members, leaving the wider public without their preferred tickets, or the 1976 Montreal Olympics where the government were paying off the debts until 2006 (Heitmann and Lóránt, 2010).

The economic motivator for event organisers and venue managers is driven by profitability (trade shows and exhibitions), raising the profile of products and brands (V-Festival, the Geneva Motorshow), covering costs and contributing to charity (The London Marathon) as well as demonstrated achievement of economic impact and developing an enduring economic legacy for a local area (the Olympic Games, the Commonwealth Games).

Direct economic impacts occur before an event in the construction of infrastructure, during the event through ticket and merchandise sales, as well as direct employment created for the event. Indirect impacts occur as a result of the event in the wider economy. Examples include visitor accommodation, additional entertainment and fringe festivals. For major events these can be extended to business development, inward investment and job creation, which then lead to increased tax revenues for the public sector. A region may, over time, develop as a tourism destination. Induced impacts include increased spending within the economy as a result of jobs created and the increased spending power of locals, showing the multiplier effect of events. This is illustrated through the legacies of events such as the Sydney Olympic Games, the Manchester Commonwealth Games and Liverpool's year as a European Capital of Culture. The World Rowing Championships at Eton generated an economic impact of £3,268,703 and the Women's World Cup Cycling Grand Prix of Wales produced £56,413. The average return was equivalent to £3.20 for every £1 spent (UK Sport, 2006). Such outcomes are powerful motivators for all stakeholders. However, negative impacts include damage to the reputation of a region if the event fails to meet expectations and potential leakage from the economy if local suppliers and businesses are not involved in the event. It is also important to note that where events are successful, they can still have a negative impact, pushing up house prices, forcing emigration from the community for those unable to afford to live there and an increase in second home ownership.

Although economic impact is often measured for events and for tourism, and much is said about the immediate short-term impact of events, 'the methods utilised in these studies are often fraught with limitations, [as they] have often become "instruments for political shenanigans" that are commissioned to legitimise a political position rather than to search for economic truth' (Crompton, 2006, p. 67). Methodological tactics used to achieve this can include the addition of local residents to poll figures, inappropriate aggregation (such as overstating positive responses by inclusion of good, very good and excellent in a single category of 'very good'), 'inclusion of time-switchers and casuals, abuse of multipliers, ignoring costs borne by the local community, ignoring opportunity costs, ignoring displacement costs, expanding the project scope; exaggerating visitation numbers, and inclusion of consumer surplus' (Dickson, 2010, p. 232).

Venue managers are motivated to use sustainability principles, CSR and legacy to demonstrate to investors that they are protecting their investment for the long term and manage their relationship with key stakeholders such as the construction industry enabling development of new facilities to embody sustainability from project initiation through to and beyond delivery. However, they often confront ethical decisions when they host controversial and environmentally sensitive exhibitions, where the venue is, in reality, only selling space.

While venue managers and event organisers may wish to plan for, and structure, events upon the principles of sustainability, from the venue management perspective implementation of sustainable management practices in the events sector can prove challenging in terms of obtaining, allocating and maintaining resources such as time, money, personnel and services. Cooperation from stakeholders such as event organisers, contractors, owners, governing bodies and staff, including volunteers, can be difficult to achieve unless close associations are created with the host organisation, underpinned by ongoing education and marketing initiatives. As an example, in today's digital world it is possible to hold a virtually paperless conference for several hundred delegates. Advertising and delegate registration can be done online and programmes, conference papers and other information distributed electronically. Similarly, post event evaluations can be conducted via electronic communications. Given the ready availability of these technologies, one could assume that delivering a paperless conference would be relatively easy. However, the reality is somewhat different. For instance at conference venues in Auckland, New Zealand delegates continue to send registrations via fax and post, and make payments by cheque; host organisations will not budge from their expectation to offer printed material for delegates such as programmes and books of papers and abstracts in delegate packs. Also, sponsors ask for 'tangible' printed material to be given to delegates, as do tourist and convention bureaux who provide material for delegates promoting the destination such as offers/discount coupons for attractions (Locke, 2012), often as part of sponsorship deals.

The achievement, then, of positive social cultural impacts is also a motivator for the inclusion of sustainability principles in events. Festivals and events are often used to promote cultural heritage, maintain traditional festivals and activities, or promote new forms of art and experience. It is argued by Bowdin *et al.* (2006) that events promote social cohesion through shared positive experiences. Events such as Gay Pride festivals allow minority groups to raise their profile, while events such as the Notting Hill Carnival allow Afro-Caribbean immigrants to reconnect with their roots and interpret their heritage for other members of the community. Mega events, for instance the Olympic Games, increase interest and participation in nationhood and community events that cluster around the core, while the growing wave of boutique festivals promotes new and alternative music genres. Events can play an important role in the education of consumers, either directly through their own communication and operating practices or indirectly, for example in green zones at concerts (Allen *et al.*, 2006). Sustainability goals for social inclusion and diversity are equally important so that many events and venues now have policies in place to manage and promote participation from the widest possible community, and include accessibility for disabled visitors. Event organisers now frequently incentivise consumer behaviour by offering rewards for collecting and turning in rubbish, offering incentives to stallholders for clearing the site after the event, for not engaging in anti-social behaviour such as urinating in public and offering abandoned tents and clothing to charity.

Negative socio-cultural impacts of events are not desirable and might be seen as de-motivators unless managed, but are predictable. They include anti-social behaviour, alcohol-fuelled behaviour, substance abuse, hooliganism, gate-crashing and overcrowding, many of which are an event management issue inside the confines of the event that need to be considered and addressed at the early stages of event planning. Event incidents in recent years include, for example, several thousand gatecrashers at the Glastonbury Festival in 2000 which led to the cancellation of the event in 2001 while security and safety was revised, nine deaths at the Roskilde Festival 2001 in Denmark, which led to the banning of crowd-surfing at many events and in many venues. However, issues outside the festival gates include damage to reputation, impact on local communities and resistance to the event. Some events are accused of losing their originality and tradition as a result of increased visitor numbers leading to over-commercialisation, resulting in a loss of authenticity. Other concerns for the community include damage to, and exploitation of, local amenities.

Environmental goals apply to both the natural and the built environment of events. Many events are developed to complement the protection of the environment where they are located, or to 'fit' with the cultural context of their location. For instance, the National Trust, a heritage conservation organisation in the UK, considers the historic nature of their properties when selecting the most appropriate types and themes of events. The economic benefits of events can help to redevelop and reinvigorate a region, or may help to pay for new infrastructure and management to protect and enhance the environment. Events may also be used by environmental charities to generate additional revenues and raise awareness of their activities. Greenpeace (2000) designed nine environmental guidelines for the Olympic Games, 2012, that can easily be applied to other events and venues. Events also provide opportunities for 'experiments in living', pathfinding for wider society and testing of technologies which may have important positive benefits for sustainability if widely adopted (Collins *et al.*, 2009).

However, events also have a negative impact on the environment, including: environmental damage, air pollution, water pollution, littering, erosion, carbon emissions, energy use, noise pollution and traffic congestion. Although travel is a major concern for any major event, many festivals take place in rural locations that have limited access options, limited sanitary infrastructure and few, but potentially sensitive, rural neighbours. This could stretch local resources and make the lives of local communities difficult, which relates back to the earlier discussion around socio-cultural impacts. As licensing applications and permissions depend upon effective management policies to control these issues, they are taken seriously by many event organisers. This need has produced specialised suppliers of event transportation for music festivals in the United Kingdom.

Today, event consumers have an expectation that considerations of, at least, environmental sustainability (recycling is the best known), CSR and legacy will be in place at an event, and thus have put pressure on organisations and managers to deliver demonstrated outcomes. It is important to note that event venues, including hotels, conference and exhibition centres, tourist attractions and festival sites must be differentiated in terms of scope and scale, since each type of venue faces its own challenges, from the CSR focus that hotels adopt, through to the issues around sustainable development that are prevalent in the tourism sector.

Implementation of sustainability practices in events and other tourism activities has been supported in recent years by many awards and industry standards in order to validate sustainability initiatives. The European Eco Management and Audit Scheme is an initiative to improve an organisation's environmental performance which recognises and rewards companies that go beyond the minimum legal compliance and continuously improve their environmental performance. A public environmental statement reporting on the performance is a requirement and the accuracy and reliability is independently checked by an environmental verifier. Other examples are ISO 14001 and ISO 20121, Green Globe, Green

Building Councils, Earthcheck and Qualmark. The Green Meetings Industry Council (USA) presents the 'Green' awards to recognise environmental commitment within the meetings industry (e.g. Green Meeting Awards, Green Supplier Awards, Green Exhibitor Awards and Commitment to the Community Awards) and BS8901 which provides specifications for a sustainability management system for events.

Conclusion

Event organisers and venue managers are social constructionists, motivated by political, socio-cultural, environmental and economic drivers. They balance positive and negative influences and impacts of their actions against those of stakeholders and consumers and are in a position of power. Altruism might suggest that the inclusion of sustainability is for the greater good – for all stakeholders, yet if an event is delivered essentially for commercial gain, then self-interest might suggest financial success comes first.

That said, there is a strong argument to suggest that the competing needs of a range of stakeholders dictate that sustainability is central to the event experience, and many large events are often commercial tools, where sponsors would not wish to be portrayed as having little or no interest in the environment. Similarly, the legislative structures within which events operate make it reasonably easy for disengaged community, concerned about the impact of an event, to place restrictions upon the event through working with local authorities. Likewise venues hosting contentious events may also put constraints upon the event organiser. The self-interest then shifts from financial success to the triple bottom line, if the event is to be repeated in the future.

References

A Greener Festival (2011) *Home Page*. Retrieved 28 June 2012 from http://agreenerfestival.com/.

Allen, J., O'Toole, W., Harris, R. and McDonnell, I. (2006) *Festival and Special Event Management* (4th edn), Milton: John Wiley and Sons.

Berger, P. L. and Luckmann, T. (1966) *The Social Construction of Reality: A Treatise in the Sociology of Knowledge*, Garden City, NY: Anchor Books.

BMU (2008) *Guidelines for Environmentally Sound Organisation of Events, Federal Ministry for the Environment, Nature Conservation and Nuclear Safety (BMU), April 2008*. Retrieved 8 December 2011 from www.bmu.de/files/pdfs/allgemein/application/pdf/broschuere_leitfaden_umweltgerecht_en.pdf.

Bowdin, G., Allen, J., O'Toole, W., Harris, R. and McDonnell, I. (2006) *Events Management* (2nd edn). Oxford: Butterworth-Heinemann.

Chalip, L. (2004) Beyond impact: A General Model for Sport Event Leverage. In B. W. Ritchie and D. Adair (eds), *Sport Tourism: Interrelationships, impacts and Issues* (Vol. 14). Clevedon, UK: Channel View Publications, pp. 226–252.

Collins, A., Jones, C. and Munday, M. (2009) Assessing the Environmental impacts of Mega Sporting Events: Two Options? *Tourism Management* 30 (6): 828–837.

Crompton, J. (2006) Economic impact Studies: Instruments for Political Shenanigans? *Journal of Travel Research* 45 (1): 67–82.

Dickson, G. (2010) Event Legacy. In P. Robinson, D. Wale and G. Dickson (2010) *Events Management*, Wallingford: CABI, pp. 225–237.

Greenpeace (2000) *Greenpeace Olympic Environmental Guidelines*. Retrieved 8 December 2011 from www.greenpeace.org/eastasia/PageFiles/301174/guideline.pdf.

Heitmann S. and Lóránt, D. (2010) Sustainability and Events Management. In P. Robinson, D. Wale and G. Dickson (2010) *Events Management*, Wallingford: CABI, pp. 181–200.

Hiller, H. (1998) Assessing the impact of Mega-events: A Linkage Model. *Current Issues in Tourism*, 1(1): 47–57.

Locke, M. (2012) *The Need for Strategic Planning and Management in the MICE Sector – A Case Study of the Auckland Region* (unpublished PhD thesis). University of Waikato, Hamilton, New Zealand.

London Organising Committee of the Olympic Games and Paralympic Games (2007) *London 2012: Sustainability Plan – Towards a One Planet 2012*. Retrieved 8 December 2011 from www.london2012.com/documents/locog-publications/london-2012-sustainability-plan.pdf.

O'Brien, D. and Chalip, L. (2007) Executive Training Exercise in Sport Event Leverage. *International Journal of Culture, Tourism and Hospitality Research*, 1 (4): 296–304.

Orams, M. (2007) The impacts of Hosting a Major Marine Sports Tourism Event: The America's Cup in Auckland, New Zealand. In M. Lück (ed.), *Nautical Tourism: Concepts and Issues*. Elmsford, NY: Cognizant Communication, pp. 97–105.

Owen, B., Lee, D. S. and Lim, L. (2010) Flying into the Future: Aviation Emissions Scenarios to 2050. *Environmental Science & Technology*, 44 (7): 2255–2260.

Smith, A. (2009) Theorising the Relationship between Major Sports Events and Social Sustainability. *Journal of Sport and Tourism*, 14 (2–3): 109–120.

Sustainable Event Alliance (2012) *Home Page*. Retrieved 28 June 2012 from www.sustainable-event-alliance.org.

UK Sport (2006) *Measuring Success 3: The Economic impact of Six Major Sports Events Supported by the World Class Events Programme in 2005 & 2006*. Retrieved 8 December 2011 from www.uksport.gov.uk/publications/measuring-success-3.

WCED (Brundtland Commission) (1987) *Report of the World Commission on Environment and Development*. Retrieved 8 December 2011 from www.are.admin.ch/imperia/md/content/are/nachhaltigeentwicklung/brundtland_bericht.pdf?PHPSESSID=8dfe0f6a3870011e7a14e3ce14c25410.

10 Strategic dimensions of hosting sustainable events

Adriana Budeanu and Elisabeth Støle

Introduction

Sustainability is an upcoming trend in the event industry, especially in relation to extensive festivities, such as world championships or the Olympic Games. Adding onto the status-value of events (Mol, 2010) the concept of sustainability brings additional prestige and makes their union, i.e. sustainable events, an appealing combination for cities worldwide. Seeking obvious benefits – new income, new jobs, unique experiences – cities are competing for the opportunity to display a responsible attitude in hosting political meetings, sportive or cultural events, of small or large stature. From local events like the Roskilde Music Festival in Denmark, to international festivities such as the British Royal Wedding in 2011 and the Olympic Games in 2012, sustainability has become a recurrent theme related to event management.

Admittedly a new field of study, a large part of the current research on sustainable events is descriptive, focusing on operational aspects and with little ambition for reflecting on the wider strategic implications for destinations. As a result, current frameworks for sustainable events fall short on explaining how sustainable initiatives in event management can have long-lasting benefits (Laing and Frost, 2010), making them seem odd, almost accidental initiatives, instead of permanent practice. Nevertheless, some destinations practice an incipient stage of strategic management related to sustainable events, involving actors and decision-making processes that aim to yield benefits for destinations. This chapter presents an inductive exploration of such a case, investigating the conditions that enable destinations to absorb the benefits and solve tensions related to hosting sustainable events.

The organisation of the fifteenth conference of the parties (COP15) for the United Nations Framework Convention on Climate Change (UNFCCC) in Copenhagen in 2009, an event with great hopes for advancing global sustainability, was also recognised internationally for its high achievements in managing the event in a responsible way. Although COP15 had important consequences for the global politics of climate change, stretching above and beyond the actual time of the event, they are left out of the scope for this research that focuses on the management of events. Exploring the contextual conditions in which COP15 took place, namely the urban system of Copenhagen city, this chapter is set out to reflect on the challenges and success factors related to sustainable events. Using information from primary and secondary sources, the chapter identifies four strategic aspects that connect destination and event management in relation to sustainable events: governance, level of change, learning and consolidation of knowledge. The main lessons crystallised from examining this case are presented in the concluding section with the hope of stimulating further research into strategic management of sustainable events.

A growing interest in the sustainability of events

The attention to the sustainable aspects of events has been growing over time. In 1992, global concerns for the long-term sustainability of human society raised at the United Nations Conference on Environment and Development in Rio de Janeiro, called for a shared responsibility for the common good that transcends current generations and legitimises the right of future generations to enjoy a high quality of life on Earth. As events are intrinsic elements of the cultural, political and civil life of communities, they were often promoted as vehicles for economic development (Angel and Hansen, 2006; Richards, 2007), consolidation of place image and cultural identities (Ooi and Pedersen, 2010). Furthermore, events can also encourage collective responsibilities and inspire behavioural changes (Laing and Frost, 2010; Pelham, 2011) that foster responsible attitudes to nature and society. Their symbolic value assigns events as good socio-political catalysts and strategic tools for ecological modernisation (Mol, 2010), reinforcing their promotion as expressions of modernity.

Starting with the Winter Olympics in Lillehammer in 1994, there was a growing interest for reducing the impacts associated particularly to sport mega-events, with the Soccer World Cup in Germany in 2006 and the Beijing Olympics in 2008 being widely acclaimed for their environmental, sporting and economic performances (Mol, 2010; Death, 2011). Following suit, the cultural sector and the performing arts adopted sustainability principles when organising their events (Andersson and Getz, 2008). Recent demands from governmental organisations (Pelham, 2011) and professional organisations indicate a weak yet noticeable cultural shift in event policies that could lead to a better adoption of sustainability principles in industry practices.

Alongside tourism, cultural and sport sectors, the meeting and events industry (MICE) is increasingly interested in adopting sustainability practices. A number of standards developed in the last decade provide necessary guidance for reducing negative impacts of events: the British standard BS 8901 for sustainable event management systems (British Standards Institution, 2012), the APEX standard of the US Convention Industry Council (CIC), the upcoming ISO 20121 standards and the Global Reporting Initiative supplement on Event Organiser Sector (Global Reporting Initiative, 2012). In addition to standards, guidelines were developed to support event planners, such as the Copenhagen Sustainable Meeting Protocol, Green Seal guidelines, US

Environmental Protection Agency Guidelines for Green Meetings, to name a few.

However, in practice, the desired contributions of events to the economic and social well-being of communities are shown to have less optimal outcomes (Hall, 1998). Studies point out the frequent incapacity of infrastructures to cope with large influxes of people (Kasimati and Dawson, 2009; Mol, 2010), inflicting damages to nature (Collins, 2009) and the social cohesion of host communities (Death, 2011). A particularly informative stream of research that focuses on the Olympic Games shows how the rhetoric of economic benefits can hijack local priorities for development, and fail to deliver on promised social, economic and environmental benefits (Collins, 2009; Kasimati and Dawson, 2009; Death, 2011; Minnaert, 2012). To such contextual challenges, operational guidelines for sustainable events listed above offer little relief or suggestions of how can destinations capitalise on events. If events should reach their long acclaimed beneficial potential, more detailed knowledge is necessary about the processes found at the interface between destinations and the event management. However, the research on sustainable events is still in incipient stages (Laing and Frost, 2010), with many studies limited to making inventories of environmental and social impacts, accompanied only occasionally by normative suggestions for corrective actions and lacking attention to the implementation conditions. Seemingly stronger and more appealing, the sustainability rhetoric praising the economic benefits of events seems to have diverted attention from the strategic considerations over the long-term sustainability of hosting events (Katusiimeh and Mol, 2011). Set to balance the focus on operational sustainability, this chapter investigates the strategic dimensions of destination involvement in managing sustainable events.

Sustainable management of events

Following the broader definition of sustainable development, Event Research International (2012) defines a responsible event as 'locality-centric in nature taking proactive measures to contribute to local sustainable development across the triple bottom-line'. For destinations, the concept of locality includes a regional and a location-specific perspective, each with their particular yet related contributions to sustainable development. While the regional perspective outlines the role of events as part of the regional socio-economic systems, the local perspective focuses on the operational aspects of event management. However, none of the two perspectives explains completely how to reach a successful regional sustainable development with a continuous interaction and exchanges of economic and socio-cultural capital between regional and local levels. A third perspective that captures the strategic integration between regional and local processes may explain how benefits of sustainable events trickle into the host destination. The next sections briefly outline the representation of each perspective in the literature on sustainable events.

Regional perspectives on sustainable events

In rather abstract terms, the regional perspective covers the role that events have in enhancing the profile of destinations and attracting foreign investment (Angel and Hansen, 2006; Richards, 2007) primarily for infrastructure developments. For larger development projects, a multiplier effect may lead to increased income and employment opportunities for local population. Certainly events increase the attractiveness of destinations for tourism and enlarge the spectrum of opportunities for its supportive sectors such as food, retailing or transportation (Ooi and Pedersen, 2010). However, the desire of destination stakeholders to maximise profits from event-related developments can lead to the commodification of cultures and a lock-in effect on non-substitutable natural resources such as land. On the other hand, high profile events like the United Nations conferences are good vehicles for mainstreaming messages about sustainability to global audiences, while cultural projects such as the Live Aid concerts draw in social engagement and a sense of collective responsibility towards global issues such as poverty, climate change and peace. Despite the logic connections between events and regional sustainability, their contribution remains difficult to isolate and measure.

Local perspectives on sustainable events

At local operational levels, the aim is to keep the socio-cultural and environmental footprint of events within acceptable limits by minimising negative impacts of transportation and logistics, contracting and sourcing, resource and waste management (Pelham, 2011). Consequently, the sustainable character of events is defined by the sum of checks on a long list of social, environmental and economic aspects that require attention (Angel and Hansen, 2006). Aiming to be exhaustive, such lists can be overwhelming and risk a quick dismissal from event managers. Shortcutting insurmountable lists of impacts other approaches focus on the reduction of single-issues aspects such as climate change (Laing and Frost, 2010) energy consumption, waste management (Katusiimeh and Mol, 2011) or social exclusion (Minnaert, 2012) in specific locations. While local perspectives enable an easier identification of key responsibilities for mitigating impacts, they often rely on technological or infrastructural solutions, such as new buildings, roads or waste management facilities. Depending on the affluence of the destinations, the costs of mitigating negative effects can lead to the subtle marginalisation or abandonment of sustainability projects related to events (Death, 2011). In order to yield their best outcomes, local perspectives on event management need grounding in the perennial strategies of destinations.

Strategic management of sustainable events

More comprehensive approaches define sustainable events by the level of adoption and integration of sustainability objectives into the planning and execution

of events (Laing and Frost, 2010). At strategic level, the focus is moved onto the planning, management and maintenance of sustainable operations, prior, during and long-term after the event (Mol, 2010). With a holistic perspective on the organisation of events in time and space, the scope of integrative approaches is to embed sustainability criteria into the planning and bidding processes. However, they are rarely seen in practice (Hall, 1998) and are mostly found as theoretical suggestions from research, with little or no reference to the practical implementation.

In essence events are concentrated time-space disturbances in the life of cities (Mol, 2010). A *sine qua non* condition for sustainable events is the ability of their hosts to accommodate events without spoiling the quality for locals or future generations (Andersson and Getz, 2008). While regional perspectives provide visionary goals for sustainable destinations as hosts of events, local perspectives allow the identification of responsibilities for action. However, there is little detailed research into the decision-making processes that translate visionary goals into practice and enable destinations to metabolise events at minimal costs for nature and communities. Typically assigned the role of sink for impacts or subject for commodification, destinations cannot be isolated from the sustainability of events (Angel and Hansen, 2006; Laing and Frost, 2010). Recent evidence indicates that destinations started to adopt strategic management approaches when organising sustainable events. Using an inductive exploratory approach, this research is set out to investigate the strategic management of sustainable events and to identify critical factors that influence it, by examining the actors, responsibilities and relationships involved in hosting the fifteenth conference of the parties (COP15) of the United Nations Framework Convention on Climate Change (UNFCCC) in Copenhagen, Denmark. The main sources of information used for this research are public records and reports about COP15, complemented by interviews with representatives of the Danish Ministry of Foreign Affairs, Wonderful Copenhagen, MCI Group Copenhagen and Københavns Kommune.[1]

Copenhagen – a gracious host for events

As the capital of Denmark, Copenhagen is home to over 1.7 million people (Region Hovedstaden, 2012) and one of world's top 20 most popular destinations for meetings, conferences, congresses and events. Its worldwide image is not only heterogeneous but sometimes controversial, combining traditional values with strong modern liberal ones (Ooi and Pedersen, 2010). More than a decade ago the municipality of Copenhagen started a series of projects intended to improve the environmental and social quality of life of its citizens. One such example was the creation of bicycle paths throughout the city, at the expense of street area. As a result, currently over 50 per cent of citizens bike every day and the municipality saves annually DKK43 million (€5.8 million) (Wiking, 2011). Another example is the successful cleantech sector in Copenhagen that had a turnover growth of 55 per cent from the year 2004 to 2009. Copenhagen city has the goal to reduce emissions by 20 per cent from 2005 to 2015 and become a carbon neutral city by 2025 (Wiking, 2011). At the same time, the city wants to attract over fifty national and international events, meetings and congresses in the years to come in order to bring an estimated income of DKK1.3 billion (€175 million) in visitor income (Juul, 2011). Aiming to reconcile these two ambitious goals, Copenhagen city subscribed to the difficult task of becoming a destination for sustainable events. The first occasion to showcase this commitment was the fifteenth conference of the United Nations Framework Convention on Climate Change (UNFCCC).

The COP15 event

The UNFCCC conference of the parties (COP) has been held annually since 1995, hosted by rotation, by the member countries (UNFCCC, 2012a). The UNFCCC secretariat is responsible for setting the requirements such as venue, security and logistics to the hosting government (UNFCCC, 2012b). In November 2006, the Danish Government launched the invitation to host COP15 in December 2009 in Copenhagen and received a positive answer in 2007 (Figure 10.1). The event was organised under the leadership of the Royal Danish Ministry of Foreign Affairs (MFA) on behalf of the UNFCCC, together with strategic partners such as the local convention bureau (Wonderful Copenhagen), the Danish National Tourist Organization (Visit Denmark), a professional congress

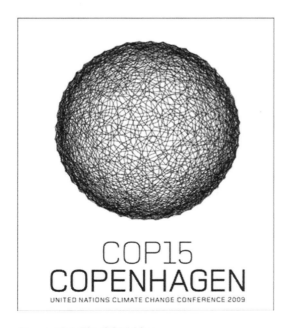

Figure 10.1 The COP15 logo.

organiser (MCI Group) and the municipality of Copenhagen city (Københavns Kommune).

The organisers expected around 15,000 delegates, almost one-third more than the actual participants to COP13 in Bali in 2007 (UNFCCC, 2009). In the end, the COP15 had 33,526 delegates present, from 192 countries, including 126 heads of state (Bigwood and Luehrs, 2010). Most meetings during the COP15 were located at the Bella Center, the largest convention center in Copenhagen, with a total capacity of 70,000 square meters of conference floor space. A supplementary 12,000 square meters conference space was added by the construction of three new large pavilions.

The organisation of the event was financed by private and public funds; the Danish Government and Copenhagen city council committed over €200 million to prepare the city for COP15. The funds were used for organising logistics, citizen information campaigns, organising security, the purchase of electric vehicles and retrofitting the infrastructure to accommodate them. An additional sum of €15.3 million was acquired from sponsorships (Bigwood and Luehrs, 2010). Nearly €932,000 was used to implement sustainability-related changes. The €537,000 saved by implementing a non-gift policy at COP15 was used to create eleven scholarships for students from developing countries to attend a postgraduate business education at Danish universities.

Strategic actions in the organisation of COP15

The decision to make COP15 as sustainable as possible by focusing on the three pillars of sustainable development: economy, society and environment, was taken by the Danish Government in line with the national sustainability strategy and its goals. Following the sustainability principles outlined in the UN Global Compact, the MFA took on the challenge of adopting the BS8901 standard and focused on administration and leadership, supplier management, stakeholder engagement, transport, high-level objectives, purchasing and sponsorships, accommodation and logistics (Bigwood and Luehrs, 2010).

The examination of the context in which the COP15 event was organised reveals important insights into the structural and institutional changes that facilitated the attempts to make it sustainable. Based on information from public documents and interviews with key stakeholders, the following section presents the most significant aspects that outline a strategic management in the organisation of COP15. The findings are presented following the main themes identified by Tidball and Krasny (2007) as strategic approaches for resilient systems in the face of concentrated disturbances such as events (Mol, 2010): self-organisation (understood as governance), level of change and learning. One additional strategic factor was identified during the research: the consolidation of success.

Governance

Governance roles and structure

The decision of the Danish Government to make events the flagship of its commitment to sustainable development, added a new layer of complexity on the shoulders of the organisers of COP15. With only a short time to convince public and private partners to adopt measures that reduced their environmental and social impacts, the organisers needed critical convincing power. Consequently, the Copenhagen Sustainability Meeting Coalition (CSMC) was created with public partners (MFA, Københavns Kommune), hospitality public partners (Wonderful Copenhagen, VisitDenmark) and private partners (the Bella Center, Novo Nordisk and MCI, the professional congress organiser).

> COP15 was not the greenest conference ever – it was created to be as sustainable as possible under the given conditions of a large international political summit.
> (Jan Christoph Napierski, Head of Section, COP15, Royal Danish Ministry of Foreign Affairs, quoted in Bigwood and Luehrs, 2010)

Following a democratic public-private partnership model (Klijn and Teisman, 2003) the CSMC had the decision power over the organisation and management of COP15 and laid out a strategic plan with congruent goals for marketing, sustainability and security, published as the Copenhagen Sustainable Meeting Protocol (CSMP). In addition, the CSM coalition had the role of coordinating the implementation of the sustainability goals by local providers. Representing a critical mass of demand, the CSM coalition was able to put forward requirements for environmental or social improvements, which hospitality suppliers, such as restaurants and hotels, could not ignore. Their success in raising, for example, the number of hotels that adopted environmental management, is yet another confirmation of the effective persuasive power of multi-stakeholder alliances in promoting sustainability goals (Kogg, 2003; Budeanu, 2009). Throughout the processes, the MCI Group offered specialised assistance, working closely with suppliers to identify opportunities for improving their environmental and social performances.

The main responsibility for organising and marketing the event belonged to the hospitality stakeholders (private and public), together with the reception and accommodating of guests upon arrival (Getz, 2008; Ooi and Pedersen, 2010). In addition, they were in charge of logistics, security, resource consumption, waste generation and infrastructure adjustments. Københavns Kommune supported their work by facilitating certain adjustments such as the supplementation and rerouting of public transport in order to avoid congestion during the event and disturbances to the quality of life for the city residents. Generalising for the sake of this discussion, three levels of governance structures could be related to COP15: a strategic level represented by the CSM coalition; an operational level

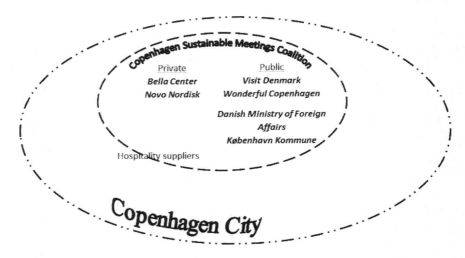

Figure 10.2 Governance structure of COP15.

represented by hospitality stakeholders; and a supportive level represented by the city of Copenhagen and the local community (Figure 10.2). Cutting across the different levels, the decision-making processes involved representatives from all levels.

The wider area of Copenhagen city, including residents, providers of commercial infrastructure and public transportation, local NGOs and guests were only marginally involved in the management of COP15. As secondary stakeholders (Andersson and Getz, 2008), they have limited involvement in decision-making but are important recipients of the indirect effects of events such as shortages of resources, congested traffic, noise, increased popularity and novel opportunities for entertainment. Before, during and after the COP15, Københavns Kommune opened physical and virtual communication channels, inviting citizens to comment on the plans made for COP15, but without much success. However, complaints from citizens and participants regarding the excessive security measures during COP15 were received later during the event. In a society renowned for its civic spirit, the low involvement of citizens in the planning of COP15 seems to be more an illustration of the Scandinavian institutional trust (Richards, 2007) than a lack of interest and civic attitude.

Public-private partnerships such as the CSM coalition are promoted as one of the most effective models for sustainability projects that involve stakeholders with diverse interests (Klijn and Teisman, 2003; Hall, 2011). However, in the field of event management they seem to be less popular, and research on sustainable events shows mostly two types of governance involved: one headed by public organisations (e.g. local municipalities) and another one dominated by private organisations (Andranovich *et al.*, 2001; Henderson, 2011). While event management policies of public institutions put emphasis on accountability and public well-being, private organisations focus more on efficiency and business profits. Studies also show the latter to have a tendency to adopt corporatist attitudes, pursuing their own interests and keeping other stakeholders at arm's-length (Andranovich *et al.*, 2001). When mixed partnerships emerge, private interests can be sufficiently strong to fast-track regulations that favour their profits (Hall, 1998) at the expense of priorities of the local communities (Death, 2011). Prior to COP15, public media suggested that internal frictions between different political fractions and ministerial bodies may have influenced the national position related to COP15. However, within the CSM coalition, participants interviewed confirm that democratic participation was encouraged, with private organisations taking the lead of implementation, and public organisations maintained a coordinating role.

Leadership and change agents

To a large extent, the environmental and social achievements related to COP15 were possible due to the visionary leadership shown by the Danish Ministry of Foreign Affairs. Besides the decision to make a worldwide statement of the Danish commitment to sustainable development, the MFA was the main investor of the event and coordinated its organisation. The role of governments in regional sustainable development is well documented by research (Hall, 2011), from top-bottom approaches with declarative statements and financial support (Andranovich *et al.*, 2001) to instances when they are merely the front cover of private interests (Death, 2011). In Copenhagen, the MFA used its legitimacy to keep the attention of stakeholders on the common goals of securing a safe and sustainable COP15 and to mediate consensus in divergent opinions. At the same time the MFA showed unmitigated commitment to sustainability goals, participating in technical and strategic meetings, finding and debating solutions, some of which were implemented within the Ministry. At the same time, the MFA was openly criticised in the media for allocating too much attention and resources to the security measures during COP15. The positive attitude of the MFA in the face of challenges, seeing them as opportunities rather than barriers, is another indicator of its role as a change agent (Kanter, 1999) and ties into the Scandinavian institutional trust (Richards, 2007).

Sustainable management of operations

Research indicates that the bulk of inputs and outputs related to events concentrate in the area where most activities take place and can be up to eight times more intense in terms of visitor numbers and commercial activity, than in the rest of the city (Richards, 2007). The sustainability-driven operational improvements during COP15 had three priority areas of action: the venue, the accommodation facilities and logistics. The key partner in the CSM coalition, the Bella Center venue committed over €2.5 million to improving environmental performance and made radical changes in its management (Bigwood and Luehrs, 2010). Using tap instead of bottled water, compostable corn resin cups and by optimising the consumption of energy for lighting, heating and cooling, Bella Center made considerable cost savings and cut 20 per cent of its CO_2 emissions, setting a precedent for its new goal of cutting CO_2 emissions by 25 per cent by 2015.

In the accommodation sector, the CSM coalition convinced and supported hotels and restaurants to adopt sustainability management procedures. As a result, the number of eco-certified hotel rooms grew to 7,200 at the time of COP15, from 12 per cent to 53 per cent of total capacity. Furthermore, over 75 per cent of the food supplied at the conference venue was organic and 100 local restaurants reduced their carbon footprint by using local produce (Bigwood and Luehrs, 2010). In terms of logistics, the main critique was the long queues at the venue entrances, caused by security measures, while public transportation was embraced by 94 per cent of the delegates. In order to accommodate this demand, Københavns Kommune worked together with bus companies to clear up the routes to and from the conference venue by diverting transportation toward peripheral areas. For individual transportation, the organisers used a fleet of over 200 low CO_2 vehicles (running on biogas, hydrogen or electricity).

> We have tried to make a new and different conference in Copenhagen. We have no bottled water, only pure, clean drinking water from the tap. Two thirds of all food here at the Conference is organic. We have tried as hard as possible to limit the carbon footprint of the conference.
> (HE Lars Røkke Rasmussen, Prime Minister of Denmark, opening speech at COP15, quoted in Bigwood and Luehrs, 2010)

By all means the overall sustainability performance during COP15 was not complete and valid critiques point out the predominant concern for environmental issues, the low profile of social aspects, the excessive flying by delegates and mostly to the disappointing outcome of the political negotiations during the event. However, from the management perspective of the event, the first attempt to organise such a large and high profile event in a sustainable manner deserves acknowledgement. As recognition, the COP15 was the first UN political summit certified according to the BS8901 Sustainable Event Management standard. A detailed account of the sustainability-driven initiatives was published by Bigwood and Luehrs (2010) in the sustainability report of COP15.

Level of change

Studies show that often infrastructure built for the sake of events ends up by being a long-term cost for the local community (Kasimati and Dawson, 2009). Wanting to avoid such a situation during COP15, the organisers decided to keep permanent structural adjustments to a minimum, replacing them with temporary structures, such as, for example, the additional 12,000 square meters of conference space, secured in pavilions that were dismantled after COP15.

One challenge for the COP15 organisers was a severe accommodation shortage, for 33,526 participants, more than double the amount estimated initially. Following the commitment to keep the level of changes in the community to a minimum, the CSM coalition decided to redirect guests towards the neighbouring city of Malmö (Sweden) despite the losses incurred by the commercial infrastructure in Copenhagen. Contrast other cases such as Los Angeles or South Africa where the commercial gains related to sport events surpassed community goals. Certainly, the size of the event made such trade-offs meaningful, which may not be the case for events that receive 500,000 visitors or more. As the capacity was still short of a few thousand beds, Københavns Kommune and the Ministry of Foreign Affairs invited residents to help by offering private accommodation to the conference guests. The response was very encouraging and over 3,000 Copenhageners offered their couches for free, a solution that was much welcomed by delegates with limited resources. Inviting residents to host COP15 guests was a good example of social inclusion, which solved the accommodation challenge while giving partial ownership of the event to local residents.

Ideally, setting acceptable levels for change in complex urban systems should rely on assessments of local resources available versus estimated (local and incoming) demand (Tidball and Krasny, 2007). Studies of sustainable regional development recommend the execution of environmental impact assessments before agreeing to host events. However, no environmental impact assessment was done for COP15 which is a shortcoming in its strategic planning. The absence of such assessments is not uncommon, as they are rather expensive and make costs of unsuccessful bids escalate (Hall, 1998) but can endanger winning bids. In 1993, Beijing lost the bid for the Olympic Games, lacking (among others) environmental action plans, only to win it in 2001 with three main themes: a green Olympics, a high-tech Olympics and a people's Olympics (Mol, 2010). Useful for informing decision-makers, assessments may also end up concluding that an event may be detrimental to a destination, a fact which may continue to hinder its use in this context. Controlling the level of change is important for reaching sustainable development (Tidball and Krasny, 2007) but it should not be confused with the absence of development. In its true meaning, sustainability means the persistence of functions over a long period of time or indefinitely, a goal followed by a strategic management of sustainable events.

Learning

Working with the sustainability goals during COP15 was a learning experience for all stakeholders involved. Starting from the adaptation of the UN Global Compact guidelines to the conditions and resources available in Copenhagen, a snowballing educational process commenced first with the partners of the CSM coalition and further onto the hospitality and utility providers. Research shows inter-organisational learning to be a strong connecting factor in multi-stakeholder groups, facilitating the creation of shared values, cooperation and innovation (Andersson and Getz, 2008) a fact confirmed during the meetings organised with hospitality stakeholders prior to COP15 to promote hotel eco-labelling and share relevant knowledge regarding sustainable events.

Research suggests that sustainable events have the potential to raise the awareness of participants and even change their behaviour (Andersson and Getz, 2008; Laing and Frost, 2010; Minnaert, 2012). A survey of the Danish Institute for International Studies on 603 Copenhagen residents shows that Danes had predominantly positive attitudes towards COP15, with nearly 57 per cent of respondents being proud of Denmark hosting it and only 13 per cent seeing it as more annoying than beneficial. Furthermore, 75 per cent of Copenhageners surveyed consider large events to be beneficial for Denmark's international reputation (Hvidt and Mouritzen, 2010). Despite these encouraging signs, there is no consistent evidence of a wider societal learning and awareness related to COP15. Activities such as the no-gift policy and the replacement of bottled water for guests were visibly successful with the participants and may have created a shared sentiment of civic responsibility.

Capitalising on success

The alliances created during COP15 built trust in the benefits of joining forces, skills and interests, while the success brought the confidence to continue. Aiming to consolidate the international image of Copenhagen as a host for sustainable events, the Danish Government offered to host the EU presidency in 2012, with a total of 100 meetings and 15,000 participants expected (Whiteling, 2011). The meetings are organised by the Danish Ministry of Foreign Affairs on behalf of the Danish Government, and will be located half in Copenhagen and half in Horsens (in Jutland, central Denmark). The strategy of dispersing the demand between two destinations is a way of avoiding infrastructure adjustments while distributing the benefits from hosting events to Danish regions less affluent than the capital city. This strategy is in contrast with the more obliging attitudes of South African hosts of the Soccer World Cup in 2010 (Death, 2011) where private interests in the economic returns kept all activities concentrated, preventing a wider distribution of benefits. The EU Presidency is expected to provide a turnover for the hotel and conference industry of DKK53 million (€7.1 million) (Dyrskjøt, 2012).

Building on the experience gained during the COP15, the Danish Government made it a top priority to organise the event in a sustainable way where possible and the MFA adopted a central approach to tender all supplier contracts in order to make sure that sustainability conditions are included in the final agreements. Aiming to secure organic food and energy efficient heating systems for over a hundred meetings at no additional costs, the MFA teamed up with private partners such as Grundfoss and Danfoss which sponsored thermostats and heat pumps for the venues used for the meetings. The final goal for the MFA is to achieve the new international ISO 20121 certificate for Event Sustainability Management System.

The cooperative public-private model was replicated once again for the hosting of the EU Presidency, with the creation of the Danish Sustainable Event Initiative as a resource for meeting planners, providing case studies and guidelines on sustainable event management. Renewing engagements and relationships developed during the COP15 event, the goal of the new initiative is to reinforce stakeholder trust and create shared values, and make Copenhagen known as a host for sustainable events. Counting on the trust of local service providers, nine more bids have been prepared for hosting events on sustainable energy management, clean air and sustainable water management in Copenhagen, between 2012 and 2018. However, the consolidation of the image of Copenhagen as a host for sustainable events will depend to a great extent on the local convention bureau, Wonderful Copenhagen, and its capacity to build the necessary skills and know-how regarding sustainable events.

Concluding remarks

The intergovernmental negotiations during COP15 had a less than optimal result with respect to global climate change initiatives. However, aside from its political achievements, which were not the subject for this exploratory research, the feedback regarding the management of the event was positive, and the organisers won (among other awards) the 'Oscar' of the meetings industry, the IMEX Green Meetings 2010 Gold Award as recognition of their efforts to reduce the environmental and social impacts of COP15 (MCI Group, 2012).

This is not to say that Copenhagen is the most advanced host of sustainable events, or that this chapter is an exhaustive account of strategies and factors related to sustainable events. Quite the contrary, the current exploration has only limited ambitions to generalise its conclusions, considering the specificity of the case in focus, namely a Scandinavian capital, with economic stability and high environmental awareness. Certain actions and strategies discussed in this chapter may be inaccessible to cities in other regions of the world. The findings presented in this chapter aim to bring proof of incipient stages of strategic management in destinations hosting sustainable events and to encourage further research into the critical factors that determine its success.

A few aspects need to be remembered from this research. First and foremost it is noteworthy that Copenhagen is committed to becoming a world renowned host for sustainable events, and launching its new image through the organisation of COP15 in 2009 was an undeniable success. However, the success went beyond the marketing campaigns and four strategic factors identified in this chapter frame the success of Copenhagen in hosting sustainable events:

- strong governance structure and public-private partnerships led by change agents truly committed to sustainable development, accompanied by a systematic management of event operations;
- keeping the changes required to accommodate events to a level that does not harm the quality of life of residents and visitors;

- inspiring inter-organisational learning and the development of specialised competences for organising sustainable events;
- consolidation of experience and practical skills.

A valid question is the longevity of the success that Copenhagen registered. While doubts may have existed after COP15, they are likely to have vanished after the city repeated the same performance in 2012, when it hosted the EU Presidency. Possibly hard to replicate, such follow-ups are good for developing local skills in sustainable event management.

Worth noting is a vague but unusual attitude that can be observed in the way that challenges raised by COP15 were met. Truth be told, the organisers of COP15 took a number of bold chances such as the heavy promotion (almost imposition) of public transportation or the no-gift policy, that could have failed and created frustration among delegates. Instead, the initiatives created a sense of solidarity and social inclusion which are desirable for sustainable events. Similarly, calling on local residents to accommodate the excess number of COP15 guests was a leap of faith on the side of the organisers, positively appreciated by locals. Uncompromising in their simplicity, such measures contrast grand structural changes customarily associated with events and show that attention to detail can contribute to reducing the environmental footprint of events. Such an attitude is yet another confirmation that often 'less is more' with regards to sustainability.

In order to survive over time, changes that enable a destination to absorb and metabolise events must be structurally suitable and institutionalised in the dynamic life of the host. A living proof of the success of sustainable living as a philosophy and everyday practice, Copenhagen is now featured as one of the world's sustainable cities and was rated as the coolest green city to visit (Styles, 2011).

Note

1 The authors gratefully acknowledge the open cooperation and insightful contributions received from representatives of the Danish Ministry of Foreign Affairs, Wonderful Copenhagen, MCI Group Copenhagen and Københavns Kommune.

References

Andersson, T.D. and Getz, D. (2008). Stakeholder management strategies of festivals, *Journal of Convention Event Tourism*, 9(3): 199–220. doi: 10.1080/1547014080 2323801.

Andranovich, G., Burbank, M.J. and Heying, C.H. (2001). Olympic cities: Lessons learned from mega-event politics. *Journal of Urban Affairs*, 23(2): 113–131.

Angel, S. and Hansen, P.J. (2006) *In Search of the Experience Economy*. Retrieved 9 October 2011 from http://meetingsnet.com/green_meetings.

Bigwood, G. and Luehrs, M. (2010). *Cop15 United Nations Climate Conference Copenhagen Event Sustainability Report*. Retrieved 2 February 2012 from www.sustainableeventsdenmark.org.

British Standards Institution (2012, 6 January) *BS 8901: Sustainability Management*

Systems for Events. Retrieved from www.bsigroup.co.uk/en/Assessment-and-Certifica-tion-services/Management-systems/Standards-and-Schemes/BS-8901/.

Budeanu, A. (2009). Environmental supply chain management in tourism: The case of large tour operators. *Journal for Cleaner Production*, 17(16): 1385–1392. doi: 10.1016/j.jclepro.2009.06.010.

Collins, A. (2009). Assessing the environmental impacts of mega sporting events: Two options? *Tourism Management*, 30(6): 828–837. Doi: 10.1016/j.tourman.2008.12.006.

Death, C. (2011). 'Greening' the 2010 FIFA World Cup: Environmental sustainability and the mega-event in South Africa. *Journal of Environmental Policy & Planning*, 13(2): 99–117. doi: 10.1080/1523908X.2011.572656.

Dyrskjøt, M. (2012, 2 January). EU-formandskab booster danskturism. *Børsen.Online*. Retrieved 10 February 2012 from http://borsen.dk/nyheder/politik/artikel/1/222566/eu-formandskab_booster_dansk_turisme.html.

Event Research International (2012, 3 May). *Responsible Events*. Retrieved 3 May 2012 from www.eventresearch.org.

Getz, D. (2008). Event tourism: Definition, evolution, and research. *Tourism Management*, 29: 403–428. doi:10.1016/j.tourman.2007.07.017.

Global Reporting Initiative (2012, 10 January). *Event Organizers Supplement*. Retrieved 12 December 2011 from www.globalreporting.org/reporting/sector-guidance/event-organizers/Pages/default.aspx.

Hall, M.C. (1998). Imagining, Tourism & Sports Event Fever: The Sydney Olympics and the Need for a Social Charter for Mega-Events. Paper presented at the *Sport in the City* conference, Sheffield, UK. 2–4 July 1998.

Hall, M.C. (2011). A typology of governance and its implications for tourism policy analysis. *Journal of Sustainable Tourism*, 19(4–5): 437–457. Doi: 10.1080/09669582.2011.570346.

Henderson, S. (2011). The development of competitive advantage through sustainable event management. *Worldwide Hospitality and Tourism Themes*, 3(3): 245–257. Doi: 10.1108/17554211111142202.

Hvidt, N. and Mouritzen, H. (2010) *Danish Foreign Policy Yearbook 2010*, Danish Insti-tute for International Studies. Retrieved 3 May 2012 from www.diis.dk/graphics/Publi-cations/Books2010/YB2010/YB2010-Danish-Foreign-Policy-Yearbook_WEB. pdfwww.standby.dk/news/27022.

Juul, F. (2011). Pænt turistår for København'. *Stand By*. Retrieved 20 January 2012 from www.standby.dk/news/27022.

Kanter, R.M. (1999). The enduring skills of change leaders. *Leader to Leader*, 13: 15–22. Doi: 10.1002/ltl.40619991305.

Katusiimeh, M.W. and Mol, A.P.J. (2011). Environmental legacies of major events: Solid waste management and the Commonwealth Heads of Government Meeting (CHOGM) in Uganda. *African Studies Quarterly*, 12(3): 47–65.

Kasimati, E. and Dawson, P. (2009). Assessing the impact of the 2004 Olympic Games on the Greek economy: A small macroeconometric model. *Economic Modelling*, 26(1): 139–146. Doi: 10.1016/j.econmod.2008.06.006.

Klijn, E. and Teisman, G.R. (2003). Institutional and strategic barriers to public-private partnership: An analysis of Dutch cases. *Public Money & Management*, 23(3): 137–146. Doi: 10.1111/1467–9302.00361.

Kogg, B. (2003). Power and incentives in environmental supply chain management. In S. Seuring, M. Muller, M. Goldbach and U. Schneidewind (eds), *Strategy and Organiza-tions in Supply Chains* (pp. 65–82). Physica-Verlag Heidelberg, Heidelberg.

Laing, J. and Frost, W. (2010). How green was my festival: Exploring challenges and opportunities associated with staging green events. *International Journal of Hospitality Management*, 29(2): 261–267. Doi: 10.1016/j.ijhm.2009.10.009.

Mair, J. (2010). The development of a conceptual model of greening in the business events tourism sector. *Journal of Sustainable Tourism*, 18(1): 77–94. Doi: 10.1080/09669580903291007.

MCI Group (2012, 9 January). *COP15 Wins IMEX Green Meetings Gold Award 2010*. Retrieved 9 February 2012 from www.mci-group.com/about/press/mci_news/MCI_IMEX_Green_Award.aspx.

Minnaert, L. (2012). An Olympic legacy for all? The non-infrastructural outcomes of the Olympic Games for socially excluded groups (Atlanta 1996–Beijing 2008). *Tourism Management*, 33(2): 361–370. Doi: 10.1016/j.tourman.2011.04.005.

Mol, A.P.J. (2010). Sustainability as global attractor: The greening of the 2008 Beijing Olympics. *Global Networks*, 10(4): 510–528. Doi: 10.1111/j.1471–0374.2010.00289.x.

Ooi, C. (2002). Contrasting strategies: Tourism in Denmark and Singapore. *Annals of Tourism Research*, 29(3): 689–706. Doi: 10.1016/S0160–7383(01)00086-X.

Ooi, C. and Pedersen, J.S. (2010). City branding and film festivals: Re-evaluating stakeholder's relations. *Place Branding & Public Diplomacy*, 6(4): 316–332. Doi: 10.1057/pb.2010.30.

Pelham, F. (2011). Will sustainability change the business model of the event industry?. *Worldwide Hospitality and Tourism Themes*, 3(3): 187–192. Doi: 10.1108/17554211111142149.

Region Hovestaden. (2012, 28 June). *Befolkning*. Retrieved from www.regionh.dk.

Richards, G. (2007). The festivalization of society or the socialization of festivals? The case of Catalunya. In G. Richards (ed.), *Cultural Tourism: Global and Local Perspectives*. New York: Haworth Press Inc.

Styles, R. (2011, 11 October). Copenhagen: Europe's coolest green city. *The Ecologist*. Retrieved 3 January 2012 from www.theecologist.org.

Tidball, K.G. and Krasny, M.E. (2007). From risk to resilience: What role for community greening and civic ecology in cities? In A. Wals (ed.), *Social Learning Towards a More Sustainable World* (pp. 149–164). Wagengingen, The Netherlands: Academic Press.

United Nations Framework Convention on Climate Change. (2009). *Fact Sheet: Minimising the Copenhagen Carbon Footprint*. Retrieved 8 February 2012 from www.unfccc.int/press/fact_sheets/items/5055.php.

United Nations Framework Convention on Climate Change. (2012a). *Background on the UNFCCC: The International Response to Climate Change*. Retrieved 8 February 2012 from http:www.unfccc.int/essential_background/items/6031.php.

United Nations Framework Convention on Climate Change. (2012b). *Fact Sheet: Copenhagen – Background Information*. Retrieved 8 February 2012 from www.unfccc.int/files/press/application/pdf/fact_sheet_copenhagen_background_information.pdf.

Whiteling, I. (2011, 10 October). Danish sustainable events initiative sets sights on green EU Presidency. *International Meetings Review*. Retrieved 9 February 2012 from http://internationalmeetingsreview.com/news/2011/10/03/Danish_sustainable_events_initiative_sets_sights_on_green_EU_Presidency.

Wiking, M. (2011, 17 October). Copenhagen – beyond green: The socioeconomic benefits of being a green city. *Mandag Morgen*. Retrieved 27 December 2011 from https://www.mm.dk/copenhagen-beyond-green.

11 Conventions and conferences
Trends and challenges in sustainability

George G. Fenich and Sandy Strick

While this textbook considers events, society, and sustainability from a broad perspective, this chapter focuses on the realm of meetings, incentive travel, conventions, and business events (MICE). The chapter begins with a discussion of sustainability and its evolution and quickly moves to a MICE focus. Discussion then proceeds to the practical economics of sustainability in MICE. That is followed by insights into the concept of 'greenwashing' as related to MICE followed by analysis of the perception of service versus quality.

Sustainability

This section of the chapter deals with the broad context of sustainability and how the concept is narrowed and focused on the MICE sector. As has been seen in previous chapters, the concept of sustainability includes social, economic, and environmental components. Yet many people do not have a good grasp or understanding of sustainability. According to the United States Environmental Protection Agency (EPA),

> sustainability creates and maintains the conditions under which humans and nature can exist in productive harmony, that permit fulfilling the social, economic and other requirements of present and future generations. Sustainability is important in making sure that we have, and will continue to have, the water, materials, and resources to protect human health and our environment.
>
> EPA (n.d.)

Given the size and breadth of the MICE industry, it impacts on a number of the aforementioned elements including: social interaction, economic activity, environmental resources, human health, the environment, and more. For example, the health issue called 'Legionnaires' Disease' was first identified when numerous attendees to an American Legion Convention were diagnosed. It was found that the disease bred in the HVAC system of the hotel and, given the concentration of convention attendees, rapidly spread among the group. In another example, one can consider that MICE traditionally used hard copy, printed material for dissemination of material. Switching to electronic distribution channels can have a huge impact. It would appear that 'sustainability' or the 'green movement' is touching the MICE industry.

What is a green meeting?

A green event is one designed, organised, and implemented in a way that mini-mises negative environmental impacts and leaves a positive legacy for the host community. In the international debate, 'greening events' include health and social concerns which should also be taken into consideration when aiming for a 'sustainable' event. It is based on the principles developed at ICLEI's Greening Events Symposium in Barcelona, September 2004. The Sustainable United Nations (SUN) unit in the United Nations Environment Programme believes that a green event is one organised in such a way that:

- emissions of greenhouse gases, such as CO_2, are minimised, and unavoid-able emissions are compensated for;
- natural resource consumption (including water and energy) is minimised and demand is adapted to available local resources;
- waste generation is avoided where possible and remaining waste is reused and/or recycled;
- biodiversity, water, air, and soil resources are protected;
- minimal environmental damage is caused while preparing and implementing the meeting;
- the local community benefits economically, socially, and environmentally both during and after the meeting, with local sustainable development encouraged to the extent achievable;
- the above principles are applied in purchasing goods and services for the meeting, the selection of the venue, transportation, catering, and accommo-dation arrangements;
- the awareness of participants, staff service providers, and the local com-munity in sustainability issues is increased, with the greening aims and measures communicated clearly to all, local hosts, regional and national authorities, sponsors, citizens groups, NGOs, business and technical experts are involved to the extent possible in order to comply with and support the above-stated principles.

(United Nations Environment Programme, 2009, Sec 2:9, p. 11)

For example, the David Lawrence Convention Centre in Pittsburgh, Pennsylva-nia (USA) was the first LEED certified convention centre in the US. LEED stands for Leadership in Energy and Environmental Design and consists of a group of rating systems for the design, construction, and operation of high per-formance green buildings, homes, and neighbourhoods. It was developed by the US Green Building Council (USGBC). The convention centre uses transparent ceiling material to admit natural sunlight thus reducing the need for electrical lighting, uses 'grey' wastewater to irrigate vegetation, natural ventilation, etc. Another example is the Vancouver (Canada) Convention Centre. Its design incorporates the largest 'green roof' in North America and uses native vegetation and habitats. Geothermal heating and cooling is achieved by utilising the constant temperature of the sea water adjacent to the centre. Grey water treatment reduces the use of potable water while translucent structural glass incorporates extensive use of daylight.

Parts of the tourism and convention industry now promote green meetings, conferences, and convention planning as demand for sustainability measures increases. Industry associations have produced standards and guides for green meetings. Government agencies and non-profit organisations also promote these practices with research, recommendations, grants, and technical support. Some private consultants in the meeting planning industry specialise in mounting green events, and industry groups and governments now sponsor awards to recognise achievements.

One notable industry group, the Green Meeting Industry Council (GMIC), is a membership based non-profit organisation which provides educational resources to planners, suppliers, and venues seeking to meet the ever-rising standards consumers set for sustainable meetings. The mission of the GMIC is to transform the global meetings industry through sustainability. The GMIC seeks to inspire, educate, and support leaders of all levels and disciplines who will manifest the transformation of the global meetings industry towards sustainability (GMIC, 2012).

Another recent initiative occurred on 28 October 2011, when the Convention Industry Council (CIC) announced that eight of the nine APEX/ASTM Environmentally Sustainable Meeting standards were complete. Thus, the meeting industry is on the cusp of embracing the very first green meetings and event standards. These standards were conceptualised and initiated by the Green Meetings Industry Council (GMIC) and the US Environmental Protection Agency (EPA). Development took place through a partnership between CIC's Accepted Practices Exchange (APEX), an initiative that focuses on industry best practices and ASTM International. The standards have been in development since 2007.

The APEX/ASTM standards will be comprised of nine individual 'sector' standards, covering all facets of event planning and management. The standards that have been ratified cover such areas as audio-visual, communication and marketing, materials, destinations, exhibits, food and beverage, meeting venues, and on-site transportation. Much of the work and research behind the standards was a result of the work done by the APEX Green Meetings and Events Practices Panel, consisting of 300 planners, suppliers, and sustainability experts from across nine time zones.

Parallel to the APEX/ASTM standards, the International Standards Organisation (ISO) is developing a sustainable events management standard, ISO 20121. The 'Global Reporting Initiative Event Organisation Sector Supplement' will provide an international framework for companies to report on their sustainability performance (Beer and Spatrisano, 2011). Sue Tinnish, ASTM liaison and chair of the ASTM committee on sustainability, is quoted in an article by Goldman (2010) as saying the standards introduce not only another level of complexity, but also another level to differentiate a meeting and to differentiate suppliers.

Another initiative relative to sustainability is exemplified in the collaboration of Green Key Global and The MPI Foundation Canada in the creation of the Green Key Meetings programme, a comprehensive assessment tool for hotel and resort properties that host meetings of any size. It was co-created by planner members of Meeting Professionals International (MPI) and reflects the needs of the business event industry. The assessment tool not only tells a hotel property what it has done to date, it provides a roadmap on how to improve. Performance is evaluated in six conference and meetings areas: (1) core areas (carbon, energy, waste, water, air quality); (2) communication (information, training); (3) activities (purchasing, auditing, community); (4) people (health); (5) exhibitions; and (6) audio/visual.

An example of private sector corporations embracing 'sustainability' was the joint announcement by two of the largest MICE industry suppliers that the Passkey 'GroupMAX' technology was being licensed by 'Green Housing Solution, Sustainable Meetings & Conventions' as its 'green' event housing solution. The technology allows processing of all hotel bookings electronically, thus lessening the environmental impact by saving resources and reducing waste. This is compatible with environmentally responsible policies and value propositions.

It would appear that 'green' conventions, meetings, conferences, and events are part of an international movement to achieve a sustainable world economy and livable planet. But is the 'green movement' really sustainable? Is this a long-term trend or a (relatively) short-term phenomenon? Or – will history repeat itself?

Repeat of history

Is 'sustainability', 'greening', or 'environmental sensitivity' a new trend? Consider the following timeline:

i   1962: Rachel Carson's *Silent Spring* comes out. It posits that the environment, economy, and social well-being are interconnected.

ii   1970: First Earth Day. Demonstrations to protest environmental abuses spark the creation of laws such as the Endangered Species Act and Safe Drinking Water Act.

iii   1972: The United Nations Conference on Human Environment is held in Stockholm. The concept of Sustainable Development is discussed and leads to many national environmental protection agencies.

iv   1974: Sherwood Rowland and Mario Molina publish their findings that chlorofluorocarbons (CFCs) can destroy the ozone molecules and may threaten to erode the Earth's protective ozone layer.

v   1987: 'Our Common Future' (Brundtland Report) is published. It says that

preserving the environment, addressing global inequities, and fighting poverty could fuel economic growth by promoting sustainable development
(NEA, 2011)

During the 1970s there was a decided focus on 'saving the environment'. This was fuelled, in part, by the 'gas crisis' (pun intended) of the early 1970s. Small, fuel efficient automobiles were all the rage, some housing was constructed to make maximum use of solar energy, photo cells appeared in roofs. But what happened? The 'green movement' faded with the economic prosperity of the 1980s and early 1990s. Much of the world became a 'throw away' society – economic prosperity allowed for the 'disposal' of waste rather than recycling, reduction, and recovery.

Is the current focus on sustainability just another phase or trend or fad? Is this trend somehow tied to the economy? Or has the developed world really 'changed its ways'? Only time will tell. The remaining sections of this chapter will provide some insights, but not answers, to this question.

The practical economics of sustainability

This section of the chapter delves into another perspective on sustainability: the economics. Everywhere meeting and event planners look these days, sustainability is a focus. Sustainability is said to be good – good for all stakeholders, constituents, and the environment. Given the size and scope of the MICE industry, it stands to reason that even the most modest sustainability initiative would have its results magnified many times. After all, a convention with thousands of attendees will eat, sleep, drink, take baths, have laundry and linen cleaned, consume cups/plates/cutlery, read from printed collateral, use transportation, etc. The impact is huge and, thus, any savings or economic efficiencies would also be huge.

It has been stated many times in the MICE industry that sustainability is good for the bottom line. 'In 2000, the EPA announced that conventions are the most energy-consuming activity compared to other leisure activities, and the second most water-consuming activity per trip because of the high dependency on hotel stays' (Park and Boo, 2010, p. 97). Thus, any reduction or cost savings will flow to the bottom line.

The following support this concept:

- Procurement or acquisition is a key factor in the ability to produce a meeting or event that saves money. The strategies employed under the acronym of the four 'R's' can help achieve these savings.
  - R1: Recycle – this strategy comes to mind most often when thinking about 'going green' and 'sustainability'. In the MICE industry, recycling can be one of the easiest cost savings strategies to request of vendors and suppliers. However, it can be difficult to convince attendees and participants to recycle. One way to help achieve attendee

participation is to use volunteers, stationed at the recycling bins and receptacles to provide assistance and instructions. Research has shown this to be an effective strategy that impacts the bottom line. However, in the MICE industry, recycling is not just a cost centre, it can be a revenue producer. Sponsors can be identified and derive benefits from being linked to 'a good cause'. They can sponsor the recycling bins, other recycling equipment, T-shirts that encourage recycling, and the training of volunteers.

- R2: Reuse – reuse items and materials that already exist. The easiest way to accomplish this is to find used items or equipment rather than 'brand new' – the effect on the bottom line is obvious. Another 'reuse' strategy that has been embraced by the MICE industry for years is 'rental' – rent items rather than purchasing them new and discarding them after the event. Some of the largest Exposition Service Contractors (ESCs) such as Freeman and GES have made their living for years on this concept. Further, even if the cost of rental matches the cost of buying new, the product is kept out of the landfill. Still another application of the 'reuse' strategy is in terms of what a product is made from – does it contain significant amounts of recycled content or 'post consumer waste'? In the case of steel or aluminum products the cost of recycled items is significantly less than new. 'Reuse' can also be implemented by undertaking an effort to 'donate' items or products at the conclusion of an event – food, clothing, carpet, etc. Name badges can be collected and 'reused' at a subsequent event thus reducing the cost for new badges. Collecting name badge holders for reuse at an event of 1,300 attendees can save approximately US$975 for the event organiser.

- R3: Reduce – cutting down on the quantity of 'stuff' used at a meeting, convention, or event can result in obvious cost savings. The MICE industry historically used printed, hard copy, for dissemination of information – at significant costs for the paper, printing, ink, shipping, and disposal; not to mention the environmental cost of the waste stream. Switching to electronic media such as CD-ROMs or memory sticks is effective; switching to an entirely electronic base such as smart phones is even more efficient and environmentally friendly. Another way the MICE industry is embracing this 'R' is by asking attendees, in advance, if they wish to receive a new tote bag for their conference materials or whether they will 'reuse' their own – and thus 'reduce' at tremendous savings to the event organisers. Some organisers even offer an incentive for NOT taking a conference bag such as an extra drink ticket for the reception. Reductions in paper products can also be achieved by changing from printed, hard copy signs to electronic. By doing so, not only is the waste stream reduced with commensurate economic advantages, but levels of service are improved through the ability to change signage in real time.

- R4: Rethink – when all of the above fail, or have been addressed, then a meeting planner must 'rethink' what they are doing. Use of 'virtual meetings' is a new, but increasingly common, approach to rethinking – do all potential participants need to 'physically' attend the event? Or can some attend using electronic means? Travel, meals, hotel, and other costs are significantly reduced. Making events shorter or more compact is another application of 'rethinking': do most association conferences need to be the typical three day/two night affairs? One can look at the expense statement for an event, line by line, to see where rethinking can be implemented (Zavada, 2011). Planners can rethink using paper or plastic by substituting real china, etc. and washing it. For example, using china service rather than disposables for a group of 2,200 attendees can eliminate more than 1,800 pounds of plastic products from being sent to a landfill.
- The Environmental Bottom Line – The four 'R's' listed above are synonymous with the term 'environmental bottom line' and they can significantly lessen the environmental impact of an event. The profit factor of an event is improved, while at the same time there are positive benefits for the environment: a win-win situation.

  The following are some hypothetical examples:
  - A large corporation might save nearly US$500,000 if it substituted water coolers instead of individual plastic water bottles at corporate events.
  - If an Association held its annual conference in a compact city centre conducive to walking it could save US$80,000 in transportation costs.
  - Reusing banners – 40,000 attendee conference, five days: US$89,250 in savings.
  - Reducing daily shuttles – 40,000 attendee conference, five days: US$60,000 in savings.
  - Reducing handouts – 1,300 attendee conference, two days: US$2,000 in savings.

So, if one believes the popular press, industry periodicals, and the concepts put forth above, planning and executing environmentally sustainable events isn't just about being environmentally responsible. They can have economic benefits for the event organiser. In fact, many environmentally friendly activities can actually save money. Or do they?

The other side of the coin (pun intended)

Most analysis of the effect of implementing sustainable or green initiatives in the MICE industry makes two assumptions that may be in error. First is the assumption that 'green' activities must be good. While this may support the notion of Corporate Social Responsibility (CSR) they may not support the bottom line. Second, the analyses tend to come from the relatively narrow perspective of 'the event itself'. In other words, the costs and benefits, or return on investment, is viewed from a single point in time. What occurs before and after the event is often not considered.

The entire investment or the entire cost is rarely considered.

Some examples:

- Bamboo is touted as a 'sustainable' alternative to plastic yet its costs of production are never included in ROI calculations.
- Large water jugs are being used as a 'green' alternative since their use eliminates individual water bottles. But where does the bulk water come from?; not the local water supply. How far does this 'bulk' water have to be trucked? What happens to these bulk water containers when they are empty? Are they reused or shipped to the landfill – just like small individual bottles? What is the cost to produce these large containers as compared to smaller, individual ones? What chemicals and energy are involved in their production?
- Much of the equipment and accessories used in green practices are very costly: LED lighting, solar panels, etc. So how long does it take for those costs to pay off? New LED lighting is claimed to last a lifetime – but what happens when these LED lights last longer than the building into which they are installed? Just think about how often a hotel, conference centre, or convention facility undergoes a remodeling – more often than once in fifty years. What happens to the lights and fixtures? How is that taken into consideration when calculating the 'practical economics?'
- It costs time and money to train employees to be part of any 'green' initiatives. How is that cost accounted for when determining the ROI or the bottom line effect of 'greening?' Further, it is assumed that these 'trained' employees are truly supportive of, and behind, these 'green' values and practices. What if they are not? Does it take them longer to do their job? What incentive is there for the employee? What is 'in it' for them? If the answer is financial, then how does that impact the bottom line?

The practical economics of sustainability in the MICE industry must take into consideration the three phases in the event process: pre-event, event itself, post-event. All costs and benefits incurred during the entire process must be taken into consideration.

Greenwashing

Sometimes an organisation feels the pressure to conform to the current societal practices and trends of promoting environmentally friendly programmes but for one reason or another cannot, or will not, actually implement those programmes. If an organisation promotes itself as having environmentally friendly programmes in order to maintain its public image, but in reality that promotion is exaggerated or used to distract attention from an organisation's less environmentally friendly activities, this is known as 'greenwashing'. As found in *Meetings, Expositions, Events and Conventions: An Introduction to the Industry* (Fenich, 2011) greenwashing is defined as:

> any misrepresentation by a company that leads the consumer to believe that its policies and products are environmentally responsible, when its claims are false, misleading, or cannot be verified. Greenwashing is also used to identify the practice of companies spending more money on the campaign to notify customers of their environmentally friendly efforts, than the efforts themselves.
>
> (p. 322)

Examples of greenwashing abound. It is very common for convention centres to place recycle bins in very visible public spaces in order to encourage attendees to recycle their unwanted paper. It is assumed that the convention centre will take the paper from the recycle bins and send it to the local recycling centre, thus reinforcing the environmentally friendly image of the facility. However, if upon further inspection in the back of the house, the planner discovers that the facility is merely emptying the recyclable paper bins in with other non-recyclables, this is greenwashing.

Another example is the transportation company that promoted itself as a 'green alternative'. When asked for an explanation, they reported as having annually planted trees to offset the carbon footprint created by their buses. However, upon further investigation, it was discovered that the transportation company had not actually planted any trees but were investigating the 'possibilities' (Wilson, 2009).

Greenwashing can take other forms as well. In some cases the supplier claiming to be green is in fact doing whatever they claim; however, it is what they don't say that causes the concern. This is the 'sin of the hidden tradeoff'. The sin of the hidden tradeoff is committed by suggesting a product or service is 'green' based on a very narrow set of standards or criteria and ignoring other important environmental issues. In such cases the product or service may be green as it is narrowly defined, but issues are ignored such as energy consumption, chemical use, or water usage. A recent study found that of 2,000 products and services claiming to be green, 98 per cent committed at least one sin of the hidden tradeoff (Barrios, 2009).

Many hotels promote their properties as being 'green' in part because they have installed low flow shower heads. However, many of these same hotels use excessive, non biodegradable packaging for their bath products – even though bulk dispensers and biodegradable packaging is available. The sin of the hidden tradeoff?

Popular products used in the MICE industry include plates made from bamboo. These are frequently used in situations where china is not practical or appropriate. Since bamboo regenerates quickly it is a 'sustainable resource' and considered a 'green' alternative to the standard paper plates. However, the use of bamboo is not at all green when considering the amount of greenhouse gas emissions, water, and toxic chemicals needed to produce these plates (Dobin, 2009).

Along the same lines as the example above is the use of corn based plates, utensils, and cups. Suppliers promote these to meeting planners as 'green' and 'sustainable' alternatives to plastic. However, corn based products cannot be mixed with plastic for recycling – they must be separated. Is this more 'eco-friendly'? And what if, as is the case in much of the US, the nearest composting facility is hundreds of kilometres away?

Today, it is common for meetings, conferences, and conventions to provide refillable plastic water bottles to attendees in lieu of individual, single use, bottles of water. This is done in an effort to be 'green'. However, some of these bottles are constructed from materials that emit unhealthy chemicals. Further, no one has studied the flow of these 'bottles' after the event. Are they really reused by attendees? Are they thrown away in the hotel room? Disposed of at home? If so, then the benefit of using bulk water and individualised bottles is minimised and it might be the case that this approach is even worse for the environment than typical pre-packaged bottles. Further, no one has assessed the cost to produce 'thick walled' reusable bottles versus 'thin-walled', single use bottles.

Another example is that of a major MICE industry convention held in the Western US. The Association organising and sponsoring the convention encouraged attendees to use the contracted 'shuttle busses' to travel between the convention centre and the host hotels. This 'green' initiative was purported as being made even 'greener' because many of the shuttles used alternative energy and were run on reduced schedules to reduce the carbon footprint. The result was that many attendees had to wait over thirty minutes or more for a shuttle – many would not wait and used taxi cabs for personal transportation. Is this greenwashing?

Another MICE industry convention selected the host city because it had a light rail system that ran through much of 'downtown', including the host hotels and the convention centre. This 'system' was extensively promoted by the local Destination Marketing Organization (DMO) as a benefit in selecting this city. However, while the light rail system did run from the front of the hotels it ran behind the convention centre. It was a six block walk from the light rail station to the main entrance to the convention centre. Greenwashing?

So what should planners do to avoid being a victim of greenwashing? According to Nancy Wilson of Meetings South (Wilson, 2009):

- Planners need to do their research and know what their suppliers are promoting. If they say they are green ask about the specifics. What practices are really in place and can they be verified?
- A clear understanding of the green terminology will help planners ask informed questions. Terms such as 'recyclable', 'post consumer waste', and 'natural' can be interpreted many ways.
- Be clear on the criteria used in marketing and certifications claims. The MICE industry has introduced quite a few, such as APEX Green Meetings,

Green Seal (US), Green Key (Canada), and Green Globe (Europe and Australasia). These are all third-party certifications that look at green operations. LEED certification looks at green construction. When researching eco-labels and certifications, look for those that use clear criteria, adopt third-party verification, and report regularly on their environmental performance.

- Don't be afraid to go behind the scenes. Plan to include green practices when doing a site inspection, and be prepared with appropriate questions. Planners should talk to convention centre employees and ask about the procedures they follow in their daily routines. This will help to verify green practices and is an effective way to ensure that venues who claim to be green are actually operating in a green manner. Ask to see the laundry room, kitchen, or the supply rooms and areas where waste is sorted. Suppliers who are proud of their green practices will be happy to show off their practices and procedures.
- Planners need to take a look at their own practices. A planner who promotes green meetings with the expectation that suppliers and vendors will be green but has not made the same commitment in his/her own office is greenwashing.
- It is important for planners to know what statements they are making, what they are buying and what they are selling. Verifying the green claims that are made is as important as any other sound business practice. It is a planner's job to make sure that declarations of green practices can be supported and not just assumed.

Greenwashing is not a new phenomenon. As far back as the 1960s there are examples of companies exaggerating their green practices in order to be seen in a favourable light by their customers. It is the planner who must be informed and vigilant and not allow unethical green practices to infiltrate the MICE industry.

Service versus quality perception in the MICE industry

Perhaps one of the largest hurdles to overcome in the effort for becoming more sustainable is the perception that green equates to inferior products and service quality. This framework dates back to the days when recycled paper had a greyish tint, was expensive, and was generally considered to be inferior in quality. In those early days other recycled products were expensive to produce and frequently had no reuse. Many of today's consumers still remember those days and it influences their perceptions of sustainability. This sometimes puts planners and convention services managers in an awkward situation. Deciding where the line can be drawn may be a function of the budget, the group, and the resources available.

Consider, for instance, a typical large three-day convention with approximately 2,200 attendees. By not pre-filling water glasses at banquet tables during three days of served lunches, attendees will conserve 520 gallons of water. That amount, by all accounts, is significant. To some attendees this is an excellent example of making a convention greener. To other attendees this is an example of poor quality service. To the convention staff, it is much more practical to pre-pour the 2,200 glasses of water before the attendees are seated so that service of the meal can be more efficient and timely without the cost of hiring extra servers. In trying to be 'greener' the same convention might opt to serve some of the meals using plates, utensils, and napery that is completely compostable. However, corn based utensils are notorious for becoming limp and flexible thus providing 'inferior' quality. There is an obvious tradeoff between 'green' and 'service quality'.

Suppose at that same banquet the planner decides to use natural centrepieces for the tables. Again, we are faced with a dilemma. If it appears that someone has stepped outside and cut down tree limbs for centrepieces this hardly seems like an appropriate table decoration for an upscale event, and it is not likely to be an acceptable substitute for cut flower arrangements (however green it may be). However, perhaps the planning staff could choose potted plants instead of cut flowers. Potted plants can be reused for other events, last longer than cut flowers, make appropriate table decor at a fraction of the price of cut flower arrange-ments, and they do not have to end up in the landfills. Another alternative may be to select a dessert that can also serve as a centrepiece. As long as the dessert is safe to leave out for the duration of the meal, this will decorate the table in a fun way and help with quick and efficient table service. However, as noted above, groups who expect table service to mean being served at the table and not self-service may consider desserts used as centrepieces as inferior as that of grey recycled paper.

If a five-day convention chooses to serve the 2,200 attendees on china instead of plastic disposables for breaks, breakfasts, lunches, and receptions, it prevents 1,890 lbs of plastic from going into a landfill according to the Convention Indus-try Council's Green Meetings Report (2010). The use of china certainly implies upscale service. However, from a venue's point of view, service for 2,200 people means owning a lot of dishes. It also means the dishes have to be washed and stored and there must be employees available to accomplish these functions. In addition, the use of china may restrict some of the more creative aspects of meal events such as boxed lunches or offsite meal events.

The debate continues even outside of the dining environment. At a recent convention of 500 corporate executives, attendees received high quality refill-able water bottles and pitchers of water were placed in multiple locations throughout the convention hall. Attendees refused to fill their own bottles and the planner ultimately requested that the convention centre provide pre-filled, single use, commercial water bottles. Unfortunately for that event the addition of the pre-filled water bottles impacted the budget by adding an additional US$5,000 in costs. Or, there was the registrant that defiantly asked the registra-tion clerk why he had to pay so much money for the conference registration only to have to download and print his own conference materials.

The service/quality perception of sustainability efforts goes beyond food and beverage. Many hotels, especially those outside the US, are using special controls that shut down the utilities in a guest room when it is not occupied. This is being promoted as a 'green' effort and organisations are selecting these hotels, in part, because of this effort. However, especially when the weather is warm, stopping the air conditioning in a guest room causes the temperature to rise. It takes some period of time after the system is 're-activated' to bring the temperature back down to the desired setting. This is perceived as 'inferior' service by many guests. In fact, some guests circumvent the systems that require the room key card to be inserted into the activation switch by obtaining duplicate key cards: one to take with them when they leave the room and the other to leave in the switch to keep it activated. The temperature vs. service issue comes up again in facilities that decide to raise (or lower) the interior room temperature by one or two degrees in order to save energy. Meeting attendees may view the higher (lower) temperature as 'inferior service'.

As has been mentioned is other parts of this chapter, convention centres are at the forefront of 'sustainability' efforts. A popular 'green' design element is the use of transparent or translucent ceiling panels. While this decreases the use of electricity for lighting it also means that rooms with such ceilings cannot be 'darkened' when electronic presentations are made. The same holds true for meeting rooms with large windows. This is viewed by some as 'inferior' service quality. Some convention planners have reduced the frequency of shuttle bus service in an effort to reduce their carbon footprint. Is this 'inferior service?'

The final analysis of the service vs. quality perception in green meetings and events

In all of these cases, educating attendees is what it takes to gain acceptance and buy-in. Getting buy-in is a process that, for most, has to evolve. For planners it is important to first understand the business objectives of both the hosting group and the attendees, and begin with efforts that take those objectives into consideration. Then market on-site. Tell attendees what the ecological objectives for the convention are and get them involved. Attendees will buy in to the efforts to go green if they understand the reason. Finally, planners have to broadcast successes. For example, attendees and even the press need know how much water and how much money were saved by using water coolers instead of pre-filled commercial water bottles. Or, how many tons of trash was diverted from the landfill due to their efforts to reduce the amount of paper handouts. Planners and organisers in the MICE industry need to 'toot their own horn' when it comes to implementation of 'sustainability' practices.

Summary

The primary goal of this chapter was to propel the discussion of 'sustainability' and 'greening' into the meetings, exhibitions, events, and conventions realm. The major themes in the discussion were: (1) sustainability and greening in the MICE industry; (2) the practical economics of sustainability; (3) 'greenwashing'; and

(4) the tension between service delivery and service perception when embracing 'greening'.

Besides these distinct themes, one over-arching issue has come to light in this chapter: the need to consider the entire life cycle ('cradle to grave', 'field to table') of sustainable or green initiatives. One must analyse the three phases in MICE management: pre-event, event itself, and post event. Thus, one cannot focus analysis or cost-benefit looking solely at the event itself. For example, it has been shown that some venues, in trying to appear green, put out recycling containers. If one looks solely at the event then the venue would be viewed as being green. But what if, after the close of the event, waste is not kept separated and recycled but commingled with all the other trash and hauled, in bulk, to the landfill. Another example is the use of bamboo as an event material. While bamboo looks very good since it is compostable and decomposes (from an event and post-event perspective) but has very high production and transportation costs at the front end (pre-event). Within the context of studying 'life cycles' are the thick plastic, reusable, refillable water bottles that have become common in registration bags. This obviously eliminates the need for individual bottles of water at the event, but no one has studied the cost of production and shipping on the front end (pre-event) or what happens to them after the event (post event).

It should go without saying – but really needs to be reiterated – meeting and event planners must (1) understand the wants and needs of the host organisation as well as attendees and (2) inform and educate hosts and attendees regarding how those needs are being met. One cannot 'assume' an attendee, inherently, knows the value of a sustainability effort nor may even know that a given initiative is green. The planner must tell them.[1]

Note

1 For greater insight see *Meetings, Expositions, Events and Conventions: An Introduction to the Industry* (Fenich, 2011), in particular Chapter 13: Green Meetings and Social Responsibility, by Sandy Strick.

References

APEX/ASTM Environmentally Sustainable Meeting Standards. Retrieved 27 January 2012, from www.conventionindustry.org/StandardsPractices/APEXASTM.aspx.

Barrios, J. (2009). How to Avoid Green Washing Sin #1: The Hidden Trade-off. *EcoVillageGreen*. Retrieved 27 January 2012, from http://ecovillagegreen.com/1002/how-to-avoid-greenwashing-sin-1-the-hidden-trade-off/.

Beer, M. and Spatrisano A. (2011, 15 December). Best of 2011: Mitchell Beer and Amy Spatrisano on Setting Sustainability Standards. *BizBash*. Retrieved 23 December 2011, from www.bizbash.com/best_of_2011_mitchell_beer_and_amy_spatrisano_on_setting_sustainability_standards/toronto/story/21828.

Convention Industry Council (2010). *Green Meetings*. Retrieved 27 January 2012, from www.conventionindustry.org/StandardsProctices/GreenMeetings.aspx.

Dobin, D. (2009). Greenwashing Harms Entire Movement. *Lodging Hospitality*, 65(14), 42–43.

EPA (n.d.). *What is Sustainability?* Retrieved 27 January 2012, from www.epa.gov/sustainability/basicinfo.htm.

Fenich, G.G. (2011). *Meetings, Expositions, Events and Conventions: An Introduction to the Industry.* Upper Saddle River, NJ: Pearson Prentice Hall.

GMIC. (2012). *About Us.* Retrieved 27 December 2011, from www.gmicglobal.org/?page=AboutUS.

Goldman, M. (2010). *The Green Standard, Green Meetings.* Retrieved 23 December 2011, from www.meetingsfocus.com/ArticleDetails/tabid/162/ArticleID/14198/Default.aspx#top.

NEA. (2011). Retrieved October 2011, from www.nea.gov.sg/cms/sei/SEIsustainabilitytimeline.pdf.

Park, E. and Boo, S. (2010). An Assessment of Convention Tourism's Potential Contribution to Environmentally Sustainable Growth. *Journal of Sustainable Tourism*, 18(1), 95–113.

United Nations Environment Programme (2009). *Green Meeting Guide 2009.* Retrieved 15 January 2012, from www.unep.fr/shared/publications/pdf/DTIx1141xPA-GreenMeetingGuide.pdf.

Webster's New Millennium Dictionary of English. (2005). 'Greenwash'. Retrieved 27 January 2012, from http://dictionary.reference.com/browse/greenwash.

Wilson, N. (2009). What is Greenwashing? *Meetings South*, p. 1. Retrieved 27 January 2012, from www.meetingsfocus.com/Topics/ArticleDetails/tabid/162/ArticleID/11625/Default.aspx#top.

Zavada, N. (2011). *Are You Saving Green? Going Green.* Retrieved 23 December 2011, from www.meetingsfocus.com/Topics/ArticleDetails/tabid/162/ArticleID/15708/Default.aspx#top.

Part IV

Insights from the field

Case studies

12 Juggling the environmental, social and economic benefits and costs of a green event

Brooke Porter and Merrill Kaufman

Introduction

Whale Day is Maui's longest free annual event. The first Whale Day was held in 1980, as a way to celebrate the founding of the non-governmental organisation (NGO) (501c3) Pacific Whale Foundation and acknowledge the community's support for whale conservation. The inaugural event, planned by the few founding staff, included a free concert, a five-kilometre pledge-walk/run, donated food concessions and informational displays at a public park. In the following years, the event expanded to include displays by other local environmental organisations and children's educational activities. The focus of the event has always been the annual migration of the North Pacific humpback whale and the surrounding marine environment, which includes important breeding grounds for these animals.

The Maui Whale Festival is designed to support the Pacific Whale Foundation's mission of protecting the oceans through science and advocacy. This is achieved in part by producing an event and festival that models innovative environmental initiatives and provides marine education to residents and visitors alike. The festival creates an innovative interface for the public to actively engage in advocacy through a combination of free and fee-based events. As a festival that prioritises conservation, The Maui Whale Festival continues to grow and evolve with the support of a small island community. The growth and expansion of what was once a small single-day event to a conservation-themed festival that now lasts an entire season is perhaps the most compelling evidence of the success of Whale Day and the Maui Whale Festival.

Events have long been used to mark global actions, celebrate change and gain support for issues. Today the spectrum of event themes is notable. Chwe (1998) finds that metaknowledge or common knowledge is a fundamental characteristic of an event and the intersubjectivity of the group is a defining factor in event participation and involvement. Rao (2001, p. 74) adds that 'public festivals have public goods aspects that go beyond pure entertainment. They [festivals] provide a socially sanctioned arena for publicly observable action.' For these reasons, festivals create a unique interface to encourage support of a specific theme. Simply stated, there is power in numbers as well as a validation of purpose and beliefs.

Building on the idea that an event has a purpose beyond entertainment, a study by Gursoy *et al.* (2004) describes four dimensions of an event: community cohesiveness; economic benefit; social incentives; and social costs. What is unique about these domains is their rankings of perceived importance. In line with Chwe (1998) and Rao (2001), the findings of Gursoy *et al.* (2004) and Yolal *et al.* (2009) suggest that the social benefits such as community cohesiveness and social incentives are of greater importance than the perceived social costs to the community. The theory of social incentives and community cohesiveness associated with events (Gursoy *et al.*, 2004) is highly applicable to the realm of environmentally minded or green events. A comparative study by Pearce and Nicholson (2001) demonstrated that the event theme was a dominating factor in the attendance motivation; therefore, when considering the attendee motivation for a green event such as those that make up the Maui Whale Festival, some commonality in participants' environmental values is assumed. From the organisational perspective, the festival and events create an interface to further an environmental message and mission.

Aside from the theme or message of an event, participant entertainment and enjoyment remain a significant factor in the overall success and sustainability of recurring events (Spangenberg *et al.*, 2006; Yolal *et al.*, 2009). The majority of events are associated with an exciting, fluid environment that is host to a mobile participant. The organisational goal is to host a flow of visitors through multiple offerings, with some events lasting only a single day. Therefore, a short-term offering that focuses on movement and fun must be supported by conveniences that are equally as mobile (e.g. food on a stick), and in many cases disposable (e.g. flat/tableware). For an environmentally minded organisation the challenge is threefold. First, the event must produce a desirable festival atmosphere (Yolal *et al.*, 2009). Second, the event must benefit the organisation by raising awareness for a mission-based issue, generating profits to support organisational goals or a combination of both. Third, the event should highlight, model and reinforce the conservation-based aspects promoted within the organisational mission. As a result, a host organisation with a conservation-based mission is faced with a juggling act of environmental, economic and social components. The question is: which ball gets dropped and why? This chapter will explore the evolution of a long-running event in Maui, Hawaii: the Pacific Whale Foundation's annual Maui Whale Festival and its associated green events. The successes and challenges of adhering to a conservation-centric mission will be described as they apply to eco-appropriate event planning, implementation and evaluation. The preparation and considerations given to the individual components of the Maui Whale Festival, and its marquee event, Whale Day, will be analysed and discussed individually.

The beginning

The fight to save the whales was a well-known conservation movement of the twentieth century. Though the fight is far from over, 'end whaling' campaigns have had a positive impact on raising awareness for global whale populations including the North Pacific humpback whale stock. By the early 1980s the previously decimated North Pacific humpback whale population had begun to stabilise (Calambokidis *et al.*, 2008) following the protection afforded by the US Marine Mammal Protection Act in 1972.

Concurrently, the scientific community began to quantify a deeper understanding of biology and behaviour (Forestell, 2007). Additionally, marine tours with the specific intent to view whales began in Maui, Hawaii. The Pacific Whale Foundation pioneered a shift in the experience from the standard cocktail cruise to educational programmes delivered by field researchers focused on interpreting humpback whale natural history and promoting marine conservation (Forestell and Kaufman, 1992). These tours allowed visitors and residents the chance to view and experience an endangered species first-hand. Increased awareness of and efforts to protect humpback whales quickly gained public support, and the 1979–1980 Hawaii whale season (November–May) marked the inaugural Whale Day celebration.

The first decade of Whale Day celebrations developed with in-kind support as the Pacific Whale Foundation and the idea of 'saving the whales' began to take hold both locally and nationally. During the 1990s, Whale Day transitioned from an event focused on raising awareness to a sustainable generator of funds for the organisation's public education and conservation efforts. In its third decade, the Foundation's mission developed a unique conservation identity within the Whale Day celebration. This evolution has led to the creation of the Maui Whale Festival, a designation of several months each year with multiple events that in 2011 represented more than 30 agencies on Maui and attracted over 20,000 participants.

Early on the Foundation began to notice repeat visitors during its annual event; a phenomena that Yolal *et al.* (2009) describe as the result of an event significantly contributing to social life. The annual 'tradition' of attending Whale Day was formally recognised in 2008 when the Pacific Whale Foundation launched a contest to honour repeat visitors by challenging attendees to wear their oldest Whale Day t-shirt. The 2012 Maui Whale Festival marks the re-branding of its 32nd marquee event as World Whale Day in recognition of the expanded international following of the host organisation, the Pacific Whale Foundation.

Calendar of events

The Maui Whale Festival calendar of events spans over six months beginning with a 'Welcome Home the Whales' celebration and ending with a 'Farewell to the Whales' send-off cruise. The Festival is timed to coincide with 'whale watch season' and includes free talks by whale experts, special VIP whale watch cruises, shore-based whale watching programmes, events for students and youth, a citizens' count of whales that can be seen from shore, as well as World Whale Day and the Run and Walk for the Whales. This diverse array of events offers multiple opportunities to prioritise conservation strategies and communicate marine conservation through minimal impact events.

The event calendar is full throughout whale season with daily activities, such as the whale interpretation stations, expanding the potential audience of participants for subsequent events. Larger events such as the Run for the Whales, Keiki E.C.O. (Educating Children Outdoors) Day, World Whale Day and the Great Maui Whale Count continue to mark major annual affairs. These major events are scheduled for three consecutive weekends each February. The design and components are continuously modified to improve the products to best support the organisation's mission while generating support and interest from attendees. For example, even the smallest components of these events such as the recycled content of the toilet paper have been considered. While such a change may go unnoticed by attendees, modifications concerning the recycled content of materials directly relate to the organisation's mission. When possible such changes are advertised via signage throughout the events presented as 'Did you know?' fun facts.

Large events rely heavily on products that are disposable and convenient (e.g. bottled water). The line between sustainability and convenience can be difficult to negotiate in terms of practicality. Sustainability initiatives may conflict with available labour, resources and profit-generating objectives, whereas convenience factors may affect overall satisfaction of participants. In an attempt to create a green event, host organisations face decisions that may compromise the mission-based conservation goals and/or undermine the community cohesiveness necessary to sustain long-term support for the event. A zero-impact event is an impossible proposition. Offset programmes may offer repentance for associated actions, although participation in such programmes does not guarantee environmentally responsible actions. The environmental consideration of the products, the potential to educate participants and evoke their support for the marine environment, as well as the economic sustainability, influence the modification of the events; compromises are a reality. The challenges of creating a green festival are critically explored through four Maui Whale Festival standalone events.

Run for the Whales

The Run for the Whales is held one week prior to World Whale Day. The event originally began with a five-kilometre (K) run and has since grown into a multiple-race event that includes a 5K run, 5K walk, half marathon and a 2K kids' fun run. The expectations of athletes participating in a sporting event limit the flexibility of the event components. Water stations, runners' packets and prizes have remained non-negotiable.

A notable idea to reduce waste at water stations included replacing disposable cups with 'rehydration' volunteers armed with water guns; however, after consultation with local running clubs it became obvious that this would compromise participant satisfaction. To date, the water station remains unchanged relying upon single-use cups. At a significant increase in cost to the organisation, paper cups were replaced with biocompostable cups. Other components of the run have been modified over the past decade to maximise the Foundation's mission. For example, standard medallions have been replaced with locally, handcrafted ceramic pendants that are strung on all-natural *ti* leaf *lei*. Replacing imported medals with locally sourced pendants has reduced the carbon footprint of the event; additionally, the nylon neck ribbons used to string the medals have been replaced with biodegradable *lei*. Event prizes include complimentary passes to a variety of the educational ecotours to promote ongoing involvement in the organisation and appreciation of the marine environment.

Trash reduction continues to be an ongoing challenge at the organisational level. To improve this aspect of the Run for the Whales, the organisation looked to in-kind donations for the use of reusable bags to package the contents of the runners' packets. Runners' packets typically include small 'freebies' for participants, and brochures and information about the organisation and sponsors. Realising that the majority of the paper in the packets is discarded, Pacific Whale Foundation strategically places numerous 'brochure recycle' containers around the event. A significant number of brochures are collected during the event and recycled for later use. Innovative products, such as biocompostable tableware (e.g. cups, plates and utensils) are utilised for post-race food service. In addition, menu items are served as finger foods to minimise the need for utensils and further reduce the overall trash.

Although flexibility of a sporting event in conforming to an environmental mission may be limited, multiple transferable strategies have been developed throughout the history of the Run for the Whales. Actions such as sourcing local artisans for production of the medals, providing meaningful and/or recyclable contents in the participant packets, modelling innovative products (e.g. biocompostable tableware) and promoting local business and environmental stewardship through the prize considerations are recommended as simple strategies for greening a sporting event.

Keiki E.C.O. Day

Children's education has been a priority of Pacific Whale Foundation since its inception. *Keiki* is a Hawaiian word used to describe youth. The *Keiki* Whale-A-Thon has been a popular component of World Whale Day that merged physical activity with education and interpretation of the migratory cycle of the humpback whale. A long-time advocate for education-based outdoor experience (e.g. Forestell and Kaufmann, 1990), in 2010 the Pacific Whale Foundation opted to expand the children's education feature of World Whale Day to a separate event the day prior to World Whale Day. The economic growth of the Maui Whale Festival in the previous years allowed the Pacific Whale Foundation to offer a day of subsidised educational field trips, including transportation to and from local schools. The new day event became known as *Keiki* E.C.O. Day. The goal of *Keiki* E.C.O. Day is to provide educational activities that promote the organisation's mission while concurrently meeting national and state science objectives.

Keiki E.C.O. Day includes a series of hands-on, outdoor learning workshops for elementary school students. The Pacific Whale Foundation works with local businesses to create educational field trip activities that promote environmentalism at the island level. All education stations are related to the broader island ecosystem, both terrestrial and marine, including the flagship species, the humpback whale. Through partnerships with local organic farmers, abstract concepts such the benefits of buying local are simplified in activities in stations such as 'Snacks You Can Grow' (see Figure 12.1). Reducing waste and minimising runoff through the use of organic fertilisers are reinforced by 'A Worm Ate My Lunch' activity. In-kind support from a local vermi-farm allows classrooms to learn the basics of vermi-composting and take a worm box back to the classroom. The role of coastal restoration and the importance of responsible beach use (e.g. keeping pets leashed) are learned through partnership with other organisations as students design and create a mock outdoor nature trail and discuss the benefits of creating controlled spaces for humans to appreciate and interact with nature.

Keiki E.C.O. Day was developed solely as a socially profitable event. The significant investment of effort and financial resources to create the infrastructure for World Whale Day is exploited for the benefit of fulfilling the organisation's mission within the local community. The majority of student participants return the following day for World Whale Day (authors' observations). This design supports the Forestell and Kaufman model (1992) by providing nearly immediate reinforcement for E.C.O. Day participants to 'try on' new ideas about nature-based learning and environmental stewardship in a setting seeded with like-minded individuals (Pearce and Nicholson, 2001).

Figure 12.1 Vince Mina of Maui Aloha Aina and Kahanu Aina Organic Sprouts gives an animated presentation to local school children about the benefits of eating local produce and growing your snacks. The participants learn how sprouts are grown and get to taste the pre-grown produce. This presentation is one of many experiential learning stations at *Keiki* E.C.O. day.

World Whale Day

World Whale Day, the marquee event held annually in mid-February, affords a unique opportunity to showcase sustainable alternatives to the usual festival challenges associated with waste generation, transportation and souvenirs. From its simple roots, World Whale Day has now become a large-scale event that aims to positively impact each of its participants through the jovial atmosphere of a festival. The event begins with a marine-themed parade and takes place entirely outdoors utilising county park space in South Maui. Each major component of World Whale Day is discussed individually.

Pacific Whale Foundation organisation tent

The organisation's booth acts as a place to bring the mission to life. Departments form the foundational pillars of the organisation: research (where the new know-ledge comes from), education (how that knowledge is disseminated to the public) and conservation (the practical application of the knowledge by making the public care about the marine resource) offer interactive displays that highlight local issues affecting the marine environment. Ecotours, as well as organisation membership and themed logo wear, are sold with all proceeds funding the ongoing research and education programmes of the organisation. These offerings provide direct communication channels to the festival attendees as well as eco-nomic benefit to the organisation; therefore, the host tent is strategically placed to ensure maximum flow of visitors.

Pacific Whale Foundation membership is offered at the event as an oppor-tunity to connect with the tone of the event and to provide participants a chance to declare a tangible connection to the mission. Pacific Whale Foundation mem-bership increases 32 per cent over a five-year average compared to other days in early February (Pacific Whale Foundation, 2011). The increase in membership registration may be an occurrence of social validation for participants as they associate themselves with the user image of the product (Jin-Soo *et al.*, 2011).

Other organisational offerings, such as the Whale Regatta, are designed to create an economic support system ahead of the event when many of the World Whale Day infrastructure costs are realised (e.g. insurance, tent, entertainment and electrical deposits). The rubber ducky race becomes a Whale Regatta by substituting bath-toy whales for ducks. Appeals for support begin months before the event to generate funds during a time when other sources of income (e.g. tourism products) are low.

Children's activities – Keiki *Carnival*

The usual games and activities of a children's carnival have been modified over the years to meet basic educational objectives. For example, the standard mallet-catapult game is now known as the krill-a-pult. The objective is to 'feed the krill' to the humpback whale by catapulting small shrimps into a large whale mouth painted on canvas. Other carnival games include a mock humpback whale competition pod, or a safe human form of bumper cars. To further the environmental message, carnival prizes including samples of reef-safe sunscreen, edible coral reef treats and 'license to migrate' ID tags that children can use to label their school packs have replaced the useless imported, plastic novelties. New for 2012 World Whale Day, *Keiki* Carnival will include 'The Whale Trail' – a self-guided walking tour on the footpath around the event grounds designed as a scaled-down humpback whale migration with stops for interactive games and exercises. By modifying existing carnival activities (e.g. games) and creating additional low budget activities (e.g. walking tours), the traditional carnival works to convey aspects of the mission to a specific audience.

Food service

Local partner restaurants purchase tent space to provide the bulk of food service. The Pacific Whale Foundation has strict requirements about the menu items served as well as the tableware used. Styrofoam, plastic, drinking straws or non-recycled paper disposables are banned items. Biocompostable flatware and paper goods with high-recycled content are provided to each food vendor by the host organisation at cost. Additionally, any restaurant partner choosing to serve seafood must conform to sustainable recommendations of the Seafood Watch Program. The Pacific Whale Foundation participates as a programme partner in Monterey Bay's Seafood Watch Program; this programme is designed to promote consumer awareness for sustainable seafood. Pocket cards that denote responsible and irresponsible seafood menu items are available throughout the event. Posted signage at each food booth highlights locally sourced products and sustainable seafood items.

One challenge that the organisation has struggled with throughout the years is water service. Single-use plastic water bottles are arguably the most convenient product for a large event. The sales generated by the purchase of water contribute significantly to the total profits; however, the waste generation from the plastic bottles remains an environmental concern. This created a three-way value dilemma between directly fulfilling the environmental promise of the mission, generating funds to support ongoing research and education, and providing a necessary hydration service to the public. During the past few years, attendees who brought their own water bottles were rewarded with free water refills. This proved only marginally successful with many people unaware of this option until the event day. For 2012, World Whale Day will introduce a new strategy by providing commemorative reusable water bottles sold with unlimited water refills, thus entirely replacing single-use plastic water bottles. It is expected that the difference in cost to the consumer will be negligible as many attendees purchase multiple beverages throughout the day. The projected decrease in revenue resultant from prioritising sustainability over profit is 3.7 per cent of beverage sales.

Entertainment

The free entertainment is a draw for many attendees (Figure 12.2). The organisation continues to develop a programme that showcases local musicians. World Whale Day provides an uncommon opportunity for residents and visitors to enjoy local entertainment, *hula halau* (school) and environmental speakers free of admission charge. There was a single centre stage for the first 29 years of Whale Day; however, for the 30th Whale Day, a second children's stage was added. In 2012, taking inspiration from the Hervey Bay Whale Festival in Queensland, Australia, in which Pacific Whale Foundation researchers participate in annually, the children's stage will promote environmental stewardship and community activism through local performances and musical acts. Professional musicians and youth performers share the day with student bands and youth groups who model healthy and environmentally engaged habits for children and families.

The entertainment is a significant component of World Whale Day as it increases the potential audience. Pacific Whale Foundation employees are approached at work and on the street as the event date nears (authors' personal observations) with future attendees seeking the coveted upcoming concert schedule. The concert scheduled is not released in order to promote a more dynamic attendee experience to those who had originally planned on coming only for their favourite performer. Though anecdotal, the importance of the free entertainment is apparent. This is in line with the findings of Jin-Soo *et al.* (2011) which describe the event programme as a strong predictor of positive emotional value associated with an event.

Figure 12.2 This picture shows an early crowd at the center stage at World Whale Day's seaside free concert. Attendees provide their own seating; as the day progresses most of the crowd is standing and dancing as the audience grows.

Made on Maui Vendor Fair

The continued success and increasing attendance of World Whale Day creates a growing demand for vendor spaces at the Made on Maui Vendor Fair. The Made on Maui fair offers local artisans one of Maui's largest audiences in which to market their crafts. A consideration that the organisation made at the beginning was to ban all shell (e.g. jewellery) and marine-life crafts (e.g. dried starfishes) from the fair. Other environmental measures include the ban on all plastic bags, excess packaging and imported goods. Within the last five years, participation has become strictly juried and the organisers now require vendors to submit an extensive application as well as to provide a donation to the organisation's silent auction. The Pacific Whale Foundation uses the vendor fair to promote awareness about negative impacts of plastic bags on the marine environment and over-exploitation of marine species (e.g. live shell harvest). Educational signs explaining these concepts are posted throughout the fair. Adherence to the organisation's standards is strictly enforced and it is not uncommon for vendors to be removed from the fair on the day of the vent due to infringements. The Made on Maui Vendor Fair not only provides a forum to model sustainable consumerism, but also creates economic benefits to the organisation generating funds through booth fees and donations for the silent auction.

Eco-Alley

Eco-Alley is an area of World Whale Day designed to inform attendees about local environmental issues on Maui. The Pacific Whale Foundation invites its programme partners (e.g. Volunteering on Vacation) and other NGO and for-profit businesses with environmentally sustainable business plans (Larson and Wikstrom, 2008). This mutual collaboration offers attendees a track to get involved in conservation through volunteerism, educational offerings or awareness raising through interactive displays that showcase sustainable products (e.g. solar panels). Organisations are provided with no-fee access to the event to promote their mission to attendees in exchange for providing free activities for children on a rotating schedule in the organisational tent.

Transportation

Laing and Frost (2010) highlight the importance of public transport in the design of a green event. The World Whale Day site location, Kalama Park, is based on proximity to the ocean and availability of free public access. Parking at the site is limited. A condition of the user permit is that organisers must provide off-site parking and shuttle services. A private shuttle bus runs from multiple satellite parking locations located one to two miles from the event site. Additionally, the municipal bus service has several stops near the event site and these are publicised on the event website. Efforts to provide incentive for riding public transport to the event have been hampered by the inability to validate the bus passage as no receipts or tickets are provided. Increasing the use of public transportation is part of the Foundation's carbon reduction policy. The Foundation is currently working with the public transportation authorities to develop a ridership documentation scheme for the event day that entitles the rider to a complimentary concession. It is assumed that the incentive-based programme may increase ridership on the event day and introduce residents and visitors to the under-utilised municipal transportation system.

Great Maui Whale Count

The Great Maui Whale Count offers participants an opportunity to participate in citizen science (Conrad and Hilchey, 2011) and affords residents and visitors an appreciation of their local community (Yolal *et al.*, 2009) and its adjacent marine environment. This ongoing, land-based count began in 1994. During 2011, the research team applied modelling techniques to historical data for the Count and has identified sources of experimental error that can be corrected. Going forward, select sites of the 13 available will be designated as scientific sites, others as public research sites. The scientific sites will feature highly trained scientific observers following a strict protocol. Others will continue to involve volunteer public observers to scan for a 'snapshot' of the overall abundance and distribution of humpback whales in Maui County waters in late February. The Whale Count is a popular event among residents and visitors alike with many volunteer repeats reserving their 'favourite' data collection site months in advance (authors' observations).

Costs and benefits

The challenge to fulfil the expectations of whale aficionados, the island community and participants who may simply stumble upon the event without any prior knowledge while upholding the organisation's mission proves to be a complex task. The environmental, social and economic benefits and costs must be considered during the planning process. An informal regression analysis of secondary data and oral histories from long-term employees involved in the planning and development of the Maui Whale Festival has provided common themes evident throughout three decades of decision-making. Table 12.1 identifies key considerations in the planning of the event and highlights important components of the decision-making process.

The tripartite design of the cost/benefit ranking table allows the user to determine the area of most profitability (e.g. social, environmental, economic) for a specific event or product. The table is designed to show increasing value by coverage. For example, the ideal event product would appear as an equal distribution across the table. The areas addressed in the cost/benefit ranking are presented at a simplistic level to provide the user with a quick evaluative tool for existing event products as well as considerations for future additions.

Table 12.1 Cost/benefit ranking of event products

Cost/benefit	Components		
Environmental	Fair trade/made with renewable/recycl-able materials	Multiple use (e.g. reusable water bottles)	Locality: Locally sourced and/or produced, highlights local businesses, benefits the local environment
Social	Educational/ innovative product	Is grounded within the community and/ or requires community support (e.g. parade, petitions)	Clearly supports mission
Economic	Price sensitive	Profits fund a specific campaign/ cause	Intangible product (e.g. membership, adopt-a-whale)

Summary

Many of the decisions made throughout the evolution of World Whale Day to the Great Maui Whale Festival were not supported by literature, but rather by the adherence to the organisation's mission. With the increasing focus on events in the literature (see Laing and Frost, 2010), it is apparent that many of these inherent actions are now explained by theory. This chapter has provided examples of creative and simplistic modifications that can be applied to any event to help conform with an environmental mission or simply to 'green' an event. It is evident that social, environmental and economic costs remain a juggling act. In the case of an event with an environmental message or mission, the prioritisation of environmental benefits assumes that increased social benefit will be realised thus partially contributing to an increase in economic benefit through long-term public support through membership and products. The environmental achievement should remain realistic and focus on a transparent least-impact rather than aim for an unattainable 'zero impact'. Compromise should be considered a necessary action within the process.

Experiences from the Maui Whale Festival reveal that events and event products can be categorised as having social, economic and environmental profits, or a combination of such. It is not to say the balance will spontaneously occur; rather when events and products are continuously developed, less economic sacrifices become necessary. For example, the careful consideration of water beverages at Maui Whale Festival Events began an intensified recycling programme at the events. The next phase will boast increased environmental and social profits by replacing a single-use product with a multi-use vessel, while generating an insignificant economic cost. Thus, by following the organisation's mission, the

Maui Whale Festival model realises the benefits of social and environmental profitability.

The Maui Whale Festival continues to focus on the marine and island environment. Many of the original components of the first Whale Days still exist in various forms throughout the festival. It is thought that the close adherence to the organisation's mission is a significant factor in generating continued and growing social support. The festival has gained national and international attention through various media and many visitors plan annual vacations to Maui to attend and/or volunteer at Maui Whale Festival events. On the international level, the staff of the Pacific Whale Foundation in Puerto Lopez, Ecuador helped launch a 'sister event' in 2011 modelled on the original Maui event – known locally as 'Festival de Las Ballenas'. The growth and expansion of what was once a small one-day event to a conservation-themed festival that has a global reputation and now lasts an entire season is perhaps the most compelling evidence of the success of World Whale Day and the Maui Whale Festival.

References

Calambokidis, J., Falcone, E. A., Quinn, T. J. *et al.* (2008). *Final report for Contract AB133F-030RP-00078 US Dept of Commerce*. Olympia: Cascadia Research.

Chwe, M. S.-Y. (1998). Culture, circles, and commercials: Publicity, common knowledge, and social coordination. *Rationality and Society*, 10(1), 47–75.

Conrad, C. C. and Hilchey, K. G. (2011). A review of citizen science and community-based environmental monitoring: Issues and opportunities. *Environmental Monitoring Assessment*, 176, 273–291.

Forestell, P. H. (2007). Protecting the ocean by regulating whale watching: The sound of one hand clapping. In J. Hingham and M. Lueck (eds), *Marine Wildlife and Tourism Management* (pp. 272–293). Wallingford: CAB International. doi: 10.1079/97818459 33456.0272.

Forestell, P. H. and Kaufmann, G. (1990). The history of whale watching in Hawaii and its role in enhancing visitor appreciation for endangered species. In M. L. Miller and J. Auyong (Chair), *Symposium conducted at the meeting of the 1990 Congress on Coastal and Marine Tourism*, Newport, OR: National Coastal Resources Research and Development Institute.

Forestell, P. H. and Kaufman, G. (1992). The anatomy of a whalewatch: Marine tourism and environmental education. *The Journal of Marine Education*, 11, 10–15.

Gursoy, D., Dim, K. and Uysal, M. (2004). Perceived impacts of festivals and special events by organizers: An extension and validation. *Tourism Management*, 25, 171–181. doi: 10.1016/S0261–5177(03)00092-X.

Jin-Soo, L., Choong-Ki, L. and Youngjoon, C. (2011). Examining the role of emotional and functional values in festival evaluation. *Journal of Travel Research*, 50, 685–696. doi: 10.1177/0047287510385465.

Laing, J. and Frost, W. (2010). How green was my festival: Exploring challenges and opportunities associated with staging green events. *International Journal of Hospitality Management*, 29(2010), 261–267. doi: 10.1016/j.ijhm.2009.10.009.

Larson, M. and Wikstrom, E. (2008). Organizing events: Managing conflict and consensus in a political market square. *Event Management*, 7, 51–65.

Pacific Whale Foundation (2011). *Annual Membership Database*. Wailuku, HI: PWF.

Pearce, D. G. and Nicholson, R. E. (2001). Why do people attend events: A comparative analysis of visitor motivations at four South Island events. *Journal of Travel Research*, 39(4), 449–460.

Rao, V. (2001). Celebrations as social investments: Festival expenditures, unit price variation and social status in rural India. *Journal of Development Studies*, 38(1), 71–97.

Spangenberg, E. R., Gursoy, D. and Rutherford, D. G. (2006). The hedonic and utilitarian dimensions of attendees' attitudes toward festivals. *Journal of Hospitality & Tourism Research*, 30(3), 279–294.

Yolal, M., Cenitel, F. and Uysal, M. (2009). An examination of festival motivation and perceived benefits relationship: Eskisehir International Festival. *Journal of Convention & Events Tourism*, 10, 276–291. doi: 10.1080/1547014093372020.

13 Jack Johnson and sustainable music events

A case study

Christian Wittlich

Music events are barely sustainable: 447.6 tons of kerosene for a single flight from New York to Sydney, just to transport 300 tons of equipment with four jumbo jets; 600,000 watts of lighting for a single concert; 100,000 kW of electricity per hour, the power consumption of a small German town. These are only some of the resources bands like the Rolling Stones, Rammstein and festivals like Rock in the Park require to create events for music fans (Irle and Koch, 2006). With facts like these, it has become clear why it is necessary to reconsider current practices within the music events industry. One possible solution to such overwhelming, resource intensive events could be a more sustainable approach to the planning, performance and post-performance aspects of the event (Irle and Koch, 2006; Jones, 2010; Raj and Musgrave, 2009).

A fitting case study of an ecologically, economically and socially sustainable music festival is the Kokua Festival in Hawaii. The festival brings together artists, teachers and community leaders to support environmental education. The festival, which features the famous surfer, songwriter, producer and moviemaker Jack Johnson, raises funds for his foundation (Kokua Hawaii Foundation) and its multiple environmental school projects. As well as the local festival, Jack Johnson's 2008 and 2010 world tours addressed similar issues by supporting local environmental organisations at all concert venues. In practice, a 'Village Green', an area in which many non-profit organisations present themselves in a tent village throughout the festival, was set up before every show (Figure 13.1).

The aim of the Village Green was to engage and inspire visitors by giving them an exclusive visitor passport with a 'visit us, participate and get your stamp' approach. The certificate, usually linked to a prize draw, served as an incentive to bring visitors into contact with these local environmental groups and encourage their participation in greening the event. Separately, an 'EnviroRider™' was included as an obligatory addition to the artist's contract, which stated that his conditions required that certain green actions were carried out before, during and after the show by the event organiser. The 2008 and 2010 tour reports published by the artist's management and available on his website (www.jackjohnsonmusic.com) bring more numeric data for discussion within this chapter.

Figure 13.1 Jack Johnson and friends performing in the Village Green before the actual show (source: photo courtesy of Jack Johnson Music archives).

Music events and sustainability

Music events are dependent on infrastructure and transport for the attendance of fans at their venue. As a result, fan, crew and equipment transport leaves a serious impact on the environment due to the production of carbon dioxide emissions (Jones, 2010). Therefore, music festivals, perceived by some (Gibson and Connell, 2005, p. 210), as 'the oldest and most common form of music tourism', are a critical issue in terms of their carbon footprint as they attract tens of thousands of national and international visitors annually. Word-of-mouth advertising and marketing campaigns have led to the attendance increasing year by year. This is beneficial for event organisers, but creates a larger carbon footprint. At the same time, music festivals can positively influence thousands of people, and change or alter their attitudes towards the environment. As a result, this may lead to participants dealing with issues of immense importance while listening to their favourite music. The original Woodstock Festival in 1969 is a good example of how musicians and participants went far beyond just playing or listening to some music. In this context, 'far beyond' relates to the political dimension of the festival. With Woodstock's '3 days of peace and music' image (as it was billed) (Gibson and Connell, 2005, p. 235), attendees emphasised the general importance of peace and protested against the participation of US soldiers in the Vietnam War. Jones (2010, p. 5) stressed this aspect by writing:

... you can influence the ongoing behaviour and attitudes of your audience, contractors, suppliers and the events industry. Running your event as sustainable as possible should underlay all operations. Combined across the event industry, the social and worldwide impact of sustainable event management should not be underestimated. [One has] the power to make change and leave participants and audience with the inspiration to also live more sustainably.

In this respect, Soares (in Jones, 2010, p. 5) speaks of a 'transforming potential' in many ways and sees the gathering of thousands of people in a limited amount of time as a good opportunity for reflection on the 'communitarian nature of species'. Similarly, the Kokua Festival tries to link visitors to environmental issues and connect them with social networks (both virtual and personal), in order to create a shared common interest. As there are only a few music festivals dealing with global issues such as climate change, the Kokua Festival has been chosen as a model of a more sustainable event: it is an event that raises funds for environmental education (economic), brings together artists, fans, non-profit organisations, teachers, volunteers, locals and like-minded people (social) and focuses on conservation and positive environmental action (ecological) in the short and long run.

The Kokua Festival

Hosted by Jack Johnson, the Kokua Festival has had a very positive social impact, as it brings together environmental organisations, eco-friendly businesses, artists, teachers and community leaders to support environmental education in Hawaii (Kokua Hawaii Foundation, 2011). Artists who have previously performed at the festival include Ben Harper, Eddie Vedder, Taj Mahal, the Hula Blues Band and Ziggy Marley. Since co-founding the Kokua Hawaii Foundation with his wife Kim Johnson in 2003, Jack has hosted six Kokua Festivals. These usually take place over the period of two days in April, at Waikiki Shell, a venue for outdoor concerts and other large gatherings in Honolulu. The Kokua Hawaii Foundation is a non-profit organisation that supports environmental education in the schools and communities of Hawaii, with several programmes such as *Actively Integrating Nutrition and Agriculture in Schools* (AINA), *3R's School Recycling*,[1] *Environmental Education Mini Grants, Kokua Earth Action Projects* (KEAP) and *Plastic Free Schools*. These were set up in order to educate students in environmental issues and foster pro-environmental actions. In addition to donations, memberships and Kokua Festival merchandising, the Kokua Festival is the major fundraiser for these programmes (Kokua Hawaii Foundation, 2011).

Results from the 2010 Kokua Festival

In total, more than 16,000 people attended the 2010 festival. Approximately 60 per cent of those visitors were locals, with 40 per cent coming from outside of

Hawaii. The majority of visitors were between 18 and 40 years of age, and families with their children. During the festival, 10,000 Kokua Festival Passports were distributed with the aim of encouraging the festival's attendees to become involved in various environmental actions. Within the Village Green (Figure 13.2), around 1,900 fans completed the passport. This led to more than 5,700 green actions on site (Kokua Festival, 2012).

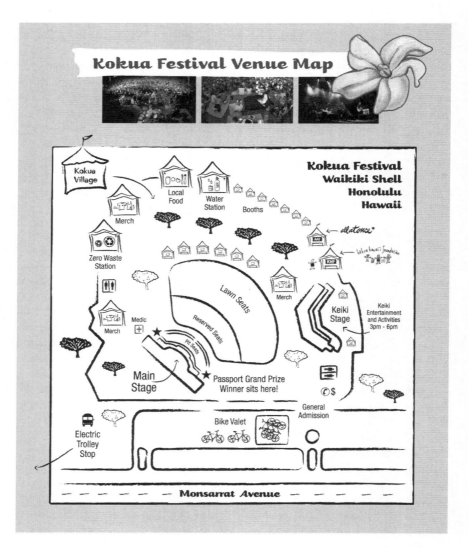

Figure 13.2 2010 Kokua Festival Passport: venue map (source: creative direction, design, map and 'greening' icons by ecoLingo. Photos courtesy of Kokua Hawaii Foundation Archives, Kokua Festival Archives and Kokua Festival Partners. Flower artwork by Julie Mealani Holland.)

With regards to drinking water consumption, fans were encouraged to bring their own empty reusable water bottles, and more than 5,600 bottles were refilled for free at the Menehune Water company stations (Figure 13.2). In total, 1,050 gallons of water were consumed, which is equivalent to diverting 8,400 16.9 oz plastic water bottles from the waste stream (Kokua Festival, 2012). As a further waste reduction measure, zero waste stations (recyclables, food waste, compostables) were set up throughout the festival grounds and separated by student volunteers. In total, 1,426 pounds of glass, 950 pounds of cardboard, 156 pounds of plastic and 52 pounds of aluminium were collected. Additionally, 20 cubic yards of biodegradables were collected and 8 cubic yards of bio waste were composted (Kokua Festival, 2012). In other activities, cameramen and photo booths in the Kokua Village documented more than 1,500 people making an Earth Day Resolution to reduce their individual footprint. About 330 cyclists made use of the Festival Bike Valet (a free and protected bicycle parking area), while 900 attendees took the electric trolley shuttle from park and ride spots to the venue. The 2010 festival introduced a new Kokua Festival shuttle while more than 340 cars participated in the festival's carpool programme (Kokua Festival, 2012). The Village Green, all production vehicles and festival generators ran on 262 gallons of sustainable locally produced bio diesel. Visitors also socialised via the 'All At Once' online platform, leading to more than 1,000 people participating in four beach clean-ups around Hawaii (Kokua Festival, 2012). Beach clean-up participants were all eligible to buy festival tickets through a presale and were entered to win two tickets per clean-up to the Kokua Festival. Moreover, Jack and Kim Johnson (a school teacher) demonstrate a keen awareness of the role of children in environmental issues, and to this end an exclusive 'Keiki Kokua Festival' ('keiki' is the Hawaiian name for kids) with more than 680 children from schools around Oahu took place on the first festival day. The invitations to the schools were directed at those who had completed environmental school projects of the Kokua Hawaii Foundation. This 'kids-only celebration' therefore recognised student efforts to care for the Hawaiian Islands. The day included special artist performances and educational activities (Kokua Festival, 2012).

Greening actions on tour

Greening actions for the Kokua Festival also inspired many actions on Jack Johnson's world tours. Each visitor to Jack Johnson's 2008 and 2010 world tours received a 'Village Green Passport'[2] (Johnson, 2011). This passport asks for fans to complete environmental actions and gives further information on the All At Once Campaign.[3] The Village Green is a combined effort of local environmental organisations that were contacted by the Jack Johnson management and were asked to represent themselves at the venue. As a result, fans and non-profit organisations were given the opportunity to meet and exchange information. As many organisations took advantage of such an opportunity, they built up a small tent village as illustrated in Figures 13.1 and 13.2. In the village fans learned about local and global environmental issues and took part in a prize draw. The organisations also had the chance to advertise for new members and accumulate donations. In addition, the Johnson-Ohana Charitable Foundation doubled every dollar donated to an organisation throughout the 2008 and 2010 world tours (up to US$2,500 per non-profit organisation). Christine von Zingler from OroVerde Germany (Bonn) was present at the 2008 concert at Loreley (Germany) and stated in a personal interview that a four-figure sum had been transferred to the organisation a few weeks after the show (personal interview at Mainz University, 2010). In addition, fans benefited from the Village Green in the following way: for every green action such as using zero-waste stations, using public transport or carpooling, refilling water, visiting a non-profit organisation, buying a CO_2 offset sticker, making a donation, making an environmental pledge at the 'Capture Your Commitment' Photo Booth or using the bicycle valet, Johnson's fans could collect stamps in their passports to be entered into a draw to win special prizes. In addition to winning skateboards and merchandise signed by Jack Johnson, two participants won the opportunity to watch the entire show from the stage. During the 2010 World Tour, '29,359 concert-goers participated in the All At Once Village Green Passport program, together completing over 105,000 individual actions, including recycling, refilling reusable bottles at water stations, carpooling, donating to local non-profit partners and more' (Johnson, 2012a). In order to promote the village, Jack and other musicians spontaneously performed some acoustic songs live in the Village Green, usually filling it with people within seconds (Figure 13.1).

Travel

The Kokua Festival offered online ticket buyers the chance to obtain an additional US$2 carbon credit to offset the emissions generated by their travel. Pacific Biodiesel, a Kokua Festival greening partner, used these credits to replace petroleum in the Maui Electric Company plant with locally produced sustainable bio diesel. Fans who travelled by airplane were encouraged to make their entire trip carbon-neutral via additional offsets. Locals from Oahu were encouraged to utilise alternative modes of transport, such as biking, walking, public transportation, carpooling, driving a hybrid or bio diesel vehicle. In addition, Kokua Festival Shuttles, with four pick-up locations around the island, brought attendees to and from the festival each day. As an incentive, all shuttle riders had the privilege of Express Entrance to the venue (Kokua Festival, 2012). The Kokua Festival also arranged for park and ride opportunities with additional free electric shuttles that ran for nine hours each day. In order to communicate the different information on transport methods to festival attendees, social networks were of great importance. A Facebook fan page, e-newsletters from the Kokua Hawaii Foundation, Jack Johnson and Brushfire Records (2011) all provided detailed information on sustainable transportation to the venue, well in advance.

With regards to the Jack Johnson World Tour, travelling has become more crucial as concerts in North America, Europe, Japan, New Zealand and Australia required long-haul flights for the band and crew. Given that different efforts have been made to green fan transport, the band and crew still have a significant impact on the environment by flying around the world, as well as buses, trucks and ships that are used to transport them and their equipment from one venue to the other. The Carbon Offset Report of the Jack Johnson 'To the Sea' 2010–2011 World Tour (Figure 13.3) shows that fan travel contributed 29 per cent of emissions, whereas freight (8 per cent), commercial air travel (22 per cent), ground transport (2 per cent) and buses and trucks (18 per cent) together made up 50 per cent of all CO_2 emissions (Johnson, 2012b).

Johnson is aware of these statistics and knows that greening measures can never completely cover the tracks artists make. Nevertheless, he believes that a complete abandonment of touring cannot be the solution:

> I struggle with that. The environmental impact with what we do leaves a big footprint during the touring step. One notion to stop doing it is stop touring and that lessens my own impact. But I feel the better thing to do is improve the music industry by trying to make the shows greener and to cooperate with musicians who care as much about the environment as we do. I think that has a greater impact in the long run.
>
> (Wittlich, 2008, 2011)

Results from Jack Johnson's 2010 World Tour: a critical consideration

As with the Kokua Festival, very similar efforts were undertaken in order to minimise the environmental impact of the Jack Johnson World Tour. Nevertheless, there is a huge difference between an annual festival taking place at a

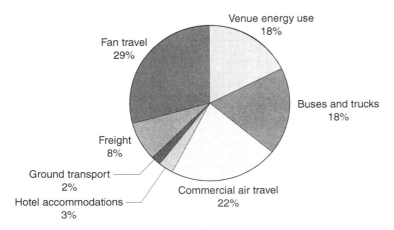

Figure 13.3 Jack Johnson 'To the Sea' 2010–2011 World Tour – Carbon Offset Report (source: Johnson, 2012b).

specific venue on an island, and a world tour. Mainly this is due to the international approach of a world tour. To be specific, management practices that work with an established team of locals need to be adapted to management practices of event organisers overseas. A very helpful instrument in this respect is the EnviroRider™ discussed later in this chapter. Another crucial aspect is that the Jack Johnson crew and partners record and analyse all green efforts that have been made throughout the festival and world tour. At the festival, data on the amount of rubbish generated and the use of bio diesel for generators for instance is more reliable than data collected that originates from multiple sources of more than 50 shows worldwide. Moreover, the complexity of measures and the complex nature of events and world tours 'make determining a true carbon footprint a near impossible task. Materials used and freight are big areas of impact but are very difficult to track as you're relying on information from contractors and suppliers' (Jones, 2010, p. 18). With respect to footprint measurements, there are hundreds of calculators available online which all lead to different results. They might be helpful for personal footprints but not for events, although the industry is working to establish internationally agreed measures (Jones, 2010). In addition, there is almost no information stating in what ways and by whom these data were collected. In contrast to music event studies conducted by universities that explain the methodology in their reports (e.g. Bottrill *et al.*, 2007), one has to be very critical with the data output. This is because data from the Kokua Festival and the World Tour originate from the artist's website, and therefore may be biased due to a lack of objectivity. Nevertheless, the textbox below illustrates the applied greening measures and relevant outcomes.

Greening measures

Fans and passports

- In total, 800,246 people attended over 50 shows in 10 countries around the world.
- Out of these, 29,359 concertgoers participated in the All At Once Village Green Passport programme, together completing over 105,000 individual actions, including recycling, refilling reusable bottles at water stations, carpooling, donating to local non-profit partners and more.

All At Once non-profit partners

- The tour collaborated with over 220 selected community groups around the world reaching over 600,000 people and adding more than 3,680 new members to these organisations.
- Over 70,000 All At Once members took over 4,000 actions on AllAtOnce.org, over 10,000 viewed non-profit videos and over 90,000 people visited the All At Once website to learn about the 2010 campaign focus areas of plastic free initiatives and sustainable local food systems (All At Once, 2012).

- All At Once connected over 14,690 interested volunteers with these non-profit organisations, which brought together 6,500 people at over 40 community events.

Giving back

- Jack Johnson donated 100 per cent of his 2008 and 2010 tour profits to charity.
- Jack Johnson's 2008 tour profits were used to establish the Johnson-Ohana Charitable Foundation, an endowment founded by Jack and his wife Kim to support environmental, art and music education now and in the future.
- The Johnson-Ohana Charitable Foundation has made over US$1.3 million in donations to date.
- As part of the 2010 *To The Sea World Tour*, the foundation donated US$525,000 directly to the 2010 *All At Once* non-profit partners.
- An additional US$700,000 was raised by these non-profit organisations through the *All At Once* matching donation programme.

Water

- Jack and his crew reduced the use of single-use plastic bottles on tour and backstage. All water came straight from the tap, filtered with filtration systems at hydration stations.
- Concertgoers filled their reusable water bottles with 6,945 gallons of filtered water. As a result, the band, crew and concertgoers saved over 55,000 single-use water bottles from being consumed and thus ending up in the waste stream.
- Concertgoers were able to fill their own reusable water bottles for free at All At Once Water Stations located throughout each concert venue and over 6,000 concertgoers took the Filter For Good pledge to become plastic free.

Recycling and waste reduction

- Backstage, Jack and the crew made every effort to make the shows low-waste events, through recycling, composting and other measures to limit waste headed for the landfill.
- Venue operators and concertgoers did their part to increase recycling and waste diversion efforts. Additionally, a parking lot recycling programme was instituted, in partnership with Live Nation, to provide bags and easy to find recycling stations in the parking lots.
- An estimated 460 tons of waste were saved from the landfill through these efforts.

Travel

- Over 26,000 gallons of sustainable bio diesel were used throughout North America to fuel tour trucks, buses and on-site generators.
- Sea freight was used for shipping gear in an effort to further reduce the carbon footprint. Many fans saved gas, money and reduced their carbon footprint by using the Jack Johnson/Zimride online ridesharing tool resulting in over 100,000 carpool miles.
- In addition, fans utilised shuttles, mass transit and bus services to travel to the shows. These combined efforts saved over 200,000 pounds of CO_2.

Catering and concessions

- As part of a Farm to Stage catering programme, tour catering worked directly with local farmers and purveyors across North America to source locally grown organic foods. In addition, many local farmers assisted in disposing of tour compost for use on their farms.
- Disposable cutlery and tableware were biodegradable and made of potato, corn or sugar cane starch.
- Over 18,000 dollars were spent on procuring organic and sustainable food from local farmers and farmers' markets in each community the tour visited.
- The All At Once Community partnered up with the Eat Well Guide, to create 33 custom guides to help fans find fresh, local and sustainable food in each city the tour visited.

Eco-friendly concert merchandise

- All tour merchandise was made from sustainable materials, with a focus on reusables and renewables. Jack and his crew used reusable water bottles and bags to reduce plastic waste. Fans purchased 2,715 exclusive Jack Johnson reusable water bottles, which if used for one year, would prevent 509,062 single-use plastic bottles from entering the waste stream.
- Fans purchased 9,605 reusable tote bags, which if used continuously for one year, would save an estimated 12.8 million barrels of oil and 14.9 million trees.
- In addition, the tour poster also consisted of recycled paper, and 100 per cent organic cotton T-shirts made in the USA were sold during the tour.

Carbon offsets

- A total of 1.8 million pounds of CO_2 were offset by over 7,000 concertgoers who took action by purchasing a Jack Johnson To The Sea offset sticker at the shows or online.

- In addition, concert venues that fully implemented the Jack Johnson Green Rider (an additional clause in the artist's contract), offset their remaining impact from the shows, totalling over 3.3 million pounds of CO_2.
- After all conservation efforts that were taken, the remaining 1,600 metric tonnes[4] of CO_2 emissions from the 2010 *To The Sea* tour were offset by supporting national and international projects like wind, solar and farm methane in communities where the tour travelled.

(Adapted from: www.jackjohnsonmusic.com, 2012)

Despite the non-scientific source of the data, the textbox shows how far-reaching these greening measures are and that they lessen the negative impact of the event(s) at least in the short run. Moreover, the concerts also aim to influence people to engage with non-profit organisations and the All At Once Community in order to support environmental activism in the long run, even though there is no information on the long-term success of such measures.[5]

Good practice needs regulations: Introducing 'The U.S. EnviroRider™'

In order to successfully green their music events, Jack Johnson and team made use of a document called U.S. EnviroRider™ for his 2008 World Tour and used a Green Rider for his 2010 World Tour. This is an environmentally responsible contractual addition to the ordinary artists' production rider. This additional contract demands obligatory and voluntary actions from the concert organiser in order to ensure sustainable music production before, during and after the event (see textbox below). This includes CO_2-reducing actions, power-saving stage equipment, thoughtful fan and crew transport, seasonal food from local farmers for the catering for the crew, free water stations for refillable bottles, recycling and waste reduction at the venue, plastic saving and many other footprint-reducing topics that were listed in the Festival and Tour Results. Thus, the EnviroRider™ can be seen as a precondition for such positive outcomes. In fact, the contract actually states that the artist will not perform if the required aspects have not been implemented. The EnviroRider™ is the result of a cooperation between Jack Johnson, environmental leaders and a company called Effect Partners (formerly MusicMatters), a pioneer in the world of sustainability marketing (see: www.effectpartners.com/).

Environmentally responsible accompaniment to production rider

U.S. EnviroRider™ – Jack Johnson World Tour 2008

DEAR VENUE/PROMOTER:
The Jack Johnson organisation is committed to reducing the environmental impact of our tour. Accordingly, we have taken many steps to ensure that our tour is produced as environmentally responsibly as possible. For example, we are using bio diesel in our vehicles, using organic cotton and recycled paper for our merchandise, providing vegetarian and organic food options in catering, composting or recycling most of our waste, and offsetting all of our remaining CO_2 emissions with regional accredited offset providers.

We are requiring all venues to support our initiative by reducing the environmental impact of the Jack Johnson concert. Our request is for you to work with us on the **underlined** actions listed in this document – and hopefully, continue these actions into the future. This list is comprised of many actions we think you are probably already doing or can easily implement – **these are a requirement for us to do the performance**. You will be required to notify the Jack Johnson organisation no later than 60 days prior to the event if there is any possibility of non-compliance with these requirements.

We have listed other actions that are optional (everything that is **not** underlined). This means we are not REQUIRING these steps to be taken, but that we would strongly encourage you to take as many of these steps that you can.

Environmental targets

- Composting and recycling of at least 50 per cent of total waste generated night of show
- Venue to purchase CO_2 offset covering all energy use for the Jack Johnson show

We are asking your assistance in tracking the environmental impact of the concert. We are tracking items such as total energy used, total waste and amounts recycled. We have attached a Greening Worksheet for you to answer these questions in the EnviroRider's Appendix.

The Greening Worksheet is due by 14 days after the concert date, or Jack Johnson has the right to require a contribution to a local environmental group that Jack Johnson specifies in an amount equal to $500 (or $500 USD equivalent) of the performance fee.

We are excited to work with you on this unique initiative aimed at reducing our environmental footprint as we travel across the world – thank you so much!

The Jack Johnson organisation

Requirements that are <u>underlined</u> in the following document are to be provided at the sole expense of the Purchaser and <u>MUST</u> be provided as part of the contract between Artist and Purchaser. All other items are 'requests' of the artist (not mandatory, but please consider).

1 Waste management and recycling requirements

The Jack Johnson World Tour 2008 production rider requires each Venue to implement a full recycling program – preferably as a general business practice – but at a minimum for the duration of the Jack Johnson 2008 World Tour engagement at the venue. As host of the Tour, each venue agrees to:

- <u>**Provide adequate waste management and recycling receptacles throughout the facility (backstage and FOH).**</u>
- <u>**Ensure your waste management vendor will properly handle all recycling**</u>, delivering it as appropriate to your local recycling facility. *RECYCLING MUST NOT BE THROWN AWAY WITH THE TRASH. THOSE FOUND DOING SO WILL BE IN VIOLATION OF THE RIDER AGREEMENT.*

2 Carbon dioxide (CO_2) emissions offsets

- <u>**PURCHASER will purchase carbon dioxide (CO_2) offsets addressing all CO_2 emissions resulting from the energy use of the show.**</u>

3 Dressing rooms

- <u>**Dressing room/backstage facilities to provide water-efficient appliances**</u> including low-flow toilets and showers (can be retrofitted with low-flow head), no leaking faucets, etc.
- <u>**All light bulbs should be compact fluorescent (CFL).**</u>

4 Production

- <u>**Turn down show lighting when no one is performing.**</u>
- <u>**Turn off speakers/monitors whenever possible as to not affect the performance of the show.**</u>

5 Front of house – general

- <u>**All light bulbs should be compact fluorescent (CFL).**</u>
- <u>**Produce signage from non-PVC, recyclable, and/or biodegradable materials, printed with soy-based inks where possible.**</u>

6 Front of house – Concessions Requests

The below Concessions Requests are not required, with the exception of recycling, however the Tour respectfully requests that the following actions are implemented where possible:

- Use reusable, biodegradable, or compostable cups and utensils for all concessions sales or reusable cups.
- Offer organic, local or fair-trade, and/or in-season food (ask/require vendors to source according to these guidelines).
    - Organic: In general, organic food is grown according to specific standards, without using pesticides/chemicals on crops and processed without radiation or the addition of preservatives. www.ota.com
    - Local: Local food is that which is grown/produced in the region in which it will be consumed, reducing the need for transportation and supporting local economies. www.foodroutes.org
    - Fair trade: In general, fair trade refers to goods produced according to social and environmental standards (such as living wages to workers). www.fairtrade.org.uk/index.htm
    - In-season: Food that is grown in its natural climate, in its natural season, thereby reducing the amount of energy it takes to produce and transport – i.e. pineapples are not in-season in Minnesota in December. www.eattheseasons.co.uk/index.htm

7 Fan/attendee interaction

The below Requests are not required, however the Tour respectfully requests that the following actions are implemented where possible.

Note: Fan travel to concerts is among the biggest contributors to CO_2 tour emissions. Help fans reduce/offset travel CO_2 – below are some to encourage more environmentally friendly ways for concertgoers to get to and from the venue.

- Set up the ability for fans to offset their emissions when they purchase a ticket (less than $1 per ticket). The Tour is coordinating this, and will provide you with the necessary information to implement this initiative at the venue.
- Encourage the use of alternative transportation, carpooling and other less CO_2 emissions-intensive ways to get to the show.

8 Management offices and administrative/janitorial

The below Requests are not required, however the Tour respectfully requests that the following actions are implemented where possible. Many of these actions can be implemented to reduce the environmental impact of daily operations, and may result in cost savings. Some of these items don't relate to our tour, but may be helpful as you host other artists and events throughout the year. Items that may result in cost savings are marked with $$$.

Waste Reduction and Recycling
Energy and Water Efficiency
Employee
Cleaning and Paper Products
Hotels
Ground Transportation

(Source: Adapted from Effect Partners, 2012)

Conclusion

This chapter focused on the Kokua Festival and Jack Johnson World Tours. By introducing greening measure results of the Festival and the 2010 World Tour, the chapter pointed out in what ways the artist and his team operate in order to contribute to the global call for sustainability. In addition, it showed how the EnviroRider™ was introduced as a contractual instrument to gently force venue organisers to act as greenly as possible. Despite the non-scientific data source, it can be seen that numerous and very different greening measures have been successfully applied before, during and after every show. Personal interviews, credible press articles from participating non-profit groups, own observations at a Jack Johnson show and ongoing debates in social networks (e.g. the All At Once forum) support this aspect. Whether these greening measures actually have long-term effects is still a question for future research.

However, genuine sustainable events are hardly possible without the willingness of stakeholders to challenge and change current practices. It is obvious that Jack Johnson has the image and charisma to positively influence fans by giving his shows a deeper meaning. He takes advantage of the gathering of thousands of people, and by adding an environmental and social concern to his music Jack Johnson uses his popularity in a very authentic and beneficial way. As specified in a *Tree Hugger* article 'most celebrity riders call for Evian water, green M&M's and a bottle of their favourite libation, Jack calls for recycling centers, the use of local foods, reusable bottles, water-refilling stations and a request that venues offset their energy consumption' (Snow, 2011). As a result, he is a role model in terms of active environmental protection and social commitment.

The chapter also pointed out how many people came to the events, how many of them made contact with the non-profit organisations, how many people and organisations are actually involved in greening the tour and how many people use the social network All At Once to organise environmental actions. Despite the negative environmental impact from touring, a fact that Johnson has himself admitted, the Jack Johnson world tours have connected tens of thousands of like-minded people worldwide and thus left a 'green belt' around the globe.

Thanks to the Kokua Festival being a major fundraiser for environmental programmes in Hawaii's schools and because of the environmental activities for kids throughout the event, the artist and his team also convey the message to the next generation. Empowering actions like these usually have long-term effects and the power to make a society more environmentally conscious. Therefore, such sustainable events influence society; society in turn influences the sustainability of events.

A good question for future research is whether lessons from the Kokua Festival and Jack Johnson world tours can be used as a model for greening other events. With regards to issues such as waste reduction, recycling, fan and crew transport, catering, energy consumption and the related carbon footprint, all issues most event organisers have to deal with, it is likely that they might serve as model events for others. In theory, such other events could also be non-music occasions, like sporting fixtures, conferences or cultural events. Around the world, lessons learned from the Kokua Festival and the Jack Johnson world tours should find practical implementation, giving every event a 'greener' look and a better reputation. What is also clear is that the music industry needs such sustainable solutions, as the industry is rapidly growing due to a general rise in living standards:

> We have more leisure time, more money, more ease of access to far-flung places. And we have far more music … As cultural consumerism has spread, the idea of the festival as a source of renewal, as break from routine, fuelled by the spirit of artistic adventure, has all but disappeared. It has been swamped by the sheer quantity of events parading under the festival umbrella.
>
> (Clark, 2000, p. 11)

Overall, the multifaceted approach Jack Johnson and his team have applied to reduce their carbon-footprint is striking, if not pioneering, and appears to be redefining the rough image of touring bands and musicians 'on the road'.

Acknowledgements

I wish to acknowledge and thank the following people for their kindness, support and fruitful cooperation: Drs Michael Lück and Tomas Pernecky for guidance and for giving me the chance to publish in their book. Furthermore, I wish to thank Karin Ourada (All At Once Campaign Direction and Kokua Festival Partnership Manager), Jessica Scheeter (All At Once Non-Profit Coordinator), Katie Pere (Director of Kokua Festival Greening) and of course Kim and Jack Johnson for their outstanding support.

Notes

1 The related 3R's Song (Jack Johnson version) stands for 'Reduce, Reuse, Recycle'.
2 See: http://jackjohnsonmusic.com/images/pages/greening/passport/JJ_AAO_Passport_WebR.pdf.
3 'All At Once' is a combination of an artist fan club, a social action network and the name of a campaign created by Jack Johnson, along with his management and crew. Moreover, it is also a virtual platform (http://allatonce.org/) for fans. At the site, interested people can easily connect with non-profit groups that get fans involved in environmental actions in their neighbourhood. At every Jack Johnson show, this social network comes to life at the 'Village Green', personally connecting fans with the non-profit organisations. The 2010 campaign featured more than 220 international non-profit organisations (see http://allatonce.org/nonprofits/) dedicated to various environmental issues. Several people and organisations have been involved to design and implement the campaign such as 'Effect Partners' (Campaign direction), Reverb (On-site activation) and Oniracom (All At Once website development). In addition to the exchange of information, the campaign also aims to 'green' the Jack Johnson World Tour in all respects and with the empowering dogma: 'An individual action, multiplied by millions, creates global change'.
4 Metric tonne = 1,000kg.
5 I.e. will new members to a non-profit organisation still act for the environment years after they have visited a Jack Johnson show?

References

All At Once (2012). *All At Once Community*. Online. Retrieved from: http://allatonce.org/ (accessed 4 February 2012).
Bottrill, C., Boykoff, M., Liverman, D. and Lye, G. (2007). *UK Music Industry Greenhouse Gas Emissions for 2007, Julie's Bicycle*. Oxford: University of Oxford, Environmental Change Institute.
Brushfire Records (2011). *Greening*. Online. Retrieved from: www.brushfirerecords.com (accessed 13 November 2011).
Clark, A. (2000). Cherish your festival idea. *Opera Festival 2000*. 11–18.
Effect Partners (2012). *Who We Are*. Online Retrieved from: www.effectpartners.com/who/ (accessed 3 February 2012).
Gibson, C. and Connell, J. (2005). *Music and Tourism: On the Road Again* (Aspects of Tourism, 19). Clevedon: Channel View Publications.
Irle, M. and Koch, C. (2006). Verbrauchsanweisung. Baden, Bremsen, Rolltreppefahren – was wirklich Energie-Verschwendung ist und wobei niemand ein schlechtes Gewissen haben muss. *Fluter*. Bonn: Magazin der Bundeszentrale für Politische Bildung, H. 19, S.24–31.
Johnson, J. (2011). *Village Green Passport*. Online. Retrieved from: http://jackjohnsonmusic.com/images/pages/greening/passport/JJ_AAO_Passport_WebR.pdf (accessed 15 May 2011).
Johnson, J. (2012a). *Tour Offset Reports*. Online. Retrieved from: http://social.jackjohnsonmusic.com/JJ_TTS_2011_OffsetReport.pdf (accessed 2 February 2012).
Johnson, J. (2012b). *Carbon Offset Report*. Online. Retrieved from: http://jackjohnsonmusic.com/archive/news/to_the_sea_end-of-tour_report/ (accessed 15 January 2012).
Jones, M. (2010). *Sustainable Event Management: A Practical Guide*. London: Earthscan.
Kokua Festival (2012). *Greening*. Online. Retrieved from: http://kokuafestival.com/eventinfo/greening (accessed 9 February 2012).

Kokua Hawaii Foundation (2011). *General Information*. Online. Retrieved from: http:// kokuahawaiifoundation.org/ (accessed 12 December 2011).

Raj, R. and Musgrave, J. (2009). *Event Management and Sustainability*. Wallingford: CABI.

Snow, S. (2011). *Green Eyes on Jack Johnson*. Online. Retrieved from: www.treehugger. com/culture/green-eyes-on-jack-johnsonatms-all-at-once-tour.html   (accessed   22 December 2011).

Wittlich, C. (2008). *Jack Johnson Interview*. STUZ, Studentenzeitung. Ausgabe 102, 20–22, Mainz: Studentenzeitung e.V.

Wittlich, C. (2011). Geographische Umweltbildung einmal anders. Ein Pop-Musiker als schülernaher Anwalt für einen besseren Planeten. *Praxis Geographie* 2, 23–27, Braunschweig: Westermann.

14 It's not just about the film

Festivals, sustainability, and small cities

Mark Rowell Wallin, Billy Collins, and John S. Hull

Introduction

Festivals and events play an important role in tourism management by attracting tourists, driving economic activity, building local community cultural capacity, and serving to enhance the image of the destination itself (Getz, 2008; Grunwell and Ha, 2008; Thomas and Kim, 2011). As a result, festivals can serve as a tool to assist in sustainable community development, simply because they have the capacity to address economic, social, and to a lesser degree, the environmental issues of destinations. This 'triple bottom line' approach has been adopted by the World Tourism Organization (UNWTO) and is the overarching paradigm by which the tourism system attempts to balance cultural and ecological integrity with economic growth and development (Dickson and Arcodia, 2010; UNWTO, 2011). The aim of this chapter is to explore the concept of sustainability as it applies to a small city film festival from several perspectives. We identify the inherent threat to event sustainability in regards to the small city film festival, explore the role of festivals in shoring up the economic and social aspects of sustainable development, and begin the process of identifying how a film festival in a hinterland destination can apply the principles of sustainability to not only survive, but to prosper. In context of the first, we will look to data collected from Kamloops Film Festival participants; while for the second, we discuss the wider impacts of festivals on community and destination.

Increasingly, destinations across North America and abroad are seeing the value of film festivals in particular as both cultural and economic instruments that add value to their overall tourism product mix. Their global emergence and ongoing popularity can be attributed to a plethora of factors, most important of which is that film festivals play a meaningful role as community-builders by sustaining socio-cultural bonds within a community, ultimately serving as a catalyst in the creation of a community's 'sense of place' (Derrett, 2003).

These large, destination festivals are not the only ones that run from year to year. As Ruling and Pedersen (2010) note, film festivals have proliferated even outside the major urban centres, with estimates placing current global numbers as high as 3,500 every year. While the internationally renowned festivals and those attached to large urban centres are undeniably successful and drivers of both economic and social capital, what is less certain is the sustainability of the small city film festival. As members of the Kamloops Film Festival (KFF), a small-scale film festival in the interior of British Columbia, Canada, we are concerned about the long-term sustainability of film-related events in a small cities context.

Literature review

To date, there is little research on the subject of film festivals and tourism management (Ruling and Pedersen, 2010). Grunwell and Ha (2008) investigated success factors in film festivals in the American Midwest; Park *et al.* (2011) probed service quality dimensions by film festivals visitors in South Korea; Ruling and Pedersen (2010) have researched film festivals from an organisational studies perspective; and Altintas (2009) looked at the socio-cultural effect of a film festival on a tourism destination in Turkey. Film festival research tends to be focused not on film festival management per se, but rather upon the broader subject of film studies. As a result, applicable theory about the sustainability of film festivals must be drawn from research in the field of what Getz (2008) has identified as event studies, and its subsequent evolution from the more applied event management stream. As Dickson and Arcodia (2010, p. 237) note, 'little has been written explicitly about events and sustainability; however there has been extensive discussion about tourism and sustainability'.

Event tourism then, at the nexus of tourism studies and event studies, is the logical place to situate film festival sustainability and its role in destination management. This destination perspective, typically seen through the eyes of a destination marketing organisation (or DMO), argues that 'events are highly valued as attractions, catalysts, animators, place marketers, and image makers' (Getz, 2008, p. 406). These events contribute significantly to a community's cultural and economic development, as they bring in new sources of capital that is often less susceptible to financial crises and longer-term economic downturns (Nurse, 2002). While the social and economic impact of events is widely studied and available, environmental impacts are rarely discussed and tend to focus on the negative (Dickson and Arcodia, 2010). However, according to Foley *et al.*, (2009, p. 13), sustainable social, cultural and environmental benefits are 'likely to preoccupy policy makers, academics and citizens as the global argument of civic boosterism is challenged for overestimating benefits and underestimating costs'.

From a community perspective, festivals provide an outlet for resident creativity but they also serve as a vehicle to demonstrate for visitors the uniqueness of the destination, diversity of cultural offerings, and special aspects of a community's culture. According to Derrett (2003, p. 52), festivals contribute to a sense of community, and in turn it has been 'observed that communities are creating festivals and events to emphasise the value they recognise in the feelings of ownership and belonging generated for resident participants'. The strength of this collective participation is in the 'social capital' created that empowers the community and its participants. As Lee *et al.* (2004) suggest, festivals have the power to animate tourists' experiences by showcasing the local community's culture, which in turn creates a unique touristic experience for the visitor. In this way, festivals act as not just tourist attractions, but as key elements of the socio-cultural fabric of a place, and in turn are vital contributors to the social sustainability of a city.

In terms of scheduling, film festivals are mainly held during the 'off-season', or slow tourist times of the year, and are often less obtrusive than other events and therefore have a lower overall impact upon the city vis-à-vis staging and logistics (Grunwell and Ha, 2008). From both economic and environmental sustainability perspectives, film festivals use existing privately owned infrastructure like theatres, hotels, restaurants, and other venues appropriate to their needs. The positive economic impact of festivalgoers' spending on a night of film can be significant (Grunwell *et al.*, 2008). In the world of festivals and events, these economic impact assessments are undertaken for a variety of reasons, the most popular of which is to consider the tradeoff between the cost of hosting the event and the tangible benefits associated with visitor expenditure and income generation (Raj and Musgrave, 2009).

While few studies of film festival demographics exist, 'motivations to attend' have been explored across event type (Getz, 1991; Backman *et al.*, 1995; Nicholson and Pearce, 2001). The fact is, shifts in attendee demographics and the impact they have on existing film festivals are problematic for the event practitioner. Customer loyalty, which is one aspect of attendee motivation, is often cited as a major factor in event success. As Petrick (2004) has illustrated, it is festival loyalty that the event organiser seeks because repeat visitors are vital to the success of any event property. Indeed, consistently satisfying the core audience of an event is of primary importance (Jago *et al.*, 2003), not just for its economic sustainability, but for event 'sociability' as well – which in turn helps to strengthen the social sustainability of the festival at the same time. As Musgrave and Raj (2009, p. 62) contend, 'festivals are an important economic sustainability concept for local authorities, to increase development in the local area by meeting the basic needs of local people and extending cultural opportunities to satisfy their aspirations for better community cohesion'.

In one of the more applicable studies, Thomas and Kim (2011) investigated the motivation factors of film festival attendees and found that 'togetherness in good environments' was the most important factor in staging a successful film festival (see also Nicholson and Pearce, 2001; Yoon and Uysal, 2005). The second most important factor was 'quality of film', followed by 'film itself' (Thomas and Kim, 2011). Socialisation, novelty, family togetherness, cultural exploration, and escape were just a few of the delineated factors identified in a summary of event motivations by Xiang and Petrick (2006). These are important elements in the creation of social and cultural sustainability because an event is based upon simultaneous production and consumption. Participants must be present and engaged in order to both co-create, and consume the festival 'product'. Therefore, from a sustainable event management standpoint, it is essential to facilitate togetherness and cultural exploration, so that improved social relationships, the building of interpersonal relationships and understandings, as well as overall social well-being can be achieved (Tassiopoulos and Johnson, 2009, p. 76). The challenge, however, is trying to measure these intangible social and cultural benefits.

Finally, a number of authors have commented on the challenges faced by festivals and events from competition and their own evolution (Hall, 1992; Wicks, 1995; Getz, 2002). While most cities tend to have just one signature film festival event, they compete for financial and other resources (such as volunteers, sponsors, funding, expertise) with other events in their community. The dilemma is that although festivals that do not innovate their product offerings ultimately risk failure, they must also be careful not to abandon their core audience along the way. As Hall (1992) observed, events that do innovate and grow can lose their community identity and original purpose. As Dickson and Arcodia (2010, p. 238) conclude, from the perspective of sustainable development, the appeal of short duration festivals as tourist attractions 'highlight the need for the event and destination to grow and develop together as a reminder that attractions do not exist in isolation and must be part of a system'.

Case study

Kamloops lies between the Cascade and Rocky Mountain ranges in the interior of British Columbia, Canada. Located 350 kilometers north-east of Vancouver and 600 kilometers west of Calgary, the city of approximately 86,000 spreads out along the confluence of the North and South Thompson rivers, which feed into the nearby Thompson Lake. The city has three significant economic engines: resource development and processing (such as lumber, pulp, biomass, and mining), Thompson Rivers University (with over 10,000 students), and the Royal Inland Hospital (City of Kamloops, 2012).

The region boasts many world-class recreational opportunities with its many mountains, rivers, lakes, and the Sun Peaks Resort. Because of its central position on the main highways running between both Edmonton and Calgary in Alberta and the British Columbia coast, Kamloops has worked to develop and brand itself as the 'tournament capital of Canada' by building many indoor and outdoor recreational facilities throughout the city.

Kamloops Film Society

Originally organised in 1971, the Kamloops Film Society (KFS) has worked to offer the community twice-a-month showings of international and independent films. Because the society and the festival are primarily organisational structures rather than physical ones, they draw upon already existing physical resources within the community. Thus, when the physical and demographic exigencies of the community have shifted, so has the film society; the society changed venues many times over the years in order to account for changes in technology and increases in demographics. Its current home, the Paramount Theatre, has proven itself to be sustainable as a cultural and economic centre for the downtown core, a strategy of resisting the political impulses to suburban sprawl, and as a concerted act of preserving the cultural centre of the city. The society membership has rejected the idea of moving to the larger, suburban multiplex venue.

Yet in spite of these concerns about Kamloop's civic and cultural sustainability, economic and logistical factors conspire against the society model. While the KFS and Kamloops Film Festival (KFF) rent the Paramount for their showings, the theatre is a second-run venue, oftentimes taking on art-house and documentary titles not claimed by the local multiplex. This three-way competition (multiplex, Paramount, society) for quality titles follows a distinct pecking order based on total revenues. With the Paramount and the society often competing for the same titles, film selection and booking challenges threaten the long-term ability of the organisation to secure quality programming.

At this point, the society's concerns are ones of economic and cultural sustainability. The demographic profile of the society is steady, in that the core is consistent and enthusiastic. That said, there is little evidence that new society members are joining to replenish the community. This hypothesis is borne out by the slow but steady decline in society film attendance over the last five years (N. Wandler, Treasurer of the Kamloops Film Festival, personal communication, 21 January 2012).

Kamloops Film Festival

The KFS, in order to take advantage of the opportunities presented by creating a major community event as well as the creative flexibility afforded by the compact delivery of the festival model, ran the first, independent KFS Festival in 1997.

While the society places no emphasis on events, the festival, from its inception, attempted to pair film with extra-cinematic activities. In the first few years, these events took on the form of workshops and lectures that patrons could pay to attend as well as securing actors and directors to introduce their films. Increasingly, in order to defray the costs that undermined previous attempts, festival events have been pegged to sponsorship activity. Additionally, the festival closing party has, over the last several years, attempted to be both a celebration as well as an independent event by partnering with local venues and sponsors to bring in entertainment with a broad appeal, particularly in the form of live entertainment. The 2012 Festival featured members of the Kamloops Symphony playing before each 7pm screening in exchange for festival promotion of the ongoing Symphony series. This emphasis on cultural sustainability emerges entirely out of the event-oriented focus of the festival, rather than the regularised consumer behaviour of the weekly society film.

While many film festivals operate in order to bring filmmakers and distributors together, often screening unreleased and premier showings, the Kamloops Film Festival draws its films largely from the same Toronto International Film

Festival (TIFF) circuit as does the society. In order to confront this obvious threat to its distinctiveness and sustainability, the festival has begun making efforts to bring in independent Canadian films; in particular, films with local or regional interest. These films, which either have been filmed in the surrounding area or feature local talent and personalities, generate a surprising amount of interest, indicating an endogenous potential inherent in local interest films, especially when paired with relevant, added-value events.

The last five years of the festival have been ones of relative growth: on the one hand, direct sales are flat to decreasing, while on the other hand profits are up substantially. The 2009 Festival was the highest attended with direct sales accounting for $20,867, and attendance has held relatively steady since then (2011 direct sales totalled $18,643). Yet despite a slight dip in direct sales, the overall profit for the festival has increased, even from its highest selling year in 2009. In 2011 the festival recorded a net profit of $4,057 as opposed to $3,318 in 2009 (N. Wandler, personal communication, 21 January 2012). The difference has been made through creative and aggressive courtship of sponsors. Sponsorship, it turns out, is essential to the economic sustainability of the festival.

Methods/results

The researchers employed a case study strategy incorporating a mixed method approach to investigate the factors that threaten the long-term sustainability of the KFF: demographic realities, perceptions of its place in the cultural mosaic of the small city, the growing emphasis on special events in the festival, and issues of quality – of service, venue, and film. Case study approaches are a preferred method when 'how' and 'why' questions are being posed, and the focus is on a contemporary phenomenon within a real-life context (Yin, 2009, p. 2). The aim of the research was to specifically understand the causal links about how and why the KFF event occurs. For the KFF, an explanatory case study approach focused on identifying the opportunities and challenges facing the KFF in the context of sustainability. In addition, an advantage of case study research, according to Jennings (2001, p. 178), is that it is also grounded in the social setting being studied. Thus, the KFF was analysed in a context of the larger structures and relations of the Kamloops community and Kamloops Film Society.

Yin (2009) explains that a case study as a research method can include a mix of qualitative and quantitative research approaches. The data set provides insights into understanding the profile of visitors, the festival experience, the marketing of the festival, and event participation during the festival.

The KFF committee conducted the annual visitor survey over the course of the festival week. The survey was announced before each film and participation in the survey enters the participant in a draw for a full pass to the next year's festival. In 2011, the paper survey (consisting of both quantitative and qualitative elements) was delivered throughout the festival period (over eight days) and delivered in the foyer of the Paramount venue, just outside the main theatre. At the close of the 2011 KFF, 145 surveys were completed. Quantitative results were analysed through frequency analysis using an Excel spreadsheet. Due to the relatively small sample size, it was not appropriate to evaluate significant relationships or hypothesis testing using regression analysis. Qualitative results from the survey were organised into key emergent themes using Excel, which were then analysed in a context of the opportunities and challenges facing the KFF. The data results are organised into the following categories: general demographics (age, sex, residency); overall experience at the festival and areas for improvement; how patrons heard about the festival; and event participation.

Demographics

Demographic questions identified the age, sex, and location residence of the respondents in order to develop a profile of KFF festivalgoers. These are key metrics to understanding the long-term challenges faced by the festival. As was previously noted, the anecdotal evidence suggested that: (a) the festival audiences were made up of mostly society members; (b) that they were primarily late middle-aged to seniors; and (c) that there was very little in the way of exogenous draw. The survey confirmed these hypotheses (see Figure 14.1). We discovered that out of 145 respondents, 110 were over 50 years of age, they were predominantly female, and 140 of them considered themselves Kamloops residents.

Overall experience and areas for improvement

The overall response to the festival in terms of areas for improvement revealed that, out of 97 responses, the top three concerns of attendees included: a need for better marketing (19), and a need to improve the quality of the films (15), while 13 commented that there was no need for improvement in the festival at all (see

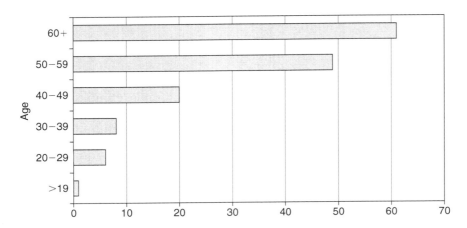

Figure 14.1 Kamloops Film Festival survey 2011 – age.

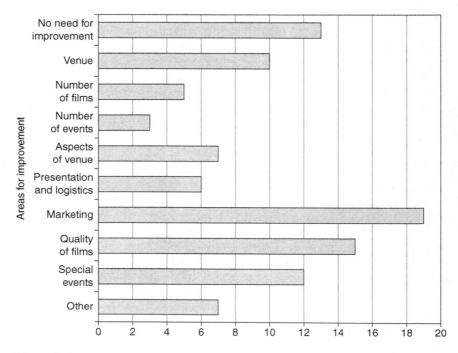

Figure 14.2   Kamloops Film Festival survey 2011 – areas of improvement.

Figure 14.2). The remaining responses indicated perceived weakness in (a) the specific aspects of the venue, (b) number of films, (c) number of events, and (d) various aspects of the festival presentation and logistics (e.g. being able to see the DVD menu as the projectionist is loading the film, long-winded introductions, parking issues, volunteer issues, and schedule conflicts between films and events).

How respondents heard about the festival

In terms of how they learned of the festival, respondents indicated that the majority of them heard about the festival (see Figure 14.3) either through 'word of mouth' (58) or 'newspapers' (44). The data indicates that there are several broad categories: respondents who have either been coming to the festival since its beginning and therefore just expect it every year (15/60), those who learned about it through the society (14/60), seeing the posters and brochures around town (9/60), and other media (4/60).

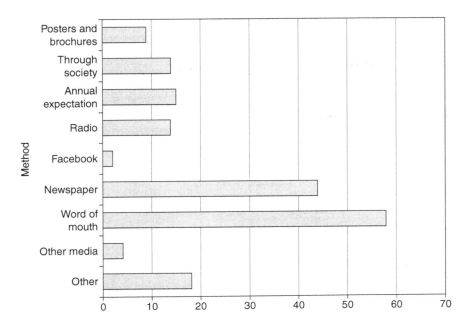

Figure 14.3 Kamloops Film Festival survey 2011 – source of information.

Events results

Over the course of the KFF, there are a number of events that are organised for visitors, including an opening reception, filmmakers' salon, and a closing gala. The two events questions indicate several important results: the majority of respondents do not attend events, but of the 69 who did attend events, the most attended one was the closing gala. The qualitative breakdown of why people did not attend events can be categorised into two main categories: time constraints and conflicts prohibited it (32/76) or lack of interest (8/76). Included in the former category are indications that events after 9pm are 'too late'.

Analysis

Visitor profile

The survey results reveal the homogeneity of the visitors in terms of age and residency. The hypothesis that the festival committee had that the vast majority of festivalgoers were over 40 years of age was born out by the survey results, which indicated that the majority of respondents were over 50 years of age. What surprised the committee, though, was the inability of the festival to draw from outside the immediate Kamloops vicinity. Over 97 per cent of respondents were from Kamloops. What this suggests is that while the small city film festival is effective in producing endogenous cultural capital, it is less able to produce exogenous, or touristic impulses at this point in time. Thus, while film festivals in larger centres can rely upon exogenous participants to bolster both their economic and cultural sustainability and influence, the small city festival may be less capable of creating such a draw. Small festivals, then, should expend their valuable resources in creating a continued and vibrant sense of community and place to draw new endogenous patrons.

In order to address the problem of an ageing audience, the festival currently seeks to engage directly with younger demographics, particularly drawing on the over 7,000 on-campus students at Thompson Rivers University, located in town. These results suggest that up to this point, this goal is not being met, at least not in terms of the films shown at the downtown venue where the survey was conducted. Of the 145 respondents, only seven self-identified as being under 30 years of age.

Overall impressions and areas for improvement

The data confirms what literature suggested: while the healthy, small-market festival has a devoted and loyal core of supporters (Petrick, 2004), patrons of the festival want more and larger events and they are concerned about the quality and comfort of the venue. It also suggests that they are willing to pay and make time for something they see as being valuable, even over a free event that they see as less desirable.

The quality of the venue and the films, as is suggested by the literature review, seems to be of continued interest and concern. While most people are extremely pleased about the quality of film provided by the Kamloops Film Festival – which reinforces Thomas and Kim's (2011) identification of the importance of film quality – the continued pressure of competing with multiple agents (including the venue hosting the festival itself) poses ongoing problems and threatens long-term sustainability. The festival has investigated several ways of ensuring that it has access to quality and recent titles, but given the nature of the industry – where the large chains are inextricably bound into complex quid-pro-quo relationships with distributors – the only option may be to try to balance access to well-recognised and 'high-buzz' titles with smaller, local interest, exclusive showings that can provide added value to filmgoers by connecting filmmakers with their audiences.

The venue expectations are a more direct issue of concern, especially when one considers the importance of the cultural location being a space of community and togetherness. Given the persistence of the lack of comfort and technical problems at the Paramount, the festival must do what it can to improve patrons' experiences in that setting. Because of the historical reluctance of the Paramount to invest in improvements, the festival must invest its own money where it can to achieve maximum effect. While the festival cannot invest in improved seating (the single, most frequent venue complaint), it can invest in materials to improve the technical experience of the film (additional and improved equipment to augment the theatre's) as well as banners, signs, lighting, and other equipment to foster more of a branded, distinctly KFF experience. As the literature suggests, festivalgoers value the sense of community, belonging, and participation in the festival (Morgan, 2008, p. 91), as opposed to just 'going to the movies'.

How respondents heard about the festival

In surveying respondents about how they heard about the festival, there was an effort to determine if the three, cost-intensive methods by which the festival has traditionally been promoted are the main ways in which festivalgoers hear about the event. As one would expect from a healthy festival, the local media community has, in the past, been somewhat supportive of the festival activities (Jago *et al.*, 2003), as is reflected in the substantial number of respondents who learned about the festival through the community's two major newspapers (*Kamloops This Week* and *Kamloops Daily News*). The fact that the vast majority of respondents either heard about the festival through word of mouth, their annual participation in the festival, or through their association with the society confirms Gordon Tarzwell's contention (G. Tarzwell, Chair of Kamloops Film Festival, personal communication, 18 January 2012) that the festival's current core is the membership of the film society. Thus, what is confounding for festival organisers is that the demographic scope of the festival is fixed, seemingly irrespective of how much money is spent promoting it. Coupled with the lack of exogenous draw, the apparent inability to attract new festival participants represents an existential threat to the economic sustainability and long-term viability of the KFF.

Events

While obviously the festival itself is an important community event, the festival has viewed the events it develops in terms of both appreciation (the opening reception) and outreach to otherwise untapped demographics (Knowledge Network Filmmakers' workshops and salon, and the closing gala).

What is striking about the events can be examined in two distinct components. First, while the Knowledge Network Filmmakers' Salon was attended by only 8 of the survey respondents, the event itself was attended by over 70 people. This discrepancy would indicate that, as the festival committee hoped, the salon was a source of outreach, bringing in participants who were not interested in attending the festival films. Second, of the respondents to the survey, those who attended events attended the closing gala over the opening reception by a factor of two to one (27/64). What is remarkable about this number is that while the closing gala requires a $10 ticket for admission, the opening reception is free. The opening reception is catered while the gala ticket includes appetisers, one complementary drink, and a band. This contrast would indicate that film-goers feel that their money is well spent for what they get at the gala and that the sense of togetherness fostered at the paid venue contributes to the overall ethos of the festival. This sensation is likely connected to the more sustained and controlled environment that is designed to foster interaction with other filmgoers but also provide a retrospective, celebratory narrative to the entire event (Morgan, 2008).

When we look at the lack of exogenous tourism generated from the festival as compared to its committed and enthusiastic endogenous support, we must also conclude that the festival works to help define identity and give Kamloops a sense of place (Derrett, 2003). Yet when this stable sense of place is confronted by the demographic realities the festival faces, the long-term viability of that civic identity is called into question. In other words, for people over 50 years of age, the KFF is a vital and rich part of their sense of place, of civic identity and engagement. The outlook is less certain for those under 50. This suggests that while the KFF holds less importance to younger audiences' sense of place, they may find other ancillary events of more value. The relative success of the closing gala and the Knowledge Network salon suggest that younger demographics may be more interested in slightly different, but related events: ones that emphasise direct engagement with the process of production (as in the salon) and those that bring together various cultural aspects, such as film, music, food, and drink (the closing gala). Such results are in keeping with Jago *et al.* (2003) as well as Lade and Jackson (2004) who point out that the diverse interests of target demographics often require diverse events and marketing tactics.

This period of transition may prove to be difficult; the festival may be forced to juggle the often contradictory expectations of several distinct groups in addition to the more traditional stakeholder mentioned in the literature review (Hall, 1992; Wicks, 1995; Getz, 2002). The concept of parallel festival structures – the traditional festival downtown at the Paramount while the edgier Dark Festival, sponsored by a local brew-pub, and filmmakers' workshops take place on the university campus – may prove to be the way to both keep an established brand viable and serve the long-standing interests of the local community (Hall, 1992) while also ensuring the long-term sustainability of the event.

Conclusions

Film festivals, when conceived and managed right, are proven cultural products that have the power to engage communities, create a sense of place, buoy up declining resource-sector economies, and help brand a destination (Jago *et al.*, 2003). As the research on film festivals grows, there are many new lines of inquiry that might be pursued regarding sustainability. One of the most pressing is the question of shifting demographics, mainly as a result of the ageing baby boomer market. How will this population's support of the arts change as they age? How will this affect future film festival audience makeup? How can and will Generation Y be convinced to support old forms of artistic expression, cultural institutions, and nostalgia for cinema in the digital age? How do film festivals, especially in small cities, re-invent themselves for a new demographic unsure or unaware of the legacy of the 'foreign film' festival model? Is it film, or film *events*, that are the key to survival for tomorrow's film festivals?

For the small film festival and the KFF in particular, the research suggests that while the event is currently healthy with a core identity and loyal customer base, demographic and economic pressures will not allow it to rest on its laurels. It is unlikely that in its current configuration the festival will act as an exogenous tourism draw, so attention should be focused on maximising the local participation and engaging across the demographic spectrum. The festival should emphasise the procurement of high-quality film, while also giving acknowledgement and recognition to smaller, independent productions of relevance to the community. Given the successes with pairing alternate venues with ancillary but film-related events, new participants may be drawn to the festival; the continued success and growth of the closing gala and the Knowledge-sponsored events would seem to confirm that continued emphasis on film-related events will pay dividends in the long run. The festival should also expend resources in an effort to improve upon the 'community experience' aspects of the festival while also augmenting the technical aspects of the theatre as much as possible. Yet the grim demography is contrasted with the steep increase in revenue moving into the festival coffers. This seeming contradiction can be set squarely at the feet of increased and larger-ticket sponsorships.

The question for the KFF has become one of sustainability. That is, when the festival confronts its various constraints – most prominent being the ageing and disappearance of its core demographic and an apparent inability to attract younger audiences to festival films – the increase in revenue from changes in sponsorship becomes a bandage on a weeping wound. Eventually, the motivations for sponsorships (as opportunities to promote to potential markets) will disappear as well and the festival will become financially and culturally irrelevant. What, then, can the festival do to stem this slow tide? How can the festival attract younger audiences in order to ensure its continuance?

Our further investigation into this ongoing phenomenon will draw upon additional and expanded survey research of the 2012 KFF and events. We also seek to theoretically augment our understanding of how film-related events exist in relation to other community events. Such a field-based approach, drawn from Pierre Bourdieu's (1993) examination of economic, social, cultural, and symbolic capital may offer insights into ways that small film festivals can position themselves and create models for sustainability.

References

Altintas, V. (2009). Antalya Golden Apple Orange Film Festival: impacts on the local community. In Raj, R. and Musgrave, J. (eds), *Event management and sustainability* (pp. 223–231). Cambridge, MA: CAB International.

Backman, K., Backman, S., Uysal, M. and Sunshine, K. (1995). Event tourism: An examination of motivations and activities. *Festival Management & Event Tourism*, 3(1), 15–24.

Bourdieu, P. and Kritzman, L.D. (1993). *The field of cultural production.* Cambridge, UK: Polity Press.

City of Kamloops (2012). *Area maps.* Retrieved 12 April 2012 from www.kamloops-info.com/areamaps.html.

Derrett, R. (2003). Making sense of how festivals demonstrate a community's sense of place. *Event Management,* 8(1), 49–58.

Dickson, C. and Arcodia, C. (2010). Promoting sustainable event practice: The role of professional associations. *International Journal of Hospitality Associations,* 29, 236–244.

European Coordination of Film Festivals. (1999). *The socio-economic impact of film festivals in Europe. Belgium: European coordination of film festivals.* Retrieved 1 February 2012 from www.a-suivre.org/.../the.socio.economic.impact.of.film.festivals.doc.

Foley, M., McGillivray, D. and McPherson, G. (2009). Policy, politics and sustainable events. In Raj, R. and Musgrave, J. (eds), *Event management and sustainability* (pp. 13–21). Cambridge, MA: CAB International.

George, E.W., Mair, H. and Reid, D.G. (2009). *Rural tourism development: Localism and cultural change.* Toronto: Channel View Publications.

Getz, D. (1991). *Festivals, special events, and tourism.* New York: Van Nostrand Reinhold.

Getz, D. (2002). Why events fail. *Event Management,* 7, 209–219.

Getz, D. (2008). Event tourism: Definition, evolution, and research. *Tourism Management,* 29(3), 403–428.

Grunwell, S. and Ha, I. (2008). Film festivals: An empirical study of factors for success. *Event Management,* 11, 201–210.

Grunwell, S., Ha, S. and Martin, B. (2008). A comparative analysis of attendee profiles at two urban festivals. *Journal of Convention and Event Tourism,* 9(1), 1–14.

Hall, M. (1992). *Hallmark tourist events.* London: Belhaven.

Jago, L., Chalip, L., Brown, G., Mules, T. and Ali, S. (2003). Building events into destination branding: Insights from experts. *Event Management,* 8, 3–14.

Jennings, G. (2001). *Tourism research.* Milton, Australia: John Wiley and Sons.

Lade, C. and Jackson, J. (2004). Key success factors in regional festivals. Some Australian experiences. *Event Management,* 9, 1–11.

Lee, C.K., Lee, Y. and Wicks, B.E. (2004). Segmentation of festival motivation by nationality and satisfaction. *Tourism Management,* 25, 61–70.

Morgan, M. (2008). What makes a good festival? Understanding event experience. *Event Management,* 12, 81–93.

Musgrave, J. and Raj, R. (2009). Introduction to a conceptual framework for sustainable events. In Raj, R. and Musgrave, J. (eds), *Event management and sustainability* (pp. 1–12). Cambridge, MA: CAB International.

Nicholson, R. and Pearce D. (2001). Why do people attend events: A comparative analysis of visitor motivations at four South Island events. *Journal of Travel Research,* 39(4), 449–460.

Nurse, K. (2002). Bringing culture into tourism: Festival tourism and reggae sunsplash in Jamaica. *Social and Economic Studies,* 51, 127–143.

Park, J., Lee, G. and Park, M. (2011) Service quality dimensions perceived by film festival visitors. *Event Management,* 15(1), 49-61.

Petrick, J. (2004). First timers' and repeaters' perceived value. *Journal of Travel and Research,* 43(1), 29–38.

Raj, R. and Musgrave, J. (2009). The economics of sustainable events. In Raj, R. and

Musgrave, J. (eds), *Event management and sustainability* (pp. 56–65). Cambridge, MA: CAB International.

Ruling, C. and Pedersen, J.S. (2010). Film festival research from an organizational perspective. *Scandinavian Journal of Management*, 26, 318–323.

Tassiopoulos, D. and Johnson, D. (2009). Social impacts of events. In Raj, R. and Musgrave, J. (eds), *Event management and sustainability* (pp. 76–89). Cambridge, MA: CAB International.

Thomas, T. and Kim, Y. (2011). A study of attendees' motivations: Oxford Film Festival. *Undergraduate Research Journal for the Human Sciences*. Retrieved 15 April 2012 from www.kon.org/urc/v10/thomas.html.

UNWTO (December 2011). *Tourism and sustainability*. Retrieved 19 April 2012 from www2.unwto.org/en/content/what-we-do.

Wicks, B. (1995). Celebrating events of the future. *Trends*, 20(2), 12–19.

Xiang, R. and Petrick, J. (2006). A review of festival and event motivation studies. *Event Management*, 9, 239–245.

Yin, R.K. (2009). *Case study research – design and methods* (4th edn, Vol. 5). London: SAGE Publications, Inc.

Yoon, Y. and Uysal, M. (2005). An examination of effects of motivation and satisfaction on destination loyalty: A structural model. *Tourism Management*, 26(1), 45–56.

Part V

Sustainable futures

Visions of action and hope

15 Sustainable strategies in the twenty-first century

Don Clifton

This chapter looks at organisational strategy from a sustainable business perspective. As organisations involved in event management are as diverse in size and scope as are events themselves, the approach taken here is generic in that it presents strategy concepts that can be applied to almost any organisation regardless of size, structure and industry sector. The approach is also critical in that, as well as presenting main-stream sustainable business narratives, it also challenges these narratives and questions whether they are capable of delivering their claimed sustainability outcomes.

The chapter begins by considering what it means for a business to contribute to the achievement of a sustainable world, that is, for it to be a 'sustainable business'. From there, we consider various strategic approaches to how a business might pursue sustainability initiatives and critically assess the extent to which these approaches may support or hinder sustainable world objectives. The analysis concludes that, although the strategic approaches we examine have their merits, they also have major failings that can work against the very sustainable world objectives they otherwise claim to support.

Sustainable business

Chapter 2, 'Critical perspectives on sustainability', considered what it means for there to be a sustainable world and identified two main streams of sustainable world thought – the reformist and the transformational approaches. Both of these approaches see the business sector as a (or the) major cause of ecological harm at local, regional and global scales and, as such, this sector needs to play a key role in solving these problems (WCED, 1987; Bruno and Karliner, 2002). But what are the characteristics of an organisation that would see it make a positive contribution to achieving a sustainable world – for it to be a 'sustainable business'?

Despite their differences, both the reformist and transformational approaches see a sustainable world having to do with:

> the flourishing of life on Earth over an indefinite time frame, incorporating human and ecological wellbeing, and with this wellbeing grounded in principles of intra- and inter-generational justice.
>
> (Clifton and Amran, 2010, p. 123)

We can call this the 'wellbeing + justice' sustainable world principle and, as a starting point, if we are to talk of sustainable business strategy, this is ultimately the end to which strategy objectives need to be focused.

Developing this line of thought further, reference to the 'phases model' of Dunphy *et al.* (2003) can be helpful. The phases model provides a framework whereby an organisation's approach to a sustainable world can be assessed depending on how it aligns with various sustainability strategies based on human and environmental practices and performance. The ideal phase, Dunphy *et al.* argue, is the 'sustaining corporation' phase (we use the term 'sustainable business' in this chapter as an equivalent), where a corporation:

> [provides] an excellent return to investors ... [but where its] fundamental commitment is to facilitate the emergence of a society that supports the ecological viability of the planet and its species and contribute to just, equitable social practices and human fulfilment.
>
> (p. 16)

Further, for Dunphy *et al.*, a sustainable business is not only committed to making a positive contribution to human and ecological wellbeing in its internal operations, but also actively advocates for change within its industry sector, in the business sector generally, in government by encouraging the development of positive sustainability policies, and in the broader social space. A sustainable business is therefore committed to progressing the wellbeing + justice sustainable world principle within its internal operations and in the broader social context. Whether in doing so a business should be advocating the reformist or transformational approach is a separate question, and one we considered in Chapter 2.

The sustainable business concept proposed by Dunphy *et al.* highlights two main ways in which the terms 'sustainability' and 'business' are connected. The first sees a focus on the business entity itself continuing as a going concern – what is sustained is the firm. The second sees the focus of what is to be sustained in terms of the wellbeing + justice principle, and the issue of interest is the role of the firm in contributing to the achievement of this sustainable world goal. Some authors (Dunphy *et al.*, 2003, for example) see these two concepts as necessarily linked in that unless a firm is actively progressing to sustainable business status, it will itself cease to be viable. Others (Van De Ven and Jeurissen, 2005, for example) are somewhat sceptical of this, pointing to various inconsistencies between corporate goals and sustainable world goals, such as return on capital objectives which are often framed around net present value calculations over time frames that can be far removed from those appropriate to sustainable world considerations, and the continued financial prosperity of some corporations even where the products and/or services they produce are fundamentally at odds with sustainable world objectives. This distinction between the two ways in which the sustainable business term is used is important to recognise. The confusion is often used deliberately in greenwash and policy debates.

One other point before we move on and discuss sustainable business strategy: is it possible for any business to be sustainable in its own right? One way to think about this is in relation to a set of 'rules' the ecological economist Herman Daly has presented as being necessary to adhere to if society is to live sustainably in ecological terms. Daly (1999) focuses on the natural resources capital base humanity needs to ensure long-term wellbeing, such as productive soils, forests, water, biodiversity, carbon cycles and so on. He proposes that the following rules need to be adhered to:

- Output rule: waste outputs must be kept within the natural absorptive capacities of the environment such that wastes do not accumulate in the environment.
- Input rules: harvest rates of renewable natural resources should not exceed regeneration rates and, for non-renewable natural resources, the rate of use must be paired to the rate of investment in renewable alternatives.

The idea is that if every generation adhered to these rules, then the generations that follow would have a natural resource base that remains intact and able to provide the needed resources for continued wellbeing.

Can any one business meet the demands implied by these rules? For example, take the output rule and consider its application to a major event such as the Olympic Games or, more broadly, to an events management company and the way it goes about running all of the events it manages. It might be possible in these settings for a range of waste reduction strategies (such as carbon emission reductions and offsets, and the recycling of waste) to be implemented in ways that are models for the industry, but whether the wastes that are still discharged meet Daly's output rule depends on what every other business is doing: it is the collective result that matters. It is this issue that brings some authors to conclude that the concept of sustainability can only make sense when looked at from a global perspective, as the positive actions by any one person, business, community or nation can easily be countered by others (Lamming *et al.*, 1999; Alcott, 2008). This is particularly evident in the small business sector where any one business may see its own ecological impacts as minor and not worthy of attention. When all small business impacts are added, however, the impact can be quite significant.

Some authors have put forward the idea of a 'generalisation principle' to help think about whether any one unit of analysis (a business, a household, a community) can be seen as sustainable. The generalisation principle proposes that human behaviour at any sub-global level is inconsistent with a sustainable world if it is one that cannot be realistically attained by the rest of humankind (WCED, 1987; Daly, 1996). The reason this is important for the strategy issues we address in this chapter is that, without the broader global picture in mind, actions within any one business to pursue a sustainable business agenda might do little more than give a feeling of achievement that, in the big scheme of things, fails to address the core issues society needs to confront.

Sustainable business strategy

A few approaches can be taken when considering a sustainable business strategy. Bonn and Fisher (2011) for example look at sustainable business practices at different levels of organisational strategy – the enterprise, corporate, business and functional levels. In this chapter however, we will focus on patters of strategic behaviour that are evident in organisations and span across all of these strategy levels. In doing so, we will use the phases model of Dunphy *et al.* introduced earlier.

The phases model categorises organisational sustainability strategies into six phases as follows:

- Rejection: Displays an exploitative view of society, employees and nature. Profit is all that matters. Sustainability pressures are actively rejected.
- Non-responsiveness: This is grounded more in an ignorance of issues concerning sustainability. Community and environmental issues are ignored where possible. Sustainability-focused actions are seen as an unnecessary cost.
- Compliance: Compliance focuses on risk reduction from failing to meet minimum standards. Attention is given to sustainability issues that have the greatest litigation risk. Tighter regulations on environmental or social issues are mostly opposed, with any calls for action by business framed within a voluntary self-regulated approach.
- Efficiency: This phase displays an increased awareness of sustainability practices. The focus is on efficiency and the resulting cost-saving benefits to business.
- Strategic proactivity: For strategic proactivity, sustainability becomes part of an organisation's core strategy. The focus is on gaining competitive advantage and long-term profitability from sustainability initiatives.
- Sustaining corporation: For this phase, sustainability values are fully internalised. The firm actively pursues ecological renewal, social equity and human welfare at the firm, industry, social and political levels. People and nature are valued for their own sake.

The first two phases, rejection and non-responsiveness, are not ones based on a firm's sustainable business initiatives: they are instead ways in which a firm is not addressing these issues. We will therefore focus on the last four strategic phases: compliance, efficiency, strategic proactivity and the sustaining corporation.

Compliance

A compliance approach to sustainable business is fundamentally a risk management strategy. The core objective is to minimise a firm's potential liabilities from any actions it might take that impact on the environment or on the wellbeing of its employees or members of the broader society on whom the firm might impact. Other activities that are unlikely to expose a firm to material risk of action against it are mostly ignored. When thinking of compliance, the first thing that comes to mind is compliance with the law; however, a broader view of compliance is 'doing what you are required or expected to do' (Dunphy *et al.*, 2003, p. 93), which sees compliance in terms of not only laws, but of other areas such as voluntary codes of conduct, and social norms and expectations. A discussion on these three dimensions – regulation, voluntary codes and social norms – now follows.

Regulation

Regulatory compliance is concerned with obeying the law and limiting the risks of harmful consequences to the firm that might result from breaching the law: fines, imprisonment, loss of licences that might be needed in order to operate, or even media exposure of regulatory breach, together with the negative impacts this might have on a firm's reputation. Although there is a clear need for a firm to comply with regulations in order to progress its sustainable business agenda, regulatory compliance, as it is conceived within this compliance phase, is quite limited in its effectiveness: it is necessary but not sufficient for a business to be a sustainable business. One reason for this limited effectiveness is that, for the compliance phase, a firm is said to adopt a general orientation to resist stronger regulation and instead advocate voluntary action to address sustainability issues. However, it is well known that regulation, or the threat of regulation, is possibly the most important driver for businesses to change and adopt sustainability strategies (Gunningham, 2002). An alternate view to this call for minimal regulation and voluntary action is proposed by Porter and van der Linde (1995) who call for stronger regulation to promote sustainability initiatives and to improve the international competitiveness of firms, industries and a nation's business sector in general. This view of Porter and van der Linde is consistent with how we described the core features of a sustainable business where we referred to the role such a business plays in promoting positive sustainability policies on the part of governments.

Another problem with a focus on regulatory compliance is that regulations are generally reactive – regulations tend to be made based on problems that have occurred, not predictive of problems that may occur:

> It is an unfortunate truth that a major incident is often the best stimulant for policy change, both in government and business. Too often policy is as good as the latest disaster was bad.
>
> (Winsemius and Guntram, 2002, p. 111)

The final point we will cover here is that it is simply not possible to regulate everything. Ultimately, sustainability is a moral issue, one concerned with issues of justice within and across generations (Rushton, 2002). In this sense, compliance with the law can be seen as merely a starting point for progressing sustainability principles within a firm.

Voluntary codes

Voluntary codes of conduct are mostly industry-based codes to which firms in that industry (or individual practitioners in some cases) agree to be bound. Often these codes require compulsory agreement to adhere to them in order to become a member of an industry association. The codes themselves are, however, voluntary in the sense that they are established by industry not by government regulation. There are a number of codes operating in the events management sector: a simple internet search of <event management code of conduct> will return a range of sites setting out various codes.

Voluntary codes have the potential to be a forceful tool in progressing sustainability principles in the business sector, especially in the light of the discussion we have had so far on the limitations of regulation in achieving this end. Whether these codes can achieve this outcome is another question and critics argue that these codes can, instead of advancing sustainability outcomes, thwart them (King and Lenox, 2000; Barraclough and Morrow, 2008; Landman, 2008). There are a number of reasons for this view, some of the main ones being as follows:

a   Voluntary codes are often used as a mechanism for warding off more stringent government regulation. In this view, industry is seen to put in place a voluntary code, designed by its own members suited to its own purposes, and use this to demonstrate to government that regulation is not needed as the industry is addressing its own issues. Further, having a voluntary code in place can give an industry group a seat at the negotiating table when regulations are being developed, providing the opportunity to dilute the impact of any regulations that might eventuate (Landman, 2008).

b   Voluntary codes can be used mostly as a means to improve the public image of an industry rather than to drive change to improve an industry's social and ecological performance. Barraclough and Morrow (2008) make this point when commenting on the chemical industry's 'Responsible Care' programme, noting:

> internal documents show[ed] the campaign was fundamentally designed to improve [the chemical industry's] poor public image (second only to that of the tobacco industry) in order to complement its policy goals of countering stricter regulations.
>
> (p. 1786)

c   There is a question of who monitors behaviour. The concern is that rather than the industry actively enforcing its code, the only monitoring of industry activity is by the public. Before anything is done by way of code enforcement, a public complaint is needed. This can mean that unless someone outside the industry acts as a watchdog, then violations of codes can continue with no action being taken. This problem is of even greater concern when firms are operating in countries with little public capacity to conduct this type of monitoring.

d   Who enforces the code and what penalties apply for breaches? Enforcement is mostly in the hands of the industry itself and critics claim that penalties are either not applied or, if they are, their impact on the violating firm is so minor as to be of little or no incentive to cease code breaches.

e   By having a code of conduct in place, firms within an industry can use the code as a justification for their behaviour, turning the code into a defence shield claiming that 'our firm was acting in full accordance with the industry code of conduct'. The point is that as industry codes are developed by industry for industry, they may only cover the issues the industry wants to address, not necessarily the broader set of sustainable world issues that firms in the industry need to confront. The code can then become a justification for not acting in ways consistent with sustainable business objectives, rather than a force driving such actions.

In summary, voluntary codes of conduct have the potential to drive significant progress in how the business sector contributes positively to the achievement of a sustainable world. However, unless issues such as those highlighted above are addressed, they can act as a barrier to progress rather than as a facilitator. We noted earlier that a sustainable business should act to progress broader sustainability outcomes in industry, government, and society at large. Being an advocate for strong and purposeful industry codes is one way in which a firm can influence the industry in which it participates to address sustainability issues.

Social expectations

Social expectation pressures come from the extent to which a firm's public image – and, from that, its reputation, product/service sales and resulting financial performance – is impaired due to public reaction to behaviours of a firm that do not meet societal expectations. Exposure of a firm's actions that may fail to meet public expectations can come from many sources: the general public, the press, activists groups or even a competitor seeking to discredit a firm's actions in order to gain an advantage in the market place.

Activism by non-governmental organisations (NGOs) is a particularly potent force on businesses to improve their performance in areas of ecological and human welfare. These NGOs range from well-established global groups such as Greenpeace, the Worldwide Fund for Nature (WWF) and Amnesty International, to small groups that focus on issues specific to the local community. Activism does not need to actually be directed at a particular firm: just the threat of it is often enough to force firms to change. In addition, a firm may be targeted by activist groups for its association with another firm that is the primary target.

The other form of social pressure issues we will address here has to do with practices that may be legal or even accepted as social norms in one country (say, a less developed country) but fall far short of what we might expect in our own home country. This is an important topic and one that is becoming increasingly relevant as firms deepen their supply chains across the globe, and outsource materials supply, manufacturing and services to countries far removed from where final goods and services are consumed. Is it right, for example, for a firm to move its manufacturing processes offshore (say, from a highly industrialised country to a less developed one) and, in doing so, take advantage of environmental and workplace laws that are less onerous than in a firm's home country? These practices raise many social justice questions encompassed in the wellbeing + justice sustainable world principle; however, the point for our current discussion is that firms who engage in this type of value chain behaviour face the prospect of having their activities (including those of their value chain participants) publically exposed, with possible negative consequences to the firm.

As is evident from the discussion above, a compliance strategy is important for any firm in order for it to progress its sustainable business agenda. This strategy, however, requires no foundation of sustainability issues within the business at any strategy level: it can be implemented as merely a risk control approach that may have little consequence to the bigger sustainability issues the firm, and society in general, needs to confront. Further, firms that stay focused only on the compliance approach expose themselves to the risk of missing out on important trends and opportunities that more comprehensive sustainable business strategies may offer.

Efficiency

The idea behind the efficiency approach to sustainable business is that, by using resources more efficiently, and by reducing waste and pollutants, both the environment and the firm win. The challenges with an efficiency approach to progressing sustainable world objectives have been covered in Chapter 2 and the key issues in that chapter dealing with productivity and production efficiency will not be repeated here. One other point to make about the production efficiency approach to sustainable business however is that, initially, firms quite often find easy gains: 'picking the low hanging fruit', as it is often termed. After this, improvements in efficiency and achievement of a win-win become increasingly harder and the costs of efficiency improvements become increasingly higher per unit of progress. This poses substantial challenges for industry in making needed improvements in resource use and waste reduction/elimination.

Baumgartner (2009) suggests that, in order for the efficiency strategy to be effective, it needs to find a base in a firm's values and be part of corporate philosophy. The efficiency strategy is, however, fundamentally an internal process strategy: it is one where the firm focuses its sustainability efforts on innovative processes, technology and monitoring and reporting systems to maximise efficiency gains with a resulting improvement in the firm's bottom line

(Baumgartner and Ebner, 2010). As such it is, on its own, a strategy that does not address the broader set of issues that businesses need to confront in order for them to become sustainable businesses.

Strategic proactivity

The strategic proactivity phase is one where a firm sees sustainability not as a cost or impediment, or as something merely to be pursued by compliance or efficiency strategies, but rather as a source of strategic business opportunities and competitive advantage. For Dunphy *et al.*, this approach requires organisations to shift their cultures, structures, reward systems and job responsibilities and build the internal capabilities to support this strategy. As with the compliance and efficiency phases, we will look at some issues with the strategic proactivity approach to consider whether it is a credible sustainable business strategy in its own right.

Entering and exiting business lines

The first issue deals with the products and/or services firms deliver. Some authors (Van De Ven and Jeurissen, 2005) propose that certain products and services simply do not belong in a society that is committed to a sustainable world (examples might include ozone depleting substances, land mines and other such forms of weaponry, inherently toxic and harmful substances). A key question here is how to respond practically to this problem in a way that achieves the needed outcome. If a firm decides to head down the strategic proactivity path and, as part of that strategic move, divests itself of a business line it sees as inconsistent with sustainable world objectives, this does not mean the product or service is eliminated from society: a divesture simply transfers ownership to another firm. Alternatively, if a firm decides to shut down its operations in a product or service line (or, for an event management firm, refuses to take on an assignment to run an event promoting these types of products or services), then unless there is some other mechanism to stop other firms from filling the space in the market place then, again, the intended outcome may not be achieved.

This poses substantial challenges for organisations seeking to embrace sustainable business principles. One of the features of a sustainable business, we proposed, is to drive social change – to advocate for change within its industry sector, within government, and within society at large to progress a sustainable world outcome. This is an example of how products and services that have no place in society may be eliminated: by organisations making a public stand and actively driving the needed social change to achieve this end. This is not to say that action by a firm to deliberately exit a business line and ensure no other firm can fill the void is easy and without financial consequences. But simply avoiding taking action because these challenges exist does not solve the core sustainable world problem. It may take some creative and innovative thinking to see the needed change come about, but if we are to progress to living sustainably, then solutions need to be found.

Some authors also suggest that organisations can pursue a strategic proactivity sustainable business agenda by deliberately seeking out business lines that have a direct link to products and services that fit with what we perceive to be sustainability practices and seeking to secure a competitive advantage from doing so (Porter and Kramer, 2006). Examples of these business lines might include renewable energy, pollution abatement and clean-up equipment, water purification systems, plantation timber rather than using native forests and so on. Although this may present some good opportunities for businesses, for a sustainable world to come about we need, as a society, to live in ways that are inherently sustainable. In this respect, it does not matter if a business makes chairs, carpets, modes of transport, provides banking services or manages events: these day-to-day aspects of life all need to fall under the sustainability banner. The point is that if organisations see themselves as being able to gain some form of competitive advantage in the market place as a result of providing a product or service that fits a model of what is 'sustainable', or can somehow promote sustainability credentials to gain a competitive advantage, then this is a demonstration that humanity is not living sustainably: if all businesses were operating sustainably, there would be no competitive advantage in being sustainable. So although we can talk of sustainability as a competitive advantage opportunity for business (as we have), this is really a transitional state to what the world would need to look like if humanity were living sustainably.

Self-interest versus doing what is right

The final point we will cover has to do with the core underpinnings of the strategic proactivity approach, namely it being based on a win-win outlook for business: good conduct in the sustainable business space is also good for business (this view also underpins the compliance and efficiency approaches we discussed earlier). But is this win-win outlook sufficient? Hoffman (1991), for example, argues that it is not always the case that doing the right thing is also in our own personal self-interest – we should do what is right for its own sake, not only if there is a win for us or our business. The point is that the compliance, efficiency and strategic proactivity approaches to sustainable business all place progressing the wellbeing + justice sustainable world principle within the context of benefits to the firm. Self-interest remains the dominant driver for action. An alternate view is to say that humans have no option but to live sustainably and, from an intergenerational justice perspective, each generation is morally bound to do so. Under this view, living sustainably must take priority and is the standard against which all human behaviour must be measured. Organisational strategies and behaviours must therefore be first and foremost consistent with sustainable world objectives. A corporation's existence then becomes conditional on sustainable business status being achieved and maintained. In this respect, none of the compliance, efficiency or strategic proactivity approaches to sustainable business is sufficient to give humanity its best opportunity to progress to a sustainable world. This is where the idea of the sustaining corporation – Dunphy *et al.*'s final strategic position – comes into play.

The sustaining corporation

Dunphy *et al.* (2003) describe the sustaining corporation phase (or, in the terminology used in this chapter, sustainable business phase) as an ideal, but one which few, if any, firms have achieved. There may be many firms that aspire to this ideal phase, but achieving it is another matter, and the change process that needs to occur both within any one firm, and within the broader social context in which a firm operates, is substantial.

Some of the key points to take from the Dunphy *et al.* description of the sustaining corporation we have referred to in this chapter are: first, sustainability principles must be embedded throughout all levels of strategy and must be an integral part of all strategy initiatives and activities. In short, for the sustaining corporation, sustainability is part of the organisation's DNA. It is the norm, the way business is done, and there is no compromise.

Second, the problems we have identified as applying for each of the compliance, efficiency and strategic proactivity phases are countered in this sustaining corporation phase. In this phase, people and nature are valued for their own sake, and actions to progress the wellbeing + justice principle are not dependent on there being a corporate self-interest benefit: if there is, then that is a bonus, but self-interest is not the overriding criteria for decision making.

In conclusion, we return to the question of what sustainability approach should a firm be pursuing and promoting in its sustainable business quest: the reformist approach or the transformational? This is an important question and one you need to ask yourself and give some deep, insightful and reflective thought to. We can all talk of how important it is to live sustainably, and how critical it is for business to be part of this quest, but to pursue an approach to a sustainable world that merely gives the illusion of progress can easily become a barrier to needed change rather than a facilitator of change.

References

Alcott, B. (2008). The Sufficiency Strategy: Would Rich-World Frugality Lower Environmental impact? *Ecological Economics*, 64(4), 770–786.

Barraclough, S. and Morrow, M. (2008). A Grim Contradiction: The Practice and Consequences of Corporate Social Responsibility by British American Tobacco in Malaysia. *Social Science & Medicine*, 66, 1784–1796.

Baumgartner, R. J. (2009). Organizational Culture and Leadership: Preconditions for the Development of a Sustainable Corporation. *Sustainable Development*, 17, 102–113.

Baumgartner, R. J. and Ebner, D. (2010). Corporate Sustainability Strategies: Sustainability Profiles and Maturity Levels. *Sustainable Development*, 18, 76–89.

Bonn, I. and Fisher, J. (2011). Sustainability: The Missing Ingredient in Strategy. *Journal of Business Strategy*, 32(1), 5–14.

Bruno, K. and Karliner, J. (2002). *Earthsummit.biz: The Corporate Takeover of Sustainable Development*. Oakland, CA: Food First Books.

Clifton, D. and Amran, A. (2010). The Stakeholder Approach: A Sustainability Perspective. *Journal of Business Ethics*, 98(1), 121–136.

Daly, H. E. (1996). *Beyond Growth: The Economics of Sustainable Development*. Boston, MA: Beacon Press.

Daly, H. E. (1999). *Ecological Economics and the Ecology of Economics*. Cheltenham, UK: Edward Elgar.

Dunphy, D., Griffiths, A. and Benn, S. (2003). *Organizational Change for Corporate Sustainability*. London: Routledge.

Gunningham, N. A. (2002). *Green Alliances: Conflict or Cooperation in Environmental Policy*. Working Paper Series. Australian Centre for Environmental Law, Australian National University, Canberra.

Hoffman, W. M. (1991). Business and Environmental Ethics. *Business Ethics Quarterly*, 1(2), 169–184.

King, A. A. and Lenox, M. J. (2000). Industry Self-Regulation without Sanctions: The Chemical Industry's Responsible Care Program. *The Academy of Management Journal*, 43(4), 698–716.

Lamming, R., Faruk, A. and Cousins, P. (1999). Environmental Soundness: A Pragmatic Alternative to Expectations of Sustainable Development in Business Strategy. *Business Strategy & the Environment*, 8(3), 177–188.

Landman, A. (2008). *Absolving Your Sins and CYA: Corporations Embrace Voluntary Codes Of Conduct*. Retrieved 27 August 2012 from www.corpwatch.org/article.php?id=15165.

Porter, M. E. and Kramer, M. R. (2006). Strategy and Society. *Harvard Business Review*, 84(12), 78–92.

Porter, M. E. and van der Linde, C. (1995). Toward a New Conception of the Environment-Competitiveness Relationship. *Journal of Economic Perspectives*, 9(4), 97–118.

Rushton, K. (2002). Business Ethics – A Sustainable Approach. *Business Ethics: A European Review*, 11(2), 137–139.

Van De Ven, B. and Jeurissen, R. (2005). Competing Responsibly. *Business Ethics Quarterly*, 15(2), 299–317.

WCED. (1987). *Our Common Future: World Commission on Environment and Development*. Oxford, UK: Oxford University Press.

Winsemius, P. and Guntram, U. (2002). *A Thousand Shades of Green: Sustainable Strategies for Competitive Advantage*. London: Earthscan Publications.

16 Imitation, positivity and the sustainable event

Niki Harré

Events are a microcosm of real life. People gather, interact, eat, consume and create. If all goes well, they engage, give something of themselves and learn from the experience. This chapter is aimed at students and researchers in event studies as well as organisers who are keen to explore how events can promote sustainability. In it, I suggest you think of events as opportunities to showcase society as you would like it to be. In this way you can not only stimulate people intellectually, but also allow them to experience an alternative to current practices. If you do it right, your attendees will leave feeling inspired, even transformed. So here is my core message – if you want to promote sustainability, make your event a peek into a sustainable way of life, which will excite and inspire people to re-make the experience in their everyday lives.

Before we get down to the details, I would like to outline what I mean by sustainability. Sustainability has been described as a 'messy' or 'complex' problem (Chapman, 2004; Westley *et al.*, 2007). Messy problems are ones in which the desired outcome is unclear, and there is considerable debate on how to get there. Will a sustainable society require radical behaviour change, such as localised food production and new ways of getting around? Or will we be able to behave as usual, saved by advanced technology such as hydrogen fuelled cars? We do not have a unified vision, because no one knows for sure exactly what is needed and how to bring about change.

From one perspective this is confusing, but from another it is liberating. If there is no single solution to the sustainability problem, then we can all play a part. To me, sustainability is about ways of living that encourage human flourishing as well as preservation of the ecosystems and natural resources on which we depend (Harré, 2011). Sustainability is not an end that we will someday reach, it is a continual process of trying to do better for each other and our planet, changing our approach as needed. It is also an inherently social endeavour, because whatever your vision, you will only be effective in promoting it if you join with others or persuade others to join with you. No one can plant enough trees to make up for the loss of the Amazon jungle, get a hydrogen car to market or offer an eco-tourism experience without help from others. But you can start small. As I said at the start of this chapter, if you offer a taste of life as it could be, hopefully you will inspire others to live a little differently, and those people will affect others and so on.

So I invite you to read this chapter while thinking of how you would like the world to be and how events can be part of the sustainability solution. If my examples do not fit with your ideals for a sustainable future, then I hope the theory I offer will give you ways to apply your own vision.

The material I offer is based on psychological research. I also attempt to live sustainability values in my work, community and personal life. For the past four years I have been involved in a waste minimisation action research project at a high school in Auckland, New Zealand, where I am based. A major thrust of our project has been encouraging the school community to separate their waste into different streams. I am also a member of a Transition Town in my suburb of Pt Chevalier. Transition Towns are grass-roots organisations aimed at promoting sustainable living within their local community (Transition Towns Aotearoa, 2012). The Transition Towns movement was initially aimed at 'energy descent', that is, planning for communities without abundant oil in which we all live more locally (Hopkins, 2008). In New Zealand, however, the focus is broader, and embraces a wide variety of initiatives including awareness raising.

Events have featured strongly in both of the projects above, and one of the key objectives of our events is to model sustainable practices. In my work with these groups I have become increasingly convinced of the power that comes from modelling the future you hope for, and giving others the opportunity to live this, even if only for an hour or two.

But, let's get back to the theory. Two psychological concepts underlie my argument. The first is the power of imitation in driving human behaviour; the second is the power of the positive. I'll discuss each in turn, highlighting the research evidence for the concept and then the implications for promoting sustainability at events.

The power of imitation

People copy each other. When we enter a social space we immediately look to see what others are doing and, often, adjust our behaviour to fit in. As the social psychologists Tanya Chartrand and John Bargh (1999) have demonstrated, we are like chameleons, only it is our behaviour rather than our colour that we change in order to blend into our surroundings. Numerous psychological studies have demonstrated this phenomenon. Newborn babies have been found to imitate facial gestures (Field *et al.*, 1982; Meltzoff and Moore, 1983), children copy their peers and adults (Bandura 1972) and even adults copy each other (Chartrand and Bargh, 1999; Brass *et al.*, 2000). This is not necessarily conscious. For example, Chartrand and Bargh's study showed that adults may mimic another's body language automatically, without deciding to, or even knowing that is what they are doing.

It is possible that our brains are set up to be particularly sensitive to what other people are doing. Intriguing recent research has suggested that people, and monkeys, have mirror neurons (Fogassi *et al.*, 2005; Iacoboni, 2009). Mirror neurons are brain cells that respond both when the person or animal is witnessing a behaviour and when they are performing the same behaviour. What this implies is that doing and watching an action are part of the same brain process. When we *watch* an action, our brains are at the ready to *perform* that action. It is almost as if all of our minds are interconnected; we cannot help but respond at some level to what other people are doing. Research has also shown that when an abstract instruction to perform a particular behaviour conflicts with the behaviour we are witnessing, we have to work hard to follow the abstract instruction (Brass *et al.*, 2000). In other words, and as we know from experience, doing what we are told when we are witnessing something different is hard work. Being smacked as a child for hitting someone is a classic example of a mixed message, and may well prime us towards hitting others rather than cure us of this. So too, is it a mixed message for events to claim to value sustainability if that claim is not matched by what is demonstrated. A friend of mine once viewed a festival display showing how much rubbish is created by disposable coffee cups, only to turn the corner and come across a coffee cart dishing out – you guessed it, disposable coffee cups!

Not only do people copy directly, they are also looking for physical cues that indicate the normal behaviour for the setting they are in. Environments often leave behavioural traces that hint at appropriate behaviour (Schultz *et al.*, 2008). This was clearly demonstrated by a study on littering in which people were shown to be twice as likely to litter in a littered car park than in a pristine one (Cialdini, 2003). A pristine environment is not only pleasant, it also says to us: 'Littering is not acceptable here. We respect our environment.'

People are also sensitive to direct feedback about normal behaviour. Prior to turning my attention to sustainability my key research focus was traffic safety. One of my students, Wendy Wrapson, found that a sign which displayed the average speed at a location, 54 km per hour, pulled the high speed drivers towards the norm (Wrapson *et al.*, 2006). Other studies have found that messages that imply a desired behaviour is normal motivate people to reuse their towels in a hotel and lower their electricity use (Schultz *et al.*, 2007; Goldstein *et al.*, 2008).

While people are always on the look-out for information about how to fit in, everyday behaviour is also driven by habitual patterns. Much of the time, people simply replicate what they did the day before. When we are in novel situations, however, without well-worn behavioural habits to follow, these imitation effects are likely to be particularly powerful. You will probably have experienced this yourself. Which food stall do you choose at a festival when they are all unfamiliar? The one which has other people in front of it perhaps? So events, which are often novel, are particularly likely sites for imitation to occur.

Therefore, if you are trying to promote sustainability values and behaviour, your event should make sustainable behaviour as visible and seem as normal as possible. Ideally, you want to create a self-replicating virtuous cycle – people behave sustainably, see others behaving sustainably, so behave sustainably again and so on. Because it is impossible to be perfectly sustainable, I also suggest putting particular effort into highly visible practices, such as the food available.

Such practices are very powerful at transmitting deep level messages that can help transform people and inspire action.

I will venture a few suggestions, although I do not presume to be an expert on event management or know exactly what you will face at your event. It starts with your promotional material and website. What behaviours are you going to emphasise? Do you communicate that walking, cycling or taking public transport are obvious ways to get to the event, with car travel being an afterthought? This is easy to do: put instructions for public transport and cycle parking first and instructions for car parking last. This is worth doing even if most people will, in fact, drive to the event. It is part of the process of shifting these options into the public eye, so they can start to be considered normal. Do you describe your strategies for minimising electricity use, water use, packaging and so on?

Next is the physical set up – not only should it allow for sustainable practices, but it should draw as much attention to these as possible. Have bike parking right at the front, car parking to the side – get people to walk in past the cycle racks. Place the recycling and compost bins in the most visible positions, with the landfill bin (if needed) slightly less obvious. Of course you'll want to provide food that is sourced from sustainable places and why not have signs that tell the story of the food, so that people cannot miss this? All massive cues that eating sustainably is what we do around here. When we provide food for our school action research project we always describe where the ingredients came from. When people eat our homemade muesli bars, we want them to be aware they contain New Zealand oats, Fair Trade chocolate and raisins, and organic pumpkin seeds.

Once you have done what you can with the physical environment, you want to tempt people into interacting with that environment as intended. With luck, you are in a position to simply not offer a less sustainable choice – do you need to sell bottled water? Can you instead provide water fountains and cheap drink bottles or reusable glasses for people who forgot to bring their own? It may also be possible to get people started by having staff or volunteers demonstrate the intended behaviour. One fun Canadian study compared the composting rates of people at a restaurant who were either exposed to just the compost bin and a sign or who were exposed to the bin and sign, and also witnessed people in front of them discussing and using the compost. The latter group were more inclined to compost (Sussman and Gifford, 2011). Living models will be especially important if the behaviour is new or different.

Not everyone can directly witness or engage in all behaviours, and this is where you can maximise attention through posted feedback. One possibility is a big sign with a running tally of the number of people who cycled, walked or used public transport to get to the event, and show the percentage (if this is the majority).

Now it is time to get personal. How far do you want to take this? Your event may demonstrate eco-credibility if you take up the suggestions above – or come up with your own ideas using similar principles. But what gives you credibility as someone who truly holds these values? It is as simple, and as difficult, as practicing what you preach. If you really believe we need to reduce the rate at which we are pumping carbon dioxide into the atmosphere, and have set up your event to encourage cycling and public transport, then how about you use a bike for moving around the space? Or if you want to be seen as a viable advocate for waste reduction, avoid grabbing a coffee on the way to the event in a disposable cup or walking around with a Pump bottle – even if you do reuse it. In our school project we bring our reusable drink bottles, cycle to the school or take the bus, and carry our cycle helmets. We do not view transport to the event as a personal affair, but as part of the package that maximises the transmission of values.

Importantly, you don't have to be secretive about your attempts to make sustainable practices seem obvious. Feel free to tell people there are models who will be demonstrating use of the compost bins and the signs on the food are to draw attention to its sustainable qualities. That will add to the fun, and may mean attendees do this too when it is their turn to be in charge. We are not trying to manipulate people through underhand means; we are trying to inspire others to become more sustainable in what they do.

A bonus in working hard at the small touches that make your event 'obviously' sustainable is that it increases your credibility. A student of mine, Adam Smith, did a study in 2011 examining young people's reaction to a presenter who opened a new bottle of water and ate a muffin wrapped in cling film while he discussed the importance of waste minimisation. Adam wanted to examine if this discordant behaviour affected the participants. Most participants didn't notice the discrepancy between the presenter's message and behaviour without promoting (a hint, Adam and I suspected, that we are used to such discrepancies and they often bypass conscious awareness). However, in a discussion afterwards they were much more negative about him than another group who had witnessed the same presentation but seen the presenter drinking from a ceramic cup and eating an unwrapped muffin. Much other research also shows that when people notice hypocrisy, they don't like it (Batson, 2011).

The lesson here is that most people will still respect you if there is inconsistency between your stated values and behaviour (and full consistency is probably impossible), but you will be on much firmer ground if you are consistent. You will be less vulnerable to criticism from those who are switched on to the issues, and a more powerful means of truly transmitting the values you hold.

Having provided a rich experience that maximises imitation potential, how can you get people to take the message of your event back into their everyday lives? Here's three ways they might do so. First, they may tell stories of your event, with stories being a core means by which people transmit practical information on behavioural norms (Boyd, 2009). Second, they may also learn new practices and set up their lives to enable these – installing a Bokashi bin, pumping up the tyres on their bike. These practices may be reinforced through products that act as behavioural cues in their new setting – a tea towel that reminds people to take their reusable coffee cup with them, a hook for their bike helmet. Another study I did in my injury prevention days involved children taking home cues to reduce their burns risk, like a sticker for the oven that showed pots with the handles turned inwards (see Harré and Coveney, 2000).

Third, they may have an identity transformation (see Harré, 2011 for a full discussion of this concept). Identity transformations can happen when we imagine or experience ourselves as different people and change our daily behaviour patterns to become that person. If you show people a glimpse of themselves as sustainable, it is possible that some will be so enticed by that vision, they become that person. That is deep level change, which is what we will need to spread sustainability values.

A positive angle

I would like to introduce one more thread to this chapter – the importance of aligning sustainability with positive ideas, emotions and outcomes. After all, sustainability is about a flourishing future, the opposite of doom and gloom, and this is what we should draw attention to. If your sustainability event is modelling the behaviour you'd like to permeate social life, you are already operating in a positive frame. You are growing the good, rather than trying to eliminate the bad, and that is how it mostly should be.

In this section of the chapter, I am assuming that you not only wish to offer an event that practices sustainability, but also that you want to stretch, inform and persuade people intellectually. This could be through displays, talks or workshops that encourage attendees to think deeply about these issues and how to take action. In these forums, it is very tempting to stress the problems – and indeed many environmental and social justice organisations habitually focus on the dark side of our current way of life. Exposing problems does have an important role in motivating action. This often results in anger and fear, which narrows our attention to the issue at hand (Fredrickson, 2001). In interviews my students and I conducted with highly committed New Zealand political activists, anger played an important role for many. For example, one said

> I think that motivated probably the last 20 years of my political activism, just the outrage really, that these people in government could just do this stuff without any consent, that they were just riding roughshod over 50 years of democratic history and had no concern for the fact that they were deeply unpopular and that nobody supported what they were doing except the very rich people who loved it.
>
> (Harré *et al.*, 2009, p. 337)

But, by narrowing our attention, these emotions also limit our imagination. Fascinating research has shown that negative emotions reduce our ability to generate a wide variety of actions or solutions to a problem (Fredrickson and Branigan, 2005). On the other hand, people who are in a positive frame of mind are more creative and generative in their thinking both when working as individuals (Isen *et al.*, 1987) and when working in groups (Grawitch *et al.*, 2003).

Importantly too, people who are encouraged to reflect on their strengths may be more willing to examine their own practices. This was shown in one study of young woman who were high caffeine users. Half the women were asked to generate a list of times when they had acted kindly, an intervention designed to make them feel good. The other half completed a neutral personality test. All the women were then told that caffeine use can produce a non-fatal but painful disease. Each woman was given the choice of three articles to read, one of which was about the negative effects of caffeine on the body. The women who had reflected on their acts of kindness were twice as quick to look at the article suggesting caffeine was a health hazard than those in the other group. They also rated themselves as more able to control their caffeine intake than the other participants (Reed and Aspinwall, 1998). This illustrates a paradox about people – they are often more willing to change when they feel they are doing quite well already.

The lesson here is clear: people are able to think more broadly and creatively if they are in a positive frame of mind, and if you want people to critically reflect on their behaviours and feel able to change to practices better aligned with a sustainable future, then getting them to focus on what they are doing right is an important first step.

Negative emotions also make us feel bad (obviously!). And people generally don't want to feel bad; on the contrary they are attracted to the promise of happiness (see Harré, 2011 for a more developed argument). If you manage to generate anger and fear in people, you may succeed in getting them to take the issue seriously and even be motivated to act, but you may also teach them to stay away from the source of that anger and fear next time. After all, it is much easier to avoid the emotion in the first place than to work to dispel it by trying to solve the underlying problem. Mathematical analyses have even suggested there is a ratio of positive to negative inputs that describes optimal individual or group functioning. This ratio ranges from 3:1 to 11:1 positive to negative inputs (Losada and Heaphy, 2004).

To get practical, when designing an event that informs people about sustainability, I suggest ensuring that communications are at least 75 per cent positive. While that is a judgement call, it is fairly obvious that a stall which shows all pictures of climate disasters or caged animals will not pass this test. In our school project, our research team delivers only positive messages about what students can do and how that will help protect other people and the planet. The bad news does creep in, as the school's student leaders want to show their peers photos of birds damaged by oil spills and tell them about the soup of plastic in our oceans. This information is important, and part of the process, but it needs to be accompanied by action suggestions. Once people have got the message that we can't continue as we are if we want a flourishing future, you don't need to keep pushing that message. Their commitment is much more likely to be maintained by the good feelings they are getting out of being part of the sustainability movement.

Uniting the 'fun' elements of your event with the 'sustainability' elements is ideal if possible. Research has shown that when people are fully engrossed in an activity that uses their skills and feels authentic, they enter a state of 'flow' and want to come back for more (Csikszentmihalyi, 1988). As I see it, a sustainable society will be full of people making music, art, performing theatre, gardening and making products with their hands and renewable resources. If you connect flow activities with protecting our future, you have passed on a durable message.

Concluding comments: bringing it all together

People have minds and bodies, and a holistic experience will offer something they can see, do and be. If your event has the opportunity for workshops, I recommend you consider a storytelling workshop in which people describe their values and sustainability-focused actions. Storytelling workshops draw attention to sustainable behaviours, thus providing models for imitation; they encourage people to reflect on their strengths, thus increasing their open-mindedness and they create a positive atmosphere. You can obtain instructions on how to run these workshops in my book *Psychology for a Better World: Strategies to Inspire Sustainability* (Harré, 2011; free to download from www.psych.auckland.ac.nz/psychologyforabetterworld).

Even if you create a wonderful experience, it is hard to ensure people will take aspects of this experience into their everyday lives. Research has shown that even 'deep ecologists' are often unable to fully live the values they are immersed in during a retreat when they return home (Zavestoski, 2003). But by providing take-home cues as to the desired behaviour, linking sustainability to activities that produce flow and giving attendees a glimpse of life as it could be, you can play an important role in creating the sustainable future you envisage.

References

Bandura, A. (1972). Modeling theory: Some traditions, trends and disputes. In R. D. Parke (ed.), *Recent Trends in Social Learning Theory* (pp. 35–62). New York: Academic Press.

Batson, C. D. (2011). What's wrong with morality? *Emotion Review*, 3(3), 230–236.

Boyd, B. (2009). *On the Origin of Stories: Evolution, Cognition and Fiction*. Cambridge, MA: The Belknap Press of Harvard University Press.

Brass, M., Bekkering, H., Wohlschlaeger, A. and Prinze, W. (2000). Compatibility between observed and executed finger movements: Comparing symbolic, spatial, and imitative cues. *Brain and Cognition*, 44(2), 124–143.

Chapman, J. (2004). *System Failure: Why Governments Must Learn to Think Differently* (2nd edn). London: Demos.

Chartrand, T. L. and Bargh, J. A. (1999). The chameleon effect: The perception-behavior link and social interaction. *Journal of Personality and Social Psychology*, 76(6), 893–910.

Cialdini, R. B. (2003). Crafting normative messages to protect the environment. *Current Directions in Psychological Science*, 12(4), 105–109.

Csikszentmihalyi, M. (1988). The flow experience and its significance for human psychology. In M. Csikszentmihalyi and I. S. Csikszentmihalyi (eds), *Optimal Experience:*

Psychological Studies of Flow in Consciousness (pp. 15–35). Cambridge: Cambridge University Press.

Field, T. M., Woodson, R., Greenberg, R. and Cohen, D. (1982). Discrimination and imitation of facial expressions by neonates. *Science*, 218(4568), 179–181.

Fogassi, L., Ferrari, P. F., Gesierich, B., Rozzi, S., Chersi, F. and Rizzolatti, G. (2005). Parietal lobe: From action organization to intention understanding. *Science*, 308, 662–667.

Fredrickson, B. L. (2001). The role of positive emotions in positive psychology: The broaden-and-build theory of positive emotions. *American Psychologist*, 56(3), 218–226.

Fredrickson, B. L. and Branigan, C. (2005). Positive emotions broaden the scope of attention and thought-action repertoires. *Cognition and Emotion*, 19(3), 313–332.

Goldstein, N. J., Cialdini, R. B. and Griskevicius, V. (2008). A room with a viewpoint: Using social norms to motivate environmental conservation in hotels. *Journal of Consumer Research*, 35, 472–482.

Grawitch, M. J., Munz, D. C. and Kramer, T. J. (2003). Effects of member mood states on creative performance in temporary workgroups. *Group Dynamics: Theory, Research and Practice*, 7(1), 41–54.

Harré, N. (2011). *Psychology for a Better World: Strategies to Inspire Sustainability*. Auckland: Department of Psychology, University of Auckland.

Harré, N. and Coveney, A. (2000). School-based scalds prevention: Reaching children and their families. *Health Education Research: Theory and Practice*, 15(2), 191–202.

Harré, N., Tepavac, S. and Bullen, P. (2009). Integrity, efficacy and community in the stories of political activists. *Qualitative Research in Psychology*, 6(4), 330–345.

Hopkins, R. (2008). *The Transition Handbook: From Oil Dependency to Local Resilience*. Totnes, UK: Green Books.

Iacoboni, M. (2009). Imitation, empathy, and mirror neurons. *Annual Review of Psychology*, 60, 653–670.

Isen, A. M., Daubman, K. A. and Nowicki, G. P. (1987). Positive affect facilitates creative problem solving. *Journal of Personality and Social Psychology*, 52(6), 1122–1131.

Losada, M. and Heaphy, E. (2004). The role of positivity and connectivity in the performance of business teams: A nonlinear dynamics model. *American Behavioral Scientist*, 47(6), 740–765.

Meltzoff, A. N. and Moore, M. K. (1983). Newborn infants imitate adult facial gestures. *Child Development*, 54, 702–709.

Reed, M. B. and Aspinwall, L. G. (1998). Self-affirmation reduces biased processing of health-risk information. *Motivation and Emotion*, 22, 99–132.

Schultz, P. W., Nolan, J. M., Cialdini, R. B., Goldstein, N. J. and Griskevicius, V. (2007). The constructive, destructive, and reconstructive power of social norms. *Psychological Science*, 18(5), 429–434.

Schultz, P. W., Tabanico, J. J. and Rendón, T. (2008). Normative beliefs as agents of influence: Basic processes and real-world applications. In W. D. Crano and R. Prislin (eds), *Attitudes and Attitude Change* (pp. 385–410). New York: Psychology Press.

Sussman, R. and Gifford, R. (2011). Be the change you want to see: Modeling food composting in public places. *Environment and Behavior*, 20.

Transition Towns Aotearoa. (2012). Retrieved 31 March 2012 from www.transition-towns.org.nz/.

Westley, F., Zimmerman, B. and Patton, M. Q. (2007). *Getting to Maybe: How the World is Changed*. Toronto: Vintage Canada.

Wrapson, W., Harré, N. and Murrell, P. (2006). Reductions in driver speed using posted feedback of speeding information: Social comparison or implied surveillance? *Accident Analysis and Prevention*, **38**, 1119–1126.

Zavestoski, S. (2003). Constructing and maintaining ecological identities: The strategies of deep ecologists. In S. Clayton and S. Opotow (eds), *Identity and the Natural Environment: The Psychological Significance of Nature* (pp. 297–316). Cambridge, MA: The MIT Press.

Index